# international
# review of
# social history

Special Issue 20

# Mediating Labour: Worldwide Labour Intermediation in the Nineteenth and Twentieth Centuries

*Edited by Ulbe Bosma, Elise van Nederveen Meerkerk, and Aditya Sarkar*

Published by the Press Syndicate of the University of Cambridge
The Pitt Building, Trumpington Street, Cambridge, CB2 1RP
40 West 20th Street, New York, NY 10011-4211, USA
10 Stamford Road, Oakleigh, Melbourne 3166, Australia

*A catalogue record for this book is available
from the British Library*

*Library of Congress Cataloguing-in-Publication Data applied for*

ISBN 9781107647374 (paperback)

*Printed in the UK by MPG Books Ltd.*

# CONTENTS

*Mediating Labour: Worldwide Labour Intermediation in the Nineteenth and Twentieth Centuries*

Edited by
Ulbe Bosma, Elise van Nederveen Meerkerk, and Aditya Sarkar

# NOTES ON CONTRIBUTORS

*Ulbe Bosma*, International Institute of Social History, PO Box 2169, 1000 CD Amsterdam, The Netherlands; e-mail: ubo@iisg.nl

*Thomas Buchner*, Department of Economic and Social History, University of Vienna, Maria-Theresien-Str. 9/4, A-1090 Vienna, Austria; e-mail: thomas.buchner@univie.ac.at

*Hannan Hammad*, Department of History, Texas Christian University, TCU Box 297270, Fort Worth, TX 76129, USA; e-mail: h.hammad@tcu.edu

*Amarjit Kaur*, UNE Business School, University of New England, Armidale, NSW 2351, Australia; e-mail: Amarjit Kaur akaur@une.edu.au

*Cassandra Mark-Thiesen*, St Cross College, University of Oxford, 61 St Giles, Oxford, OX1 3LZ, United Kingdom; e-mail: Cassandra.mark@history.ox.ac.uk

*Enrique Martino*, Institute of Asian and African Studies, Humboldt University Berlin, Sophienstraße 22–22a, 10178 Berlin, Germany; e-mail: enrique.martino@gmail.com

*Alexander Mejstrik*, Department of Economic and Social History, University of Vienna, Maria-Theresien-Str. 9/4, A-1090 Vienna, Austria; e-mail: alexander.mejstrik@univie.ac.at

*Elise van Nederveen Meerkerk*, International Institute of Social History, PO Box 2169, 1000 CD Amsterdam, The Netherlands; e-mail: enm@iisg.nl

*Christoph Rass*, Institute for Migration Research and Intercultural Studies (IMIS), Osnabrück University, Neuer Graben 19/21, 49069 Osnabrück, Germany; email: chrass@uos.de

*Magaly Rodríguez García*, Vrije Universiteit Brussel/FWO, Pleinlaan 2-5B 407d, 1050 Brussels, Belgium; email: mrodrigu@vub.ac.be

*Aditya Sarkar*, Centre for Modern Indian Studies (CeMIS), Georg-August-Universität Göttingen, Waldweg 26, 37073 Göttingen, Germany; e-mail: bhochka2@gmail.com

*Cristiana Schettini*, Instituto de Altos Estudios Sociales, National University of General San Martín/Instituto Interdisciplinario de Estudios de Género, University of Buenos Aires, Paraná, 145, 1er piso, Buenos Aires, Argentina; e-mail: cschettini@hotmail.com

*Sigrid Wadauer*, Department of Economic and Social History, University of Vienna, Maria-Theresien-Str. 9/4, A-1090 Vienna, Austria; e-mail: sigrid.wadauer@univie.ac.at

*IRSH* 57 (2012), Special Issue, pp. 1–15 doi:10.1017/S0020859012000430

# Mediating Labour: An Introduction

Ulbe Bosma

*International Institute of Social History, Amsterdam*

E-mail: ubo@iisg.nl

Elise van Nederveen Meerkerk

*International Institute of Social History, Amsterdam*

E-mail: enm@iisg.nl

Aditya Sarkar

*CeMIS, Georg-August University, Göttingen*

E-mail: bhocka@gmail.com

SUMMARY: The essays in this volume aim to explain the evolution and persistence of various practices of indirect labour recruitment. Labour intermediation is understood as a global phenomenon, present for many centuries in most countries of the world, and taking on a wide range of forms: varying from outright trafficking to job placement in the context of national employment policies. By focusing on the actual practices of different types of labour mediators in various regions of the world during the nineteenth and twentieth centuries, and by highlighting both the national as well as the international and translocal contexts of these practices, this volume intends to further a historically informed global perspective on the subject.

Maria came to the United States with some 50 other Filipino nationals who were promised housing, transportation, and lucrative jobs at country clubs and hotels under the H2B guest worker program. Like the others, Maria dutifully paid the substantial recruitment fees to come to the United States. But when she arrived, she found that there was no employment secured for her. She did not work for weeks, but the recruiters seized her passport and prohibited her from leaving their house. She and other workers slept side-by-side on the floors of the kitchen, garage, and dining room. They were fed primarily chicken feet and innards. When the workers complained, the recruiters threatened to call the police or immigration.[1]

Maria is but one of millions who in recent times have fallen prey to illegal trafficking agents who promise migrants work in return for a substantial

---

1. US Department of State, *Trafficking in Persons Report* (June 2011), p. 34, http://www.state.gov/documents/organization/164452.pdf; last accessed 13 April 2012.

payment. Though varying a great deal, estimates by several institutions indicate that between 1997 and 2009 an average of between 500,000 and 4,000,000 people per annum were victims of human trafficking worldwide.[2]

Apart from those who are victims of outright illegal forms of labour migration and trafficking, many other workers fall victim to various forms of deceit or coercion. Since remittances have become the largest global monetary flow after oil, and since increasing migration control has raised the costs of entering the labour markets of rich countries, labour recruitment has become a global business powerful enough to resist most international legislation attempting to protect the rights of migrant labourers.[3] One way or the other, the global trade in labour relies on local patterns of recruitment and on local intermediaries: the village notables, family heads, and other brokers who cater to the demands of the professional "headhunters". The activities of the latter can in turn often count on the tacit or sometimes even explicit support of governments keen to receive either precious foreign exchange or cheap and willing labour.[4]

This is by no means a new phenomenon, though its determinants have changed over time. Over the past five centuries, if not longer, and in all parts of the world, workers have been attracted, lured, tricked, coerced, and even raided into specific labour regimes, which themselves often featured coercive conditions. Mediators, ranging from free job agencies, contractors, subcontractors, and jobbers, to traffickers of human beings, played a crucial role. This special issue of the *International Review of Social History (IRSH)* focuses on labour intermediaries, the persons or agencies who interceded between employers and workers, for which they received payments and commissions. Their practices played a crucial role in the recruitment of both free and forced labour, and frequently blurred the boundaries between the two. In the labour historiography, mediators constitute an intriguing category, operating in the interstices between labour and capital. Both labour

2. Figures presented by UNESCO. The wide range reflects the fact that the estimates were compiled by different institutions, including national governments and NGOs such as the ILO. UNESCO, http://www.unescobkk.org/fileadmin/user_upload/culture/Trafficking/project/abc/ Selected_Articles_and_Publications/Graph_VT_Trafficking_in_Person_01.pdf; last accessed 13 April 2012.
3. In fact, it is even debated to what extent protective international legislation is favourable to labour migrants, as measures sometimes seem to harm the target groups as well as to increase the phenomenon of trafficking; Michele Ford, Lenore Lyons, and Willem van Schendel, "Labour Migration and Human Trafficking: An Introduction", in *idem* (eds), *Labour Migration and Human Trafficking in Southeast Asia: Critical Perspectives* (London [etc.], 2012), pp. 1–22.
4. Two glaring examples of such governmental complicity were the Marcos and Suharto dictatorships in the Philippines and Indonesia respectively. See, for example, Rachel Silvey, "Transnational Domestication: State Power and Indonesian Migrant Women in Saudi Arabia", *Political Geography*, 23 (2004), pp. 245–264, and Daromir Rudnyckyj, "Technologies of Servitude: Governmentality and Indonesian Transnational Labor Migration", *Anthropological Quarterly*, 77 (2004), pp. 407–434.

and capital have tried to monopolize the placement of labour, a struggle in which the state often joined as a third party. The central question posed in this special issue is how we can explain the emergence and persistence of, and variations in, labour intermediation practices.

Historically, recruitment practices have often had translocal consequences, changing the social landscapes of migrant-sending and migrant-receiving regions. Obvious examples are the 12.5 million Africans who made the middle passage and the other millions who were traded across the Sahara or the Indian Ocean. These flows altered both sending and receiving societies to a great extent, as did the indentured ("coolie") workers sent all over the world.[5] Moreover, forms of slave labour and indentured labour have also coloured the debate about the "labour recruitment problem" in the colonial era.[6] What constitutes free as opposed to unfree labour migration, and the nature of the line dividing one from the other, have been matters of intensive debate. Some historians, such as Tinker, apply a broad definition, whereas others regard any consensual migration as free migration.[7]

The first may be problematic, since it tends to conflate indentured labour with slavery, while the latter might gloss over cases of severe coercion or deceit. It is no coincidence that the definition of trafficking used by ILO and UN agencies includes the possibility of consent by the victim.[8]

---

5. See, for example, Piet Emmer (ed.), *Colonialism and Migration: Indentured Labour Before and After Slavery* (Dordrecht, 1986); Pat Manning (ed.), *Slave Trades, 1500–1800: Globalization of Forced Labour* (Aldershot, 1996); Yoko Hayashi, "Agencies and Clients: Labour Recruitment in Java, 1870s–1950s", IIAS/IISG CLARA Working Paper, No. 14 (Amsterdam, 2002), available at http://socialhistory.org/sites/default/files/docs/publications/clara-wp14.pdf (last accessed 13 April 2012); and Andreas Eckert (ed.), *Europe, Slave Trade, and Colonial Forced Labour* (Munich, 2009).

6. Jan Breman, *Taming the Coolie Beast: Plantation Society and the Colonial Order in Southeast Asia* (Delhi, 1989); Paul Baak, "About Enslaved Ex-Slaves, Uncaptured Contract Coolies and Unfreed Freedmen: Some Notes about 'Free' and 'Unfree' Labour in the Context of Plantation Development in Southwest India, Early Sixteenth Century–Mid 1990s", *Modern Asian Studies*, 33 (1999), pp. 121–157; Dennis D. Cordell and Joel W. Gregory, "Labour Reservoirs and Population: French Colonial Strategies in Koudougou, Upper Volta, 1914 to 1939", *Journal of African History*, 23 (1982), pp. 205–224, 213–221. For a more recent historiographical account of the "recruitment problem" and the role of internal slavery in Africa, see Gareth Austin, "Cash Crops and Freedom: Export Agriculture and the Decline of Slavery in Colonial West Africa", *International Review of Social History*, 54 (2009), pp. 1–37, 8–12.

7. For a broad understanding of coercion and slavery see Hugh Tinker, *A New System of Slavery: The Export of Indian Labour Overseas 1830–1920* (London, 1974). For a more limited understanding see David Northrup, *Indentured Labor in the Age of Imperialism, 1834–1922* (Cambridge, 1995).

8. ILO, Report of the Director-General, *Stopping Forced Labour: Global Report under the Follow-up to the ILO Declaration on Fundamental Principles and Rights at Work*, International Labour Conference 89th Session 2001; Report 1 (B) (Geneva, 2001), pp. 47–48, available online at http://www.ilo.org/wcmsp5/groups/public/—dgreports/—dcomm/—publ/documents/publication/wcms_publ_9221119483_en.pdf (last accessed 13 April 2012).

4 Ulbe Bosma, Elise van Nederveen Meerkerk, and Aditya Sarkar

Other historians reject the entire dichotomy between free and unfree as artificial, and Eurocentric, if not utterly naive.[9] Nonetheless, one could argue that recruitment practices usually lead to less freedom of movement for workers once they become engaged. One might even suggest that this is their raison d'être, the reason why employers are prepared to accept the transaction costs of the recruitment process. From that perspective a distinction between free and unfree labour, or a sliding scale from slavery at one end and a direct labour contract between employer and labourer, without any extra-economic pressures, at the other, might help us delineate the space in which recruiters operated. Recruitment practices that blurred the lines between coercion and consent may, it seems, have played a major role in shaping modern labour markets deeply marked by ethnicity, gender, and age.[10]

The essays in this special issue of the *IRSH* aim to explain the emergence and persistence of, and changes in, practices of indirect labour recruitment. We have added the adjective "indirect" to exclude explicitly forms of direct recruitment by employers, though we do not mean to suggest that these forms always imply freedom for the workers involved. Several other questions arise in the course of analysing labour intermediation. Under what conditions did job intermediaries operate around the world and throughout history? What regional and occupational similarities and differences can be found in labour recruitment practices and methods? What role did economic factors (transaction and information costs, scarcity of labour, for instance) play? To what extent did cultural factors and colonial discourses about traditional labour recruitment patterns play a role in the use of labour intermediaries? What does a focus on indirect labour recruitment contribute to our knowledge of the tenuous and shifting lines of division between "free" and "coerced" labour, as these came to be constituted historically across a range of local and global contexts? What role did gender, ethnicity, and age play in the particular practices of labour recruitment around the world?

This special issue deploys a translocal perspective on the emergence and persistence of intermediation. In so doing, it seeks to extend the debate on this practice as a global phenomenon, transcending the dichotomy between "traditional" labour-supplying societies and "modern" labour-demanding

9. Jairus Banaji, "The Fictions of Free Labour: Contract, Coercion, and So-Called Unfree Labour", in *idem, Theory as History: Essays on Modes of Production and Exploitation* (Leiden, 2010), pp. 131–154.
10. See, for example, Samita Sen, "'Without His Consent?': Marriage and Women's Migration in Colonial India", *International Labor and Working Class History*, 65 (2004), pp. 77–104; Karen Tranberg Hansen, "Labor Migration and Urban Child Labor During the Colonial Period in Zambia", in Kristoffel Lieten and Elise van Nederveen Meerkerk (eds), *Child Labour's Global Past, 1650–2000* (Berne [etc.], 2011), pp. 595–612.

societies that is usually adduced to explain it. The "transitional" character usually attributed to the labour intermediary, as a temporary institution in the development from pre-industrial to industrial society, will be questioned. Though globalization may have challenged labour market inefficiencies and information asymmetries,[11] the same process also created new asymmetrical relations and new barriers. The introduction of new means of transport, more stringent job requirements, and increasing immigration control raise the costs for migrants and make them more reliant on debt contracts and smuggling. This might all explain why the labour contractor or recruiter is not, therefore, simply a relic of the past.[12] Moreover, the rise and persistence of labour intermediation cannot be explained by mere analyses of the *need* for capital or labour, because labour mediation itself has often become a powerful institution, capable of defending its interests in spite of increasing transaction costs.[13] This special issue focuses therefore on the actual practices of labour mediators in various regions of the world, while also taking into account power relations between the various actors.

## HISTORIOGRAPHY ON LABOUR INTERMEDIATION

Recruiting agents and agencies, contractors and subcontractors, slave traders, traffickers, jobbers, headmen, and labour agencies are all part of the broader phenomenon of labour intermediation. The different terms relate, however, to different academic orientations that, until recently, were linked hardly at all to one another in the context of this particular subject. Labour intermediation over the past few decades has featured prominently in studies on labour issues in industrializing countries, but it rarely figures in the historical literature.[14] Trafficking is widely used to connote contemporary people smuggling, but few scholars have endeavoured to provide historical depth to the subject by relating it

---

11. David H. Autor, "Introduction", in *idem* (ed.), *Studies of Labor Market Intermediation* (Chicago, IL, 2009), pp. 1–23, 4–10.
12. Tirthankar Roy, "Sardars, Jobbers, Kanganies: The Labour Contractor and Indian Economic History", *Modern Asian Studies*, 42 (2008), pp. 971–998, 997.
13. *Ibid.*, p. 976.
14. For migration history see Christoph Rass, *Institutionalisierungsprozesse auf einem internationalen Arbeitsmarkt: Bilaterale Wanderungsverträge in Europa zwischen 1919 und 1974* (Paderborn, 2010). For labour management and control see John F. Wilson, *British Business History, 1720–1994* (Manchester [etc.], 1995), pp. 32–34; Dick Kooijman, "Jobbers and the Emergence of Trade Unions in Bombay City", *International Review of Social History*, 22 (1977), pp. 313–328; Rajnarayan Chandavarkar, *The Origins of Industrial Capitalism in India: Business Strategies and the Working Classes in Bombay, 1900–1940* (Cambridge, 1994); *idem*, "The War on the Shopfloor," *International Review of Social History*, Supplement 14 (2006), pp. 265–277; *idem*, "The Decline and Fall of the Jobber System in the Bombay Cotton Textile Industry, 1870–1955", *Modern Asian Studies*, 42 (2008), pp. 117–210.

to slavery.[15] The role of foremen is almost invariably studied within one specific cultural zone – the work on brickmakers by Jan Lucassen, which stretches from India, to Russia and western Europe being an important exception in this respect.[16]

Recently, it has been pointed out that labour recruiters were also a widespread phenomenon before the rise of industrial capitalism, both in Europe and in other parts of the world.[17] Armies and navies, for example, have deployed recruiters throughout history, and in very different cultural zones.[18] Moreover, subcontracting was widely employed to mobilize migrant labour, ranging from brickmakers in Europe and south Asia to tin miners in south-east Asia.[19] Furthermore, existing patterns of recruitment and subcontracting can be subsumed under new labour regimes. In Asia, in particular, all kinds of informal debt-contracting arrangements, such as the *kangani* systems of southern India or the *kongsi* systems found in China, were "regulated" by the colonial state, in the sense that it gave legal status to labour contracts issued by official recruiters and imposed penal sanctions on employees leaving work without their employer's consent.[20] Thus, they limited labour's freedom of movement, an abstractly upheld value, to address what in their eyes was a greater evil. To combat

---

15. Suzanne Miers, *Slavery in the Twentieth Century: The Evolution of a Global Problem* (Walnut Creek, CA [etc.], 2005); Michael Zeuske, *Handbuch Geschichte der Sklaverei. Eine Globalgeschichte von den Anfängen bis heute* (Berlin, 2012).

16. See, for example, Jan Lucassen, "Brickmakers in Western Europe (1700–1900) and Northern India (1800–2000): Some Comparisons", in *idem* (ed.), *Global Labour History: A State of the Art* (Berne, 2006), pp. 513–572.

17. By, for example, Catharina Lis and Hugo Soly, "Subcontracting in Guild-based Export Trades, Thirteenth-Eighteenth Centuries", in S.R. Epstein and Maarten Prak (eds), *Guilds, Innovation, and the European Economy, 1400–1800* (Cambridge, 2010), pp. 81–113; Baak, "About Enslaved Ex-Slaves".

18. "Fighting for a Living", a three-year research programme on military recruitment in Europe, the Middle East, and Asia, 1500–2000 CE, conducted by a team led by Erik Jan Zürcher at the International Institute of Social History, is currently investigating this phenomenon.

19. Jan Lucassen, "The Brickmakers' Strikes on the Ganges Canal in 1848–1849", in Rana P. Behal and Marcel van der Linden (eds), *Coolies, Capital, and Colonialism: Studies in Indian Labour History* [Supplement 14, *International Review of Social History*, 51] (Cambridge, 2006), pp. 47–83; Mary F. Somers Heidhues, *Bangka Tin and Mentok Pepper: Chinese Settlement on an Indonesian Island* (Singapore, 1992).

20. Jan Breman, *Koelies, planters en koloniale politiek. Het arbeidsregime op de grootland-bouwondernemingen aan Sumatra's Oostkust in het begin van de twintigste eeuw* (Dordrecht, 1987); Peter Robb, "Labour in India 1860–1920: Typologies, Change and Regulation", *Journal of the Royal Asiatic Society*, Third Series, 4 (1994), pp. 37–66, 48; Baak, "About Enslaved Ex-Slaves", pp. 136–137, 152; Vincent Houben *et al.*, *Coolie Labour in Colonial Indonesia: A Study of Labour Relations in the Outer Islands, c.1900–1940* (Wiesbaden, 1999); Roy, "Sardars, Jobbers, Kanganies", p. 972; Adam M. McKeown, *Melancholy Order: Asian Migration and the Globalization of Borders* (New York, 2008).

the continuation of outright slavery, and in order to regulate labour conditions and separate "bona fide" from "mala fide" recruiters, they had to allow employers to include penal sanctions in labour contracts. Nonetheless, informal methods of debt contracting continued to exist in the Atlantic world, as Gunther Peck has shown.[21]

The negative connotation attached to labour recruitment in Africa and Asia, and the efforts by colonial authorities to regulate recruitment, originated with the struggle against slavery. At the same time, colonial authorities recruited massive numbers of labourers for public works schemes and turned a blind eye to – or even openly allowed – plantation owners to send recruiters to entice labour to work on their estates. In this context, recruitment as a form of intermediation merged with practices that already existed in Europe, where even then they had a quite negative connotation. "Recruit", a word derived from the French in the seventeenth century (*recruer*, "reinforce"),[22] signified the strengthening of the army and navy by crimping men in several ways, some more "decent" than others.[23] In the Asian and African contexts, historians have often described recruitment as part of the effort to force colonies along the path of economic development, of the "*mise en valeur*" of colonial wealth. In the same vein, the role of intermediaries was considered essential to feed emerging industries, such as the jute industry in Bengal, or ports, with labour. Labour intermediation in these regions would have been one way to solve this issue, thus also mediating between "modern" industrialized (often urban) businesses or plantations and "traditional" clan- or family-based (usually village) communities.[24] This interpretation tends to regard labour mediation as a distinct phase in the transition towards an industrial society.

However, this traditional–modern dichotomy falls short of an explanation in at least two respects. First of all, labour mediation existed in pre-industrial

---

21. Gunther Peck, *Reinventing Free Labor: Padrones and Immigrant Workers in the North American West, 1880–1930* (Cambridge, 2000).

22. A.S. Hornby, *Oxford Advanced Learner's Dictionary*, 7th edn (Oxford, 2005).

23. For a historical typology of the recruitment of military labour, see for instance, Jan Lucassen and Erik Jan Zürcher, "Conscription as Military Labour: The Historical Context", *International Review of Social History*, 43 (1998), pp. 405–419. For the maritime sector see Paul van Royen, Jaap Bruijn, and Jan Lucassen, *"Those Emblems of Hell"?: European Sailors and the Maritime Labour Market, 1570–1870* (St Johns, 1997).

24. See, for example, Ranajit Das Gupta, "From Peasants and Tribesmen to Plantation Workers: Colonial Capitalism, Reproduction of Labour Power and Proletarianisation in North East India, 1850s to 1947", *Economic and Political Weekly*, 21:4 (January 1986), pp. PE2–PE10; Dipesh Chakrabarty, "Conditions for Knowledge of Working-Class Conditions: Employers, Government and the Jute Workers of Calcutta, 1890–1940", *Subaltern Studies*, 2 (1983), pp. 259–310. Further examples can be found in the historiographical overview given by Baak, "About Enslaved Ex-Slaves", pp. 121–124.

societies; second, the phenomenon is still widespread today.[25] Secondly, it implies a teleological view of the development of societies, with the rise of capitalism from "traditional" to "modern", with labour intermediaries representing the link between these two paradigmatic poles. This involves too rigid and linear a view of the development of industrial capitalism, as well as one-dimensional depictions of pre-industrial societies.[26] That there is no linearity here can be illustrated by the long battle against slavery and trafficking, whose roots stretch back to the abolitionist struggles of the early nineteenth century and which led to increasingly complex international labour legislation in the twentieth century targeting commercial recruitment, with the ILO emerging as the central agency. Even in Europe, commercial recruitment has never been rendered extinct, and is now more present than ever. While in 1926 the ILO succeeded in regulating the recruitment of maritime labour to combat deceitful and profiteering recruiters,[27] in other segments of the labour market intermediaries emerged, with or without the involvement or explicit encouragement of national governments.

In fact, since the time of the guilds labour placement had been a means to regulate the supply of labour and, thereby, control wage levels. Labour organized itself collectively to refuse work when employers offered inadequate wages, while employers tried to organize labour recruitment to increase labour supply and reduce wages. Labour intermediation became an instrument of control both for unions and for employers. Attempts by labour unions in late nineteenth-century Europe to control intermediation failed in most countries, however, and an equilibrium emerged in which unions, employers, and governments collaborated to control the labour market. The temporarily unemployed received unemployment benefit, but only on condition that they registered as being available for work.[28] As Wadauder *et al.* explain in this special issue, labour intermediation became a means to separate those who were able to work from those who were unfit. As we shall now see when discussing the contents of this special issue, labour intermediation practices, both legal and illegal, public as well as private, have been ubiquitous, both in terms of time and place.

25. *Ibid.*; Austin, "Cash Crops and Freedom".
26. See also Roy, "Sardars, Jobbers, Kanganies", p. 976.
27. ILO Convention No. 9, "Placing of Seaman Convention 1920", and Convention No. 22, "Seaman's Articles of Agreement Convention, 1926".
28. Ad Knotter, "Mediation, Allocation, Control: Trade Unions and the Changing Faces of Labour Market Intermediation in Western Europe in the Nineteenth and Early Twentieth Centuries", in Sigrid Wadauer, Thomas Buchner, and Alexander Mejstrik (eds), *History of Labour Intermediation: Institutions and Individual Ways of Finding Employment* (currently under review).

## INDIRECT RECRUITMENT OF WORKERS ACROSS THE WORLD IN THE NINETEENTH AND TWENTIETH CENTURIES

The contributions to this special issue display a wide geographical and thematic scope. The temporal framework is largely confined to the end of the nineteenth and the twentieth centuries. National and supranational concerns with labour intermediation are addressed in the articles by Rodríguez García (League of Nations), Rass, and Wadauer *et al.* (Europe). The African continent is particularly well represented, in the case studies by Hammad (Egypt), Mark-Thiesen (Ghana), and Martino (Rio Muni and Nigeria). Schettini's article explores the Brazilian and Argentinian entertainment business, and Kaur's contribution addresses issues of labour intermediation in south-east Asia. All sectors of the economy are discussed: agricultural (plantation) labour (Martino) and mining (Mark-Thiesen); industrial labour (Hammad, Rass, Kaur, Wadauer *et al.*); and the service sector (Kaur, Rodríguez García, Schettini). All the articles implicitly or explicitly also address the indistinct boundaries between "free" and "unfree" as well as between "formal" and "informal" labour.

In this wide-ranging set of contributions a fairly limited set of actors can be identified that operate at three different levels. First, recruitment relies on existing authority within the family and/or the local community, whose members might act as mediators between workers and employers, and between labour and employers or professional recruiting agencies.[29] In her contribution Hanan Hammad describes how, in the emerging Egyptian textile industry at the beginning of the twentieth century, workers themselves were able to secure jobs for their relatives and village connections, which enhanced their position within the villages of origin and within the factory. Mechanisms such as these can be found all over the world, and have been recorded for India and Java as well.[30] Apart from in mediation, these connections were also useful in the informal training of newcomers in the factory, and in finding someone to share a place to live. Likewise, Enrique Martino describes how the Spanish authorities considered each contract labourer who had finished the first term of their contract on the cocoa plantations of Fernando Pó to

---

29. See, for example, John Ingleson, "Life and Work in Colonial Cities: Harbour Workers in Java in the 1910s and 1920s", *Modern Asian Studies*, 17 (1983), pp. 455–476, 456; Ernst Spaan, "Taikongs and Calos: The Role of Middlemen and Brokers in Javanese International Migration", *International Migration Review*, 28 (1994), pp. 93–113; Ruth Rosenberg (ed.), *Trafficking of Women and Children in Indonesia* (Jakarta, 2003); Graeme Hugo, "Migration in Indonesia: Recent Trends and Implications", in P. Graham (ed.), *Horizons of Home: Nation, Gender and Migrancy in Island Southeast Asia* (Clayton, VIC, 2008), pp. 45–70; Roy, "Sardars, Jobbers, Kanganies".
30. See, for example, Ingleson, "Life and Work in Colonial Cities".

be a potential recruiter for other labourers, through their networks of kinship and ethnicity.

Apart from the workers themselves mediating for their relatives, the family realm might more generally be the locus of labour intermediation. This could range from simply selling their children into captivity or for prostitution, to more subtle and less obvious forms of child exploitation by parents, which could include sexual exploitation. Cristiana Schettini's contribution is highly illuminating in this respect, indicating how difficult it is to a draw a line between the family theatre and entertainment business and the abuse of children's dependence on, and loyalty to, their parents. In some cases, parents acted as the agents (or, at times, outright pimps) of one or more of their children, usually daughters, either directly mediating with customers or making arrangements with employers in the theatre business. Under the influence of a worldwide campaign against white slavery, and the abduction of women for prostitution, this kind of labour recruitment came to be framed by moral anxieties, and removed from the purview of the ILO.[31]

In her contribution to this special issue, Magaly Rodríguez García discerns a similar attitude within the League of Nations towards the worldwide recruitment of prostitutes, which she appropriately typifies as the "moral recruitment" of women. She shows that the question of morality pervaded the approach of the Advisory Committee that was established by the League of Nations in 1922 to gather information on the trafficking of women and children. This committee ordered an extensive investigation into the matter by a body of experts, including "studies on the spot", in order to compile official and unofficial information on the prostitution milieu.

Next-of-kin and neighbourhood or village ties were also important in processes of labour intermediation and recruitment at the level of village communities. Cassandra Mark-Thiesen turns our attention to recruitment practices in the Ghana gold mines, where local headmen recruited "gangs" of young workers in their home villages. As these headmen exerted a degree of authority over other village members, not only because of their political and symbolic function but also through creditor–debtor relations, they possessed the power to mediate between their subjects and employers' representatives. Her contribution has a long pedigree and can be supplemented by other cases. In this respect, mention should be made of the work of Babacar Fall, Dennis Cordell, Gareth Austin, and Carolyn Brown. Though the practice of requisitioning labour through village headmen diminished after the signing of the Forced

---

31. Suzanne Miers, "Contemporary Forms of Slavery", *Canadian Journal of African Studies*, 34 (2000), pp. 714–747, 717.

Labour Convention of 1930, in some areas these practices continued after World War II.[32] Paralleling the types of brokership based upon the political authority of village headmen is the authority of other village notables, such as priests. Brokership for recruitment based on religious authority is not discussed in this volume, but it has been extensively recorded for rural Java and West Africa in the literature.[33]

The second level of actors is the ensemble of public and private agencies of labour mediation at the local or regional level. At the level of the firm, employers regularly made use of commissioned recruiters, agents who were not formally employed by the company itself. This happened, for instance, in the Egyptian Misr textile firm, but also at factory gates throughout Europe. As Wadauer *et al.* note, the first agencies in Europe offering job placement arose in the eighteenth and early nineteenth centuries. Most of these associations had a philanthropic or confessional background, and labour mediation typically constituted only one of its many activities. Only towards the end of the nineteenth century, when debates about the problem of unemployment intensified, did labour exchanges come to be seen as the solution. In some countries, such as Switzerland, the Netherlands, Belgium, and Germany, these agencies were initiated, set up, and financed mainly by municipal authorities. Private agencies continued to exist too, although in some countries and some periods they were looked upon as problematic, and in many countries (Italy being one) legislation to restrict or even forbid the existence of these agencies was introduced. Outside Europe too, colonial governments set up local agencies for job placement, for instance in Africa and India. However, informal practices of labour intermediation persisted everywhere, because of their lower costs and because they allowed for greater control of labour, as was the case for instance with the *kangani* in India, as Kaur notes in her contribution.

The third set of agents comprises national and international agencies involved in labour intermediation, both as direct providers and as regulators of mediation practices. Examples here include the nation state and the colonial state, but also supranational agents such as the League of Nations

32. Babacar Fall, *Sénégal: Le Travail au XXe siècle* (Amsterdam, 2010); *idem*, *Le travail forcé en Afrique Occidentale française (1900–1945)* (Paris, 1993); Frederick Cooper, *Decolonization and African Society: The Labor Question in French and British Africa* (Cambridge, 1996); Gareth Austin, *Labour, Land and Capital in Ghana: From Slavery to Free Labour in Asante, 1807–1956* (Rochester, NY, 2005); Carolyn A. Brown, *"We Were All Slaves": African Miners, Culture, and Resistance at the Enugu Government Colliery* (Oxford, 2003); Cordell and Gregory, "Labour Reservoirs and Population".
33. C. Babou, "Brotherhood Solidarity, Education and Migration: The Role of *Dahiras* among the Murid Muslim Community of New York", *African Affairs*, 101 (2002), pp. 151–170; Celia E. Mather, "Industrialization in the Tangerang Regency of West Java: Women Workers and the Islamic Patriarchy", *Bulletin of Concerned Asian Scholars*, 15:2 (1983), pp. 2–17.

and the ILO. As mentioned earlier, the end of the nineteenth century witnessed a growing debate in Europe on the issue of unemployment and labour market intermediation. During that period, when the "nation state" was established and consolidated, the role of the state in unemployment policy, social welfare, and job placement became increasingly important in Europe, as Wadauer *et al.* note in great detail. While they emphasize the variety of developments in state-run and national unionized labour exchanges in the various countries, they also point to the remarkable, and almost universal, involvement of the nation state in these facilities in the period 1880 to 1940. Although they do not offer a specific explanation for this phenomenon, other than what they call "a type of intrinsic logic", we believe that the phenomenon of globalization can help us here. It was precisely during this period that, after years of relative international political stability on the continent in the first few decades after 1815, Europe's nation states started to carve out a role for themselves on the international arena. This process extended, of course, to areas outside Europe, where large empires were built and extended, also by relatively "new" colonial powers. During this process, the protection of *national* labour markets became important, both as part of the urge to stand out but probably also in response to the insecurities of increasing globalization. Each country reacted to these challenges in fairly similar ways, while evidently closely watching each other's moves.

At the same time, the colonial rulers in Asia and Africa attempted to control the increasing international labour flows following the processes of industrialization and globalization. As Amarjit Kaur notes in her contribution on brokerage in south-east Asia, British intervention in the region in fact brought about an integration into global networks, while also developing "manpower supply chains" connecting India, China, and Malaya. Similar labour flows had been created by the Dutch colonial state with the introduction of "coolie labour" both within the Indonesian archipelago and between separate parts of the empire.[34] Remarkably, these interventions, aimed at creating a "freer supply of labour" in the region, simultaneously entailed highly unfree and even forced recruitment practices and labour relations.

As in Asia, Africa's colonial authorities intervened in issues of labour migration and recruitment. Cassandra Mark-Thiesen argues, however, that the colonial state's relationship to the labour intermediation of European mining firms, through African headmen and gangs, was ambivalent. On the one hand, it aimed to develop certain industries, for which a steady supply

---

34. See, for example, the contributions to Houben *et al.*, *Coolie Labour*; and Thio Termorshuizen, "Indentured Labour in the Dutch Colonial Empire, 1800–1940", in Gert Oostindie (ed.), *Dutch Colonialism, Migration and Cultural Heritage* (Leiden, 2008), pp. 261–314.

of labour was needed; on the other, the state was confronted both with the persistent influence of African mediators, and with the fact that these types of indentured labour contract went against their professed desire to ban coercive labour relations throughout the British Empire. Unlike the British, the Spanish colonial state seems to have been more reluctant to relegate slave-like labour conditions to "the island of no return", as Fernando Pó was called. In his contribution, Martino shows that, while other empires, as well as the ILO, condemned these outright inhuman recruitment practices, the Spanish authorities failed to intervene, and in some cases even encouraged the persistence of coercive labour conditions.

Thus, the challenges presented by globalization and colonialism were taken up too by supranational entities, both in the form of NGOs and of bilateral agreements between various states. Both Schettini and Rodríguez García stress the concern of international associations, such as the ILO and the League of Nations, with the international trafficking of women and children. Rodríguez Garcia's article, in particular, highlights the tensions between concepts of "free" and "unfree" recruitment in this respect, as the (usually bourgeois) members of the Advisory Committee on the Traffic in Women and Children automatically assumed each woman to have been a defenceless victim of deceit and forced to enter the prostitution business. Indeed, the increasing migration flows caused an ever-growing and more visible stream of women and girls being trafficked for the sex industry. However, as the author convincingly shows, without wanting to deny the social and psychological damage inflicted by trafficking in general, while the Committee officially battled against trafficking, by defining any prostitute as a victim of forced recruitment it implicitly made a case against the moral vices of prostitution in general.

As Christoph Rass's contribution notes, it was not only international organizations that were concerned with regulating international labour migration. Equally, supranational agreements could be reached by means of bilateral or multilateral agreements between states. In the context of rapidly changing economic structures and demographic regimes – both in terms of natural population growth and migration patterns – in the period 1919 to 1975, European countries were confronted with new labour market problems. On the one hand, the need for flexible (often unskilled) labour increased in what Rass calls the "core economies of north-western Europe"; at the same time, unlimited migration flows increasingly came to be perceived as undesirable. One – historically underexplored – way of regulating this international labour migration was through bilateral agreements. Rass argues that nation states instigated these agreements in order to retain as much control over international migration flows as possible, but that ultimately these bilaterals actually contributed to setting international standards. More implicitly, his contribution can thus also explain how the ILO standards that emerged were predicated upon specific "European" developments and therefore hardly relevant to migration patterns and conditions elsewhere in the world. Rass's analysis ends in the 1970s, and so we cannot see how these international standards subsequently developed. But Kaur concludes that, at least in south-east Asia, the "second wave of globalization" in the post-Independence era led to transnational labour migration becoming both regionalized and more global.

By and large, the contributions to this special issue of the *IRSH* identify powerful mechanisms that maintain systems of labour recruitment. The combination of indebtedness, family loyalties and needs, the pressure exerted by local authorities, and even national interests is a constellation of forces hard for individuals to withstand, and probably more difficult to withstand for women than for men in patriarchally organized societies. We do not want to give the impression, however, that the women and men who are recruited are just helpless victims. Even in cases where their recruitment could hardly be considered voluntary, their hopes and expectations, and the forms of agency they were able to fashion, are as historically significant as their experiences of exploitation, subjugation, and deceit. This is shown clearly in the articles by Rass, Schettini, and Rodríguez García, all of whom stress the agency and hopes of the recruited migrants, as well as the exploitation and control they suffered. This ambivalence also becomes clear in more recent accounts of contemporary domestic workers, who not only feel a responsibility to take care of their families at home, but also dream of a better life for themselves and their children.[35]

Apart from the desire for economic betterment, there is also the question of women's agency in a context marked by both male domination and by capitalist exploitation and precarity. Earning their own living, whether in a "respectable" or "immoral" job, may expose women to new forms of subjection and uncertainty, but it might also offer them a degree of economic independence, and at least partially free them from the prior constrictions imposed by the household and local community.[36] Again, the uncertain, and shifting, boundaries between free and unfree labour, and between agent and victim, become apparent.

## SOME CONCLUDING REMARKS

Each contribution to this special issue of the *IRSH* endeavours to explain the emergence and persistence of practices of indirect labour recruitment.

---

35. Rhacel Salazar Parreñas, *Servants of Globalization: Women, Migration, and Domestic Work* (Stanford, CA, 2001).
36. See the contributions by Rodríguez and Schettini in this issue. This could be the case not only for young unmarried women, compared with their position in the parental household, but also for married women. See Sen, "'Without His Consent?'".

It emerges from those contributions that three powerful interest groups are involved. First of all, there are the people who have authority over the labourer (a family member, a spouse or lover, a village head, relatives already employed by a plantation, factory, or at a port). Secondly, there are the professional intermediaries. These were already operative long before a third player emerged on the scene: governments, which, from the nineteenth century, in the wake of the abolition of the slave trade, tried to address and control the phenomenon. This happened at the same time that governments in Europe became involved in labour mediation, which had so far been a contested area between labour collectives and employers. The dual and often contradictory interests of governments become quite clear from the contributions, whether in the case of a colonial administration or of a democratically elected government. In both cases they have to enforce legislation against trafficking and coerced labour conditions, but they also feel responsible for facilitating enterprise in dire need of cheap labour. There is the same dual tension at the family or village level; parents are responsible for the well-being of their children, and village heads for that of their communities; at the same time, they are interested in the income-generating capacities of their kin. This is precisely what makes labour mediation ubiquitous and persistent. At the same time, however, impartial mediation does not exist, and this quite often gives it morally disturbing features.

*IRSH* 57 (2012), Special Issue, p. 16 doi:10.1017/S0020859012000764
© 2012 Internationaal Instituut voor Sociale Geschiedenis

# Mediating Labour: An Introduction
# CORRIGENDUM

ULBE BOSMA, ELISE VAN NEDERVEEN MEERKERK, AND ADITYA SARKAR

---

doi: 10.1017/S0020859012000430, Published by Cambridge University Press, 24 August 2012.

The email address for the third author, Aditya Sarkar is incorrect. This should be bhochka2@gmail.com

## Reference

Ulbe Bosma, Elise van Nederveen Meerkerk, and Aditya Sarkar, "Mediating Labour: An Introduction", *International Review of Social History*, 57 (2012), Special Issue, pp. 1–15.

*IRSH* 57 (2012), Special Issue, pp. 17–38 doi:10.1017/S0020859012000405
© 2012 Internationaal Instituut voor Sociale Geschiedenis

# The "Bargain" of Collaboration: African Intermediaries, Indirect Recruitment, and Indigenous Institutions in the Ghanaian Gold Mining Industry, 1900–1906*

CASSANDRA MARK-THIESEN

*St Cross College, University of Oxford*

E-mail: Cassandra.mark@history.ox.ac.uk

SUMMARY: This article argues that during the formative years of the colonial state in Ghana, European employers established new collaborative mechanisms with African intermediaries for the purpose of expanding the modern mining sector. They were forced to do so on account of severe labour-market limitations, resulting primarily from the slow death of slavery and debt bondage. These intermediaries, or "headmen", were engaged because of their apparent affluence and authority in their home villages, from which they recruited mineworkers. However, allegiances between them and managers in the Tarkwa gold mines considerably slowed the pace towards free labour. Indeed, a system in which managers reinforced economic coercion and repressive relationships of social dependency between Africans, allocating African labour contractors fixed positions of power, resulted from the institutionalization of purportedly traditional processes of labour recruitment into the modern market.

During the "industrialization" of gold mining in colonial Ghana at the turn of the nineteenth century, after two decades of a vexing labour shortage and one disastrous attempt at the large-scale import of indentured labourers from elsewhere in the British Empire, mine managers around Tarkwa finally felt compelled to pull in migrant labourers from various enclaves of West Africa. Modern forms of mining would in future rely strictly on African labourers. Several of these men arrived in the interior

---

* Previous versions of this article were presented at the African Economic History Workshop held on 2–3 May 2011 at the Graduate Institute of International and Development Studies, Geneva, and at the 4th European Conference on African Studies, Uppsala, 15–18 June 2011. I would like to thank Jan-Georg Deutsch, Deborah Mason, Alexander Thiesen, and Rouven Kunstmann for their comments. I gratefully acknowledge the Janggen-Pöhn Foundation in Switzerland for research support.

mining district in search of wage jobs from the nearby coastal regions of the colony and its protectorates. Others had travelled from remote villages in Liberia, Nigeria, and Sierra Leone. The Fante, Apollonians, Moshi, Krepi, Wangara, Basa, Kru, Vai, Yoruba, Hausa, Mende, and Timmani were among the social groups turning up in the mining towns.

A considerable number of these young men did not enter modern worksites on an individual contract basis. Rather, they served as members of a gang of roughly twenty-five men, each gang being recruited by and subcontracted to a headman from a shared home village or region. Various scholars have observed that in British West African colonies, the slow death of slavery and debt bondage overlapped with a period of rapid industrialization, often leading to the incorporation of traditional institutions of labour mobilization into large-scale industry.[1] Carolyn Brown has demonstrated that to get hold of "free" labour to serve the construction of the railway from Port Harcourt to Enugu in colonial Nigeria during the labour scarcity of World War I, managers frequently went through village authorities for recruits "under the assumption that requests through 'native chiefs' would be accepted by their subjects who, it was alleged, were accustomed to serving their customary labour needs".[2]

This article aims to shed new light on the industrial labour history of Ghana by exploring the system arising from the formal subsumption of such coercive patterns into colonial commodity capitalism during a boom period in the mining industry. It investigates two sets of vertical political relationships. Firstly, those between European mine managers and African workers; and secondly, those between African workers, particularly between headmen and the members of their gangs, engaged in mining for wages as part of their livelihood. The case of indirect recruitment in colonial Ghana demonstrates how, in defiance of an abolitionist rhetoric that put modern commerce on a pedestal, social bondage could be just as

1. For studies on the role of African authorities, in particular chiefs, in labour mobilization for various government services in colonial Ghana, see Kwabena O. Akurang-Parry, "Colonial Forced Labor Policies for Road-Building in Southern Ghana and International Anti-Forced Labor Pressures, 1900–1940", *African Economic History*, 28 (2000), pp. 1–25; *idem*, "'The Loads Are Heavier Than Usual': Forced Labor by Women and Children in the Central Province, Gold Coast (Colonial Ghana), ca.1900–1940", *African Economic History*, 30 (2002), pp. 31–51; *idem*, "African Agency and Cultural Initiatives in the British Imperial Military and Labor Recruitment Drives in the Gold Coast (Colonial Ghana) During the First World War", *African Identities*, 4 (2006), pp. 213–234; David Killingray, "Labour Mobilization in British Colonial Africa for the War Effort, 1936–46", in *idem* and Richard Rathbone (eds), *Africa and the Second World War* (London, 1986), pp. 68–96. After 1906, administrative officials increasingly made direct arrangements with chiefs to recruit labourers from northern Ghana to serve government services and colonial commerce.
2. This was a method known as "political labour" or the "local method"; Carolyn A. Brown, *We Were All Slaves: African Miners, Culture, and Resistance at the Enugu Government Colliery* (Cape Town, 2003), p. 78.

constraining following the region's deeper incorporation into the global capitalist market.

In the late 1890s, with the backing of the Foreign Office, the colonial government in Ghana embarked on a mission of social and economic development. As in other parts of British West Africa, particular industries were pinpointed and supported in the hope of economic prosperity. Out of this situation mine managers also anticipated that colonial administrators would begin to groom African workers in the ways of the free market. By the turn of the century, the gold mining industry in Tarkwa, previously desperately beseeching the colonial administration for additional support in infrastructure and government services, was now suddenly a core element in the administration's economic agenda.[3] However, the proliferation of wage labour in commercial companies was evidently taking a unique path. During this period of economic urgency, headmen became a common feature of the labour supply chain in Ghana's mining sector. Not only did these intermediaries recruit labourers, they also moved into the position of ethnic broker, caretaker, and de facto supervisor of the members of their gang for the entire duration of their contract.

In what follows, this article examines the transformation of African authority once it was used for the purpose of industrial labour mobilization. It attempts to discern the changing socio-economic position negotiated by such intermediaries, ambiguously situated between "labour" and "capital", by illuminating their interrelations with the aforementioned groups at various stages of the recruitment process: starting at the point of contact in the village, during the journey towards the mining centre, continuing throughout the contractual period, and even anticipating the extension of relationships between the members of a gang once they had completed a contract, due to shared home ties. The following questions will be addressed. What kind of authority did headmen hold over the larger population of African workers whom they had recruited from a shared home village or region? To what degree was such authority dictated by unwavering loyalty versus complex social negotiations? How did African social relations interact with the beliefs of European managers and officials? Why did managers employ these intermediaries? Moreover, why did European employers not simply fade them out to gain more authority over the labour market?

Methodologically, this study fits into a school of thought that regards European collaboration with indigenous authorities as lying at the heart of imperial policy around the globe.[4] In Ghana, the expansion of industrialized

3. Raymond E. Dumett, *El Dorado in West Africa: The Gold-Mining Frontier, African Labor, and Colonial Capitalism in the Gold Coast, 1875–1900* (Athens, OH [etc.], 1998), p. 289.
4. Studies exploring collaboration theory in imperial history include: Ronald Robinson, "Non-European Foundations of European Imperialism", in Roger Owen and Bob Sutcliffe (eds), *Studies in the Theory of Imperialism* (London, 1972), pp. 117–140; *idem*, "European Imperialism and

mining fostered, even demanded, new allegiances between Europeans and local authorities. In turn, these new relations also influenced the socio-economic landscape of the expanding wage labour market.

## CHANGE AND CONTINUITY IN MIGRANT SOCIAL RELATIONS

Migration was not a novel feature of the Ghanaian economy. Rather, the story of the twentieth-century mining industry was one of concentrated mass migration. Annually, several thousand labourers streamed from their villages in remote areas of West Africa to find wage jobs in the mines of south-west Ghana. They contributed to an estimated 15,000 African employees in Tarkwa and Obuasi, a neighbouring mining centre, around the first decade of the twentieth century.[5] This number included casual piecework labourers, permanently urbanized labourers, and, most of all, subcontract labourers who were bonded by agreement for six to twelve months. They were employed for "surface work which would include cutting firewood, clearing bush, making excavations, moving loads, and in the various underground duties entailed in ore-extraction".[6] Together they comprised a cluster of men of diverse cultural, economic, and regional backgrounds, speaking a multitude of languages.

The list of innovative rituals, relations, and beliefs shaping migrants' identities in the colonial mines of Africa has prompted the research of many scholars.[7] For Carola Lentz's studies on migrant miners in Tarkwa from northern Ghana, colonial ethnicization has been a driving force of these new politics.[8] For young male migrant labourers, life in a cosmopolitan area was at once both invigorating and terrifying. Novelty, for example, came in the form of newly acquired liberties and power relative to other

Indigenous Reactions in British West Africa, 1880–1914", in H.L. Wesseling (ed.), *Expansion and Reaction* (Leiden, 1978), pp. 141–163; Anthony E. Atmore, "The Extra-European Foundations of British Imperialism: Towards a Reassessment", in C.C. Eldridge (ed.), *British Imperialism in the Nineteenth Century* (London, 1984), pp. 106–125; Jane Burbank and Frederick Cooper, *Empires in World History: Power and the Politics of Difference* (Oxford, 2010).

5. An annual report from 1908 suggests that the number of African employees in the mining industry "was about 15,300 of which 540 were European". However, the available statistics are hardly precise; Gold Coast Departmental Report for 1908, National Archives of Ghana in Accra [hereafter, PRAAD], ADM 5/1/17.

6. Migeod to Governor Rodgers, Semi-Official and Private Letters concerning the Transport Department, no. 661/06, 28 April 1906, Royal Commonwealth Society Library in Cambridge, [hereafter, RCMS], 139/10/3.

7. See for example Patrick Harries, *Work, Culture, and Identity: Migrant Laborers in Mozambique and South Africa, c.1860–1910* (London, 1994).

8. Carola Lentz, *Ethnicity and the Making of History in Northern Ghana* (Edinburgh, 2006), pp. 1–13; *idem*, "Colonial Constructions and African Initiatives: The History of Ethnicity in Northwestern Ghana", *Ethnos*, 65 (2001), pp. 107–136.

social groups.[9] Lentz demonstrates that in spite of historical tensions and competition, groups from different localities encountered one another on a more or less equal footing in the mining centres.[10] These "new political structures, rituals and discourses were attractive [...] to migrant workers [...] who sought the same status and respect as colleagues [...] from pre-colonial kingdoms".[11] Among other guarantees, they now received equal pay for equal work and had access to similar legal rights. In conjunction with this shift, she contends that migrant men had simultaneously to establish affiliations to serve and protect self-interest along lines "often containing ethnic overtones, that emphasised ties extending beyond the boundaries of the [...] home village".[12]

Another driving force of colonial ethnicization in the urbanizing centres was the development of new political institutions with an ethnic identity at their centre. These new identities were further normalized through administrative routines led by European officials. Within this ensuing social structure, the headman served as the spokesperson for his ethnic kin.[13] He was in charge of negotiations between ethnic groups. In addition, during periods of occupational discontent, he was the one to voice the opinions and grievances of his countrymen. In cases of emergencies, illness, accidents, or death, even in "ordinary small palavers", he stood as their representative.[14] At the same time, scholars have pointed out that he was in the service of, and accountable to, the European mine managers.[15]

Yet, more than a few studies analysing miners' identities in colonial Africa highlight that they were not dictated by innovation alone, but that older modes of social organization continued to guide the way in which they organized themselves. For instance, D.T. Moodie argues that migrant gold miners on the Witwatersrand imported into modern enterprise a moral order from home. They constructed "new life-worlds out of fragments of the old".[16] Similarly, William Beinart emphasizes that many

9. Lentz states that in colonial Ghana "ethnicization" within migrant populations paralleled changes within broader society; Lentz, *Ethnicity and the Making of History*, pp. 2–3.

10. *Ibid.*, p. 34.

11. *Ibid.*

12. *Ibid.*, p. 2.

13. Carola Lentz and Veit Erlmann, "A Working Class in Formation? Economic Crisis and Strategies of Survival among Dagara Mine Workers in Ghana", *Cahiers d'Études Africaines*, 29 (1989), pp. 69–111, 95; Carola Lentz, "The Chief, the Mine Captain and the Politician: Legitimating Power in Northern Ghana", *Africa: Journal of the International African Institute*, 68 (1998), pp. 46–67, 64.

14. "Aufargah Mutiny", Letter Book, 9 October 1903, RCMS 139/4/30.

15. Lentz and Erlmann, "A Working Class in Formation?", p. 95; Jeff Crisp, *The Story of an African Working Class: Ghanaian Miners' Struggles, 1870–1980* (London [etc.], 1984), pp. 9–10, 76.

16. T. Dunbar Moodie with Vivienne Ndatshe, *Going for Gold: Men, Mines, and Migration* (Berkeley, CA [etc.], 1994), p. 42.

other groups of migrant workers in South Africa "retained deep roots" that continued to influence identity and self-organization.[17] The connection to older forms of a socio-political order was not solely abstract either. In her study of industrial coal miners in Nigeria, Carolyn Brown illustrates the persistence of an intimate connection to social hierarchies in the home villages. "Both the state and the industry used men whom they designated as local 'leaders' to control their populations."[18] Following similar observations in Ghana, Jeff Crisp recorded that, for European employers, "the easiest and most satisfactory way of dealing with Africans" was through African authorities.[19] Older institutions rooted in the context of a rural environment continued not only to influence migrants' identity and self-organization on a personal level, but also the operative system of labour regulation within modern mining companies.

Still, in the existing literature on Ghana's industrial history there is little mention of social hierarchies among migrants that predated their arrival in these urban areas. The business activities of headmen outside the mines, i.e. their roles as labour recruiters and contractors, are rarely discussed.[20] The discussion of colonial ethnicization, with its "new forms of classification and self-understanding",[21] has apparently overshadowed socio-political relationships that may have cut across ethnically homogenous groups in the mines, and that had roots in older power structures and institutions visible across the rainforests, savannas, and deserts of West Africa.

Closely related to the subject of continuities of power structures during the late nineteenth and early twentieth century is, naturally, abolition.[22] Around this period, the lives of African workers were under two trajectories of major transformation. Firstly, there was the slow death of slavery and debt bondage. The abolition of the legal status of slaves was granted in 1874. However, following a tradition of scholars who have regarded emancipation

17. William Beinart, "Worker Consciousness, Ethnic Particularism and Nationalism: The Experiences of a South African Migrant, 1930–1960", in Shula Marks and Stanley Trapido (eds), *The Politics of Race, Class and Nationalism in Twentieth Century South Africa* (London, 1990), pp. 286–309, 305. See also Charles Van Onselen, *Chibaro: African Mine Labour in Southern Rhodesia, 1900–1933* (London, 1976).

18. Brown, *We Were All Slaves*, p. 97.

19. J. Dickinson, *Notes for the Guidance of Europeans in the Gold Coast* (Accra, 1939), cited in Crisp, *The Story of an African Working Class*, p. 69.

20. Lentz and Erlmann mention, but do not elaborate on, the provision of job opportunities for new migrants by headmen; Lentz and Erlmann, "A Working Class in Formation?", p. 102.

21. Lentz, *Ethnicity and the Making of History*, p. 6.

22. Gareth Austin discusses the limited attention being paid to the subject of abolition in the field of West African economic history in his "Cash Crops and Freedom: Export Agriculture and the Decline of Slavery in Colonial West Africa", *International Review of Social History*, 54 (2009), pp. 1–37, 2.

as an uneven and slow transformation, Trevor Getz has argued that this "watered-down" piece of legislation "resulted for most slaves only in a gradual re-evaluation of dependent status rather than massive liberations".[23]

Further, Getz advanced the notion that political ties between European colonial officials and African authorities were a crucial motivation to the dilution of emancipatory legislation. During the era of emancipation, colonial administrators were, according to him, acutely aware of their need for the support of African authorities in political and military matters in the colonies.[24] Thus, just as the reliance of African authorities on the British for military support had quelled violent uprisings in the aftermath of the emancipation proclamation, in turn the British colonial government put forward the pretence of radical transformation in the metropolitan areas whilst maintaining their political allegiances to the same group of African elites for whom slave ownership continued to be integral to wealth, status, and power.[25]

On a perspective that coincides with Getz's in time and concept, Peter Haenger asserts that along with a colonial administration that unsuccessfully attempted to "steer a middle course" in dealing with the issue of slavery, other groups of Europeans in colonial Ghana were equally baffled by the complexities of realizing emancipation.[26] In particular, he portrays the Basel missionaries as often lacking a straightforward strategy in dealing with the liberation of slaves as they encountered resistance from among their own group of religious followers.

Ronald Robinson, an original voice on the subject of collaborative relationships between Africans and Europeans, has stated explicitly that colonial rule was built upon neither hegemony nor control. More accurately, he declared that it hinged on the establishment of collaborative mechanisms between the British and indigenous peoples. However, economic relationships in Africa, and for that matter also in Asia, were essentially undifferentiated from socio-political ones.[27] Thus, here, collaboration was not "in the export-import sector but among essentially non-commercial, ruling oligarchies and landholding elites".[28] Therefore, it

---

23. Trevor R. Getz, *Slavery and Reform in West Africa: Toward Emancipation in Nineteenth-Century Senegal and the Gold Coast* (Oxford, 2004), p. 160.

24. *Ibid.*, pp. 56, 113.

25. *Ibid.*, pp. 111–117. Other colonial governments around Africa took an equally ambiguous stance on ending slavery and debt bondage. For late nineteenth-century East Africa, Deutsch demonstrates that the institution of slavery was hardly challenged, and even supported, by the German colonial government in Tanganyika; Jan-Georg Deutsch, *Emancipation without Abolition in German East Africa, c.1884–1914* (Oxford, 2006), pp. 97–144.

26. Peter Haenger, *Slaves and Slave Holders on the Gold Coast: Towards an Understanding of Social Bondage in West Africa* (Basel, 2000), pp. x, 61–102.

27. Robinson, "Non-European Foundations of European Imperialism", pp. 129–130.

28. *Ibid.*

is hardly unusual that with the expansion of the industrial wage labour market, the second major trajectory of transformation, European employers established collaborative relationships with men who they believed already held enough authority to mobilize others.[29] Given their apparent affluence in their home regions, powerful African intermediaries were hired as labour recruiters and contractors to produce wage labourers for the industrial gold mines around the Tarkwa area.

For the period 1900 to 1906, it is useful to distinguish between larger political bodies formed mainly according to European design in the context of the mines, i.e. the councils, from smaller groups of socially homogenous gangs whose formation predated their arrival at the mines. To examine social relations within these smaller "gang" units, this article moves beyond the topic of ethnicity to compare the gang system with older institutions for labour mobilization.

## RELATIONS BETWEEN "CONTRACT BOYS"[30] AND HEADMEN

Associations between headmen and labourers may have been temporary in a professional sense, but in most cases their personal relationship extended far beyond the setting of the gold mines. Some headmen may have already been in the employment of industrial mines before setting off on the lengthy journey of labour recruitment. Nevertheless, they all initiated the "collection", or "shepherding", of migrant workers in their rural home region.[31] Though they may have shared similar lifestyles in that environment, by the time a gang reached the urban workplace distinctions between a headman and his labourers were evident and visible even in dress. The headman was in Western clothing: cotton T-shirt, full-length trousers, and cloth cap so typical of a contemporary industrial worker;[32] typical "unskilled" workers, in turn, were still sighted in loincloths and traditional cloth garb.[33] Many of the recruits chosen to engage in the tasks of drudgery and menial labour would have been young men

29. Writing about various types of labour recruiters in India, Tirthankar Roy explains that the ensuing imperfect wage markets "[created] space for individuals already enjoying economic or political power of some kind to try to become monopolistic suppliers"; Tirthankar Roy, "Sardars, Jobbers, Kanganies: The Labour Contractor and Indian Economic History", *Modern Asian Studies*, 42 (2008), pp. 971–998, 978.

30. For an original usage of this term, see "Inspector General of Police v. Seiden Wangara", July 1918, PRAAD, ADM 27/4/60, pp. 276–277.

31. These contemporary terms were used to describe the system of indirect recruitment serving the mines.

32. See Figure 1.

33. For an image of "unskilled" Liberian and Ghanaian labourers in Ghana around 1895–1905, see Dumett, *El Dorado*, p. 260.

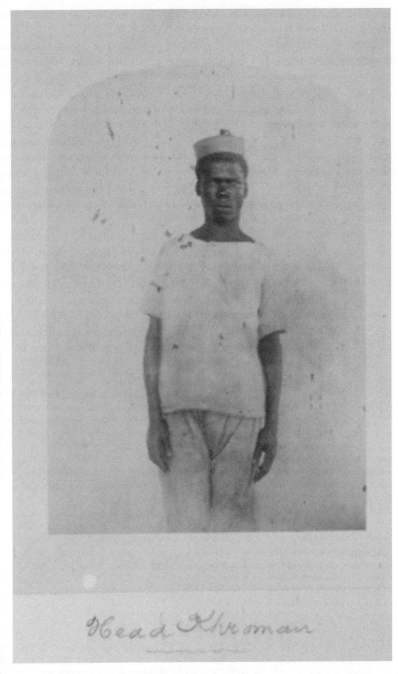

Figure 1. Kru headman on the Gold Coast (c.1876–1877).
*National Archives of the UK: ref. CO1069/29/34. Used with permission.*

belonging to a more socially vulnerable class of the community, or possibly even former or current slaves.[34]

In sum, labourers would likely have felt an obligation to their headman that surpassed modern-day employer–employee relationships. Just as some chiefs regularly managed to call on their followers for communal labour within the *corvée* system, so too social pressure could be utilized to mobilize industrial workers.[35] However, European imaginings of submissive African subjects failed to capture this relationship in its full complexity. A headman gained only a small fraction of his authority by virtue of a natural and self-affirmed affiliation between him and the labourers rooted in home ties. Indeed, indigenous economic institutions that could enforce coercive labour arrangements were far more vital to the amelioration of the pervasive labour scarcity, as seen in the widespread use of credit for the purpose of industrial recruitment.

Polly Hill shows that credit relationships were an integral part of rural-based economic production and development in parts of West Africa going back to "time immemorial".[36] Borrowing between farmer-traders was indeed an extension of the social hierarchy. Those individuals who had available surplus became creditors whilst the remaining population became debtors in order to raise starting capital for their enterprises. Such credit relationships were established in many forms, and were settled in an equally diverse number of ways.[37] For example, one of the patterns by

34. Dumett posits that some of the "generalized" barriers to long-term permanent wage labour for local labourers were even stronger for industrial mining. He gives three key reasons for this aversion, which was rooted in historical socio-cultural beliefs. Firstly, during the nineteenth century it was a taboo for the Akan to mine for gold. Rather, especially for the more dangerous tasks, they employed slaves. Secondly, there was a general awareness that mining was still an extremely dangerous occupation. Thirdly, even during pre-colonial times, the bulk of the workforce in the mines were migrants. These hindrances, along with the fact that no resources had to be exchanged upfront, speak to a higher proportion of local men from the poorest classes of society being extended credit to serve as wage labourers, relative to those who were granted credit for rural-based economic activities; Dumett, *El Dorado*, pp. 144–148; Polly Hill, *Development Economics on Trial: The Anthropological Case for a Prosecution* (Cambridge, 1986), p. 83; *idem*, *The Migrant Cocoa-Farmers of Southern Ghana: A Study in Rural Capitalism* (Oxford, 1997), p. 186.
35. For the pre-colonial period in parts of Ghana, *corvée* was used for everything from gold mining to agricultural labour and road maintenance; Gareth Austin, *Labour, Land, and Capital in Ghana: From Slavery to Free Labour in Asante, 1807–1956* (Rochester, NY, 2005), pp. 112, 185–189; Dumett, *El Dorado*, pp. 71–72; *idem*, "Precolonial Gold Mining and the State in the Akan Region: With a Critique of the Terray Hypothesis", *Research in Economic Anthropology*, 2 (1979), pp. 37–68, 44–47.
36. Hill, *Development Economics on Trial*, ch. 8.
37. Hill describes some ways in which loans were executed by rural dwellers: through the supply of temporarily borrowed farms, grains for the harvest, short-term loans for trading expeditions, produce to be sold for profit, animals for transportation to trading sites, and the mortgaging of farms to gain starting capital for business activities; Hill, *Development Economics on Trial*, pp. 89–90.

which poorer debtors repaid richer creditors was in non-monetary form, as in labour. Hill recognized that, "Grain may be granted to farm labourers who repay, over a period, in terms of work".[38]

Nonetheless, just as the number of credit relationships increased with commercial expansion,[39] so did the variety of their manifestations. Relevant here is the adaptation of such credit schemes for urban-based economies during the early colonial period as debtors were routinely recruited as wage labourers for large-scale mining. In order to engage twenty-five men for wage work in the urbanizing areas, it was often necessary for headmen to first loosen their economic constraints in the home villages. Before a gang could depart, it was therefore expected that the labour recruiter would provide each man with an advance payment. These funds were "primarily for the purpose of paying his debts (not for supporting his family) as otherwise his creditors, and natives have creditors, would not allow leave", remarked one European official.[40] Settling debts with local creditors granted large groups of indebted young men the mobility to pursue work for cash beyond the confinement of their home villages in order to improve their social status, among a broad spectrum of ambitions. Nevertheless, a migrant's debts were never simply written off. This financial exchange was rather equivalent to a switching of patrons.

Assuming the workers' debts, often amounting to several British pounds per individual, was invariably an expensive and risky business. Yet, it allowed the headman-creditor to solidify his authority over the members of his gang. He now possessed the power of economic coercion over them. To be more precise, it served the headman by compelling a recruit to continually sell his labour power in the mines until the debt had been paid off in its entirety.[41] Since in actuality the terms of lending

38. In addition to labour, repayment could occur in monetary form, or through produce and products; *ibid.*, p. 89.
39. For studies confirming the positive relationships between the availability of "trust", or credit, systems between Europeans and Africans and the spread of commerce in West Africa, see *ibid.*, pp. 89–90; Martin Lynn, *Commerce and Economic Change in West Africa: The Palm Oil Trade in the Nineteenth Century* (Cambridge, 2002), pp. 67–68; Ray Kea, *Settlements, Trade and Politics in the Seventeenth-Century Gold Coast* (Baltimore, MD, 1982).
40. "Memorandum on the Concession Labour Bill" enclosed in Confidential dispatch, William B. Griffith to F.W.H. Migeod, No. case 714, 25 March 1904, RCMS 139/12/11.
41. The coercive nature of this system should not undermine the fact that many labourers decided to work voluntarily. Nor should it overshadow the fact that many African workers were driven by more crippling economic pressures. For example, for those men from the border regions of French West African colonies in particular, the pressure to work for wages predominantly stemmed from the poll tax imposed by their colonial government. In spite of efforts by French administrative officials to keep such men within their administrative boundaries as a pool for forced labour, migrants made their way to Ghana, where wages were higher, allowing them to pay their taxes and still have enough money left over to participate in economic activities such as trade; Austin, *Labour, Land, and Capital*, pp. 401–402.

seemed to have largely rested in the headman's hands, he could spread the period of repayment, during which he gradually deducted this sum along with other fees and fines from his men's wages, as he saw fit (but likely with the limitation of a few months).[42] Although it is uncertain what amount of capital headmen possessed before their service engagement, the prevalence of this form of inducement to labour indicates that, at the very least, when he was in need of cash, mine managers were eager to provide him with enough money to conduct recruitment activities seamlessly. There is further documentation of African employers in the timber industry taking a similar approach to recruit labourers.[43] In addition to such capital tying labourers to headmen, once they used it to pay off their pre-existing debts, young men incurred additional debts during their journey to the mines.

There is no evidence that in the course of migration any labourers travelled with much, if any, remuneration. Firstly, potentially severe transportation costs, as required by travelling by train in 1903, for example, were initially the headman's responsibility, though they were later deducted from the workers' wages.[44] Secondly, small rations of fresh produce, grain, and water[45] were of limited use for what could range from several days to weeks of trekking on foot over hundreds of kilometres, or travelling for several days upon a German steamer, as was usually the case for labourers from Liberia. Therefore, in contrast to the self-financed journey home,[46] during which migrant workers usually had to purchase their own food and water and pay their own fares,[47] a headman would

42. It was also routine to wait until labourers had reached the mines before assigning them a concrete rate of pay; Migeod to Governor Rodgers, 28 April 1906.

43. "Quow Hammah v. Mahoma Nuhu", Criminal and Civil Record Book, District Commissioner's Court, 1894, PRAAD, ADM 27/4/41, pp. 39–42. Hammah testified: "I live at Abosso and I am a petty trader and I am also a contractor for firewood for the Abosso Company. One the Wednesday last I counted £24 [intended to be given] to a man Quamina Amman to take to the coast to advance labourers."

44. For example, one colonial official declared, "the cost of the steamer and the headmoney [for the Liberian government] is usually and properly paid by the employer. Sometimes, however, it is deducted from the men's wages"; Migeod to Governor Rodgers, 28 April 1906.

45. In 1914, an administrative official reported witnessing many gangs en route to Kumasi. They "are usually conducted by a native who had been to Kumasi before, and their members each carried with them a scanty supply of food and very little else"; Report on the Northern Territories, "Immigration and Emigration", Gold Coast Departmental Report for 1914, PRAAD, ADM 5/1/23.

46. Even Kru labourers who were imported by steamboats were responsible for their own return fares.

47. The colonial administration was concerned with the effect that rising food prices would have on the flow of migrant labourers into Ghana. The voyage home could be especially precarious. "During the dry season a soldier on his way to Kumasi on leave from Northern Nigeria informed [the District Commissioner] on his arrival that he had paid no less a sum than £2 for water since he had entered the Protectorate at Bawku"; Report on the Northern

also have been expected to offer the aforementioned provisions in subsistence and travel. Offerings of this kind ensured the labourers' arrival in
a good healthy condition. At the very least, gang members had to be
strong and energized enough to contribute to the building of their own
housing, which they were permitted three days on full pay to complete.[48]
The relationship of dependency that was established with indirect recruitment eventually carried over into the subcontracting period.

Formal sources of credit stemming from European employers eventually
became entangled with the financial institutions established between
Africans. Before embarking on a single day's work, or even witnessing
conditions in the mines first hand, labourers were getting themselves deeper
in debt by around 20 shillings.[49] In this case, the cash was a straightforward
economic incentive, and could be spent arbitrarily. Administrative reports
noted that men from the urban coastal regions of Ghana found offers
of this kind particularly attractive, despite the negative impact on their
final wages. It was evident that, "£2 a month with an advance of 20/- is
more desirable than £2.10/- a month with no advance".[50] Many companies
even used competitive advances of up to 30 shillings, far surpassing the 10
shillings suggested by the administration, to attract workers.[51] The accep-
tance of such credit stood as a ratifying seal of approval upon a worker's
consent to serve.[52]

Nevertheless, there was a more dubious side to this competition since
labour recruiters frequently used these cash advances to induce desertion
from competing concessions. This tactic may have been fair game for the
recruitment of casual labourers. However, secret talks had to be held with
the highly favoured "agreement boys". The ensuing conversation mirrored parts of the negotiation process that would have occurred in the
home villages. The covering of debts, future wages, transportation costs,
lifestyles on site, and the supply of advances were initial items to be
settled out of the earshot of potential informers to local management.[53]

Territories, "Immigration and Emigration", Gold Coast Departmental Report for 1914,
PRAAD, ADM 5/1/23.
48. Migeod to Governor Rodgers, 28 April 1906.
49. Griffith to Migeod, 25 March 1904.
50. "Concession Labour Ordinance", Letter Book, Sekondi, 3 December 1903, RCMS 139/4/57.
51. *Ibid.*
52. Often when a labourer was brought before the court and charged with desertion it was
emphasized that he had not only entered into contract with a particular mine, but also that he
had accepted an advance of a given amount.
53. For example, during the hearing of one allegedly illicit recruiter, the "underground boy"
Albert Kofi testified: "I know Bonsa Kwamin the accused. I knew him a week ago. Accused
came to me and asked me if I worked. I told him yes. He said he wanted people to work on
timber with him and that they would get plenty of money to pay our debts. Seven of us went
with him. He advanced us one pound each. We gave him, accused, a paper for the advance.

This apparently pricey service was a low cost to bear for mine managers since, as shown above, the wages of those miners who had accepted advances were appropriately adjusted and lowered. However, this calculation panned out only after roughly two to three months of continual work; ultimately employee retention was key. In all this, general management delegated to the headman the difficult and murky undertaking of tracking the multiple balances carried by each of the members of his gang. African authorities, officially insignificant auxiliaries to management, hereby mediated a share of the formal payment structures, another credit-based system.

Mine management may have preferred written contracts under the Master and Servant Ordinance of 1893, yet, before 1906, most contracts were still "under hand",[54] and for the length of their six to twelve month contracts mineworkers were subject to extended payment. This meant that they simply did not "draw their pay until the final completion of their contract".[55] In the meantime, similar to older forms of dependency that existed with the institution of nineteenth-century slavery or debt bondage, labourers acquired clothes, small sums of money, and other items by bargaining with their headmen.[56] This method of extended payments not only strengthened relationships of dependency by temporarily putting the labourers in the seat of "creditor", it also gave mine managers some peace of mind on the issue of retention. In 1903, one administrative official concluded that "a labourer does not desert when he has some money standing in his credit, except the provocation on part of his employer be unendurable; and there being no monthly payment in his case he does not take two or three days off after pay day to enjoy himself".[57]

Yet, there remained some room for manoeuvre. Rather than depending strictly on allowances from their headmen, some workers managed to

His clerk told us we would not get a full advance from accused. He refused to pay our train here. We asked him to pay what the mine at Tarquah owed us when we left at his request. He complained to the F.M. at Abosso and he sent us all to the police. Accused spoke to me first at Tarquah and said if I left the mine we would get plenty of money on timberwork" ;"Inspector General of Police v. Bonsa Kwamin", Criminal and Civil Record Book, District Commissioner's Court, 1919, PRAAD, ADM 27/4/61, pp. 223, 25; "Inspector General of Police v. Mana Wangara", Criminal and Civil Record Book, District Commissioner's Court, 1914, PRAAD, ADM 27/4/54, pp. 246–252.

54. "Coolie Labour", House of Commons Papers, Accounts and Papers (1906), pp. 1–50, 34. Therefore, Herbert Bryan, the Acting Governor, argued, "labour is seldom 'indentured' in the strict legal interpretation of the word".

55. "Rates of Wages and Cost of Living", Gold Coast Departmental Report for 1904, PRAAD ADM 5/1/13.

56. Akosua A. Perbi, *A History of Indigenous Slavery in Ghana: From the 15th to the 19th Century* (Accra, 2004), pp. 49–50.

57. "Report on the Transport Department, 1903", Rhodes House Library, Oxford [hereafter RHO], 7ss.14 s.10.

secure loans from individuals from the Fante coast of Ghana.[58] This option, nonetheless, proved of limited satisfaction. Labourers commonly became discontented after a six-month period under such constraints.[59] Having taken these limitations into account, one European employer asserted, "I do not care that they be bound for longer, as much trouble arises in consequence".[60] Certainly, migrants could find ways to finance a variety of entertainment: gambling, drinking, and sexual relationships. Yet, there existed constant reminders of their bondage.

At the end of a contractual period, when the time came to hand over payment, there also remained, as earlier implied, large scope for abuse since all payments went through the headman.[61] Referencing labour contractors in South Africa around the late nineteenth and early twentieth centuries, Alan Jeeves has posited that they "preferred this system rather than that where the mine paid the workers directly because it enabled them to discount wages in various surreptitious ways".[62] In Ghana, some headmen were just as conniving, managing to lengthen their men's service by continuously and strategically raising fines.[63] In one especially bad case, a particular headman refused payment to his entire gang after several months of hard labour.[64]

These strategies of tying workers for (relatively) short terms were pervasive throughout the recruitment process during the first years of the twentieth century. Supported by collaborative mechanisms between European employers and African headmen for the purpose of labour recruitment, these schemes were not, however, carried out in a facile manner with obedient followers, albeit perceived as "traditional". They required a high level of financial and social management. Nevertheless, indirect recruitment had a counteractive effect on the ambitions of contemporary "agents for change" for free labour. It obscured and weakened such humanitarian efforts since headmen could solidify and enhance their positions relative to the larger population of African workers. Considering that under British protection no individuals were supposed to be working under coercive conditions any longer, and at the very least they were to be

---

58. In a 1910 letter one headman complains about the damaging consequences of his men taking credit from "Fanti" people; Letters from Natives of West Africa, 1904–34, Letter no. 3, Essikadoe, Sekondi, 3 February 1910, RCMS 139/12/52.

59. "Report on the Transport Department, 1903", RHO, p. 472.

60. *Ibid.*

61. Criminal and Civil Record Book, District Commissioner's Court, 16 April 1902, PRAAD, ADM 27/4/43, pp. 330–331.

62. Alan Jeeves, *Migrant Labour in South Africa's Mining Economy: The Struggle for the Gold Mines' Labour Supply, 1890–1920* (Kingston, ONT, 1985), p. 97.

63. "Tarquah Mining & Exploration Company v. Kukoboa", Criminal and Civil Record Book, District Commissioner's Court, 18 November 1909, PRAAD, ADM 27/4/48, pp. 762–763.

64. *Ibid.*, pp. 297–299.

working by agreement, an investigation launched by the House of Commons into the state of these indentured labourers in 1906 indicates that many Europeans still had major concerns about the virtues of the gang system.[65] The nature of relationships between members of a gang remained hauntingly ambiguous. So, why did mine managers accept the infusion of "traditional" authority into the labour process?

RELATIONS BETWEEN MINE MANAGERS AND HEADMEN

In the setting of the formative colonial state, Europeans relied on African employees for a wide range of essential duties. According to Lawrance, Osborn, and Roberts, these were Africans who "held positions that bestowed little official authority, but in practice the occupants of these positions functioned, somewhat paradoxically, as the hidden linchpins of colonial rule".[66] Europeans hired these men in spite of realizing that African intermediaries would have to tackle the competing interests of serving their professional appointments whilst also satisfying their personal ambitions in the accumulation of power, wealth, and honour. In modern industry too, they faced these challenges. Mine owners in early colonial Ghana therefore had to negotiate their continual dependence on the authority of these individuals for daily functions, with the long-term goal of abolition and the spread of free wage labour.

Language barriers were one obstacle that few European officials, let alone entrepreneurs, had the time or boldness to cross. In the formal setting of the colonial state, such as offices and courts, European employers could rely on educated African middlemen, who sometimes spoke multiple European languages along with indigenous ones. Also in the wide and often tumultuous landscape of the goldmines, managers were incapable of looking over the shoulders of all the men working on a single concession. Difficulties in controlling the often hundreds of workers were multiplied as European mine managers had to deal with a wide range of languages and dialects. Thus, to minimize some of these problems within the organizational hierarchy in the mines, managers required that their headmen spoke at least some English, perhaps just enough to give and take orders.[67]

Keeping track of workers alone was a daunting task for mine managers, who often lacked an overview of the individuals in their employment at a

65. "Coolie Labour", pp. 1, 34–35.
66. Benjamin N. Lawrance, Emily Lynn Osborn, and Richard L. Roberts (eds), *Intermediaries, Interpreters, and Clerks: African Employees in the Making of Colonial Africa* (Madison, WI 2006), p. 4.
67. Official Correspondence and Papers, Gold Coast Transport Department, 2 December 1904, RCMS 139/11/8.

given time and in a given place. This issue remained infinitely more difficult where the workers were predominantly subcontracted, as opposed to having individual contracts under the Master and Servant Ordinance of 1893.[68] Individual registrations would have been costly and the colonial government continuously dodged shouldering such a burden. Instead, they pointed to the lack of cooperation between mines as the origin of the continual desertion problem. Administrators were certainly not convinced of the benefits of a fixed class of wage earners. This was, after all, a period in which colonial institutions were already stretched thin. Indeed, they could barely monitor who was entering and leaving the colony throughout the year. As a result, the difficulties of labour supervision grew proportionately with the number of African workers put to work. Given the frequent and widespread turnover in labourers, at least on an annual basis, this problem would not necessarily improve with time. In 1905, in neighbouring Asante, for example, a mine manager noticed to his own terror that "there was a much larger number of natives employed [there] than [they] had any idea of owing to the system of contracts whereby only one name appeared on the books".[69]

If European employers were not even clear about who was part of the workforce in their own companies, there was hardly any chance of them exercising adequate supervision themselves. This should not imply that the benefits of more extensive supervision by Europeans over single gang units were not regularly discussed.[70] Still, the financial burden of implementing such an operation remained unsustainable. The manpower was simply not available at a reasonable cost. In actuality, aside from senior management, white staffers generally also worked on an annual basis in administrative jobs in accounting, or technical jobs such as surveying. Moreover, there were usually only two mine captains under the direction of a chief mine captain. They were the ones in charge of supervising the

---

68. Around the late nineteenth and early twentieth centuries, some workers from Nigeria and Sierra Leone executed contracts under the Master and Servant Ordinance for roughly six months. However, predominantly Liberian Kru workers were "enlisted in their own country informally, and the agreement [was] properly drawn up under the Master and Servant Ordinance on their arrival in this Colony". This generally obligated them to twelve months of service. Arriving on steamboats at Sekondi, they were much easier to capture and register by local district commissioners before they made their way up to Tarkwa; Migeod to Governor Rodgers, 28 April 1906.
69. "Report by Mr. Mann", Mines Correspondence Inwards, 10 January 1905, London Metropolitan Archives, Ms 14171 v.11, pp. 48–54.
70. Migeod asserted that "the value of a gang of labourers varies with the ability of the European in charge. One will condemn a gang as worthless, while another will get most excellent result out of it. Probably under efficient supervision, or if possible working on a fair system of daily task work, a day's work will be performed at will for the expenditure compared favourably with that of an unskilled labour in other countries"; "Report on the Transport Department, 1903", p. 472.

activities of roughly 100 to 200 underground miners, who laboured in the extraction and hauling of ore, as well as surface miners, who worked in the various mills spread across a concession. Reducing the chance of adequate surveillance even further, among the handful of staff at each individual mine there was a frequent rotation of white men having to take to their sickbeds due to the harsh rural environment.[71] In practice, European supervision in the mining industry was no more than a delicate "thin white line".[72]

As a consequence of the practical limitations of European supervision, during the height of headship, in 1904, it was suggested that to avoid desertions "a native (who would more easily recognize native faces than a European) could be employed, constantly inspecting labourers at the different mines, paying special attention to all newcomers".[73] Additional lines of inspection by Africans would also have the effect of curbing the illegal activities of African clerks, who were suspected of producing artificial names on the timesheets, and later withdrawing the earnings of these dummy employees.[74] To this purpose, managers at the Ashanti mine contemplated the employment of four junior clerks. However, by and large, individual headmen administered other African wage earners and stood as their principal barrier to desertion. In fact, when there were runaways, headmen were first in charge of searching for and collecting these absconders.[75]

After carefully examining the devices that mine managers in south-west Ghana utilized to regulate labour migration, Raymond Dumett put forward the view that, contrary to the South African case around that period, they did not manufacture a system of oscillatory migration as a means of influx control.[76] "Rather they relied on it because it was the only

71. Dumett claimed that "rotating field management, the inevitable result of illness, frequent rest leaves, and convalescences in Europe, which saddled [mines] with heavy operating costs and destroyed continuity in administration" debilitated mine management in nineteenth-century Wassa; Dumett, *El Dorado*, p. 207.
72. Sara Berry, *No Condition is Permanent: The Social Dynamics of Agrarian Change in Sub-Saharan Africa* (Madison, WI, 1993); Anthony Kirk-Greene, "The Thin White Line: The Size of the British Colonial Service in Africa", *African Affairs*, 79 (1980), pp. 25–44.
73. Griffith to Migeod, 25 March 1904.
74. For example, in the case against John D. Coleman and William Dunn it was alleged that "they on about Feb. 26th [and] April 1st 1916 at Abbontiakoon in the Tarquah district did obtain the sum of £1-12-10 [and] £1-14-8 from Abbontiakoon by falsely pretending that one Kwaku, a labourer in the Abbontiakoon Mine, worked during the months of February [and] March 1916 whereas [...] in fact he had not worked during those months." Both men pleaded guilty; 6 May 1916, PRAAD, ADM 27/4/56, p. 595.
75. "Aufargah Mutiny", 9 October 1903.
76. Following Dumett, the narrative of "cheap labour theory" does not fit the case of nineteenth-century colonial Ghana. He has convincingly argued that there is no indication that mine managers deliberately constructed a non-permanent migrant labour force to lower wages and to enhance labour control; Dumett, *El Dorado*, pp. 224–225, 233.

alternative".[77] In reality, the majority of European companies struggled to retain workers, in particular those engaged in underground mining. An irregular labour market "cost them far too much money in lost time and skills and the continuous training of new workers".[78] In the long term, most workers were not dependent on wage labour for their reproduction, and their freedom to sell their labour power to whomever they desired kept wage rates comparatively high. To make things worse, as mentioned earlier, mining companies failed to cooperate with each other, probably because they had no support from the state when it came to solving the free-rider problem, i.e. in policing agreements among companies. Rather, these entrepreneurs used various shrewd tactics to steal workers from one another, often employing the services of labour recruiters to get men from neighbouring concessions with the attraction of better pay and food. This threat was particularly acute in the first weeks of employment, when workers still had credits to pay off.[79] Although African workers had mixed incentives to work for wages, a (more) regular workforce was of high priority for most businessmen.

Consequently, during the mining boom in early twentieth-century Ghana, the industry fostered institutions led by headmen that became a pivotal part of managerial strategies. By now it had become noticeably easier for men to enter the wage labour market as a member of a gang, as opposed to on an individual basis.[80] Naturally, some wage labourers did travel to find work in the gold mines by themselves.[81] However, given that nobody was sufficiently familiar with them to vouch for them or to supervise and protect them, European employers believed that they were much more likely to abscond from their contracts, leaving behind outstanding debts, and forcing companies to acquire replacements. The gang system aligned smoothly with widespread contemporary European perceptions of "traditional" African culture, which was based on small-scale tribal society. Individual labourers generally fell under the undesirable and suspicious category of "casual labourer". Gangs, by contrast, promised stability and order.

The incorporation of this modified form of "traditional" African authority at once aided early industrialization and made more elusive a comprehensive "market-oriented" approach to economic development

---

77. *Ibid.*, pp. 269–270.

78. Rumsey (1882) in *ibid.*, p. 270.

79. According to the Chief Officer of the Transport Department, it was "exceptionally rare" for a labourer to desert after several months of work; Letter Book, July–December 1903, RCMS 139/4/75.

80. Uttering his dislike for casual labourers, one administrative official complained: "They stay with an employer so long as it suits them and when the inclination takes them to make a change they merely await pay day to leave"; Migeod to Governor Rodgers, 28 April 1906.

81. Individual workers from Sierra Leone and Nigeria were reputed to travel to Ghana "on their own initiative" to look for jobs; *ibid.*

in Ghana. This was because the type of "progress" that was occurring in the mining industry around the early twentieth century modified labour relations in ways that increasingly followed market principles, but also remained based on social incentives. Employers' incorporation of institutions into industry, as opposed to individuals, would perpetuate a growing yet undifferentiated market for wage labourers.

Nevertheless, irrespective of whether they embraced indirect recruitment as a best practice for a tribal society, for most managers around the early 1900s it was merely a temporary solution which detracted from their long-term objective of better-organized management of wage earners in the colony, with the assistance of state law.[82] In other words, only as long as radical intervention in the lives of African workers was not a priority of the administration would most businessmen continue to respond crudely to the conditions of the labour market.

## CONCLUSION

The urgent expansion of modern enterprise in Ghana overlapped in time with the slow death of slavery and bonded labour. Yet, the existing literature on industrial labour in Ghana has overlooked the persistence of social hierarchies as it transpired between labourers in modern industry, following the emancipation of slaves. As African colonial employees in the "industrialized" mining sector, headmen initially emerged as labour recruiters and contractors in the Tarkwa region when European mine managers and officials, pressurized by labour shortages during a boom period, were unable to bring large numbers of young men into the labour market with wage incentives. These intermediaries were responsible for recruiting thousands of labourers from within an expansive West African network. Although they would lose influence with time, in the earliest decades of industrialization these types of African authorities enjoyed extraordinary autonomy over the larger population of African workers. In contrast to African colonial employees in government houses, i.e. educated Africans, the headmen derived power from home ties. Mine managers depended on these supposedly "traditional" authorities as they could use their relationships to mobilize other African workers.

It is unclear what percentage of these recruits were slaves. However, modern enterprise certainly adapted to a market wherein African workers

---

82. The Mine Managers' Association, a collective body of Tarkwa managers founded in 1902, attempted in vain to convince the government to approve the mandatory individual registration of workers in their centres. The Concession Labour Bill sought to curb desertion and other irregularities consistent with the lack of oversight of the workforce at the time; "Concession Labour Ordinance", Press Copy Book, 3 December 1903; RCMS 139/4/57. See also R.G. Thomas, "Forced Labour in British West Africa: The Case of the Northern Territories of the Gold Coast 1906–1927", *Journal of African History*, 14 (1973), pp. 79–103, 80, 87.

were driven by mixed incentives, some of which remained coercive in nature. An even closer look at indirect recruitment and subcontract labour further reveals that African authority, rooted in the home villages, not only remained relevant, but was further strengthened as it was built into managerial strategies. A novel feature of the modern industrial economy, headmen managed to acquire additional personal security and power through the formal and informal structures surrounding the organization in the mines, as they positioned themselves with European employers as natural leaders of "rural" societies.

Indeed, indirect recruitment for the purpose of colonial commodity capitalism mirrored colonial policies of administrative indirect rule in many ways, as social control in the mines was enacted through modified forms of African "customs" and "traditions", whether invented, imagined, or simply practised. Nevertheless, greater emphasis ought to be placed on the recognition that headship was modelled on a system of contested mutual rights and obligations between people as had existed in older times, as opposed to one hinging solely on natural submission. Caretaking and supervision were the rewards for loyalty and hard work. Further, both parties remained in a vulnerable situation due to shifts in debts and finances.

Similarly, the "pulling and tugging" that occurred within the vertical political relationships between European businessmen in colonial Africa and their indigenous intermediaries was certainly not hegemonic.[83] Some managers may have preferred to use modified forms of pre-industrial productive relations. However, it is unclear whether they could intervene in a radical fashion: whether any amount of investment in the mining industry would have sufficiently affected the contemporary state of the labour force, and, more significantly, the socio-political dynamics defining it. Rather, as a system of new rule, headship seems to have resulted from a pragmatic assessment of the condition of the labour market, where British industrial employers had little other choice.

In south-west Ghana, the "paradox" of allegiances between African intermediaries and European employers was that they simultaneously served to expand colonial commerce and to restrict the growth of free labour. On the one hand, it was the headmen's embeddedness within rural networks, and older types of socio-economic institution, that made them fundamental to industrial labour recruitment. On the other hand, it was the enhancement of their powers within such institutions that made them a threat to radical economic transformation and humanitarian ambitions,

---

83. In his introduction to Burbank and Cooper, *Empires in World History*, p. 14, Cooper describes the study of intermediaries as that "of people pushing and tugging on relationships with those above and below them, changing but only sometimes breaking the lines of authority".

as a considerable segment of the African labour force would remain directly accountable to other Africans, and not to European employers. Social submissions were reproduced. As a consequence, the colonial state would invest much time and effort in regulating indirect recruitment, rather than directly empowering and policing workers. This was the "bargain" of collaboration as manifested in the modern industry of early colonial Ghana.

*IRSH* 57 (2012), Special Issue, pp. 39–72 doi:10.1017/S0020859012000417
© 2012 Internationaal Instituut voor Sociale Geschiedenis

# Clandestine Recruitment Networks in the Bight of Biafra: Fernando Pó's Answer to the Labour Question, 1926–1945*

## ENRIQUE MARTINO

*Institute of Asian and African Studies, Humboldt University Berlin*

E-mail: enrique.martino@gmail.com

SUMMARY: The "Labour Question", a well-known obsession pervading the archives of Africa, was posed by colonial rulers as a calculated question of scarcity and coercion. On the Spanish plantation island of Fernando Pó the shortage and coercive recruitment of labour was particularly intense. This article examines two distinct clandestine labour recruitment operations that took hold of Rio Muni and eastern Nigeria, on the east and the north of the Bight of Biafra. The trails of the recruitment networks were successfully constructed by the specifically aligned "mediators" of kinship, ethnicity, money, law, commodities, and administration. The conceptual focus on flat "mediators" follows Bruno Latour's sociology of associations and has been set against the concept of an "intermediary" that serves to join and uphold the structure/agency and global/local binaries.

A disappearing Spanish Empire had wedged itself into the Bight of Biafra. Charted by Portuguese navigators and bound by the slave trade, this corner of the Atlantic was for the first two-thirds of the twentieth century embroiled in the colonial struggle for "manpower". The so-called "Labour Question", a well-known obsession pervading the archives of Africa, was

* This research has benefited from the financial support of ERC Starting Grant no. 240898 under Framework Programme 7 of the European Commission, which funds the Research Group "Forced Labour Africa: An Afro-European Heritage in Sub-Saharan Africa (1930–1975)". I am most grateful for the generous suggestions and corrections of Alexander Keese, Andreas Eckert, Sabine Scheuring, Ineke Phaf-Rheinberger, and Joel Glasman, and of course to the editors of the present Special Issue. Most of the sources referenced are from one Spanish archive, for which the following abbreviations have been used: AGA = Archivo General de la Administración, Alcalá de Henares, Spain, IDD 15, Fondo África; C = Caja; E = Expediente; DGMC = Dirección General de Marruecos y Colonias (Colonial Office, Madrid); GG = Gobernador General de Guinea (Governor, Santa Isabel); GG Bata = Subgobernador General de la Guinea Continental (Lieutenant Governor, Bata); Curaduria = Curaduría Colonial (Labour Office, Santa Isabel); Cámara = Cámara Agrícola de Fernando Póo (Agricultural Chambers of Commerce, Santa Isabel).

posed by colonial rulers as a calculated question of scarcity and coercion. In Spanish Guinea the shortage and compulsory recruitment of labour was unusually pronounced. On the island of Fernando Pó *la cuestión bracera* had revived the economic logic of the Caribbean plantation. With the indigenous Bubi population decimated by disease and forced labour, the island's economy came to depend on imported *braceros* – the Spanish term for agricultural contract workers derived from the word for arms. Towards the end of the Atlantic slave trade and the long imperial nineteenth century, these *braceros* included Cuban political prisoners and freed slaves, "coolie" workers from China, itinerant Kru sailors from the Windward Coast contracted into bondage, and, most infamously, tens of thousands of indentured labourers from Liberia.

Recruitment and even labour migration to the sole remnant of equatorial Spanish colonialism, by then reduced to the size of Belgium, was explicitly prohibited by all other European empires. The labour supply from the Republic of Liberia was cut off in 1930 after a well-publicized intervention by the International Labour Organization (ILO), whereupon the obscure colony became popularly known, from Monrovia to Geneva and from London to Lagos, as "the island of no return". Surrounded by boycotts and their own notoriety, the planters on Fernando Pó, who were producing about 2 per cent of the world's cacao, sought out underground labour suppliers in an attempt to scramble themselves out of the paralysing labour shortage on the island. As the archival material unearthed here will show, planters relied on two distinct and successive clandestine labour recruitment operations in Rio Muni and Nigeria to the east and north of the Bight of Biafra. The scale of clandestine recruitment was, in its region, period, and proportionate dimension, unparalleled.[1]

In 1926 Fernando Pó turned to its continental exclave Rio Muni, and transformed the border zones with Gabon and Cameroon into a labour reserve for Spanish recruiters. What Catherine Coquery-Vidrovitch called "the plague of recruiters" unleashed decades earlier across the hinterlands of resource-extraction works in central and southern Africa reached Rio Muni with a time-lag, and a vengeance.[2] As a Spanish territory, it had

---

1. The techniques used by the island's recruiters, which at the least can be described as audacious and cunning, have their parallels throughout colonial constellations of capital and labour. See, especially, Alan Jeeves, *Migrant Labour in South Africa's Mining Economy: The Struggle for the Gold Mines' Labour Supply, 1890–1920* (Johannesburg, 1985); the Peru case study in Tom Brass, *Towards a Comparative Political Economy of Unfree Labour* (London, 1999); and the case study of a plantation island in New Guinea in Marcel van der Linden, *Workers of the World: Essays Toward a Global Labor History* (Leiden, 2008), pp. 339–358.
2. Catherine Coquery-Vidrovitch, "The Colonial Economy of the Former French, Belgian and Portuguese Zones, 1914–35", in Adu Boahen (ed.), *General History of Africa*, VII, *Africa Under Colonial Domination 1880–1935* (Paris [etc.], 1985), pp. 351–382, 363; André Gide, *Voyage au Congo* (Paris, 1927), p. 72.

been a haven for Fang escaping German and French forced-labour regimes, but in just a few years the Spanish were close to subjecting the entire male population of working age to forced labour on the mainland and to contract labour on the island. The first part of this essay covers the period of the Primo de Rivera dictatorship and the Second Republic, which lasted from 1931 to 1936, and will document the free rein given to private recruiters and their lawless methods, to which the Spanish authorities turned a (permissive) blind eye. The labour reforms initiated at the end of the short-lived republic led to the dispersal of the Spanish recruiters of Rio Muni and prompted the transition to complete dependence on Nigerian recruiters.

The second part of the essay traces the recruitment constellation that took hold of Nigeria's eastern provinces. From Calabar and Victoria to Santa Isabel, the trickle of small traders and recruiters, using counterfeit papers on ferry boats, turned into a wholesale smuggling network on canoes which brought over tens of thousands of Ibibio and Igbo workers. The outbreak of the Spanish Civil War left the then fascist island of Fernando Pó financially and diplomatically isolated until the end of World War II, which entrenched the illegal canoe trade along the sharpest edge of the Bight of Biafra. Around 1940, in the aftermath of the Great Depression in Nigeria, and with Calabar's merchants seeking profitable new ventures, the proportion of illegally recruited workers stood, astoundingly, at 10 per cent of Nigeria's wage-employed population.[3] Even in the post-World-War-II decades, the amount of migrant labour, disenfranchised and doubly discriminated against in Spanish Guinea, was large enough to contradict Frederick Cooper's or Carolyn Brown's positing of the late colonial period as a time when wage labourers turned to nationalist protest and claimed entitlements through orthodox class-based means.[4]

While only the "long decade" of the 1930s falls within the scope of this essay, this important period signals the beginning of labour reforms in most African colonies, as labour departments and protective legislation were widely introduced after a spate of ILO treaties on forced labour, and

3. Heinrich Wieschhoff, *Colonial Policies in Africa* (Philadelphia, PA, 1944), p. 38; Granville St John Orde-Browne, *Labour Conditions in West Africa* (London, 1941), p. 79. The figure in 1938 for those in waged employment was 182,600, of which 50,000 each were employed in mines and government, in a Nigerian population of 21 million. For mines, see William Freund, "Labour Migration to the Northern Nigerian Tin Mines, 1903–1945", *Journal of African History*, 22 (1981), pp. 73–84.
4. Frederick Cooper, *Decolonization and African Society: The Labor Question in French and British Africa* (Cambridge, 1996), see esp. parts 2 and 4, as well as his ongoing research; Carolyn A. Brown, *"We Were All Slaves": African Miners, Culture, and Resistance at the Enugu Government Colliery* (Oxford, 2003). For an overview see Andreas Eckert, "Geschichte der Arbeit und Arbeitergeschichte in Afrika", *Archiv für Sozialgeschichte*, 39 (1999), pp. 502–530.

the recruitment of and contracts for "indigenous workers".[5] In a pro-
gressivist narrative the interwar years would mark the transition from
unfree to free labour in African history.

In terms of labour recruitment, empires in Africa sought to shorten the
distance from the Asian-based indentured labour market and to hasten the
end of their "initial" – drawn-out and recurring – stage of administratively
directed forced labour. The replacement would be a framework where
employers could hire voluntary workers under the guidance of state-
regulated international conventions and licensed agencies. The two
recruitment constellations examined here fall into neither of those temporal
"stages" because they cannot be categorized by the binary pairs of
free/unfree and legal/illegal correlated by the modern state. That constant
and shady borderland was home to a para-state, quasi-open market of
trafficking entrepreneurialism. By operating on the edges of the Bight of
Biafra the illegal recruiters circumvented the police state and disrupted
the institutionalization of regulated labour markets. They pocketed an
enormous share of the colonial economy of the island, which they also
underpinned. The recruiters were paid, but through a series of very
elaborate transactions they had to pay the costs of displacement, and every
cent and metre had to be accounted for.

The empirical tracing of the recruitment networks leads to a prolonged
focus on the institution of bridewealth in the Fang societies of Rio Muni and
the trading and merchant structures of the Igbo and Efik of south-eastern
Nigeria. The often underestimated role of kinship and ethnicity in structur-
ing labour migration and recruitment has been highlighted by Ravi Ahuja.
His unique research on South Asian maritime labourers has wonderfully
reconstructed how colonial "networks of subordination" were accompanied
by the "networks of the subordinated", that were neither "surviving elements
of pre-capitalist societies nor solely infrastructures of resistance".[6] However,
as the empirical tracing of the recruitment networks includes the even more
often underestimated role of non-human actors, such as currencies, travel
documents, labour laws, and contraband goods, the theoretical inclination in
this piece relies on Bruno Latour's sociology of associations rather than on
the conceptual reservoirs of social history.

Latour's controversial method prohibits scientific "purification" that
reduces socio-technical processes to singular causes, such as the nature of

5. Only Portugal refused to even sign the ILO conventions of 1930, 1936, and 1939, and while
only Britain ratified them expeditiously, they carried a rhetorical and international legal weight.
See part 1 of Cooper, *Decolonization and African Society*.
6. Ravi Ahuja, "Networks of Subordination–Networks of the Subordinated: The Ordered
Spaces of South Asian Maritime Labour in an Age of Imperialism (c.1890–1947)", in Ashwini
Tambe and Harald Fischer-Tiné (eds), *The Limits of British Colonial Control in South Asia:
Spaces of Disorder in the Indian Ocean Region* (London, 2009), pp. 13–48, 33.

the market or class, power, and imperialism. With Latour, phantom master concepts are deflated and demystified to the extent that they can no longer be causally posited "below", nor be used as shortcuts to explain deductively almost everything else as mere effects, expressions, and reflections thereof. In Latour's laboratory the privileged lens that splits the abstract from the concrete to attain largely hollow structures disintegrates and, as if with the wave of a wand, hitherto passive actors and restricted contexts come to life in "a world made of concatenations of mediators where each point can be said to fully act". The magic comes from a *flat* ontology and a radicalized empiricism that "tries to replace as many causes as possible by a series of actors – such is the technical meaning of the word 'network'".[7]

A "network" is not merely the loose and uninspiring middle ground between structure and agency or the local and the global. In Latour's methodological terms, after "localizing the global" and, with equal weight, "dislocalizing" or "redispatching the local", comes the work of "connecting sites". Even though Latour rejects the term "actor-network theory", preferring instead a magmatic totality of a "plasma of actants", he endorses its famous acronym. ANT encapsulates his methodological maxim: to follow the actors, and to do it as painstakingly as ants might, had they been set to work on the shelves of an archive. An ANT approach has been enabled by the Africa collection in the Spanish archive as it is actually "un-archived": the bulk of the documentation was never filtered or indexed. In this text, the aim has not been to mirror the already purified form of the well-structured colonial reports occasionally encountered, but, with the sources of all scales side by side, to reflect in method, map-making, and writing, the data cascades contained in a series of archival sheets, files, and boxes.

## RIO MUNI OVERRUN BY RECRUITERS, 1926–1935

In the main square in Santa Isabel there once stood a statue of Governor Ángel Barrera signing the 1914 labour treaty with Liberia, surrounded by the Gothic cathedral, the mission, the Governor's Palace, and the offices of the John Holt Company. The treaty was briefly renounced by Liberia in 1926, and finally annulled in 1929, after which a fact-finding ILO

7. Bruno Latour, *Reassembling the Social: An Introduction to Actor-Network-Theory* (Oxford, 2005), p. 59. This network-theory direction is a response to the insistent cues of Frederick Cooper's critique of the term "global", found in its most programmatic form in Frederick Cooper, "Back to Work: Categories, Boundaries and Connections in the Study of Labour", in Peter Alexander and Rick Halpern (eds), *Racializing Class, Classifying Race: Labour and Difference in Britain, the USA and Africa* (London, 2000), pp. 213–232, and idem, "Networks, Moral Discourse, and History", in Thomas Callaghy, Ronald Kassimir, and Robert Latham (eds), *Intervention and Transnationalism in Africa: Global-Local Networks of Power* (Cambridge, 2001), pp. 23–46.

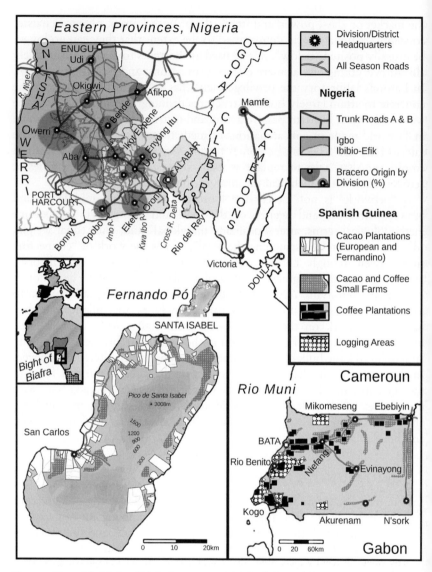

Figure 1. Map of the Bight of Biafra in 1940. For Nigeria all five eastern provinces, including the Cameroons, a British Mandated Territory, are visible. Each province was subdivided into several divisions, whose borders are not drawn, although their relevant headquarters are. The circles indicate the origin of Nigerian *braceros* by division. The road network is a good proxy for population density. For Fernando Pó, land use is to actual size.[8]

8. The map of Nigeria in 1940 is adapted from "A Ten-Year Plan of Development and Welfare for Nigeria", National Archives of the UK, London: Public Record Office [hereafter, TNA, PRO], CO 657/53. The maps of Spanish Guinea are adapted from Jaime Nosti Nava, *Notas*

commission discovered that contract workers had "been recruited under conditions of criminal compulsion scarcely distinguishable from slave raiding and slave trading".[9] Liberia's first treaty retraction cut the plantation labour figures by half, and in response the new governor, General Miguel Nuñez del Prado, orchestrated the military occupation of Rio Muni.

Before 1926, Spanish control on the mainland was limited to the coastal towns and most of the 100 European residents had been German factory shop owners and arms dealers who bought up hardwood, wild rubber, and ivory. In the years that followed, with *prestación personal* (*corvée*) in lieu of tax, some 500 kilometres of roads and bridges were built, dotted with garrisons of the colonial guard. At any given moment, up to 4,000 Fang were working unwaged on such public works, and the dictates of forced labour meant that people were shuffled off to the plantations by the colonial guards on any pretext of disobedience.[10] Systematic disempowerment and induced indebtedness were also fostered by the colonial courts, who summarily distributed heavy fines or sentences of forced contract on Fernando Pó, so that during the three months approaching the harvest season in 1926 some 4,500 *braceros* and 1,181 accompanying and working women were sent there.[11] Alongside such forced labour schemes, the aggravated labour scarcity on the island activated a private recruitment industry.

---

*geográficas, físicas y económicas sobre los Territorios Españoles del Golfo de Guinea* (Madrid, 1942), pp. 120–122. Data on the origin of Nigerian *braceros* can be found in C.W. Michie, "Labour Conditions in Spanish Guinea" (28 February 1941), TNA, PRO, FO 371/26908. Jaime Nosti Nava, *La agricultura en guinea española* (Madrid, 1955), p. 153, writes that "at least fifty per cent of contracted *braceros* are Ibo from Owerri". In 1940 18 per cent of the island was under cultivation, 26,340 hectares or 71 per cent by Europeans, and 10,600 hectares or 29 per cent by Africans. There were some 270 cacao producers, 100 of whom did not employ migrant labour. See Günther Wolff, "Ein Beitrag zur Wirtschaft von Fernando Poo", *Beiträge Zur Kolonialforschung*, 1 (1942), pp. 93–110.

9. "Slavery Conditions in Liberia", *New York Times*, 27 October 1930. See the foundational work of Ibrahim Sundiata, *From Slaving to Neoslavery: The Bight of Biafra and Fernando Po in the Era of Abolition, 1827–1930* (Madison, WI, 1996), pp. 117–122.

10. Gustau Nerín, *La última selva de España. Antropófagos, misioneros y guardias civiles: Crónica de la conquista de los Fang de la Guinea Española, 1914–1930* (Madrid, 2010), p. 218. In the early twentieth century there were other forced labour schemes also subjecting the indigenous Bubi populations of Fernando Pó. See Gonzalo Sanz Casas, "Los finqueros y el uso del trabajo forzado en la agricultura colonial de la isla de Fernando Poo", *Arxiu d'Etnografia de Catalunya*, 3 (1984), pp. 123–136; and Dolores Garcia Cantus's ongoing research. The small historical literature on Equatorial Guinea has focused almost exclusively on Fernando Pó and on the pre-1930 period.

11. These women worked unwaged as cooks and cultivated food plots near plantations; GG to DGMC, 12 October 1926, C-81/07646. For indictments against the entire colonial institutional apparatus, see Curaduria to GG, 27 July 1932, C-81/8125, E-4; Nerín, *La última selva de España*, p. 225. This is the only published work, beyond the very few sentences in other publications, dealing with labour issues in Rio Muni. It does not, however, cover the activities of the private recruiters.

## Reclutadores, ganchos, *and the money trail*

The start-up funds for the recruiter-entrepreneurs were easily provided by wealthy planters. The 10,000 tonnes of cacao exports were guaranteed to be sold in Spain at protectionist prices three times higher than the global market rate.[12] The existing harvest on the 36,000 hectares under cultivation already filled the subsidized cacao quota, and so all that was needed was to ring the labour-scarcity alarm and invoke the spectre of rotting crops and a bankrupt colony to perpetuate the exploitation of a just-in-time labour force that would be procured by any means necessary.

While a short-lived decree gave the Cámara Agrícola de Fernando Póo (Agricultural Chamber of Commerce, hereafter Cámara) a recruitment monopoly in Rio Muni that aimed "to avoid the recruitment of indigenous workers being bastardized and converted into an illicit trade, to the benefit of the recruiters", the allocation of any incoming labour by the Cámara suited only the so-called aristocratic planters, consisting of the early Catalan settlers, Spanish Cuban exiles, and the large corporate-owned plantations. The owners of the other major plantations were Spanish, Portuguese, German, and Fernandino – African immigrants originating from the nine-teenth-century Portuguese Empire and British West Africa. Feeling their own hands were tied, the planters decided to force through the reintro-duction of "FREE RECRUITMENT as the only solution". In December 1927 the governor of Fernando Pó conceded and even extended "free recruitment to all territories outside the colony".[13]

The new logging lobby of Rio Muni entered the fray over labour in the late 1920s by denouncing the deleterious effects of the island's recruiters, both in demographic terms and for its own commercial interests. There were fewer than 100,000 Fang in Rio Muni, and in 1930 80 per cent of the 5,000 annually contracted *braceros* were sent to the island.[14] That pro-portion was slowly being reversed as Fang workers much preferred

12. William Gervase Clarence-Smith, "African and European Cocoa Producers on Fernando Póo, 1880s to 1910s", *Journal of African History*, 35 (1994), pp. 179–199, 197; Jordi Sant Gisbert, "El modelo económico colonial y sus contradicciones: Fernando Poo (1900–1936)", *Afro-Hispanic Review*, 28 (2009), pp. 57–80, 65. In 1930 the Cámara blocked the granting of any further land concessions for almost two decades. For a broad overview, see Alicia Campos Serrano, "Colonia, derecho y territorio en el Golfo de Guinea: Tensiones del colonialismo español en el siglo XX", *Quaderni Fiorentini*, 33 (2005), pp 1–27.
13. Sebastian Llompart Aulet, *Legislación del trabajo de los Territorios Españoles del Golfo de Guinea* (Madrid, 1946), p. 108; Finqueros to Cámara, 4 February 1927, AGA, C-81/08096, E-28; Llompart Aulet, *Legislación del trabajo*, p. 109. For an overview of the conflict see Gonzalo Sanz Casas, "Política colonial y organización del trabajo en la isla de Fernando Poo: 1880–1930" (Ph.D., University of Barcelona, 1983), pp. 241–248; and in the local media "¿Monopolio, No? ¿Exlusiva, Si?", *La Guinea Española*, 25 March 1927.
14. For the census tables and much more, written up by a wizard of statistics and founder of a Braudel-like structuralism in Spain, see Román Perpiñá Grau, *De colonización y economía en la*

employment in the closer and better-paying expanding logging concessions of Rio Muni. With the final withdrawal of Liberian workers, the
labour shortage on the island peaked. In the speculation and bidding wars
for *braceros*, the commission paid by the cacao planters of Fernando Pó to
the recruiters rose from 50 pesetas in 1926 to 500 and even to 800 pesetas
in 1931, of which 200–300 pesetas was pure profit. Considering that the
average income of Europeans was 500 pesetas a month, that "margin of
profit actively sustain[ed] a large army of intermediaries, direct and
indirect, who by all possible means made sure they directed the workers
to ensure the best agricultural interests of the island".[15]

There were at least 60 European *reclutadores* operating at any one time.
Professional recruiters could sign off up to 100 *braceros* a month at the
Curaduria (labour office) in Bata, whereas the part-timers could manage
around 10 *braceros*. The latter group of *reclutadores*, more numerous,
were start-up planters "who found in this activity the resources to cover
the costs of running their coffee plantations" until the seedlings grew
large enough to bear fruit, which would take at least three years.[16] The
first coffee plantations were dotted along the new road between Bata
and Mikomeseng, and land concessions were more readily granted than
private credit. In contrast to other European colonies, there were no
immigration restrictions to Spanish Guinea to discourage – to use early
twentieth-century census categories – "undesirable" Europeans of the
"vicious" classes from settling.

During the 1920s the colony experienced an economic boom and
"served as a landfill site for Spaniards of the worst class who wanted to
enrich themselves, quickly and easily", who wanted to "prosper and find a
fortune".[17] The *reclutadores* are described by Republican and Victorian
authors as "callous, sleazy [and] spiritually barren", and, in one recruiter's
own words, they were "merciless and criminal".[18] Their methods were
"legally prohibited but perfectly known".[19] In Rio Muni the recruiters not

*Guinea Española: Investigación, sobre el terreno, de la estructura y sistema de colonización en la Guinea Española* (Barcelona, 1945), p. 101.

15. Cámara Bata to GG, 11 August 1931, AGA, C-81/8095, E-17. In the late 1930s, 20 per cent of labour costs disappeared into recruiters' pockets, 20 per cent covered wages, 45 per cent went into imported food rations, and the remainder went for housing, sickness, death, and flight; Román Perpiñá Grau, "Mano de Obra Africana: Factor de coste colonial", *Cuadernos de Estudios Africanos* (1947), pp. 127–144, 128.

16. Curador to GG, 16 June 1931, C-81/08125, E-2.

17. A. Victor Murray, *The School in the Bush: A Critical Study of the Theory and Practice of Native Education in Africa* (London, 1929), p. 25; Guillermo Cabanellas, *¡Esclavos!: Notas sobre el África negra* (Valencia, 1933), p. 19.

18. Curador to GG, 16 June 1931; Francisco Madrid, *La Guinea incógnita: Vergüenza y escándalo colonial* (Madrid, 1933), p. 89.

19. GG to DGMC, 28 December 1935, AGA, C-81/06867, E-5.

only had free rein over Africans, but even established a mafia-like power of intimidation over European managers and administrators, even to the point of assaulting the labour officer if he dared question the true age of a *bracero* or the legitimacy of a contract's "signing". Some recruiters also operated illegal rackets to import alcohol and rifles, essential items needed by all the recruiters entering into negotiations with the local chiefs.[20]

The crucial interlocutors between all these mediators of the money trail were the *ganchos* (runners or literally "hooks"). Each *reclutador* operated with up to six *ganchos*, who were usually skilled labourers or employed as foremen in the Rio Muni plantations. These African intermediaries tended to be Kombe and Balenke who lived in the Bata area and had acted as porters in the first colonial expeditions. The coastal Ndowe groups had some trading and marital relations with the Fang, whose territory began at Niefang, although there were tensions between them, as after the end of the slave trade – which the Fang had largely evaded – there was a history of the Fang displacing the Ndowe further along the coast.[21]

## Fang clan chiefs, regalos, and bridewealth

The recruiters operated with two related tools that mediated their work of recruitment in a situation where there was no spontaneous market for voluntary labour. First, the *regalo* – literally "gift" but actually a full wage advance – used for the payment of bridewealth, and second, the payoff of the African labour intermediary. In the African social history literature that is less inclined to dwell on kinship, the practice of bridewealth and the figure of the collaborating chief are often tabooed and demonized and then treated as if they were expected to have operated by themselves.[22] In such a detached functionalist view, the common commercial and missionary reading of "women being bought" and "chiefs selling the bachelors" takes over. Instead, with ethnographic patience and by taking the long detours and time lapses that the archive allows, it becomes possible to trace how labour recruitment was a product of a continuous thread of translations between wage advances, colonial

---

20. Madrid, *La Guinea incógnita*, p. 89; Gustau Nerín, *Un Guardia Civil en la Selva* (Barcelona, 2008), p. 117.

21. Muakuku Rondo Igambo, *Conflictos étnicos y gobernabilidad: Guinea Ecuatorial* (Barcelona, 2006), pp. 30–41; Nosti Nava, *Notas geográficas*, pp. 51–60.

22. Even where the focus on the sites of wage labour has been dispersed to the home and hinterlands, as for example in chs 3 and 4 of Brown, *We Were All Slaves*, on recruitment in Eastern Nigeria, she does not dwell for long on the non-industrial ethnographic literature. The main works employed here, alongside the available sources, are Jane Guyer, *Marginal Gains: Monetary Transactions in Atlantic Africa* (Chicago, IL, 2004), pp. 27–49; Jonathan Parry and Maurice Bloch (eds), *Money and the Morality of Exchange* (Cambridge, 1989), pp. 1–29.

currencies, monetized bride-prices, the colonial state, and chiefly accumulation. In non-coastal Equatorial Africa it

> [...] was not only a calculation and political power that created the spatial geography of exchange but also the ideology of transformation that undergirded it. The capacity to define, institutionalize, take advantage of, technically control, and symbolically represent conversions is at the heart of the extensive regional transaction systems that every autonomous polity built up in the stepwise relations that connected the interior to the changing currency flows of the great trade routes.[23]

Of course, such conversions or translations, tightly binding together money, gender, and power across different polities, were not always indispensable for labour recruitment. With state-directed forced labour, non-dialectical violence worked. To be sure, the private recruiters managed to break into the scene only after two sweeping acts of foundational colonial violence, namely military pacification and the imposition of a new colonial currency as a measure of value. Alongside the ongoing military invasion, recruiters often dressed up in uniform or otherwise made use of the aura of intimidation derived from systematic police brutality to hoax and coax entire villages. Alongside the imperial occupation, the Spanish colonial authorities prohibited the use of previous currencies. A proletarianizing poll tax was not yet in place, but the peseta coin came to be quickly translated by the Fang for the purpose of bridewealth payments.[24]

In several sources the *ganchos* and the *reclutadores* unanimously describe the process of recruitment in formulaic terms. They would drive along the Bata to Ebebiyin Road, on or near to which the Fang population had been told to relocate their "villages, strung out like beads upon the arteries of commerce by the colonial administration".[25] The *ganchos* would inquire in a mix of Fang and Pidgin English if any men could be supplied. The resident chief would categorically answer in the negative until a sufficient combination of cash and goods were promised – the expected rate was 100 pesetas – and would include items such as salt,

23. Guyer, *Marginal Gains*, p. 39. For a similar stepwise analysis of the emergence of a labour market in a nearby logging industry, see Christopher Gray and François Ngolet, "Lambaréné, Okoumé and the Transformation of Labor along the Middle Ogooué (Gabon), 1870–1945", *Journal of African History*, 40 (1999), pp. 87–107.
24. Fernando Muakuku Rondo Igambo, *Guinea Ecuatorial: De la esclavitud colonial a la dictadura nguemista* (Madrid, 2000) p. 48; Nerín, *La última selva de España*, pp. 225, 249; Guyer, *Marginal Gains*, p. 30. In the early twentieth century currencies included iron arrowheads, tobacco, guns, and German and French money.
25. James Fernandez, "Fang Representations under Acculturation", in Philip D. Curtin (ed.), *Africa and the West: Intellectual Responses to European Culture* (Madison, WI, 1974), pp. 3–48, 17.

tobacco, textiles, a bottle of brandy or wine, or even a rifle. To seal the deal, a 300 peseta on-the-spot *regalo* was advanced to anyone signing up for contract labour. The recruiters negotiated and spoke in commercial situations and terms, and in the sources they hardly reflect on how they unwittingly mobilized labour through the extensive mediations of currencies and polygamist clan chiefs.

Fortunately, there is a subaltern reflection in a singular interview transcript dated July 1931. The first republican labour officer, branded a Bolshevik by the planters, took it upon himself to ask each of the 165 *braceros* who were waiting at his Curaduria for the steamship to Santa Isabel how they had been recruited. The majority said they had come because of the 300-peseta *regalo* for *comprar mujer*, the adopted Hispanicized term for bridewealth, or literally "buy wife", which was needed to fund a marriage either for themselves or a brother, or required to settle the debt of a divorced sister or mother.[26] Of those interviewed, about one-quarter admitted to being French subjects, who had then illegally crossed the border with a *gancho* as they were attracted to the lower bride-prices in Rio Muni.[27]

Marriage was strictly exogamic to the patrilineal descent group or clan. A series of intermarrying clans would tend to form a grouping, such as the Ntumu Fang who lived in the northern half of Rio Muni, southern Cameroon, and the Woleu-Ntem province of Gabon.[28] While at that time there was no overarching authority between clans, nor any institution of slavery, there was considerable economic inequality and intense prestige competition between clans, and both were heightened by the influx of recruiters. For any important social events between Fang clans, men engaged in a performative *bilaba*, a milder type of potlatch, or "total prestation", that required an exorbitant but "honourable level" of gift-giving by the hosts.[29]

---

26. Curaduria Bata, July 1931, AGA C-81/8125 E-2; of the *braceros* in the group 20 per cent were under the age of fifteen.

27. There were several thousand French-African subjects in Spanish Guinea. France had denounced illegal recruitment before the League of Nations almost annually between 1929 and 1933, and encroaching *ganchos* were given ten-year prison sentences in Duala and Libreville; GG to DGMC, 28 December 1935, AGA C-81/06867, E-5. See Maurice Mveng, "Note sur l'emigration des Camerounais à Fernando Po entre les deux guerres mondiales", *Abbia*, 23 (1969), pp. 35–43.

28. Clans, made up of discontinuous family-based hamlets, were of highly variable size but tended to fall into the three-figure range. The Ntumu Fang are a subgroup of the Fang, who in turn are subcategorized into the broader linguistically defined Beti-Pahuin peoples. See *Wikipedia* or Georges Balandier, *The Sociology of Black Africa: Social Dynamics in Central Africa* (New York, 1970); Augusto Panyella, *Esquema de etnología de los fang ntumu de la Guinea Española* (Madrid, 1959).

29. Nerín, *Un guardia civil en la selva*, pp. 90–96; Guyer, *Marginal Gains*, pp. 40–41; Balandier, *The Sociology of Black Africa*, p. 28.

The most substantial way to increase food production and the network of alliances was through, in Lévi-Straussian terms, the exchange of women. Marriage was an exchange of female labour and reproductive potential. A son without a sister could not have a wife, and wives worked more than sisters and much more than men.[30] Paying the bride-price was not an act of buying, as a wife could usually neither be "sold on" nor converted into common commodities. Also, a married woman remained strongly linked to her lineage and, as solidarity in kinship was extended to the entire lineage and clan, should a woman become divorced the money to reimburse the bridewealth would be acquired by one of her brothers. This was the situation for one-third of the respondents.

Divorce rates were on the increase, as due to the rising bride-prices remarriage was a more lucrative option for a wife-giving clan. It tended to be only the *nkukuma* or "clan chief" – a recent term for the title, meaning "wealthy" in Fang – who could afford the new bride-price and who would accumulate wives. When the *gancho* arrived, the *nkukuma* would either marry off wives or collect the outstanding debt of another clan who had already received one of his wives, effectively leaving him with the 300-peseta *regalo* of the recruit in addition to the 100-peseta bonus. That was the case with half the respondents, most of whom also said that their brides had been accompanied to their patrilocal villages by one of her new in-laws, as otherwise they feared she would suffer harassment or be tempted to remain on Fernando Pó doing alternative work. Polygamy was not a matter of increasing the labour input of the village economy, for the increase in the practice as well as the act of "selling on" divorced wives were innovations boosted by the recruiting process.[31]

In terms of the usual categories of labour mobilization, rather than opposing them or stipulating a hidden "articulation" between them – that is to say between the domestic mode of production or acquiring labour through marriage, and the capitalist or contractual wage relationship – both can be seen as a continuous translation between non-equivalent

---

30. In the basic stereotype, women would work the subsistence farms and market goods, while men would help in the yearly slash-and-burning of a new plot, raise domestic animals, and fish or hunt; Joaquín Mbana, *Brujería fang en Guinea Ecuatorial* (Madrid, 2004), pp. 13–24; Nosti Nava, *Notas geográficas*, p. 51. Men also supervised children, engaged in craft metalworking, and most famously in sculpting (and selling) *biere*, statuettes that guarded the ancestral bones and which populate all ethnographic museums in Europe and even inspired Picasso's first cubist painting. See Guyer, *Marginal Gains*, p. 45, who adds that "to the Fang, the real value was in the bones, not the statues".
31. Jack Goody, "Polygyny, Economy and the Role of Women", in *idem* (ed.), *The Character of Kinship* (Cambridge, 1974), pp. 175–190. This procedure, in which the chief controls the circulation of women to mobilize a labour force for capital, forms a basis of the articulation of modes of production theory in anthropology. See Claude Meillassoux, *Femmes, Greniers et Capitaux* (Paris, 1975).

bridewealth and equivalent abstract labour, standardized through quantifiable colonial money across cultural norms. Such translations, which drove the recruitment of remunerated unskilled *braceros*, in turn depended on the monetization by legislative fiat of the reproduction of Fang socio-economic life. With the sudden prohibition of other currencies and the forced introduction of the peseta, within just a few years the bride-price had risen from about 50 pesetas to 300 in 1929, at which point this price became fixed by government decree. However, as one of the recruits told the labour officer, the 300 pesetas was the bride-price only for a "divorced woman belonging to a chief". Like several others among those interviewed, the recruit had given the *regalo* to his family to save for the 500-peseta bride-price for a wife acquired directly from an almost extortionist future father-in-law. The state's monetary policy and "price regulation" was crucial to speeding up the *regalo* method of recruitment as it stabilized both the powerful intermediary position of the chiefs and the burgeoning labour costs for the employer.

### *Trickery, the work contract, and fines*

The *ganchos* and *braceros* interviewed also revealed some of the tricks of the *reclutadores*, on whose actions the somewhat spineless backbone of the recruitment system was based. *Ganchos* were told to pretend that they were recruiting for the logging industry in Rio Muni or otherwise to claim falsely that they were working for a reputable planter in a "good area" located near a town and with no sleeping sickness. The most appallingly deceitful method employed by the recruiters was to refer to the 300-peseta wage advance as a *regalo*. Over half the recruits were induced to believe that the *regalo* was literally a gift, while to those who knew full well that the *regalo* would be deducted from their pay the *reclutadores* insisted that due to the scarcity of labour it was now indeed a "gift". The wages for a *bracero* on the island were 20 pesetas a month, one-half of which was paid monthly, while the remaining 240 pesetas were released at the end of a two-year contract. If the *braceros* had not been saving their monthly wages, then at the expiry of the contract the planters would force them to renew their contract to repay the remaining 60 of the 300-peseta *regalo*.[32]

An employer could be chosen or changed only in the rarest of cases. To top it off, the working day was measured by a foreman's estimate of "a day's work". Piecework was a managerial strategy that served to replace constant supervision with occasional performative threats and actual assaults that would often lead to 12-hour workdays shot through

---

32. Curaduria to GG, 28 November 1933, C-81/08126, E-21. In the case cited, the Labour Officer refused to renew a debt-bondage-based contract, but the planter was outraged enough to make it clear that this extortion was usual.

with violence.[33] Those features of the labour contract led to misery among the workforce and sustained the high fees of the recruiters. The republican labour officer in Rio Muni knew that the labour scarcity was not a matter of some sort of conflicting African work ethic, but rather that it was the paltry wages and the constant deductions from them, as well as the isolating and brutalizing contract conditions, that kept potential workers at bay. Colonial "laziness" tropes were popular merely in the colonial metropole and the media, and were only intermittently appealed to to legitimize violent exploitation.

Privatized recruitment in Rio Muni wound down in the final years of the republican period. Fines were finally dealt out to *reclutadores* for violations of the labour code (that since 1912 had prohibited payments to chiefs), and for causing speculation by selling on individuals already recruited. The industry's profit margin was slashed, and while the recruiters and their emissaries and accomplices disbanded, the highest bidders in Fernando Pó looked elsewhere. In just a few years the number of *braceros* contracted to Fernando Pó's plantations from Bata dropped to fewer than seventy, while the desertion rate among Fang labourers in Rio Muni increased.[34] Eventually the *regalo* wage-recruitment system was abolished altogether because of the escalation in cases of "serial" recruits – those who continually went to different recruiters or employers to receive the *regalo* only to disappear again.[35]

The republicans sought to "humanize recruitment and suppress inter-mediaries", and to "attract rather than capture" wage labour, but in order to "stimulate voluntary and spontaneous immigration", bridges needed to be built for a surplus proletariat to cross closely policed imperial borders.[36] Those bridges were conveniently constructed by an ensemble of Nigerian recruiters, as an outgrowth of stratified social groups and the

---

33. There is much evidence of this in the archives, and a good quarter of the planters and/or their overseers could be described as brutal. For fines and working conditions see AGA, C-81/08128, E-14; C-81/08129 E-2. On the anomalous position of Fernando Pó in West and Central African colonial history, in terms of the long two-year labour contracts and the extremely harsh vagrancy laws, see William Gervase Clarence-Smith, "Cocoa Plantations and Coerced Labor in the Gulf of Guinea, 1870–1914", in Martin Klein (ed.), *Breaking the Chains: Slavery, Bondage and Emancipation in Modern Africa and Asia* (Madison, WI, 1993), pp. 150–170.

34. Perpiñá Grau, "Mano de Obra Africana", p. 129. The figure in 1941 was very high; more than 20 per cent fled once they had received the *regalo*; idem, *De colonización y economía*, p. 365. The 1930s saw the complex disintegration/reinvention of Fang political life through the *alar ayong* or "pan-clan" anti-colonial movement and the famous, drug-fuelled reformative *bwiti* cult popular in the logging labour camps. See James Fernandez, "The Affirmation of Things Past: Alar Ayong and Bwiti as Movements of Protest in Central and Northern Gabon", in Robert Rotberg and Ali A. Mazrui (eds), *Protest and Power in Black Africa* (New York, 1970), pp. 427–457.

35. Cámara Bata to GG, 30 July 1946, AGA, C-81/08130, E-1.

36. GG, 1 October 1934, AGA, C-81/08126, E-1; Curador to GG, 16 June 1931; DGMC to GG, 4 June 1932, AGA, C-81/06415, E-2.

continuing decline of the colonial economy of south-eastern Nigeria during the long decade of the 1930s, from the Great Depression until the end of World War II.


## THE NIGERIAN CONNECTION, 1935–1945

From the Calabar coastline the silhouette of the volcanic peak of Fernando Pó is clearly discernible on the horizon. The Nigerian recruiters navigating the stretch to the island were a motley crew of former labourers and traders, and professionalized gangs run by canoe-owning coastal merchants. While the former continuously slipped in and out of small-scale recruitment, it was the latter, the commercial elite of Calabar Province, who paved the way for this clandestine sea lane across the bay, on both steamers and canoes. While the traffic on such different vessels was simultaneous, there was a clear break during the Spanish Civil War when the numbers of *braceros* arriving on colonial ferry boats dried up, only to rise exponentially on the tide of large sea-going canoes. In the post-Spanish-Civil-War section below, the social structures within which the Nigerian recruiters operated are contrasted, specifically between the kinship-based networks of Igbo traders and former labourers and the patronage-based Efik wards in Calabar and the caste-class axes of Ekpe, their "secret society".

Why both those groups of recruiters threw themselves at the opportunity afforded by Fernando Pó's planters can be understood only by constant reference to the material consequences of the solidification of British colonial rule and the palm oil depression, that is, the development of a transport infrastructure which reversed the fortunes of canoe-owning middlemen as well as the "remorseless decline" of prices for palm products offered to farmers by the European import-export factories.[37] Awaiting them at the Curaduria in Santa Isabel were guaranteed payments of between 500 and 800 pesetas (or £10 to £16) per *bracero* delivered.[38] Most of the commission being profit, their activity was lucrative indeed; even the lower figure was the equivalent of around 5 months' work as an individual trader or a year's work on a plantation. In 1935 there were 5,000 Nigerians on the island, one-half of whom were *braceros*.[39] By 1940 some 10,000 Nigerians were under contract

---

37. Susan Martin, *Palm Oil and Protest: An Economic History of the Ngwa Region, South-Eastern Nigeria, 1800–1980* (Cambridge, 1988), p. 88. Martin deduces (p. 119) that in 1933 palm oil was worth only 17 per cent of its barter terms of trade levels of 1912 and that Eastern Nigeria was in a long depression between 1914 and 1945.
38. This was double the rate of recruiting agencies operating in other African colonies; see Orde-Browne, *Labour Conditions in West Africa*, p. 11. For the largest recruitment treaty, in the early 1930s the Union of South Africa paid the Portuguese Empire £5 per head for almost 100,000 labourers annually for 12-month contracts.
39. Nosti Nava, *Notas geográficas*, p. 20. Census data for the island's resident Africans in 1936: Bubi or Fernandino, 9,348; Rio Muni, 6,800; Nigeria, 4,819; French Cameroon, 4,200;

in Spanish Guinea, a figure that had doubled by the final year of World War II. In those years, during the period of tax collection in Nigeria, coinciding with the cacao harvest and the canoe season between October and March, the number of new contracts exceeded 1,000 per month.[40]

Including family members and other professions, two-thirds of the 40,000 residents on Fernando Pó were Nigerians, who for the most part had arrived outside the purview of the British colonial authorities, either with the help or through the deceit of recruiters.[41] The displacement of mostly unmarried *braceros* was accompanied by trafficking in sex workers. For many women departing under the guise of a wife or daughter it was "not difficult to imagine their ultimate occupation in Spanish territory".[42] Fernando Pó was a very male-centric place, with almost 80 per cent of West African and European immigrants being men, whose hetero- and homo-socialities and sexualities were quite at odds with domestic or missionary moralities.[43]

### Ferry boats, bribes, and papers

From 1901 on it was forbidden for British West Africans to take up work as plantation labourers in Spanish Guinea. The first Nigerian Labour Ordinance in 1929 had included severe penalties for "unlicensed recruiting for foreign territories", by which was meant Fernando Pó.[44] In

São Tomé, 209; Liberia, 175; Sierra Leone, 155; Annobon and Corisco, 146. At that point most non-Spanish African migrants were skilled labourers or traders of all sorts rather than *braceros*, and were regarded with some hostility for not making themselves "useful" to the plantation economy. See GG to DGMC, 12 June 1933, AGA, C-81/06467 E-19; "Hospitalidad Excesiva", *El Defensor de Guinea*, 2 November 1933.

40. British Consul to GG, 10 July 1946, AGA, C-81/08130, E-1.
41. Akinjide Osuntokun, *Equatorial Guinea –Nigerian Relations: The Diplomacy of Labour* (Ibadan, 1978), pp. 36–40. This book is the only published work dealing even partially with this period, but Osuntokun had no access to the Spanish archives. For 1940s census data, see Sebastian Llompart Aulet, *Anuario estadistico de los Territorios Españoles del Golfo de Guinea* (Madrid, 1945), p. 195; and Wolff, "Ein Beitrag zur Wirtschaft von Fernando Poo", p. 108.
42. Michie, "Labour Conditions in Spanish Guinea" (28 February 1941). The quotation is from a 1943 newspaper article cited in David Pratten, *The Man-Leopard Murders: History and Society in Colonial Nigeria* (Edinburgh, 2007), pp. 166–167. Calabar was the central recruiting ground for prostitution networks that spanned Nigeria and British West Africa; see Laurent Fouchard, "Urban Poverty, Urban Crime and Crime Control: The Lagos and Ibadan Cases, 1929–1945", in Steven J. Salm and Toyin Falola (eds), *African Urban Spaces in Historical Perspective* (Rochester, NY, 2009), pp. 291–320, 300.
43. Llompart Aulet, *Anuario estadistico*, p. 29. For so-called "unnatural acts" between men on the plantations, see British Embassy to Ministerio de Asuntos Exteriores, 5 December 1945, Archivos del Ministerio de Asuntos Exteriores, Madrid, Archivo Renovado [herafter, AMAE], R 2370, E-11.
44. David Aworawo, "Decisive Thaw: The Changing Pattern of Relations between Nigeria and Equatorial Guinea, 1980–2005", *Journal of International and Global Studies*, 1 (2010), pp. 89–109, 95. The nine prosecutions in 1939 of illegal recruiters by the Calabar courts rose to over 100 in 1941; British Consul to GG, 10 July 1946, AGA, C-81/08130, E-1.

spite of the £500 fines or 5 years' imprisonment, the illegal recruiters were adept at outmanoeuvring the half-hearted attempts to police them. In the early 1930s the role of the recruiters was to act as a "conductor of the recruits through the network spread by the police in Nigeria to prevent their emigration", and they were akin to "publicity agents for the island, not so much misrepresenting the conditions on the island as failing to mention that employment conditions were unlike Nigeria".[45] The recruiters paid for ferry tickets, bribes, the necessary counterfeit paperwork, and other travel expenses, but the recruits were "made to sign an I.O.U. acknowledging that should they fail to take up contract on the island they would owe three pounds to the recruiter".[46] Hundreds of new recruits arrived every month on the ferry boats, but the IOU made backtracking on arrival prohibitively expensive for them. Furthermore, being an immigrant without a work contract on the island was not a legal option. In 1933 vagrancy laws, targeting unemployed and self-employed migrants, established that those who did not "seek work within 15 days" or pay for their own deportation should be sent to the "disciplinary brigades" of the prisons and used as labour for public works.[47]

In 1934 a petition signed by seventeen "Ibibio Boys" entitled "THE ATROCITIES OF THE SPANISH IN FERNANDO POO" reached the British Consul in Santa Isabel. The Consul visited the plantation from which the complaint had emerged and after talking to the Nigerian *braceros* he concluded that "their chief grievance seemed to me to be that they had been tricked by the recruiters into farm work against their wishes [… and expectation] to being apprenticed to some trade, and that they had no share in the bonus paid by their employer to the recruiters".[48] The first public alarm was raised in a letter to the editor in a 1936 issue of the important journal the *West African Review*:

> British Subjects in Africa have known freedom from slavery for nearly one hundred years. We have seen Abyssinia and Liberia under reprimand for this offence, yet little or nothing has been said about the trade still carried on by Spain in her territories in the Gulf of Guinea. [...] The unlawful activities of people employed by Spain to recruit men chiefly in Calabar and other parts of

45. T. Farley Smith, "Report on Employment of Nigerian Labour in Fernando Poo. Submitted after a visit lasting from June 5th to July 4th, 1939", 21 September 1939, TNA, PRO, FO 371/23171.
46. A.E. Yapp, "Report On Employment of British Coloured Labour in Fernando Po, as the Result of a Visit made August 29th–September 1st, 1936", 17 September 1936, TNA, PRO, CO 554/105/3. An IOU, or "I Owe You", is an informal document acknowledging debt.
47. Llompart Aulet, *Legislación del trabajo*, p. 131. For the creation of this law, see GG, "Extranjeros en la Colonia", AGA, C-81/08156, E-6.
48. British Vice-Consul to the Resident of Calabar Province, 13 September 1934, TNA, PRO, FO 458/126.

Nigeria […] is more than obvious in Fernando Poo, where there are thousands of Ibos. […] Cannot something be done to stop this illegal traffic in human cargoes?

The letter was signed anonymously by "Salvador" (Saviour), but the author was quickly arrested in Santa Isabel after a visiting correspondent from the Nigerian *Daily Times* "Mr. J.S. Olu Georg who when a special degree method was used on him, disclosed the name of the writer of the article".[49] Salvador was revealed to be Samuel Babington Macaulay, a Fernandino from Lagos but born on the island, and from prison he somehow managed to get hold of a typewriter and in a letter to the British Vice-Consul claimed that "the boys thus recruited I am cocksure are brought here through the aid of the falsified permits manufactured one way or the other by the RECRUITERS".[50]

The British Consul General for the region was then sent on an investigative tour of the island. The British captain of the steamer that took him there showed him forged police permits, which acted as passports for legitimate traders to embark on ships destined for Santa Isabel. The forgeries "were very clever ones but not clever enough to deceive the Captain who pointed out three slight errors in it". While on that day the recruiter and the eighteen recruits "hastily and unceremoniously left the ship", the British captain confessed that:

> […] the temptation held out to a [ship's] Master was so alluring that even he might fail. [The Captain] said if he wished to work with the recruiters he could clear a 100 pounds every crossing. The passage money he said to Fernando Po was 10/- [shillings]: any recruiter would readily pay him an extra 10/- or more per head if he agreed to accept the boys illegally. He could carry 200 each passage.[51]

In Calabar "vendors of second hand and forged passports made a lucrative income".[52] As for acquiring original permits, two recruiters from

---

49. Salvador, "Slavery in Spanish Guinea", *West African Review*, May 1936; "Sensational Arrest at Fernando Po", *Sierra Leone Daily Mail*, 16 September 1936. The Salvador piece was reprinted with a commentary by the media mogul and first president of Nigeria Nnamdi Azikiwe, who noted ironically, "Let Fernando Po's inhumanity be spotlighted. Let Spain explain its slavery. But then Spain is a Colonial Power and a European State at that, which explains a lot"; Zik, "Inside Stuff: Fernando Po", *The African Morning Post*, 27 May 1936.
50. Samuel Babington Macaulay to British Vice-Consul, 30 August 1936, TNA, PRO FO 458/127.
51. Yapp, "Report On Employment of British Coloured Labour", 17 September 1936. 20 shillings = £1. Similar observations can be found in W. Benson, "The Fernando Po Labour Demand", February 1936, TNA, PRO, CO 554/105/3. See also W. Benson, "Some International Features of African Labour Problems", *International Labour Review*, 39 (1939), pp. 34–45.
52. Rev. Ewart Shepherd, "Nigerian Labourers in Fernando Po: Dr. Haden Guest Misinformed? Allegations of Slavery Cannot Be Substantiated", *West Africa*, 19 May 1939.

Eket "boasted [to the Consul] that they will never have trouble in Calabar as they pay the Native Police Inspector WULOBI (or some such name) 1 pound per head".[53] The dealers in paperwork also bought up and resold "permits of return", issued by the British Consulate in Santa Isabel, which enabled new recruits to travel under the false names of those leaving the island with no intention of returning.[54] The Spanish colonial state was "lazy", and while the British attempted to regulate labour recruitment by generating paperwork, documents were quickly forged, circulated, or evaded by a series of mediators, to the detriment of a significant proportion of Nigerian recruits, who while arriving voluntarily were not expecting to encounter the desolate drudgery of the *bracero*.

## The Spanish Civil War and the palm oil belt

Fernando Pó was overrun by Francoist mutineers in July 1936, the first month of the Spanish Civil War. Within the next two years it was "impossible to bring braceros from Calabar" as recruiters ceased their operations since all foreign exchange was to be rerouted to Spain for the fascist front.[55] During those years *braceros* were regularly forced to renew their contracts as they were told by the Curaduria that "'We got no money, You better go back to work – contract for two more years – we will not let you walk in the streets' – or something to this effect".[56] The export of all currency was suddenly prohibited and recruiters or traders leaving the island were thoroughly harassed at customs and subject to intrusive searches. Even though their money was well hidden, small fortunes were confiscated by the Spanish nationalists.[57] Traders stopped trading and as a result the British ferry lines cut off their services to Santa Isabel, a withdrawal that "presented the canoe owners with a practical [transport] monopoly, of which they have not been slow to take advantage".[58] For non-Spanish recruiters and *braceros*, half of their fee and wage was paid in British money, and some £2,000 a month were finally earmarked for the Curaduria in Santa Isabel in 1938. The recruiting networks sprung back, and profits rose because there was no

53. British Vice-Consul to the Resident of Calabar Province, 13 September 1934.
54. Only 50 "permits of return" were issued in 1936, and by 1939 the British Vice-Consul was issuing 150 a month; British Vice-Consul to the Resident of Calabar Province, 14 January 1939, TNA, PRO, CO, 554/119/5.
55. Cámara to GG, 1 April 1937, C-81/08129, E-2; Junta de Importación y Exportación to GG, 22 May 1937, AGA, C-81/08056, E-1. For a thorough overview see William Gervase Clarence-Smith, "The Impact of the Spanish Civil War and the Second World War on Portuguese and Spanish Africa", *Journal of African History*, 26 (1985), pp. 309–326.
56. Yapp, "Report On Employment of British Coloured Labour", 17 September 1936. As a result of the Liberia Treaty and to make immigration more attractive, the Labour Code stipulated that half the wages of foreign workers were to be paid in sterling.
57. British Vice-Consul to British Legation, Monrovia, 11 July 1938, TNA, PRO, CO 554/114/10.
58. Michie, "Labour Conditions in Spanish Guinea" (28 February 1941).

expensive paperwork to pay for on the canoes and because wartime Spanish monetary policy had intensified the labour shortage.

The recruiting fee represented a clear leap in income and social mobility, which is why "every labourer who has completed his first term of contract [was] a potential recruiter. Frequently also the older hands [on the plantations were] given advances in sterling to pay for recruiting expenses".[59] Back in Nigeria, recruitment paths were shaped through kinship ties and the ethnically redefined immigrant associations proliferating in urban areas. These "home-town" associations served many extended community needs. They were always, for example, the first port of call for new arrivals seeking employment opportunities.[60]

Almost all recruits were Owerri Igbo or Southern Ibibio from the "palm oil belt" provinces, where land scarcity was acute and the population density was one of the highest in Africa. In the 1930s Calabar Province contained a little over 1 million people, while some 2 million lived in Owerri and subsistence levels were nowhere very high. Palm, and increasingly cassava, the main cash crops, were grown in between food crops on family farms. In colonial cartographic categories, in some of the districts of eastern Nigeria there were over 100 "taxable males per square mile", as opposed to approximately a single 1 per square mile in Rio Muni.[61]

The reasons for migration are portrayed in the general and regionally specific literature, as well as often by migrants themselves, around two poles, a liberal and ethnographic narrative and a Marxist and materialist storyline. On the one hand, there is the genre of *Wanderlust*, of adventurous youth propping up exchange and prestige value with the eventual aim to "deproletarianize" and reintegrate into home communities, but at a step up. On the other hand, there are the constant reminders of the struggle of the poverty-stricken upon whom responsibility falls for covering payments such as taxes and bridewealth.[62] After the invasion by

59. *Ibid.*; Casa Drumen to GG, 21 October 1938, C-81/08126 E-1.
60. W.T. Morrill, "Immigrants and Associations: The Ibo in Twentieth Century Calabar", *Comparative Studies in Society and History*, 5 (1963), pp. 424–448; Richard Henderson, "Generalized Cultures and Evolutionary Adaptability: A Comparison of Urban Efik and Ibo in Nigeria", *Ethnology*, 5 (1966), pp. 365–391; Howard Wolpe, *Urban Politics in Nigeria: A Study of Port Harcourt* (Berkeley, CA, 1974), pp. 56–81; Brown, *We Were All Slaves*, pp. 182–187.
61. Martin, *Palm Oil and Protest*, pp. 90–96. For the overlap in recruitment in Owerri and Bende for the Enugu mines, which in this period employed some 2,400 workers, see Brown, *We Were All Slaves*, pp. 155–160.
62. Segun Osoba, "The Phenomenon of Labour Migration in the Era of British Colonial Rule: A Neglected Aspect of Nigeria's Social History", *Journal of the Historical Society of Nigeria*, 4 (1969), pp. 515–538, 524. See the editor's introduction in Samir Amin (ed.), *Modern Migrations in Western Africa* (Oxford, 1974), pp. 93–118, and Aderanti Adepoju (ed.), *Internal Migration in Nigeria* (Ife, 1976). For oral history see Chima Korieh, *The Land Has Changed: History, Society and Gender in Colonial Eastern Nigeria* (Calgary, AB, 2010), pp. 268–282.

British colonial armies, the interwar period in Nigeria witnessed political stabilization and a massive pauperization that enabled an increase in mobility. Those who had to look outside the village economy were often younger sons, who would be the last to receive their disappearing share of land and whose bride-price could no longer be afforded as it had risen to as much as £25 in some Igbo areas.[63] The internal Igbo diaspora of colonial Nigeria was enormous, numbering in the millions, and to the long list of tenant farms, mines, trades, administrative, and urban jobs we should append Fernando Pó. It should be noted that the cumulative extent of migration from the eastern provinces, on the rise until the 1970s, has largely been forgotten.

The Igbo recruiters came in much smaller groups than the more QJ;professionalized Calabar recruiters, and in the many testimonies of Igbo recruits available in the archives most said they had come "with a relative".[64] That would mean someone from the same village group, although if an individual had already worked elsewhere in Nigeria and been perceived as a "foreigner" kinship terms would encompass much larger groupings. Migrants would usually have to walk, but with the recruiter's advanced fee, buses, trains, and canoes were used to reach Oron, from where the ocean-going canoes would sail in convoys to the island. Each canoe could seat up to forty people, including the ten paddlers, and carry several tons of contraband goods. The logistics of this traffic were managed almost exclusively by the Efik of the Cross River Delta.[65]

### The Efik recruiters and the towns of Calabar

While the recruiters were setting up their trade, the governor generals, the Spanish embassies, and the Cámara initiated, but unsuccessfully, labour treaties intended to bring indentured labour from India (1928, 1947), China (1928), Indonesia (1928), Morocco (1929), Romania (1929), São Tomé (1929, 1931), Cameroon (1934), Congo (1945), Haiti (1934, 1949), from Liberia again (1949), and persistently from Angola (1930, 1939, 1945, 1952).[66] Personalized recruitment was more reliable and cheaper

63. Martin, *Palm Oil and Protest*, p. 100.
64. In the Curaduria and police files at AGA there are over 100 witness statements about numerous incidents in which Nigerian labourers were always initially asked to give details of their route and arrival.
65. Michie, "Labour Conditions in Spanish Guinea" (28 February 1941). The journey took thirty-six hours. Oron was a small fishing village that became an important trading centre, with local fishermen selling many large ocean-going canoes; Ekong E. Ekong, *Sociology of the Ibibio: A Study of Social Organization and Change* (Ibadan, 1983), p. 92.
66. Most of these far-fetched plans were false starts, while others crumbled, for numerous reasons, at the outset or after being signed. The archive is filled with un-histories of a standardized global indentured labour market. Even until the 1960s, Spanish Guinea was desperate

than the lump sums prescribed by indentured labour treaties. Already, in the early 1930s, the Fernandino R. Barleycorn had a regular supply of workers brought by Money Ekambi and King Ndumbe from Douala on their launch.[67] At the same time, the British firm Ambas Bay used its launch to bring workers from the rubber plantations in Calabar paid for by the Cámara.[68] The main German planter on the island, W.A. Moritz, was provided with workers from the plantation of a family friend located near Mount Cameroon.[69] According to the testimony of one "Freeboy Calabar", the important Fernandino planter J.W. Dougan was supplied with large numbers of workers from the Eyamba ward in Calabar.[70]

The professionalized recruiters were predominantly Efik and they brought over Ibibio and Igbo canvassed by the riverside markets of their hinterland and, certainly at first, the surplus of slave descendants from their own towns. The word Efik literally means "oppressor" in the Ibibio languages, of which the Efik language is a dialectical group. It is no surprise that most of the dedicated recruiters lived in Calabar and Umuahia near Bende,[71] for between those two towns was a well-worn trading route along Enyong Creek, the main tributary of the Cross River that connects Itu, Bende, and Afikbo, all of which had had large slave markets. In the late eighteenth century the route became one of the main arteries of the Atlantic slave trade that poured out of Old Calabar, until the British government restrained its own slave traders.[72] By the mid-nineteenth

---

to disentangle itself from complete dependency on Nigeria and continued to pursue indentured labour treaties throughout the world, asking for at least 10,000 workers on 5-year contracts. See AMAE, R 887 E-52, R 3215 E-56; AGA, C-81/08095, C-81/08147, C-81/12373; and Max Liniger-Goumaz, "La cuestión bracera. Ciento cincuenta de búsqueda de mano de obra en Guinea Ecuatorial", *Estudios de Asia y Africa*, 22 (1987), pp. 497–534.

67. The Resident of Cameroons Province to GG, 31 October 1931, AGA, C-81/08146, E-1.

68. Curaduria, 3 November 1932, C-81/08125, E-4; Cámara to GG, 16 December 1930, 81/08095, E-18.

69. German planters in Cameroon complained of the "efforts of Fernando Poo's planters, to whisk away our workers"; see Westafrican Plantation Company Victoria to Kemner, 20 May 1926, Bundesarchiv, Berlin-Lichterfelde [BArch], R 1001/3504.

70. Curaduria, 6 June 1932, C-81/08126, E-21. Members of the Eyamba family, from the most commercially and politically powerful lineage of Calabar, had settled on Fernando Pó in the late nineteenth century; Ivor Miller, *Voice of the Leopard: African Secret Societies and Cuba* (Jackson, MS, 2009), p. 128. For the rise of the free marketeers of the Eyamba ward at the expense of the "landed interests" of Duke Town, see Patrick Manning, "Slave Trade, Legitimate' Trade, and Imperialism Revisited: The Control of Wealth in the Bights of Benin and Biafra", in Paul E. Lovejoy (ed.), *Africans in Bondage: Studies in Slavery and the Slave Trade* (Madison, WI, 1986), pp. 203–233.

71. List of forty known recruiters in Michie, "Labour Conditions in Spanish Guinea" 28 February 1941); list of another forty recruiters and hundreds of canoe paddlers in Policia Colonial, 12 December 1942, AGA C-81/15865, E-12.

72. For the role of the Aro traders and the failed abolition along the same route, see G. Ugo Nwokeji, *The Slave Trade and Culture in the Bight of Biafra: An African Society in the Atlantic*

century the seven Efik towns had a slave population of 95 per cent, and it was they who produced food surpluses and operated the canoes transporting palm oil.[73]

Duke Town had grown to be the wealthiest Efik town due its advantageous location on the Cross River. Duke Town was called Old Calabar by British merchants and was the site of the first British missionary establishments and later the capital of the Southern Nigeria Protectorate. In the years following World War I, with the construction of a railway from Enugu to Port Harcourt, extensive road building, the emergence of small-scale Igbo bicycle traders, and the market occupation by a handful of European import-export firms, the hitherto obligatory economic passage point of Calabar was eclipsed. Merchants from the coastal trading groups found themselves virtually transformed from "wealthy entrepreneurs to petty traders".[74]

While a large proportion of Efiks were employed in colonial administration or in British mercantile firms across Nigeria, for others with a status less guaranteed by the quid pro quo of colonial rule, the only choice was to continue to deploy their canoes and reposition themselves as middlemen in new markets.[75] The Efik gentry who had maintained their wealth invested in urban property, acquired lorries, and "owned most of the canoes that plied the river and sold most of the spirits that were found in the market".[76] The new sources of income from recruitment were accompanied by downward social mobility of low-caste Efiks, who aspired in the opposite direction from agricultural labour, which was

World (New York, 2010); Adiele E. Afigbo, The Abolition of the Slave Trade in Southeastern Nigeria, 1885–1950 (Rochester, NY, 2006), pp. 33, 156. British merchants continued to dock in Old Calabar for palm oil; see Martin Lynn, Commerce and Economic Change in West Africa: The Palm Oil Trade in the Nineteenth Century (Cambridge, 2002), pp. 37, 61.

73. Slaves continued to be sourced from districts such as Bende and Uyo; Rosalind Hackett, Religion in Calabar: The Religious Life and History of a Nigerian Town (Berlin, 1989), pp. 20–30; Geoffrey Johnston, Of God and Maxim Guns: Presbyterianism in Nigeria, 1846–1966 (Waterloo, ONT, 1988), p. 275. For an overview of the extensive and classic literature on the history of the Efiks, see Paul E. Lovejoy, Transformations in Slavery: A History of Slavery in Africa (Cambridge, 2000), pp. 102–104, 187–189.

74. Anthony Nwabughuogu, "From Wealthy Entrepreneurs to Petty Traders: The Decline of African Middlemen in Eastern Nigeria, 1900–1950", Journal of African History, 23 (1982), pp. 365–379. This powerful middleman status was lost by many coastal groups across much of West and Central Africa.

75. Adiele E. Afigbo, The Warrant Chiefs: Indirect Rule in Southeastern Nigeria, 1891–1929 (New York, 1972), pp. 27–31. D. Simmons, "An Ethnographic Sketch of the Efik People", in Daryll Forde (ed.), Efik Traders of Old Calabar (London, 1956), pp. 1–26.

76. Nwabughuogu, "From Wealthy Entrepreneurs to Petty Traders", p. 369. For the famous "canoe-houses" west of Calabar, see Patrick Manning, "Merchants, Porters, and Canoemen in the Bight of Benin", in Catherine Coquery-Vidrovitch and Paul E. Lovejoy (eds), The Worker of African Trade (Thousand Oaks, CA [etc.], 1985), pp. 51–74.

heavily stigmatized as work for slaves. While he was in Santa Isabel, an Efik recruiter named Ben Bassey submitted a letter of complaint to the British Vice-Consul:

> On Tuesday I happened to meet my younger brother unexpectedly in the street. I requested how they manage to come here. I was to understand that they were brought here by one trader [known as the "Dahomey woman"] who deceived them that they will be employed as shop-boys on Fonda-sellers [African grocery store]. On this account the children followed her. But now she wishes to sign them in the farm. They are boys and do no farm work because they were in school all the time.[77]

The most competitive side of Efik social organization emerged from the internal dynamics of the Ekpe society. This politico-religious organization spanned all seven towns, all men could and were pressured to be members, and wealth accumulated from trading was the primary criterion for determining status. A large sum of money was required to rise higher than the "young adult" rank of the first two gradients, a rank which also tended to mark the upper limit of membership for individuals from former slave families.[78] Above that was the "middle-management" level of monetized membership that was central in propelling recruitment, as ambitious Ekpe members could draw upon the patronage of and hire the canoes owned by the wealthy elite. Even the Ekpe society's musicians propagated or at least ideologically reflected recruitment, as the lyrics of an Ekpe chant attest: "You say you are unemployed, if you are jobless let's go to *Panya*".[79]

The hierarchical networks of labour mobilization that were organized from Calabar came into competition with the much more decentralized recruitment activities of Igbo former labourers and petty traders. The emerging economic prominence of Igbo migrants in Calabar was met with hostility, even to the point of a spate of public attacks on the "foreigners".[80] In light of that competition, but only after the eruption of a media scandal

---

77. Ben Bassey to British Vice-Consul, 2 December 1935, TNA, PRO CO 554/105/3; British Vice-Consul to the Resident of Calabar Province, 15 January 1936, TNA, PRO, CO 554/105/3.

78. Daniel A. Offiong, "The Functions of the Ekpo Society of the Ibibio of Nigeria", *African Studies Review*, 27 (1984), pp. 77–92, 80. For the different composition of the "leopard" society in Annang country around Ikot Ekpene, which was also called "Ekpe", see Pratten, *Man-Leopard Murders*.

79. Panya was the Pidgin rendering of España or Spanish Guinea, cited in Miller, *Voice of the Leopard*, p. 128. The song was recorded in Calabar in 1982, by which time the Ekpe society had been largely reduced to recreational and entertainment activities.

80. Pratten, *Man-Leopard Murders*, p. 194. For the settings of urban economic politics see Ute Röschenthaler, "A 'New York City of Ibibioland'? Local Historiography and Power Conflict in Calabar", in Axel Harneit-Sievers (ed.), *A Place in the World: New Local Historiographies from Africa and South Asia* (Leiden, 2002), pp. 87–110.

that sought to break the traffic, L.O. Esien Offiong wrote to the Governor
of Fernando Pó, proposing that as a

> [...] retired member of the Nigerian civil service [...] belong[ing] to the
> Eyamba House, of the ruling houses in Calabar [he would be] qualified as an
> experienced and responsible man to run a Labour Recruiting Organisation in
> Nigeria [which would] remove the abuses, unpleasantness and inconvenience
> caused by the unlawful system of canoe recruiting and solve finally the labour
> problem in Fernando Po.[81]

## Shanghaiing, brandy, and World War II

Esien Offiong's proposal was rejected by the Spanish Governor, while cases
of "shanghaiing" – a quintessentially British imperial term for being kidnapped to work offshore – shocked the Nigerian media. In Britain, the
scandal echoed its way into all major newspapers and even into the House
of Commons, and numerous letters of concern were dropped through the
letter box of the Colonial Secretary in London by the Anti-Slavery Society.
The *Nigerian Eastern Mail* sparked the controversy in an exposé of

> [...] the smugglers posing daily at Oron as canoe ferry men [in which] travellers
> run the risk of unknowingly falling into the hands of the "slave dealers". [...]
> It is to be deplored that this wicked practice should have been resuscitated
> by those who thought they could eke out an existence at the expense of the
> freedom of others.[82]

The recruits were variously described by Nigerian journalists as "unemployed and down and outs", "innocent and unsophisticated Africans"
"belonging to the lower walks of life", who were "inveigled", "tricked
and bamboozled", "lured – in most cases actually kidnapped by agents
who thought of nothing else but the prospect of earning the promised
commission on the transaction".[83]

It is quite certain that at least 10 to 15 per cent of Nigerian *braceros* on
the island had "been taken there without their being willing to go there".
That figure was estimated by Timothy Farley Smith, a colonial administrator from Nigeria sent to investigate labour conditions on the island
after the media scandal. He arrived at his estimate after "listening to
complaints and making inquiries on the Island" and he even excluded

81. L.O. Esien Offiong to GG, 14 June 1939, AGA C-81/08131.
82. "The Nigerian Eastern Mail Alleges Slavery in Oron", *The West African Pilot*, 21 January
1939; newspaper clippings in TNA, PRO, CO 554/114/10.
83. Shepherd, "Nigerian Labourers in Fernando Po"; "The Fernando Po Slave Traffic", *The
Nigerian Eastern Mail*, 25 February 1939; "Matters of Moment, by Observer", *The Nigerian
Daily Times*, 15 July 1939. For further bad press, with commentators and student groups even
calling for an invasion of the island, see Bolaji Akinyemi, "Nigeria and Fernando Poo
1958–1966: The Politics of Irridentism", *African Affairs*, 69 (1970), pp. 236–249.

from it those "for whom it is natural that having gone willingly and finding they do not like the conditions make as good a story as possible in their efforts to return to Nigeria before completing their contracts". From Farley Smith's impression, only

> [...] in isolated cases have recruiters been able to lure fully grown men into going to Fernando Po without their knowing that they were going there, but I am certain that the recruiters have induced a considerable number of youths to leave their homes on promises of work in Nigeria or the Cameroons under British Mandate and have taken them to the Island. The usual procedure is to bring the recruits at night down to some small village on the coast or creeks of Calabar province and tell them that in order to get to their destination they have to cross a wide river. [...] The recruits then embark in the canoes and next morning they are well out at sea and it is too late for them to be able to take any action to get away from the recruiter.[84]

Between the canoe owners and the planters on the island there was another set of dedicated intermediaries taking their slice by acting as translators and managers of the recruits. In the words of the most infamous *reclutadora*, the "Dahomey woman [who the Consul was told] by various Calabar natives here, [was] a notorious recruiter", would act "as a counsellor and friend to the boys in their journey to Fernando Poo".[85] Louisa Sousa, or the "Dahomey woman [was] regularly going to Nigeria by canoe" and she continuously reappears in the archive as one of a large handful of shanghaiing culprits. One of her victims was Friday Akpan, whose complaint was pithily transcribed by the British Consul:

> I was brought here six months ago by a canoeman named Godwin of Abak, Uyo Division. I asked to him to take me to Calabar to join my brother Christian Nkere, but he took me here and handed me to Serra [a large Portuguese planter in San Carlos whose labour manager was Louisa Sousa]. I have not been paid for three months. I went to a farm and reported my trouble to my relative. I was caught there and sent to prison. I am still in the prison. My employer said that she paid a fat sum to Godwin and that I am her slave.[86]

In Calabar there were "huge public notices warning Natives against going to Fernando Po" that highlighted the risk of canoes being capsized by tornadoes near the island's shark-infested waters.[87] The newspapers pressed

84. Farley Smith, 21 September 1939.
85. British Vice-Consul to the Resident of Calabar Province, 15 January 1936, TNA, PRO, CO 554/105/3.
86. Consul General to Governor of Nigeria, 3 March 1943; "General Report No. 3 on Situation in Fernando Po", TNA, PRO, FO 371/34772; British Consul to Consul General, 30 November 1944; "Native Labour, Monthly Report", TNA, PRO, FO 371/49598.
87. British Vice-Consul to the Resident of Calabar Province, 14 January 1939, TNA, PRO, CO 554/114/10.

both governments "to accelerate action against this abominable canoe traffic, in order that some plan be formulated whereby Nigerians could travel like human beings, and not after the manner of sacks of palm kernels".[88] In the summer of 1939, during his inspection tour of Fernando Pó, Farley Smith had already initiated the meticulous drafting of a labour treaty in accordance with the recently ratified ILO conventions. But with the outbreak of World War II the incipient canoe traffic, which the new treaty had aimed to replace, turned into a bazaar-like bonanza.

The smuggling of labourers had become embedded in the increasingly profitable contraband trade, where "anyone, with enough money to hire a canoe and paddlers [went] into this business. [...] There is no one central organisation, the smuggling is almost universal". Those allegedly involved in smuggling were "the rank and file of police, customs and immigration officers, [who] are exposed to enormous temptation", as well as "Senior Police, Europeans and prominent Africans".[89] The smuggling was an open secret hovering across colonial Calabar. A contemporary anthropologist, undertaking fieldwork in Eket, noted that her informants were "extremely reluctant to reveal their true incomes, [...] to reveal certain illegal sources of revenue, notably Brandy smuggling from Fernando Po".[90] The "Santa Isabel–Oron–Calabar traffic in contraband goods [went on to become] the heaviest along the coast of Nigeria and indeed of West Africa".[91] During World War II, the island was wholly dependent on Nigeria for foodstuffs and other vital commodities such as pesticides, petrol, and motorcycles, while barrels of palm oil and rubber were even re-exported to Spain. In exchange, all sorts of Spanish goods were brought back on the canoes, but the bulk of the return cargo was brandy. Thousands of crates found their way into all corners of Nigeria.[92]

88. Shepherd, "Nigerian Labourers in Fernando Po".

89. Commissioner of Police to Governor of Nigeria, "Illicit Traffic between Nigeria and Fernando Po", 2 June 1944, TNA, PRO, FO 371/39661.

90. Anne Martin, *The Oil Palm Economy of the Ibibio Farmer* (Ibadan, 1956), p. 17. Brandy, along with "the fear of high tax assessments" from clip-board-holding anthropologists, made the on income the least satisfactory part of [Martin's] budget enquiry". There is even a popular adolescent's book about the seedy Calabar smuggling dens: Rosemary Uwemedimo, *Akpan and the Smugglers* (Lagos, 1965). For food smuggling from Aba to Fernando Pó and elsewhere, see Gloria Chuku, *Igbo Women and Economic Transformation in Southeastern Nigeria, 1900–1960* (New York, 2005), pp. 110–112.

91. "Smuggling – Nigeria's curse", *Drum*, January 1961. By then, the commercial Efik class had lost its last vestige of autonomous economic power. "The Cross River and its main tributary the Enyong Creek [had] become notorious highways for smuggling of goods, including alcohol tobacco, drugs, and cloth from Fernando Po. Calabar remains the base of this illegal trade which [was] dominated by Bende Ibos"; Reuben K. Udo, *Geographical Regions of Nigeria* (Ibadan, 1970), p. 91.

92. Imported gin from northern Europe declined tenfold between 1929 and 1939; Dmitri van der Bersselaar, *The King of Drinks: Schnapps Gin From Modernity to Tradition* (Leiden, 2007)

The chief of the Calabar police, investigating the labour trafficking, had good reason to claim that there was "great difficulty in enlisting the help and cooperation" of the public.[93] Calabar was the site of the first Nigerian naval base, established there expressly to stop illegal recruitment and liquor smuggling, as customs revenues from alcohol constituted the golden lining of the colonial treasury. However, no patrol launches were available until the final years of World War II, and in any case they were ineffective in stamping out the canoe convoys, which would scatter in all directions if pursued. The canoe operators came to know the timetable of the naval patrols – so they set off only when the launch was being refuelled! Furthermore, the innumerable twisty creeks of the Cross River Delta were impossible to police, and even if they did catch the smugglers "the four naval officers [found it] difficult to take up to 40 Africans in belligerent mood aboard the vessel".[94] The British Empire controlled the eastern Atlantic, and even throughout World War II the vast shipping routes were regulated by sailing permissions or "navicerts", but imperial ticketing systems were powerless in the Bight of Biafra.

*The labour treaty agency, blood papers, and* reenganchos

Meanwhile, Farley Smith's labour treaty was being drafted and re-drafted, before finally being signed by the British and Spanish colonial authorities in December 1942.[95] The attempt to redraw, standardize, and supervise the recruitment trajectory involved the construction of an obligatory passage point for all labour intermediaries. All contract formalities and medical tests would be processed by the British authorities before boarding. The John Holt Company in Calabar was put in charge of hiring licensed recruiters, under the "newspeak" organizational name of the "Anglo-Spanish Agency for Contracting and Protecting Calabar Labourers".[96] The agency set out to become a monopoly, but it had scant

p. 187. And for how much was at stake in terms of colonial revenues, see especially Chima J. Korieh, "Alcohol and Empire: 'Illicit' Gin Prohibition and Control in Colonial Eastern Nigeria", *African Economic History*, 31 (2003), pp. 111–134, 119.

93. "The Nigerian Eastern Mail Alleges Slavery in Oron", *The West African Pilot*, 21 January 1939.

94. Commissioner of Police to Governor of Nigeria, 2 June 1944. This is similarly recounted in the memoir of a marine officer, P.J. Odu, *The Future That Vanished: A Biafra Story* (n.p., 2009), p. 70: "I never once caught a smuggler".

95. Colony and Protectorate of Nigeria and Spanish Territories of the Gulf of Guinea, "Treaty Regarding the Recruitment in Nigeria of Native Labourers for Working in the Spanish Territories of the Gulf of Guinea", 9 December 1942; available online at: http://treaties.un.org/doc/Publication/UNTS/LON/Volume%20205/v205.pdf (last accessed 15 April 2012). For the long series of drafts, disharmonies, and scribbles, see AGA, C-81/08131. The Spanish fascist government suspected that the treaty was an imposition by "Geneva" conspiring against them.

96. Nkparom Ejituwu, "Anglo-Spanish Employment Agency: Its Role in the Mobilization of Nigerian Labour for the Island of Fernando Po", in A.I. Asiwaju, B.M. Barkindo, and

success as the recruiters circumvented the new requirements of the treaty, which prohibited individual planters from paying premiums. Even one official licensed recruiter stationed in Opobo, handing out flyers with pictures of model plantations, would bring the recruits to Sambo Ekpo, a canoe operator in Oron, instead of to the agency's transit camp.[97] For the first few years only around 150 monthly work contracts were overseen by the agency, and it was only in the late 1950s that *braceros* brought in under the new arrangements began to outnumber illegally recruited workers.[98]

The treaty's first article, which was also its stated aim, prohibited those arriving outside the protocols of the treaty from being placed under contract. However, those already working on the island before the treaty was signed could renew their contracts, although the majority did not.[99] Those finishing their contracts turned to trading or left the island and sold their Spanish medical examination results or "blood papers" to the counterfeit dealers in Calabar. With those "blood papers", the new recruits arriving clandestinely on canoes would start working under false names as re-contracted pre-treaty labourers. While many of those arriving saved themselves the trouble and claimed they had set off from the French Cameroons, for those *reenganchos* (officially under a second contract) the wages were 60 pesetas a month, twice that of *braceros* under a first, or a treaty contract.[100] The increase in pay had been put in place to prolong the contracts of workers who were already familiar with the labour-intensive procedures of cacao production, which entailed constant

R.E. Mabale (eds), *The Nigeria-Equatorial Guinea Transborder Cooperation* (Lagos, 1995), pp. 42–57. It was later renamed the "Anglo-Spanish Employment Agency", and the "branding" talk very consciously avoided the term "recruitment".

97. British Consul to Don Juan, 11 June 1946, AGA, C-81/8130 E-1; Consul General to Governor of Nigeria, 3 March 1943; list of licensed recruiters in Nigeria, "Annual Report of the Department of Labour, Nigeria, for the year 1944", TNA, PRO, CO 657/53.

98. British Consul to Consulate General, 6 July 1943, TNA, PRO, FO 371/34772; Esteban Hanza to GG, June 1962, AGA, C-81/08214 E-1.

99. Wolff, "Ein Beitrag zur Wirtschaft von Fernando Poo", p. 98. Wolff was stuck in Fernando Pó at the outbreak of World War II, and he wrote that "usually the Gastarbeiter returned home with three to five pounds in savings". Spanish officials used the resulting statistically high recontracting rate as "proof" of the good working conditions.

100. Some planters even offered a lump-sum bonus, a real *regalo*, for recontracting for another two years. In 1944, it was 1,000 pesetas or £20, higher that the first two years of wages; British Labour Officer at Fernando Po to Consul General, 26 May 1944, TNA, PRO, FO 371/39661. Food rations, housing, and health costs were covered by the plantation owners. Living expenses were very low compared with the cost of living in Nigerian cities and towns. There were also many opportunities by which workers could increase their income. It was very common for Nigerian *braceros* to sell a combination of their imported food rations as well as any bush-meat, river crabs, and fruits gathered from the shadow trees planted alongside the cacao. That was the main reason why an employer near the road or town was much to be preferred.

clearing of vegetation, maintenance of plant nurseries, transplanting seedlings, spraying trees with sulphate, estimating ripeness, harvesting cacao pods with long-handled sickles, fermenting and drying the fruit, and classifying and bagging the beans.

Forgery of second contracts was what kept illegal recruitment going, as without the *reengancho* bonuses wages on the island were, by the end of World War II, lower than in Nigeria, as "due to army separation allowances and the present food produce prices, there [was] plenty of money in circulation and it [was] possible for a labourer to earn a favourable living locally".[101] Planters regularly used the contracts of *braceros* who had died to sign up clandestine recruits under false names.[102] On the surface, the Curaduria had to have its paperwork appropriately ordered to accommodate the Treaty's stipulations and the British Consul's inspections. By 1945 the Calabar police had arrested hundreds of smugglers, and at the

> [...] Nigerian end, the labour smuggling [that remained was] in the hands of a chosen few, [among whom was] the Dahomey woman, who [was still] notorious as a smuggler of labour and contraband goods, [...] as is the case on the Island where the traffic [was] controlled entirely by about 3 persons with the full knowledge and connivance of Officials in High Authority.

It was both the chief of the Spanish police and his brother the labour officer whom a handful of the most important recruiters had in their pockets.[103] As the supply of "blood papers" was dwindling, Sebastian Llompart Aulet (the labour officer until the 1960s), would, for a 50-peseta bribe, stamp forged contracts that made it appear that the new recruits were re-contracting. "As with the smuggling of contraband goods, the sum of 1000 pesetas is collected by the chief of police and 500 pesetas by the owner of the beach where the canoes arrive", who would also take the recruits "over to San Carlos for distribution".[104]

Polite requests – almost amounting to injunctions – to shut down illegal recruitment were made by the British Consul in almost every communication with Spanish officials. The Cámara would of course point to the inevitability and indispensability of the clandestine recruiters, as "the supply of labour is

101. F. Shepherd to British Consul, 6 December 1944, AGA, C-81/08130, E-1. The official wage on Fernando Pó until 1946 was 30 pesetas, or 14 shillings, 6 shillings short of £1.

102. Fernando García Gimeno, *Fernando el africano* (Madrid, 2004), pp. 45–50. This is the memoir of a humble and unpretentious Spanish settler who spoke "Pichinglish" and who, between 1950 and 1964, managed 600 Nigerian *braceros* at any one time for several Portuguese and Bubi planters.

103. British Consul to Consul General, 30 December 1944, TNA, PRO, FO 371/49598.

104. British Consul to Consul General, 23 July 1944, TNA, PRO, FO 371/39661. The supply chain was geared towards the remote San Carlos and to the large Fernandino and Portuguese planters, who had been cut out by the official recruitment channels which prioritized Spanish planters.

far less than the demand [… and besides] Nigeria is overpopulated". To make its point quite blatantly, in 1945 the Cámara petitioned the British Consul to increase the Treaty quota from 400 labourers a month to 1,200 for the island in addition to a further 3,400 monthly contracts needed for the projected growth of logging works and coffee plantations in Rio Muni, and signed off with an impertinent bottom line of 55,000 *braceros* per year.[105]

## CONCLUSION – AGENCY, MEDIATORS, AND INTERMEDIARIES

The basic lesson in economics given to the Consul by the Cámara should not be mistaken for a conclusive hypothesis for the underlying explanation as to why clandestine recruiters enjoyed such success in the Bight of Biafra. The single cause of exploitation and efficiency is formulated by experts through a variety of legitimated formulae, and only then can labour surplus/scarcity be seen as a wave "simply transported without deformation through a chain of intermediaries".

To study empirically the metrics of capitalism-imperialism, it can be helpful to abandon the contrivances of Marxist schemata and the idea of roaming but placeless *homines economici*. Replacing those with the actual toil of constant action and constant connection, without which the contorted landscapes of history would not have come into existence, allows for a precise account of the delicate and brutally imposed contours of world-systemic economic trajectories. Only once a great many material instruments and ideological scripts have been mobilized can a configured network give the impression of being either something "local" or a durable global structure commanding predictable intermediaries to do its bidding.[106] ANT provides the methodological tools to unfold structures, flatten the global, and to disperse or "dislocalize" action. By following the procedures of ANT we are led to the conceptual dissolution of binary pairs and of the manifold sociological compromises – their "dialectical mutual constitution", or their "interdependence" – that keeps them intact.

The single scope and object of analysis in Latourian ANT is the actor-mediator, or "actant", which transports and translates a network that is

105. British Consul to Cámara, 20 October 1948, AGA, C-81/08124, E-1; Consul General to Governor of Nigeria, 12 February 1945, "Native Labour, Monthly Report, No. 12", TNA, PRO, FO 371/49598. At this time about one-third of the still comparatively smaller workforce in Rio Muni was from Nigeria.

106. Latour, *Reassembling the Social*, pp. 60, 204. For this line of post-structuralist thinking, where "movements and displacements come first, places and shapes second", and that should not easily be dismissed as a mere symptom of the neoliberal World Wide Web "age" but treated as a theory of history that diverges scientifically and politically from the critical style of analysing "global capitalism", see also J.K. Gibson-Graham, *The End of Capitalism (As We Knew It): A Feminist Critique of Political Economy* (Minneapolis, MI, 2006).

always on site, being performed, stabilized, undermined, or reconstructed. As noted in Graham Harman's wonderful book on Latour, for Latour there exist only more or less powerful actants. In the autonomy- and resistance-defined notion of agency, agency is a human privilege that lies below a constraining structure. However, if power, structure, and agency are released from humanisms and dualisms and are said to be distributed throughout a socio-technical network, it does not mean that they are diffuse or horizontal.

The *braceros* were literally surrounded, and even though they had to enter into and go through what could be described as the ordeal of colonial modernity, they never lost the ability to move and to become mediators themselves. In Rio Muni, the theft of *regalos*, flight, and border crossing eventually led to the abolition of the whole wage-*regalo* recruiting arrangement. Nigerian *braceros* increased their share of wealth produced in the Spanish colony by unflinchingly supplying markets with second-hand documents and contraband commodities. It was their initiative to bring to official attention the abuses of the recruiters by submitting complaints to the Consul and by exposing stories to journalists, and therefore of creating the traces that populate the archives.

A good critique of ANT is that it tends to protagonize exceptional actors and "winners", such as colonialists or recruiters, as their victory depends on being part of the dominant associations that leave behind the most traces and sources.[107] The colonial economic project could spread by aggressive force and maps of battlefields, through plenary imperial mandates and administrative paperwork or in racist and intimidating legal-symbolic status regimes. Within geo-imperial coordinates the activities of Fernando Pó's recruiters working with their allies, compatibilities and preconditions could unfold, specifically through, in Rio Muni, Fang gender and status hierarchies, bridewealth, and peseta coinage; and in Nigeria through the logistical infrastructure of merchants in Calabar, the legacies of the Atlantic slave trade, and the relentless cutting of prices in the palm-product market.

The position of the clandestine recruiters as indispensable and quite durable relay points for the mobilization of labour across the Bight of Biafra was meticulously created by a long list of mediators which cannot be disentangled and formalized into the purified combinatory matrix characteristic of structuralist social theory. Rather, in a diagrammatic

107. For a critically sympathetic view see Graham Harman, *Prince of Networks: Bruno Latour and Metaphysics* (Melbourne, VIC, 2009). Apart from Latour's work, Harman's book has been the most inspiring for an attempt at ANT-inflected historical social science research, although the British branch of ANT is more closely associated with illuminating the operations of imperial expansion. See, for example, John Law, "On the Methods of Long Distance Control: Vessels, Navigation and the Portuguese Route to India", in *idem* (ed.), *Power, Action and Belief: A New Sociology of Knowledge?* (London, 1986), pp. 234–263.

fashion, to deploy themselves, the labour intermediaries aligned with the organizational standards of and translations between kinship, ethnicity, money, gender, psychology, law, bureaucracy, religion, war, commodities, and so on.

The composition of the recruitment trajectories partially followed up on in this article included: subsidized Spanish chocolate; the currencies deemed acceptable for paying bridewealth; police uniforms; the control of wealth by chiefs; *regalos* and the colonial state's currency and price regulations; the structure of the contract; the ability to make false promises and convincingly deceive; the fraternal relations between the Spanish police chief and the labour officer; the documentation required for boarding ships and taking up contracts; IOUs; bombs bought with foreign exchange reserves dropped by the Francoists in Madrid; bottles of brandy; home-town associations; the organization of Ekpe membership; forged second contracts; and the one navy vessel that was transporting Nigerian soldiers during World War II instead of patrolling the Cross River Delta.

It was *within* these serialized mediators, not adjacent to some sort of wider context or below pre-produced structures or somewhere outside the concrete, that the recruiters organized a treacherous path between capital and labour – or, with the details unfolding, between this mediated capital and that mediated labour.

*IRSH* 57 (2012), Special Issue, pp. 73–96 doi:10.1017/S0020859012000429

# Making and Breaking the Working Class: Worker Recruitment in the National Textile Industry in Interwar Egypt*

HANAN HAMMAD

*Department of History, Texas Christian University, Fort Worth*

Email: h.hammad@tcu.edu

SUMMARY: This article examines how worker mediation to secure jobs for relatives and co-villagers in the nationalist textile industry influenced working-class formation in interwar Egypt. Mediation was conducted out of a sense of communal commitment or for commission, or indeed both. The fact that rank-and-file workers were able to intervene in the recruitment process reveals that workers were successfully able to manoeuvre in such a way as to balance their unjust work relations with the huge mill and to manipulate its system. On the other hand, this method of recruitment became a source of violence among workers when they fought one another, sometimes fatally, whenever one side failed to respect the terms of the financial arrangements agreed. In most cases it strengthened the communal solidarity based on kinship and geographical origin. In both cementing and distracting from working-class solidarity, worker interference in the recruitment processes was part of the developing sense of social transformation and bonding among a distinctive and connected professional community that hoarded its own bargaining power.

This article examines the process of worker recruitment for the modern national textile industry in interwar Egypt. Under the banner of nationalism and opposition to British occupation and foreign economic domination, Bank Misr established the largest Egyptian-owned textile factories in several locations during the interwar period. Bank Misr itself was established in 1920 to finance Egyptian-owned, large-scale industrial enterprises under the slogan, "An Egyptian bank for Egyptians only".[1] Thousands of male and female agricultural labourers and landless and near landless peasants of all

---

* I am indebted to the editors of this volume, especially Aditya Sarkar, for their useful comments on previous drafts of this article.
1. For a meticulous history of Bank Misr and its pioneering "national-capitalist" role, see Eric Davis, *Challenging Colonialism: Bank Misr and Egyptian Industrialization, 1920–1941* (Princeton, NJ, 1983).

ages were brought from their villages to work in those factories, thus becoming industrial labourers and urban dwellers.

The rapid and impressive expansion of Bank Misr's companies was not associated with any systematic recruitment or training of workers. Workers themselves intervened in the apparently chaotic process of labour recruitment, securing jobs for their relatives and co-villagers. Sometimes this mediation was conducted out of communal commitment, and frequently the new workers were committed to pay a commission or a percentage of their salaries to the older colleague who had helped them get the job. This practice had long-term ramifications. On the one hand, the fact that rank-and-file workers were able to intervene in the recruitment process reveals that workers were successfully able to manoeuvre to balance their unjust work relations in huge factories and to manipulate its system. On the other hand, this method of recruitment became a source of antagonism and violence among workers. Workers fought one another, sometimes with fatal consequences, whenever one side failed to respect the terms of the financial arrangements agreed. In most cases it strengthened the communal solidarity among workers based on kinship and geographical origin. Spontaneously, workers were divided into fighting and competing groups, while their communal bonding facilitated their adaptation to industrial work and to coping with the urban setting.

Through the historical experience of the Misr Company of Spinning and Weaving in al-Mahalla al-Kubra (MCSW), I trace this recruitment process of rank-and-file workers and its consequences for both workers' interrelations and relations with the company. Contesting the ideas that employers had absolute power in choosing labourers in the abundant labour market, and that vehement, loud labour activism was the only efficient method for labour empowerment, the experience of the MCSW sheds light on the agency of seemingly powerless workers and their strategies for negotiating power within the gigantic company and nationalist, capitalist system.[2] It also juxtaposes nationalist discourses on progress and modernization as embodied in the company with the opposing reality of the company's random and chaotic work practices. I argue that the modern, industrial disciplinary process of recruiting and training labourers in nationalist, capitalist factories were the site where both economic functioning and cultures interacted to shape the formation of an industrial working class and the development of its consciousness. Worker interference in the recruitment processes was itself part of the developing sense of social transformation and bonding as a

---

2. For a comprehensive treatment of the gap between discourse and practices of nationalist capitalism in interwar Egypt, see Robert Vitalis, *When Capitalists Collide: Business Conflict and the End of Empire in Egypt* (Berkeley, CA, 1995).

distinctive and connected community that hoarded its own bargaining and negotiating power.

Ever since E.P. Thompson's seminal work, *The Making of the English Working Class*, scholars on working-class formation have been divided over the position of pre-capitalist ties and cultures in the development of working-class consciousness. Scholars acknowledge capitalists' utilization of racial and ethnic divisions among workers to distract them from working-class solidarity.[3] In many cases, however, shared ethnicity between workers and capitalists did not halt the development of working-class solidarity among workers who led labour protests against entrepreneurs of the same ethnic group.[4] Yet, the issue of communal bonding throughout the processes of working-class formation is still problematic in the historiography.

Chakrabarty and others launched a sweeping critique of the Marxist analysis of labour history in Asia and Africa.[5] Noting that, in particular circumstances, the most feudal system of authority can survive at the heart of the most modern of factories, they criticized the Marxist approach to working-class consciousness as one that undermined and even misunderstood culture, and criticized its assumption that working classes everywhere follow the European script for working-class formation.[6] The historiography of the Middle Eastern working classes has been limited to the political activism and labour movements of factory workers and alienated social culture and its crucial rule in working-class formation.[7] How "primordial" ties facilitated workers' adaptation to urban life while simultaneously promoting sectarianism has been treated as a dramatically exceptional case in Lebanon's torn society.[8]

In the case of Egypt, which this article focuses on, the available scholarship has treated the Egyptian working class as a Cairo-based phenomenon, with some attention given to Alexandria, Egypt's second-largest metropolis.[9]

---

3. Lex Heerma van Voss and Marcel van der Linden, *Class and Other Identities: Gender, Religion and Ethnicity in the Writing of European Labour History* (New York [etc.], 2002).
4. See, for example, Daniel Hiebert, "Jewish Immigrants and the Garment Industry of Toronto, 1901–1931: A Study of Ethnic and Class Relations", *Annals of the Association of American Geographers*, 83 (1993), pp. 243–271.
5. Dipesh Chakrabarty, *Rethinking Working-Class History: Bengal, 1890–1940*, 2nd edn (Princeton, NJ, 2000), and Peter C.W. Gutkind (ed.), *Third World Workers: Comparative International Labour Studies* (Leiden, 1988).
6. Chakrabarty, *Rethinking Working-Class History*, p. xi.
7. For a good critique of the limitation of the Middle East working-class historiography, see Sherry Vatter, "Militant Journeymen in Nineteenth-Century Damascus: Implications for the Middle Eastern Labour History Agenda", and Assef Bayat, "Historiography, Class, and Iranian Workers"; both in Zachary Lockman (ed.), *Workers and Working Classes in the Middle East* (Albany, NY, 1994), pp. 1–20 and 165–210 respectively.
8. Samir Khalaf, *Lebanon's Predicament* (New York, 1987).
9. Examples of this historiography include Joel Beinin and Zachary Lockman, *Workers on the Nile: Nationalism, Communism, Islam, and the Egyptian Working Class, 1882–1954* (Princeton,

The workers' journey from recruitment to transformation into industrial labourers has been overlooked, together with their daily lives and routines inside and outside workplaces and trade unions, their interaction with other social groups, and the question of whether or not their experiences were distinct from the rest of the urban population.[10] In the existing literature, the peasant origin of most Egyptian industrial workers is neither denied nor well examined. Rather, it is merely cited as a source of limitation for the labour movement, and workers hailing from rural traditions are usually categorized as "unconscious and backward".[11] To fill this gap, I examine how workers' social origins, informal labour mediation strategies, and communal networks impacted their transformation into labourers within a new urban, industrial milieu, and shaped their working-class formation and identity.

## RECRUITMENT FOR NATIONAL SUCCESS

From the eighteenth century onward, the town of al-Mahalla al-Kubra, in the middle of the Nile Delta, emerged as an important textile industry centre in Egypt and the Ottoman Empire. In 1927 the Egyptian nationalist economist and founder of Bank Misr, Tal'at Harb, chose the town as the site for the MCSW. This was the first large, Egyptian-owned textile factory in Egypt, and it remains one of the biggest today. The MCSW also became Bank Misr's flagship company and most successful enterprise, employing the largest number of industrial workers in the country. By the end of 1930, the factory's products had successfully gone to market, which encouraged the owner of Bank Misr to expand it continually. The workforce rapidly increased from approximately 2,000 workers in 1930 to 10,000 in 1938, and then to 27,000 in 1945. Such rapid expansion helped construct the company within Egyptian nationalist discourse as an emblem of national success and progress in the face of foreign political and economic domination. Throughout the 1930s and 1940s, commercial advertisements frequently appeared in Cairo's press, promoting and exalting the MCSW as a national icon by stating, for example, "Every dress you wear that is made in the Misr Company is a banner of our

NJ, 1988), and Ellis Goldberg, *Tinker, Tailor, and Textile Worker: Class and Politics in Egypt, 1930–1952* (Berkeley, CA, 1986). The notable exception in terms of greater consideration being given to working conditions in al-Mahalla, rather than to the labour movement there, is Joel Beinin's chapter "Fikri al-Khuli's journey to al-Mahalla al-Kubra", in *idem, Workers and Peasants in the Modern Middle East* (Cambridge, 2001), pp. 99–113.

10. Samer Said Shehata, *Shop Floor Culture and Politics in Egypt* (Albany, NY, 2009), is a notable exception in terms of how it broadens the discussion on working-class formation to include social networking and social dynamics on the shopfloor.

11. See Taha Sa'd 'Uthman, *Mudhakkarat wa-watha'iq min tarikh 'ummal Misr: Kifah 'ummal al-nasij 1938–1947* [Memoirs and Documents from the History of Egypt's Workers: The Struggle of Textile Workers, 1938–1947], 2 vols (Cairo, 1982–1983).

national freedom". However, that rapid and impressive expansion was not associated with any systematic recruitment or training of workers.

At its beginning, the company sent dozens of technical school graduates to Europe for training to prepare them to train others upon their return to Egypt. It also depended on experienced handloom weavers among the local population of al-Mahalla to train unskilled workers with no previous experience of industrial practices. The local townspeople's expertise in handloom weaving was one obvious reason why Bank Misr chose al-Mahalla for its flagship textile company. In his 1924 inauguration speech for the Bank Misr branch in al-Mahalla, Tal'at Harb expressed great admiration for the people of al-Mahalla and their commitment to education and industry, particularly the textile industry. He pointed out that 57 per cent of al-Mahalla's population worked in industry (and almost one-third of the population worked in the textile industry), while only 26 per cent worked in agriculture and 17 per cent in commerce, which he considered the ideal balance in terms of economic activity.[12] The theory was that the textile industry had become so much a part of the culture of the town that its children were effortlessly predisposed to acquire its skills and traditions, and that consequently the shift from handloom to mechanical weaving should not be difficult.[13]

The prospect of working at the MCSW was not initially attractive to the townsmen due to its poor wages and night shifts. Handloom weavers who joined the company and contributed to the training of its pioneer workforce quit shortly after realizing that their company wages were less than they had earned in the handloom workshops. The MCSW sent low-ranking, white-collar workers from Bank Misr to rural villages to recruit workers from among the peasantry. Despite their lack of industrial skills, workers from rural areas were seen as an asset because they were believed to possess a simple, obedient character, making them more inclined to submit to rigid discipline.[14] The white-collar workers dispatched to recruit peasants were *afandiyya*, the modern, educated middle class of Egypt. They used a strong nationalist discourse and lured peasants with promises of a comfortable urban life with guaranteed living accommodation.

A recruitment visit by an *afandi* to a village typically began with a meeting with the head of the village (*'umda*), whose cooperation was the

12. Tal'at Harb, *Majmu'at Khutab Muhammad Tal'at Harb* [A Collection of Tal'at Harb's Public Speeches] (Cairo, 1927), p. 101.
13. Nawal Isma'il, "Madinat al-Mahalla al-Kubra: Dirasa fi jughrafiyyat al-'umran" [The City of al-Mahalla al-Kubra: A Study in Urban Geography] (M.A. thesis, 'Ain Shams University, Cairo, 1965), pp. 18–19.
14. Frederick Harbison and Ibrahim Abdelkader Ibrahim, *Human Resources for Egyptian Enterprise* (New York, 1958), p. 69.

key to the success of the recruitment mission. He also met local school teachers, bureaucrats, and students – with whom he shared the title of *afandi* and the nationalist drive and championing of Bank Misr and its industrial enterprises. Although Bank Misr was ostensibly founded to help Egyptian landowners diversify their investments and was technically under their control, it was primarily embraced by the rising, educated middle class, the *afandis*. In keeping with the traditional method for publicizing news and information among illiterate villagers, public cryers roamed the villages to urge men and women, children and adults, to gather in the courtyard (*dawwar*) of the *'umda*. There, the *afandi* recruiter spoke to the rural poor about abundant job opportunities in Bank Misr's big new textile factory in al-Mahalla al-Kubra.

In their discourses, *afandiyya* mixed their recruitment agenda with their nationalist mission, in which the ultimate goal was to attract rural peasants into urban, industrial work and immerse them in nationalist ideology. *Afandiyya* preached how great it was to have an Egyptian-owned factory buy the Egyptian cotton that Egyptians cultivated to make clothes that Egyptians could wear. Thus, "everything would be from Egypt for Egyptians", rather than having the British buy Egyptian cotton only to resell British-manufactured clothes to Egyptians. Such nationalist discourse was not only disseminated among peasants by employers of Bank Misr but also by the *'umadas* (village mayors), political activists, and local *afandis* residing in villages, such as professionals, techno-bureaucrats, school teachers, and high school and college students. For example, leftist labour activist Muhammad Shata, who joined the MCSW in the early 1930s as a twelve-year-old boy, learned about the factory in al-Mahalla from his elementary school teacher.[15] In his Arabic composition lessons, the teacher gave lectures about Bank Misr, its textile factory in al-Mahalla, and the bank founder and nationalist economist Tal'at Harb. Even in villages where *afandiyya* recruiters did not visit, others urged those who wished to earn a living to join the al-Mahalla factory.

Landless peasants may have needed to be informed about job opportunities in al-Mahalla, but it is doubtful whether the massive numbers that joined the MCSW did so in direct response to the recruiters' nationalist discourse. Owing to the increasing concentration of land ownership, more peasants became landless agricultural labourers, or struggled to secure small landholdings through seasonal agricultural labour. Working at the MCSW thus seemed an attractive solution to their unemployment problem. The recruiting *afandiyya* and village cryers promised that peasant children would learn a good profession (*san'ah*) by becoming

---

15. Rif'at al-Sa'id, *Arshif al-Yasar: Sirra zatiyya li-munadili al-yasar* [The Archive of the Left: An Autobiography of the Fighters of the Left] (Cairo, 1999), pp. 283–288.

industrial workers in al-Mahalla, and that good wages would be paid to anyone who completed the training. The *'umadas* endorsed these promises as well as announcements publicizing the time and place from which the *afandiyya* would transport those who wanted to work in the factory.[16] Stories about children going to work in al-Mahalla and then returning to their home villages a few months later wearing new clothes also persuaded the rural poor to believe the rhetoric about better urban living standards, higher wages, and better work conditions in the factories. Moreover, the prospect of working at the factory meant permanent work and rescue from the elements instead of seasonal, agricultural labour in outdoor fields.[17]

The sight of big trucks arriving to pick up those willing to leave their homes to join the factory in al-Mahalla was already very familiar in these villages. It was almost identical to the sight of trucks picking up and transporting landless village peasants to work in distant fields. Land ownership became increasingly concentrated in the late nineteenth century, particularly after the onset of British occupation in 1881, and labour contractors seasonally shipped male and female labourers from villages with large numbers of landless peasants to work on large farms or construction sites hundreds of miles away.[18] These seasonal workers were known in their home villages as *tarahila* (roaming workers), whereas people in their host villages sometimes derogatorily called them *gharraba* (aliens). During these seasonal trips for work, men, women, and children worked long hours under the harsh sun in the summer and in the cold in the winter. They slept in hasty, makeshift shelters made of thin burlap and rags. Given this history, it is unsurprising that the *Mahallawiyya* (townspeople of al-Mahalla) likewise referred to the new influx of poor villagers arriving to work at the factory as *gharraba* and *shirkawiyya* (people of the company).

The profession of labour contracting was understood to be restricted to men. However, the archival records on which this study relies reveal that there were also female labour contractors and subcontractors in areas surrounding al-Mahalla al-Kubra. Those female contractors performed the same tasks of recruiting village labourers for agriculture and construction

---

16. Fikri Al-Khuli, *al-Rihla* [Journey], 3 vols (Cairo, 1987–1991), I, p. 17.

17. Al-Sa'id, *Arshif al-Yasar*, p. 288.

18. For the history of agricultural workers, *Tarahila*, see Sawsan el-Messiri, "Tarahil Labourers in Egypt", in Alan Richards and Philip L. Martin (eds), *Migration, Mechanization, and Agricultural Labor Markets in Egypt* (Cairo, 1983). See also Fatimah 'Alam al-Din Abd al-Wahid, *Tarikh al-'Ummal al-zira'iyyin fi Misr, 1914–1952* [History of Agricultural Labourers in Egypt, 1914–1952] (Cairo, 1977), and 'Atiyyah al-Sayrafi, *'Ummal al-tarahil* (Cairo, 1975). In his social-realist novel, *al-Haram* [Sin] the Egyptian author Yusuf Idris deals exclusively with the moral and material dilemma of a female *Tarahila* worker; Yusuf Idris, *al-Haram* (Cairo, 1965).

sites, and riding trains and pick-up trucks to escort them to other villages and towns. Among these women was 'Aziza Hassan al-Tiryaqi, who agreed to recruit labourers for the 1937 cotton season and share the profit with a male labour contractor, al-Birins Mirsal al-Sudani. When al-Birins failed to comply with their agreement, paying her only EGP 1.4 instead of the agreed EGP 3 (half the profit), she sued him and won her case.[19] Another female labour contractor was Fatima Ali al-Dali, who recruited workers to harvest cotton in the 1945 season in the nearby village of al-Mu'tamadiyya. She had to accompany male and female labourers to their work sites and wait with them until the end of the workday. She ran the risk of having some of her recruited labourers rejected by farm managers due to poor health or bad reputation. She was also robbed by some of the workers she recruited.[20]

With the integration of Egypt into the global market as a cotton exporter in the late nineteenth century, labour contractors also shipped the rural poor to work in cotton gins. The work was seasonal, and many of the labourers were women and children. The Deputy Director of the International Labour Organization, Harold Butler, noted in his 1932 report that women and children worked in cotton gins in deplorable conditions, and workers of all kinds were not only poorly paid but often cheated out of their meagre earnings by unscrupulous employers and labour contractors.[21]

Formal labour contractors were absent in the transportation of peasants seeking work at the MCSW in al-Mahalla. This, in itself, implied that the peasants recruited would receive the full share of their wages. However, the *afandiyya*'s promise that the company would provide workers with accommodation proved false. What the MCSW actually provided at the beginning was permission for workers to sleep in the company's courtyards for a few weeks.[22] The rapid increase in the workforce population and the company's incessant drive for expansion were used as excuses by the company for making workers arrange their own accommodation. Many workers slept inside bakeries, animal sheds, marketplaces, and alleys, and along railway lines and canal banks.[23]

After the company became highly publicized across Egypt as a major job provider, thousands of peasants travelled on their own from all over

---

19. Al-Mahalla Civic Court Records 1939, file 6612, case 2503, Archive of Dar al-Mahfuzat al-'Umumiyah bil-Qal'ah.

20. Al-Mahalla Misdemeanour Court Records 1945, file 7795, case 3389. Hereafter this source will be cited using the following format: "Misdemeanour 1945/7795/3389".

21. Harold Butler, *Report on Labour Conditions in Egypt with Suggestions for Future Social Legislation* (Cairo, 1932), p. 14.

22. See al-Khuli, *al-Rihla*, I, pp. 28–31, and al-Sa'id, *Arshif al-Yasar*, p. 284.

23. Misdemeanour 1938/899 and Misdemeanour 1936/6767/1762.

the country to al-Mahalla, hoping to be employed. The company's demand for labourers was relentless due to its rapid expansion and the high labour turnover rate. It was common for workers to quit and then return later to the company.[24] The greatest rates of absenteeism occurred during workers' first week of employment, the most difficult period of adjustment for those who had never operated heavy, industrial machinery. Adjustment to factory routine, operational training, group work, and abusive foremen was difficult, and was aggravated by the lack of a worker-orientation programme. Many workers assumed factory employment did not require their presence every day. If they had families with small landholdings, or if their landlord offered temporary work during the planting or harvesting seasons, workers – particularly new recruits – might remain in their villages for a few days, thinking they could resume work at the factory when they had finished with their agricultural job.

As early as April 1931, just four months after the MCSW produced its first piece of cloth in December 1930, the administration started to complain about the extraordinary absence of workers "without an excuse, which forces the company to train others".[25] Many workers joined the company with the intention of returning to their home villages once they had saved some cash. Many more quit when they discovered the promises of the *afandiyya* recruiters to be false. Bad working and living conditions spurred even more workers to quit. The problem was so acute that the company perpetually had to train more workers than it needed just to be ready to cover those who would drop out. In 1941 the MCSW administration finally objected, stating that "large numbers of our trained workers leave our factory every day with one group following another".[26] This time, the reason for the high turnover rate was clear, and the administration admitted that workers were "seeking higher wages".[27] The high rate of worker absenteeism and resignations resulted in a tangible reduction in production in 1943, when the company attributed the phenomenon to seasonal agricultural work and the attractive wages offered by other new, competing factories.[28]

That many workers would actually prefer agricultural work, known to be among the lowest-paid occupations, over factory work at the MCSW revealed the irony that wages for menial agricultural labour were still

24. MCSW, *Sijil Tarikhi Sharikat Misr lil-Ghazl wal-Nasij* [Historical Record of the Misr Company for Spinning]. It comprises unpublished undated documents.
25. *Ibid.*
26. *Sharikat Misr lil-Ghazl wal-Nasij: al-Taqrir al-Sanawi li-Majlis Idaratiha al-Muqadam lil-Jam'iyya al-'Umumiyya lil-Musahimin* [Misr Company of Spinning and Weaving: Annual Report of the Board submitted to the General Meeting of Shareholders] (Cairo, 1941).
27. *Ibid.*
28. MCSW, *Sijil Tarikhi Sharikat Misr.*

higher than those that the company was prepared to pay. Yet another irony was that, while the company preferred workers of peasant origin due to their perceived submissiveness, many such workers considered factory work at the company merely a reserve occupation for when there was a shortage of agricultural work. There is no question that meagre pay and severe working conditions precluded worker loyalty to the company and commitment to industrial work. Returning to agricultural work whenever it was available was in effect a form of resistance against the company's injustices in the manner that James Scott describes as "everyday forms of resistance" among oppressed peasants, and that Asef Bayat calls "quiet encroachment of the ordinary" among the urban poor.[29] Quitting work was one way of resisting the unjust work relationship with the MCSW, and it exposed the dire lack of a systematic company policy for recruiting and retaining workers.

## RECRUITING GOOD SUBJECTS

MCSW job candidates regularly waited in the company yard, where a uniformed officer, typically a retired, high-ranking army official employed by the company to police its workforce, would randomly chose new workers.[30] Candidates did not fill out forms or job applications. Rather, the officer would simply select from among the gathered candidates those whom he judged to be good subjects and determine, again using his own judgement, at which section they were qualified to work. Records show that young men between the ages of sixteen and twenty-five were usually chosen for the weaving section, and older men were directed to the yarn sections or to work as porters. Children were also often directed to work in the yarn and preparation sections.

Department heads reserved the right to judge the suitability of candidates before submitting them for medical examination and criminal background checks. The arbitrary, haphazard selection process was based on individual officers' experience and personal judgement in discerning who would be a docile worker. Candidates who showed any hint of alertness or aggressiveness were branded as potential troublemakers and

---

29. James C. Scott, *Weapons of the Weak: Everyday Forms of Peasant Resistance* (New Haven, CT, 1985), *idem*, "Everyday Forms of Peasant Resistance", *Journal of Peasant Studies*, 13:2 (1986), pp. 5–35, and Asef Bayat, *Street Politics: Poor People's Movements in Iran* (New York, 1997).
30. The recruiting scene given here is based on many court cases; Muhammad Yusuf al-Mudarrik, *Hawla Mushkilat 'Ummal al-Mahalla* [On the Problem of Workers in al-Mahalla] (Cairo, 1947), and the memoirs and autobiographies of four pioneer workers. See Asma Halim, *Kikayat 'Abdu 'Abd al-Rahman* [The Story of 'Abdu 'Abd al-Rahman] (Cairo, 1977); 'Atiyyah al-Sayrafi, *Sirat 'Amil Mushaghib* [An Autobiography of a Trouble-Making Worker] (Cairo, 2007); al-Sa'id, *Arshif al-Yasar*; and al-Khuli, *al-Rihla*.

bypassed.[31] From the early moments of recruitment, *ghafar* (guards) practised their disciplinary mission by using batons to line the job candidates forcibly into rows and keep them quiet until the officer had completed his selection.[32] The primary mission of company guards and police was to control workers rather than guard the company's property. City policemen were always visible around the MCSW's property, and at the routes leading to its facilities, to control traffic and push people away from the company gates. Police forces were always willing to help control workers, and workers often complained of excessive and cruel police harassment.[33]

A few years after its establishment, increasing demand for factory work led the MCSW to develop a system to exclude candidates with criminal records, anyone who had previously joined the company and been fired or quit, and anyone with incurable health problems. This exclusion policy was applied with particular rigidity against job candidates with tuberculosis or poor vision.[34] When a job candidate was selected by the officer at the company gates, a form was completed with his name and place of origin (*balad*), and the candidate's photograph attached. The completed form would be sent to the respective department manager to determine whether the nominated candidate was a good fit. The candidate would then undergo a medical examination to screen for diseases and to ensure that his or her sight was sufficient. A clerk would pore through company files to see whether the candidate had previously worked there and been fired or quit. Candidates with criminal records were screened out by a background check of government records, a procedure for which the candidate had to pay 13 piastres.

If the candidate's record was clean, that person would finally be confirmed for a job at the factory and receive a worker ID card with name, photograph, and serial identification number. The demand for work was so high that the company at first had to conduct the selection session a few times a week, and then once a month. The hiring process forced candidates to cover the procedural costs of criminal background checks and photographs themselves. In 1947 the cost of such a file was 24 piastres, equivalent to nearly two weeks' wage for the average worker.[35] The high costs served to deter workers from quitting the company after a few days, particularly

31. Harbison and Ibrahim, *Human Resources for Egyptian Enterprise*, p. 74.

32. For one of the many incidents in which *ghafar* injured candidates while forcing them to line up, see Misdemeanour 1942/6792/2649.

33. Misdemeanour 1945/7793/1865, and Misdemeanour 1938/6776/2177.

34. Sharikat Misr lil-Ghazl wa al-Nasij al-Mahalla al-Kubra, *Taqrir 'ann al-a'mal al-tibiyya* [Misr Company of Spinning and Weaving: A Report on Medical Activities] (Cairo, 1951), p. 5.

35. Al-Mudarrik, *Hawla Mushkilat 'Ummal al-Mahalla*, pp. 13–14.

when they discovered that they had to pay the same costs each time they left and tried to rejoin the company.

Informal labour mediators emerged in this chaotic, multi-step hiring process to assist others in winning company jobs. A delicate balance between formality and informality was, arguably, negotiated daily through mediation. The formal regulation at the factory – the presence of police officials, medical inspection, and worker registration – provided opportunities for subversion and manipulation by workers and others, and thus established the possibility of informal mediation. In most cases mediators were company workers who had experience of the hiring system, enjoyed good connections with bosses, and had access to company labour files. They helped candidates skip the humiliation of having to endure the long hours of the selection process by the company gates, and they even helped candidates who did not pass the selection.

After quitting school and migrating to al-Mahalla to seek a company job, Muhammad Shata joined other job candidates by the company gates for several days, but the recruiting officer never selected him. Eventually, a factory worker offered to help him get a job in return for two weeks' wages. Shata's wages were 1 piastre a day for a 13-hour shift.[36] The clustering of "corrupt" or "informal" practices was a consequence of the nature of formal regulation at the factory and encouraged informal mediation. Mediators also helped those who failed to join the company owing to their having a criminal record or poor health. Workers, who were supposed to be powerless subjects, were thus able to manipulate the system and expose its limitations. The company's hiring process was so ineffective that many workers with criminal records and others with a history of quitting were able to sidestep the process to get hired.[37]

Among the many cases of individuals with criminal records joining the company, the case of al-Yamani Zahran al-Gallad provides insight into the extent to which mediators were able to subvert the system. Twenty-three-year-old MCSW employee, al-Yamani, lived in the workers' slum of Muhammad 'Ali Street.[38] On 14 August 1943, while strolling along Railway Station Street (the largest boulevard in the modern commercial centre of al-Mahalla), al-Yamani was spotted by 'Ali al-Dib, a policeman, who was familiar with his criminal record. The policeman was suspicious because al-Yamani was known for committing theft and violent crimes (*I'tida' 'ala al-nafs wa al-amwal*), so he took him to the police station to investigate how he made a living. Al-Yamani said he worked for the MCSW and showed his worker ID card. The ID card displayed his

---

36. Al-Sa'id, *Arshif al-Yasar*, pp. 282–288.
37. Tanta Criminal Court Record 1943/7455/2731, Archive of Dar al-Mahfuzat al-'Umumiyah bil-Qal'ah.
38. *Ibid.*

photograph under the alias 'Abdulla Ibrahim al-Mansi, and al-Yamani confessed that he adopted that name because he had a criminal record that would have prevented him from getting the job. Company sources indicated he had been working under that alias since 18 June 1943. Clerks had followed the usual criminal record investigation procedure (*fish wa tashbih*), with the Department of Identification reporting that his record was clean. To show the level of the system's inefficiency, 'Abdulla Ibrahim al-Mansi turned out to be a real person living in the village of Shunu in the province of Kafr al-Shaykh.

Workers with criminal records who joined the company with help from mediators were discovered only when they were apprehended for unrelated incidents. Police discovered that the eighteen-year-old factory worker Hilmi Muhammad Khattab had a criminal record when he was arrested for pickpocketing Batta 'Abd al-Latif.[39] Similarly, when thirty-six-year-old Hilmi Hamuda al-Zayyat was arrested in July 1938 for attempting to steal a piece of cloth from the MCSW, it was revealed that he had a criminal record, with four previous arrests, and was consequently given a harsh sentence of four months in jail with six months' probationary surveillance.[40] Al-Zayyat's colleague, twenty-eight-year-old Zakariya Ali al-Bilihi, was also caught hiding a piece of MCSW cloth under his clothes in late 1940, and al-Bilihi was discovered to have committed three crimes in the past. He was sentenced to four months in jail for a previous offence in August 1940. Police records had labelled him a suspected criminal (*mashbuh*) earlier that year, but despite his extensive criminal record mediators enabled him to join the company and pass the background check. Al-Bilihi was also sentenced to six months in jail and given three months' probationary surveillance.[41]

As a way of augmenting their income, some experienced workers took advantage of the hiring process by deliberately seeking random individuals searching for work and helping them secure jobs in return for one-off, fixed fees. They showed their company IDs to convince potential candidates of their ability to guide them through the hiring process. Ma'addawi Ibrahim Galalah charged Abd al-Qadir Ghazi Salamah 150 piastres in exchange for a position as either a factory worker or guard after passing the medical examination. Upon being caught, Salamah was sentenced to four months in jail, with labour, and bail was set at EGP 5.[42]

---

39. Misdemeanour 1939/6779/47.
40. Misdemeanour 1939/6779/138.
41. Misdemeanour 1940/2007. For more incidents involving workers with criminal records, see Misdemeanour 1945/7791/363 and 7791, and 1938/6775/100 and 775. See also Tanta Appeal Court Record 1948/7564/1365, from which it appears that Salih Mas'ud Khairallah, who was caught stealing a piece of cloth, had nine crimes on his record.
42. Misdemeanour 1935/6783/4613.

Some mediators specialized in helping job candidates who failed the medical examination; they navigated the internal networks and used bribery to help candidates pass. Others made a living from counterfeiting medical reports and ID cards. Mediators bribed officials in the Department of Health, for example, to pass unqualified candidates. In one particular case, a mediator convinced a candidate that he could get him the required medical report if he gave him EGP 1.5 to bribe the doctor; the mediator took the money and disappeared.[43] Administrators at the MCSW Labour Office eventually discovered that some candidates who had failed the medical examination were able to get jobs in the company without ID cards. After an investigation, thirteen-year-old Ibrahim Muhammad Zarra was caught with a fake ID card, complete with company seal. Zarra had migrated from his village of Shubra Babil to al-Mahalla hoping to join the company workforce. Though he had passed the preliminary selection process at the company gates, his application was rejected because he had failed the medical examination. Two of his colleagues, whose names were not revealed in the investigation, sold him the fake ID, which enabled him to join the company and get paid.[44] The ID card displayed the fraudulent signatures of two high-ranking company administrators, which indicates the degree to which the mediators were familiar with the company administration and internal system.

Though the names of the mediators were not disclosed in the case of Zarra, cases such as his indicate that at least some of these mediators were mid-level, white-collar workers, and administrators at the company's Labour Office, with access to company records. The case of job candidate Girgis Salib presents yet another example. Salib gave his photo to 'Abd al-Hamid Ahmad Badr, a cook who acted as his mediator.[45] Salib paid a fixed fee in return for a counterfeit company ID, complete with his photograph, company seal, and signature of the Labour Office head. Curiously, all the workers caught with fake ID cards were men, while no reports exist of female workers being caught for such fraud. Considering that there were about 2,000 women among the company's workforce of 20,000 people, it may be assumed that some female workers might have secured their factory positions through a similar mediation system but were simply never caught. The fact that no women were reported indicates that either none were caught, or that their cases were settled before reaching court. It is also reasonable to assume that female workers with fake company IDs were fewer in number, and female job candidates were more likely to look for other jobs in smaller textile factories or domestic labour if their applications were rejected.

43. *Ibid.*
44. Misdemeanour 1936/6767/1069.
45. Misdemeanour 1936/6767/1495.

Mediators also helped workers sidestep the company's policy of not rehiring those who had quit or dropped out of work. The most common trick employed to do this was to change their names every time they needed to rejoin the company. The company's fingerprint system failed to catch them, unless they were arrested for some incident.[46] Others were able to take advantage of the company's inefficient bookkeeping to add fake names to the payroll lists and claim wages for non-existent people. Company worker Rushdi As'ad Rufa'il was able to add twenty names to the payroll before being caught. With fake ID cards and seal stamps, he collected money for non-existent workers and for others who did exist but had never actually worked at the company. His fraud was very successful, and he embezzled 427 piastres between September 1935 and February 1936. He was caught only by chance when his landlord found his fake stamps and ID cards.[47]

Not all worker mediation was conducted in exchange for a commission or percentage of wages. Workers also mediated to secure company jobs for their relatives and co-villagers. In the early 1940s, 'Atiyyah al-Sayrafi was forced to quit his studies at the Zaqaziq Islamic School owing to poverty and to search for work while still a child.[48] After failing to find a job in his hometown of Mit Ghamr, his mother planned to take him to al-Mahalla to secure a job at the MCSW. While she waited for the train at the Delta Railway Station in Zifta, along with workers from various provinces on their way to al-Mahalla, al-Sayrafi's mother asked how she could find a job in the factory for her son. The workers volunteered to take care of the boy through the early morning selection process and get him a job. She gave them 20 piastres to support her son until he got paid. The workers accommodated 'Atiyyah al-Sayrafi in their room in the workers' slum of Abu Gahsha, and at 7 am the following day they escorted him to the company gates, where he was selected for work in the spinning section. He went to the company's Labour Office to register his name and personal information so as to start work the following day. In his memoir published in 2007, 'Atiyyah al-Sayrafi, a veteran labour activist, reflected on the humiliation he felt during the initial selection process at the gates:

> In an atmosphere of terror, about 300 new workers were driven by the factory guards to a big yard, which was [like] a bazaar for the sale of human workforce for MCSW. Workers who came to sell their labour were asked to sit down on the floor so that their [physical] features could be inspected, as if they were

---

46. Misdemeanour 1938/6775/100 and 775; Misdemeanour 1939/6779/47 and 138; Misdemeanour 1940/2007; Misdemeanour 1945/7791/363 and 7791.
47. Misdemeanour 1936/6766/852.
48. Al-Sayrafi, *'Amil Mushaghib*, pp. 68–70.

slaves in a slavery market. In that dehumanizing exhibit, guards lashed obscene words to our faces although we were totally silent.[49]

In 1929, at the age of twenty, 'Abdu 'Abd al-Rahman earned a diploma from a vocational high school in the town of Damanhur.[50] He worked on his uncle's estate for three years before migrating to al-Mahalla, where he started working at the MCSW in 1932. The day he arrived, a porter at the railway station recommended that he go to a coffee shop located next to the company buildings, where he could find people who could secure a job for him. At the coffee shop, al-Rahman ran into an old schoolmate from Damanhur, Muhammad Fahmi.[51] Fahmi and his roommate, 'Ali Muhammad, took 'Abd al-Rahman's birth certificate and school diploma to the factory administration and secured a job for him immediately. On the following day, when he went with them to work, he discovered that both of them had arranged everything for him and exempted him from all the hassles of the screening process. He operated a loom for 7 piastres a day for a 10-hour shift. In the case of 'Abd al-Rahman, kinship, geographical origin, and collegial ties played a key role in his labour mediation.

Another example of how workers were able to negotiate the system to help each other gain jobs and promotion is that of pioneer worker, Fikri al-Khuli. In his three-volume memoir, al-Khuli gives a vibrant account of his experiences working at the MCSW, spanning the period of his early days at the age of eleven until he was fired and imprisoned in 1942 for participating in labour activism.[52] Although al-Khuli's memoir contradicts the nationalist narrative, his depiction of working and living conditions in al-Mahalla is consistent with contemporary documents published by leftist activist Yusuf al-Mudarrik in 1947 as well as with the court records utilized for this study and the oral testimonies I collected in al-Mahalla.[53]

Fikri al-Khuli travelled as a child from his village of Kafr al-Hima to al-Mahalla searching for two friends who had gone to work at the factory. He met them at the factory gates at sunset as they arrived to start their night shift (between 8 pm and 7 am), and walked with them as they went inside the factory. On the busy shopfloor, one of the bosses came and registered al-Khuli's name among the workers present and instructed him, and the other children, to pick up bobbins from the spinning machines. This was how he accidentally joined the MCSW, to become a child labourer in the factory's spinning section.[54] A few weeks later, al-Khuli

49. *Ibid.*, p. 69.
50. Halim, *Kikayat 'Abdu 'Abd al-Rahman*, p. 5.
51. *Ibid.*, pp. 28–30.
52. Al-Khuli, *al-Rihla*.
53. On the position of al-Khuli's account in the nationalist narrative, see Beinin, *Workers and Peasants in the Modern Middle East*, pp. 99–113.
54. Al-Khuli, *al-Rihla*, I, pp. 23–24.

wandered into the weaving section out of curiosity. The weaving machines were smaller than the spinning machines, and the workers were a bit older. He asked the section boss to allow him to join that section. Initially, the boss refused because al-Khuli was too young and too short. After some begging, with al-Khuli claiming he was an orphan who needed a higher wage to support his mother, the boss relented and ordered one of the weavers to train him. Thus, al-Khuli became a weaver at the factory, and his daily wage increased from 1 piastre to 2.5 piastres.[55]

His room-mates and friends in the spinning section then asked him to help them join the weaving section since they had helped him join the company. The following day, he went with them to his section boss, asking for them to be hired as well. They pleaded that they were room-mates from the same village and needed to work in the same section in order to accompany one another on the walk between work and home. The boss relented and allowed them to work in the weaving section as well.[56] An older, skilled weaver from the same region as the children trained them with enthusiasm. Later, the three children joined that older worker in the conflict with the people of al-Mahalla (*Mahallawiyya*) who attacked factory workers in a desperate attempt to drive them out of town. Al-Khuli and his friends are thus prime examples of the informality embedded within the process of recruitment and of mediation based on loyalty to geographical origin.

Behind the seemingly arbitrary system of recruitment, there were intricate structures at work. Agrarian pressures on land made labour abundant, and kinship, friendship, and geographical origin became crucial to acquiring an industrial job. In a milieu of corruption and informality, the selection process allowed workers who enjoyed good relations with their supervisors to mediate in the process to help others get jobs. The fact that a rank-and-file worker was able to mediate in the selection process was a significant sign of how so-called powerless workers were willing and able to manipulate the system to their advantage, thereby acquiring a measure of balance in their unjust relations with the giant company. It was further remarkable that rank-and-file workers were able to secure jobs for others while powerful politicians and rich businessmen failed to do so.

The unwritten policy was to ignore the recommendations and endorsements of outsiders.[57] Top-level personnel were recruited from among Cairo-based, government civil service employees with higher education and technical training. They viewed themselves as part of the modernization

55. *Ibid.*, pp. 50–51.
56. *Ibid.*, p. 54.
57. Harbison and Ibrahim, *Human Resources for Egyptian Enterprise*, p. 73.

and nationalism ethos.[58] Their experience in public administration brought
with it the assets as well as many of the shortcomings of bureaucratic
organization. They demonstrated the national aspiration to create modern
subjects through authoritative coercion. As highly skilled technicians, these
top managers were hardworking and opposed nepotism. Notables of the
town, including company board members, often failed to mediate the
hiring process to get people jobs. 'Abd al-Hayy Pasha Khalil – politician,
wealthy businessman, and MCSW board member – failed, for example, to
secure jobs for a retired policeman and a bankrupt handloom weaver.[59]

## MAKING AND BREAKING CLASS SOLIDARITY

The informality of recruitment practices had contradictory implications for
shopfloor relationships among workers and between workers and their
superiors. On the one hand, it led to the reproduction of relations of
dependence and indebtedness right down the chain of social relationships
in and around the factory. On the other hand, providing assistance with
recruitment in return for wage-sharing became a widespread practice, tying
the mutual economic advantages into the mechanisms of social solidarity
that enabled workers to exercise such influence over recruitment.

Yet, in many cases, worker intervention in the processes of recruitment
and hiring created a potential source of violence among workers. When
mediation was conducted out of communal commitment, it served to
strengthen communal identity based on geographical origin and kinship,
but also consequently weakened class solidarity. When mediation was
based on a financial agreement, workers fought violently, sometimes
causing fatalities, when someone failed to respect the terms of the
arrangements agreed. We can trace violent incidents reported to the court
and peaceful incidents mentioned in less than a handful of available
biographical sources, noting that many other violent and peaceful incidents must have escaped these records.

One of the most violent confrontations over such a financial agreement
occurred between two twenty-five-year-old workers, 'Abd al-Salam
al-Sayyid and al-Sayyid 'Uthman al-Samanudi, from the nearby town
of Samanud.[60] Al-Sayyid helped his co-villager, al-Samanudi, secure a job
at the company, and, based on what had become convention, al-Sayyid
assumed it was his right to receive a portion of al-Samanudi's wages.

58. In dedicating *The Mahalla Report*, the American researcher William Morris Carson
depicted Abd al-Hamid Hamdy, the general manager of the MCSW, as "Egypt's enlightened
captain of industry".
59. 'Abdin Archive in Dar al-Watha'iq al-'Umumiyah, Mahfazah, 441, "Iltimasat talab wazifa,
1939–1944" [Petitions on Job Requests, 1939–1944] and Mahfazah, 402, "Iltimasat i'anat,
1947–1949" [Petitions for Financial Aid, 1947–1949].
60. Tanta Criminal Court Record 1939/7443/1864.

Al-Samanudi refused to pay, which troubled their co-villager colleagues. On 29 August 1939, al-Samanudi and al-Sayyid confronted each other on their way to work and got into a violent fight. Three of their colleagues witnessed the fight but decided not to intervene and continued on their way to work. In the course of the fight, al-Sayyid broke al-Samanudi's skull, causing al-Samanudi severe, permanent disability. The injury to his skull exposed al-Samanudi to infection, endangering his life. Al-Samanudi also struck al-Sayyid but caused him only minor injury that required less than twenty days' treatment.

In yet another case, seventeen-year-old Lutfi Hamid Muharram travelled from his village to al-Mahalla so that his co-villager, Salama Muhammad Mustafa, could help him get a factory job at the MCSW.[61] Their financial agreement extended beyond mediation in the hiring process to include shared housing and living costs. Such agreements were common among workers and were always strictly verbal. Financial disagreement between the two broke out, however, soon after Muharram acquired a job. Although Mustafa willingly chose to leave his own room, the two got into a violent confrontation during the moving process. Muharram stabbed Mustafa three times with a knife, causing him serious injury.

Even in cases where both sides honoured their financial agreements and the hiring process passed off peacefully, newly hired workers often felt exploited by their colleagues, whether or not they were co-villagers. Mediators were able to manipulate the system to augment their incomes, but such opportunistic acts came at the cost of the welfare of their fellow workers. These acts placed great financial burdens on their peers, exploiting them and depriving them of a portion of their much-needed incomes. As Muhammad Shata's biography reveals, it was simply too difficult for those forced to pay a percentage of their meagre, hard-earned wages to feel any solidarity or unity with their mediating co-workers.[62] Some of them resented the exploitation by their co-workers even more than the exploitation by the company.

A representative case is that of weaving-section worker, Ahmad al-Tur. Following the first major workers' strike in 1938, al-Tur was the only worker to testify against his striking colleagues, which led to the conviction of fifty-two people.[63] After the trial, al-Tur enjoyed favourable treatment by the company's administration, particularly from the company guards and officers. He took advantage of his heightened status to mediate for those who sought jobs in the company in return for a fixed fee. As a reward for spying on his colleagues, his mediation efforts were always accepted.

61. Tanta Criminal Court Record 1940/7443/1905.
62. Al-Sa'id, *Arshif al-Yasar*, p. 284.
63. Misdemeanour 1938/6776/1865.

He was despised by his colleagues and over time became a burden on the administration. He was sent to trial when he was caught stealing company property. Among the many workers who testified against him were those forced to pay him for getting them jobs.[64]

The clustering in particular neighbourhoods of family members and co-villagers working at the company was a by-product of the workers' ability to participate in labour mediation. Moreover, living and working conditions served to cement the groupings of workers. The lack of official training, orientation, and industrial safety systems made such groupings vitally important for the safety and protection of unskilled workers with no prior machinery experience. Although the MCSW was quite generous in providing top managerial and administrative employees with overseas training, it invested little time and resources in the training of rank-and-file workers. Workers had to learn by watching others. The philosophy, as described by one administrator, was: "The worker is like a person who has never been swimming and is thrown into the river. He either sinks or swims purely on the basis of his own instincts."[65] Such practices evoke the contemporary system of Bengal's jute factories.[66]

The general practice was to assign new workers to help older workers. If the new recruit was a good observer and imitator, he might acquire the skills necessary to perform the job. Older workers, on the other hand, were often reluctant to teach new recruits their skills out of fear that they might be replaced by younger workers earning lower wages.[67] If the new worker was a relative or came from the same village, however, the senior worker might take an interest. Training in such cases was likely to be based upon personal considerations and kinship. This system emphasized communal bonding and deepened divisions among workers, which fragmented their sense of solidarity rather than built a sense of professionalism. Meanwhile, bosses and supervisors were irritated by these kinship groupings, believing that they disrupted the company work system. For example, Lutf allah Rizq went to check on and help his newly recruited brother, and when twenty-year-old section supervisor 'Abd al-'Aziz Hassan al-Mallah caught Rizq doing this, he hit him with a handloom shuttle.[68]

Groupings could develop not only from communal-based hiring mediation and informal skills training but also the sharing of living arrangements. Since newcomers often relied on their relatives and co-villagers to get them

64. Misdemeanour 1942/6790/960.
65. Harbison and Ibrahim, *Human Resources for Egyptian Enterprise*, p. 84.
66. Chakrabarty, *Rethinking Working-Class History*, p. 92.
67. In one such case, Ahmad Muhammad 'Isa refused to train Nasr Muhammad al-Sayyad; then the latter punched him; Misdemeanour 1941/6789/1362.
68. Misdemeanour 1937/6774/3728.

jobs, they also very often shared housing. This led to the tendency for clusters of workers from the same village to share rooms or live in the same area. Such communal concentrations served several purposes simultaneously. Accompanying each other on their trips between work and home provided them with much-needed protection and a sense of familiarity. Dividing the cost of rent also reduced their living costs and ensured communication with their families because a room-mate visiting their home village could carry money, messages, and other provisions between roommates and those families.[69]

This is not to say that such groups did not experience internal disagreements and fights. A geographical cluster could even be shattered, depending on the severity of a disagreement between two individuals in the group. For example, seven teenage workers from the nearby town of Samanud mediated for each other in securing positions at the company. Thanks to the mediation of one supervisor among them, they all succeeded in acquiring jobs. They all worked in the yarn section of shopfloor number 3 and shared a single room as living accommodation. One night, two of them started to argue over possession of a mat they used to sleep on. When others intervened to contain the fight, the entire group split into two opposing sides, and they all suffered physical injuries.[70]

Workers were likewise divided into competing groups. Geographical origin, as I have demonstrated elsewhere, played a divisive role among the factory workers of al-Mahalla in a manner similar to racial divisions among American workers.[71] Yet, kinship was also a significant factor in the creation of a violent atmosphere at the factory and in workers' slums.[72] For example, supervisor Aziz Ghubriyal *afandi* beat teenage worker 'Ashmawi Muhammad 'Ashmawi during his night shift. At the end of the shift 'Ashmawi and his father, who was working the same shift, along with four other company workers (their neighbours from the adjacent workers' slum of 'Izbat Abu Gahsha), waited for Ghubriyal at the company gates. Armed with sticks, they dragged Ghubriyal and threatened to kill him in revenge for beating 'Ashmawi's son. Ghubriyal was lucky that a policeman intervened and saved him.[73] In a similar case,

---

69. Although this pattern of communication between workers in al-Mahalla and their families in their home villages took place efficiently on a regular basis, court records show that it was not always risk-free. In some cases workers did not pass on money to their families or provisions to their co-workers; in other cases a group of villagers fought over splitting the cost of transporting provisions.

70. Misdemeanour 1938/6775/620.

71. Heerma van Voss and Van der Linden, *Class and Other Identities*, pp. 1–41, and Hanan Hammad, "Mechanizing People, Localizing Modernity: Industrialization and Social Transformation in Modern Egypt" (Ph.D. thesis, University of Texas, 2009).

72. Hammad, "Mechanizing People, Localizing Modernity", especially ch. 5, pp. 173–245.

73. Misdemeanour 1939/6779/727.

Ahmad al-Su'udi rushed to help his brother when he heard him screaming on the shopfloor. Al-Su'udi forced the supervisor, Suliman Mar'i, to stop hitting his brother with a stick. After work, the two brothers and the supervisor met outside the company gates for another round of violence, in which al-Su'udi was injured.[74]

It is reasonable to assume that such dramatic confrontations widened the rift between rank-and-file company workers and the supervisors and guards (*ghafar*). Two brothers, Abbas and Ali Fahmi 'Isawi as-Su'udi, exchanged blows with company guard Muhammad Musa Khalifa on 23 March 1938. A few anonymous other workers participated on the side of Khalifa, who reported that the fight erupted between him and one of the brothers because the latter was allowing a third person to enter his house while he was away.[75]

What was even more dangerous was the daily agitation among rank-and-file workers that extended beyond the shopfloor and into their homes and on to the roads between the two destinations. A disagreement broke out on the shopfloor between sixteen-year-old Husayn 'Ali al-Zini and his colleague, Qasim Ahmad 'Abd an-Nabi, on 7 March 1939. On their way back to their homes in the workers' slum of 'Izbat Raghib, al-Zini and the twenty-two-year-old fellow company worker Yusuf, along with eight other people, waited in ambush in a dark alley to attack 'Abd an-Nabi with a hammer. 'Abd an-Nabi received blows to his head; he lost the vision in his right eye. Al-Zini was sentenced to two years in jail, with hard labour, and had to pay EGP 50 in compensation to the victim.[76]

A similar, explosive confrontation took place in the weaving section, with two brothers clashing with two other workers. The incident began with a disagreement between Muhammad Mahmud al-Minufi and Musa 'Abd al-Maqsud Abu an-Naga in the weaving section, and a fight erupted when al-Minufi's twenty-year-old brother, Tawfiq, and others joined in. Abu an-Naga hit Tawfiq on the head with a large piece of heavy wood. Tawfiq was taken to hospital in a critical condition, and underwent surgery. Doctors had to remove pieces of Tawfiq's skull from his brain, which impaired his ability to work and placed his life in danger from exposure to brain infection. Tawfiq's injury resulted in a permanent disability, and Abu an-Naga was sentenced to five years in prison.[77]

Despite the importance of worker solidarity based on geographical origin, bonds based on kinship usually prevailed. The brothers 'Abdu and Ibrahim Mahmud Ghayra (twenty-eight and twenty-three years old respectively) met their rivals Muhammad 'Ali Darwish and Muhammad

74. Misdemeanour 1938/6777/1742.
75. Misdemeanour 1938/6776/975.
76. Tanta Criminal Court Record 1939/7441/879.
77. *Ibid.*

Muhammad al-Qutt after work on the al-Mahalla-Samanud road (all of them hailed from the village of Samanud). After an argument, the brothers stabbed their rivals, who were riding a bicycle, causing them serious injuries.[78] The privilege of kinship was also evident within the same geographical cluster. The brothers Fathi and 'Abd al-'Aziz Hassan al-Muslimani, company workers aged sixteen and twenty respectively, struck their co-worker and room-mate Muhammad al-Sayid Fadil because he failed to bring home the food they had ordered him to bring.[79] Geographical origin and kinship thus worked together in simultaneously cementing and dividing workers' groupings. In March 1936 a group of company workers became involved in a confrontation against several townspeople from al-Mahalla (*Mahallawiyya*) in the workers' slum of 'Izbat al-Sa'ayda; three brothers sided with the workers and two sisters sided with the *Mahallawiyya*.[80]

## CONCLUSION

Workers who mediated in the MCSW hiring process to obtain and maintain jobs for themselves and others manifested their ability to empower themselves in the face of the giant, nationalist company. They mediated to select and train their kin and co-villagers, manipulated the hiring process to embezzle money by adding fake names to the payroll, and secured jobs for those who did not meet the company's medical and legal qualifications. In doing so, workers augmented their income through commission, graft, or fraud, and they brought their social networks from their native villages to their new home town. The familial and village groupings that developed as a by-product of worker mediation resulted in explosive moments of violence among workers. Occasionally, financial disagreement between workers and their mediators led to violent confrontation. Polarization based on kinship prevailed among groups of alien workers.

It must also be noted, however, that working and living in an environment dominated by exhaustion, alienation, and disorientation among young workers was commonly the main, underlying trigger for daily arguments and disagreements even within the same group of kin or co-villagers. Diverse geographical origins and social cultures combined with the experience of having to live in overcrowded and dilapidated urban slums caused workers' groups to lack cohesion based on social codes or authoritative reference to solve disagreements in a calm or non-violent manner.

78. Tanta Criminal Court Record 1939/7442/1222.
79. Misdemeanour 1945/7791/232.
80. Misdemeanour 1936/6767/1019–1025. For similar cases see Misdemeanour 1942/6791/1628 and Misdemeanour 1937/6770/572.

Although familial and communal groupings served to divide workers, these groupings also facilitated their transformation and adaptation to urban industrial life and shaped their social consciousness as a distinctive urban group. Sharing skills on how to operate machinery safely and providing protection at work and at home reduced the feeling of alienation for many workers, and gave them a much-needed sense of familiarity in their lives in al-Mahalla. More importantly, the groupings provided them with work and helped to sustain them in their jobs. As in the case of interwar India, kinship and village connections added an economic function to "primordial" solidarity and provided workers with accommodation and shelter during times of sickness and hardship.[81]

During the major workers' strikes of 1938 and 1947, workers living in slums survived on a system of credit. Co-villagers and relatives sheltered newcomers until they were able to secure jobs in the company. Worker mediation in the company hiring process to secure employment for others empowered labourers in the face of the capitalist factory, but also created divisions among the workers themselves. Worker empowerment and division formed their consciousness as a distinct community – much like a separate class – in relation to the local capitalist system and their new urban surroundings.

---

81. Chakrabarty, *Rethinking Working-Class History*, pp. 205–206.

*IRSH* 57 (2012), Special Issue, pp. 97–128 doi:10.1017/S0020859012000442
© 2012 Internationaal Instituut voor Sociale Geschiedenis

# The League of Nations and the Moral Recruitment of Women*

MAGALY RODRÍGUEZ GARCÍA

*Vrije Universiteit Brussel/Research Foundation Flanders (FWO)*

E-mail: mrodrigu@vub.ac.be

SUMMARY: This article analyses the debate on trafficking and policies to combat the recruitment of persons for commercial sex within the Advisory Committee on the Traffic in Women and Children of the League of Nations. Its main argument is that the Committee's governmental and non-governmental representatives engaged in what might be called a "moral recruitment of women". This form of recruitment had a double purpose: to protect females from prostitution through the provision of "good employment", and to repress intermediaries of prostitution by means of criminalization. Three elements of the Committee's internal debates and concrete actions will receive special attention. Firstly, the ideological framework (feminism, social purity, humanitarianism, abolitionism, regulationism, and/or class); secondly, the gender dynamics (differences of opinion between the Committee's male and female representatives); and thirdly the degree of gendering (construction or reinforcement of gender roles and relations).

World interconnectedness increases not only the mobility of people, customs, resources, and ideas within and across national borders, but also the fear of spreading crime and diseases. Tougher controls and repression are the inevitable corollary of such a process. As noted by the former Secretary General of the United Nations, Kofi Annan, in the foreword to a report on the 2000 Convention against Transnational Organized Crime,

* I am indebted to Jean-Michel Chaumont for his generous sharing of information about the League of Nations Archives [hereafter LNA] at the United Nations Office, Geneva; and to Olivier de Maret, Daniëlle De Vooght, Anneke Geyzen, Paul Knepper, Lex Heerma van Voss, and the editors of this journal's special issue for their constructive remarks and reading suggestions. Needless to say, the opinions expressed in the present study are my own. I would also like to record my special thanks to Jacques Oberson and Lee Robertson for their professional and friendly assistance during my research in the Geneva archives; and to Paul Bullard for his careful proof-reading of this article. I am a Postdoctoral Fellow of the Research Foundation Flanders (FWO), Belgium, which facilitated my stay in Geneva by the award of a mobility grant.

"if crime crosses borders, so must law enforcement";[1] special attention is paid to the recruitment of persons for prostitution.[2]

Alarming reports on international crime, and human trafficking in particular, are not new, however. Since the nineteenth century, trafficking in women and girls for prostitution has attracted great attention.[3] Information about the so-called white slave trade – initiated by British reports on the "abduction" of English women to continental brothels and the "sexual slavery" of European females in South America – spread rapidly during the 1870s and led to the formation of the first anti-trafficking movement.[4] At the end of the nineteenth and beginning of the twentieth centuries, efforts to prevent and combat trafficking in persons resulted in the organization of a series of conferences and the passage of national laws and international conventions.

During the interwar period, the League of Nations strengthened the legal instruments aimed at the suppression and prevention of international crime.[5] In 1921 – in cooperation with anti-traffic voluntary organizations – it first addressed the recruitment of persons for purposes of prostitution by approving the International Convention for the Suppression of the Traffic in Women and Children. In subsequent years, the League and its anti-traffic committee contributed to perfecting a "global prohibition regime"[6] against international sex trafficking and the direct or indirect recruitment for prostitution that endures to this day.[7]

1. United Nations Convention against Transnational Organized Crime and the Protocols Thereto, United Nations, 2004, p. iii, available at: http://www.unodc.org/documents/treaties/UNTOC/Publications/TOC%20Convention/TOCebook-e.pdf; last accessed 29 November 2011. For a comprehensive overview of cross-border crime and crime control, see Peter Andreas and Ethan Nadelmann, *Policing the Globe: Criminalization and Crime Control in International Relations* (New York, 2006).
2. "Annex II: Protocol to Prevent, Suppress and Punish Trafficking in Persons, Especially Women and Children, Supplementing the United Nations Convention against Transnational Organized Crime", in United Nations Convention against Transnational Organized Crime and the Protocols Thereto, p. 42.
3. Paul Knepper, *The Invention of International Crime: A Global Issue in the Making, 1881–1914* (London, 2010), p. 98.
4. Donna J. Guy, *White Slavery and Mothers Alive and Dead: The Troubled Meeting of Sex, Gender, Public Health and Progress in Latin America* (Lincoln, NE [etc.], 2000); Stephanie A. Limoncelli, *The Politics of Trafficking: The First International Movement to Combat the Sexual Exploitation of Women* (Stanford, CA, 2010).
5. Paul Knepper, *International Crime in the 20th Century: The League of Nations Era, 1919–1939* (London, 2011).
6. Ethan A. Nadelmann, "Global Prohibition Regimes: The Evolution of Norms in International Society", *International Organization*, 44 (1990), pp. 479–526. For the application of the concept of global prohibition regimes in the fight against sexual trafficking in contemporary Greece, see Georgios Papanicolaou, "The Sex Industry, Human Trafficking and the Global Prohibition Regime: A Cautionary Tale from Greece", *Trends in Organized Crime*, 11 (2008), pp. 379–409.
7. The UN Protocol to Prevent, Suppress and Punish Trafficking in Persons, Especially Women and Children (in force since December 2003) contains much of the League's gendered logic with

This article analyses the debate on trafficking and policies to combat the recruitment of persons for commercial sex within the Advisory Committee on the Traffic in Women and Children of the League of Nations (henceforth "Committee").[8] The Committee seldom used the word "recruitment". Most often, its members used verbs such as to "incite", "entice", and "lead away", or the term "intermediary of prostitution", probably to emphasize the illegal and presumed exploitative character of the recruiters' activities. "Recruitment" and "intermediary of prostitution" are used in this article to encompass all persons who directly or indirectly facilitate women entering the world of prostitution. As the narrative unfolds, the difference between traffickers, procurers, brothel keepers, and *souteneurs* (pimps), as well as the Committee's proposals to punish them, will be specified. With the exception of its US experts, the Committee almost invariably used the word "*souteneur*" instead of "pimp". This was most likely a result of the common usage of French during the Committee's meetings. In this article, I will employ both terms for the activity of pimping. As with the word "prostitute", I am aware of the pejorative connotation and vague definition of the terms "pimp" or "*souteneur*". Those involved in the prostitution milieu often use the less deprecating – but also less clear – words "boy" and "girl" instead of "pimp" and "prostitute"; furthermore, they make no distinction between procurers and pimps. Since this article primarily focuses on the debates within the League of Nations, I prefer to adhere to the terms used within the Committee.

The main argument of this article is that the Committee's governmental and non-governmental representatives engaged in what might be called a "moral recruitment of women". This notion is inspired by Howard Becker's concept of "moral entrepreneurs" and Ethan Nadelmann's "transnational

regard to traffic and prostitution in general. Unlike the 1949 UN Convention for the Suppression of the Traffic in Persons and of the Exploitation of the Prostitution of Others, the new convention includes the issue of coercion and deception in its definition of trafficking. However, the definition is so broad that it could include cases in which the question of force or consent is unclear; United Nations Convention against Transnational Organized Crime and the Protocols Thereto – Conference of the Parties to the United Nations Convention against Transnational Organized Crime, available at http://www.unodc.org/unodc/en/treaties/CTOC/index.html#Fulltext; last accessed 29 November 2011. For a critical view on the negotiations for the UN Trafficking Protocol, see Jo Doezema, "Who Gets to Choose? Coercion, Consent, and the UN Trafficking Protocol", *Gender and Development*, 10 (2002), pp. 20–27.
8. This League of Nations unit adopted various names during the 1920s and 1930s: Advisory Committee on the Traffic in Women and Children (1921–1924), Advisory Committee on Traffic in Women and Protection of Children (1924–1925), Advisory Commission for the Protection and Welfare of Children and Young People – Traffic in Women and Children Committee (1925–1936), and Advisory Committee on Social Questions (1936–1939). These changes reflect the Committee's shifting focus, from a specific issue within commercialized sex – trafficking – to prostitution in general; Victor Yves Ghébali and Catherine Ghébali, *A Repertoire of League of Nations Serial Documents, 1919–1947* (New York, 1973), p. 610.

moral entrepreneurs", meaning "those who 'operate with an absolute ethic' in seeking to create new rules to do away with a perceived great evil".[9] Proselytism plays a key role within the process of rule creation and enforcement, as reformers follow their morals when attempting to make rules or to alter the existing ones that do not satisfy them. But, as Becker comments, a reformer is not merely a "meddling busybody, interested in forcing his own morals on others". Reformers are often concerned with humanitarian issues and believe that the reform they propose "will prevent certain kinds of exploitation of one person by another". He also noticed that reformers are commonly "more concerned with ends than with means" and rely on the advice of experts for drawing up rules.[10]

As the Committee's discourse revealed these two dimensions – morality and humanitarianism – and as its concrete initiatives on behalf of prostitutes placed great emphasis on the provision of "good employment"[11] for women, I believe the notion of a "moral recruitment" fittingly depicts its commitment to fight sex traffic and – albeit not officially – prostitution in general. This form of recruitment was meant to rescue females from "social evils connected with prostitution",[12] and to repress intermediaries of prostitution by means of law enforcement principles.[13] The Committee perceived these moral/humanitarian and repressive approaches as complementary, although there was a clear hierarchy. Law enforcement would be guaranteed by international and national authorities (through international conventions aimed at the convergence of national legislations), while protection and rescue work would be the main concern of non-governmental organizations. Whether the proposed measures effectively protected persons from being trafficked and punished genuine criminals, or rather triggered legal and social means that ended up limiting the freedom of alleged victims and offenders, is open to debate. Further research and a different sort of primary source are required to shed more light on this issue.

9. Howard Becker, *Outsiders: Studies in the Sociology of Deviance* (New York, 1963), p. 148; Nadelmann, "Global Prohibition Regimes", pp. 481–482, n. 4.

10. Becker, *Outsiders*, pp. 148, 150.

11. League of Nations Advisory Committee on the Traffic in Women and Children, Minutes of the First Session [hereafter, "Committee, Minutes of ..."], Geneva, 28 June–1 July 1922, p. 8, LNA C.445.M.265.1922.IV.

12. League of Nations, *Report of the Special Body of Experts on Traffic in Women and Children*, 2 parts (Geneva, 1927), Part 1, p. 6, LNA, C.52.M.52.1927.IV.

13. Investigation and prosecution of traffickers on the one hand, and protection of and assistance to the victims of trafficking on the other, are also included in the UN Trafficking Protocol of 2003. For a critical analysis of the current debate on and campaign against trafficking, see Brenda Carina Oude Breuil *et al.*, "Human Trafficking Revisited: Legal, Enforcement and Ethnographic Narratives on Sex Trafficking to Western Europe", *Trends in Organized Crime*, 14 (2011), pp. 30–46.

The article's structure follows Ethan Nadelmann's "evolutionary pattern" towards global prohibition regimes. The first section examines the situation prior to 1927, when the Committee largely ignored the issue of recruitment. The second section focuses on the affirmation of the existence of trafficking in women and the redefinition of recruitment for prostitution "as a problem and as an evil".[14] The third and fourth sections analyse the Committee's activism and the problems involved in it for the identification and criminalization of recruitment on the one hand, and for the protection of victims and potential victims on the other. In every section, three elements of the Committee's internal debates and concrete actions will receive attention: firstly, the approaches (feminism, social purity, humanitarianism, abolitionism, regulationism, and/or class) that provided the framework in which the Committee operated; secondly, the gender dynamics (differences of opinion between male and female representatives within the Committee); and thirdly, the degree of gendering (construction or reinforcement of gender roles and relations) and the basis of the Committee's dichotomous view of (female) "victims" and (male) "perpetrators" in the sex industry.

## THE ORIGINS OF ANTI-TRAFFICKING AND THE COMMITTEE'S INITIAL ACTIVISM

The campaign against human trafficking can be traced back to the second half of the nineteenth century. However, the first anti-trafficking movement was not monolithic.[15] Abolitionism – the movement to eliminate state-regulated prostitution – appeared for the first time in Great Britain and gained strong support among feminist organizations from various parts of the world. Opponents of regulation viewed this form of state control of women not only as morally unacceptable and inefficient (clandestine prostitutes and male clients were not part of the system), but also as dangerous because it allegedly promoted "national and even international traffic and commerce in prostitutes".[16] A shift from the original purpose of abolitionism became clear as abolitionists began to draw a stronger link between licensed prostitution and trafficking.[17]

---

14. Nadelmann, "Global Prohibition Regimes", pp. 484–485.
15. Limoncelli, *Politics of Trafficking*, p. 7.
16. Sheldon Amos, *A Comparative Survey of the Laws in Force for the Prohibition, Regulation and Licensing of Vice in England and Other Countries* (London, 1877), quoted in League of Nations, *Report of the Special Body of Experts*: Part 1, p. 7. For an overview of the involvement of the first leader of the abolitionist movement, the British feminist Josephine Butler, in the campaign against the "white slave trade", see Susan Mumm, "Josephine Butler and the International Traffic in Women", in Jenny Daggers and Diana Neal (eds), *Sex, Gender, and Religion: Josephine Butler Revisited* (New York, 2006), pp. 55–71.
17. Petra de Vries, "Josephine Butler and the Making of Feminism: International Abolitionism in the Netherlands (1870–1914)", *Women's History Review*, 17 (2008), pp. 257–277, 259–260.

By the late 1890s, a movement for the suppression of "white slave traffic" emerged in Britain and was institutionalized under the name International Bureau for the Suppression of Traffic in Women and Children [hereafter, "International Anti-Traffic Bureau"].

One important difference between the two organizations was that the International Anti-Traffic Bureau did not denounce state-regulated prostitution – perceived as a necessary control mechanism – and focused solely on international trafficking. Furthermore, the first-generation abolitionists were strongly influenced by liberal ideas that opposed patriarchal oppression and state intervention in private matters, while social purity dominated the International Anti-Traffic Bureau's campaign against trafficking.[18] However, from the early twentieth century onward, the social-purity discourse gained ground among abolitionists and feminists.[19] For its part, feminism itself was by no means homogeneous; many different views on questions of morality existed among internationally organized women.[20]

After some successes at national level, the anti-trafficking movement proceeded to the international arena to press for the suppression of traffic in women. In the early twentieth century, the first international agreements against "white slave traffic" were approved.[21] At the end of World

18. Anne Summers, "Which Women? What Europe? Josephine Butler and the International Abolitionist Federation", *History Workshop Journal*, 62 (2006), pp. 214–231, 217; Limoncelli, *Politics of Trafficking*, pp. 44–48, 57–58.

19. Deborah Stienstra, "Madonna/Whore, Pimp/Protector: International Law and Organization Related to Prostitution", *Studies in Political Economy*, 51 (1996), pp. 183–217, 187–188; De Vries, "Josephine Butler and the Making of Feminism", p. 260. Limoncelli, *Politics of Trafficking*, tends to portray the first anti-trafficking movement in binary terms: the International Abolitionist Federation is perceived as feminist, progressive, humanitarian, and transnational, while the International Anti-Traffic Bureau, along with the religious voluntary assessors and delegates from regulationist countries represented in the League's Committee, are often depicted as conservative, repressive, and nationalist. A thorough analysis of the Committee's anti-trafficking activity reveals a more complex picture.

20. For instance, most of them supported a single moral standard for both sexes, but many women interpreted it in different ways. One feminist brand supported female sexual integrity as the desired norm for both men and women, while another group understood the common standard as implying greater (sexual) permissiveness for women, akin to that for men; Leila J. Rupp, *Worlds of Women: The Making of an International Women's Movement* (Princeton, NJ, 1997), pp. 150, 154. Evidence from the minutes and reports of the League's Committee indicate that most female representatives tended to read the single moral standard for men and women in terms of continence. According to the representative of the International Women's Organizations and well-known French feminist/abolitionist Avril de Sainte-Croix, it was "the duty of parents to bring their sons up in the same atmosphere of purity as their daughters"; Committee, Minutes of the Fifth Session, Geneva, 22–25 March 1926, p. 92, LNA C.233.M.84.1926.IV.

21. In 1904, the International Agreement for the Suppression of the White Slave Traffic was adopted. It included the appointment of central authorities to gather information on trafficking, the supervision of employment agencies that sent women abroad, and the vigilance of ports and railway stations for putative procurers and victims. In 1910, the International Convention for the Suppression of the White Slave Traffic was signed, covering the offence of procuring adult

War I, Article 23c of the League of Nations Covenant entrusted the League with monitoring the agreements on the traffic in women and children. A survey revealed that many countries had not complied with the 1910 Convention, so the League proceeded to organize an international conference in June 1921.[22] Four important decisions were taken during this conference. First, the racialized term "white slave traffic" was replaced by "traffic in women and children".[23] Second, governments and voluntary associations were requested to send annual reports on trafficking and on the legal and social measures taken to suppress it. Third, a new convention was proposed. Fourth, the conference suggested the establishment of a special committee to investigate and to advise the League's Council and Assembly on conditions and measures against the international traffic in women and children.[24]

In September 1921, the International Convention for the Suppression of the Traffic in Women and Children supplemented the provisions of earlier international agreements by extending the protection to women of twenty-one and to minors of either sex.[25] An Advisory Committee on the Traffic in Women and Children was set up, consisting of government delegates and five non-governmental assessors representing the main international organizations that dealt with the suppression of traffic.[26] The Committee often made use of lawyers, experts on criminal and

women by means of fraud, violence, or other forms of compulsion, and of women under the age of twenty even with their consent; League of Nations Advisory Committee on Social Questions [hereafter, "Committee on Social Questions"], Report of the Sub-Committee entrusted with the drawing up of the Second Draft of a Convention for Suppressing the Exploitation of the Prostitution of Others, Geneva, 16 August 1937, pp. 2–3, LNA, C.331.M.223.1937.IV.

22. Karen Offen, *European Feminisms, 1700–1950* (Stanford, CA, 2000), p. 355.

23. As Leila Rupp, *Worlds of Women*, pp. 211–212, 216, comments, several women's organizations objected "to the lumping together of women and children", but they celebrated the League's initiative to continue the fight against traffic. The treatment of women and children as one group with comparable problems or facing similar dangers symbolizes the paternalism of the League's system. Many within the League of Nations seemed to have believed that women and children needed protection because they were "the least able to look after themselves"; Committee, Minutes of the Third Session, Geneva, 7–11 April 1924, p. 25, LNA C.217.M.71.1924.IV.

24. League of Nations, *Report of the Special Body of Experts*: Part 1, pp. 5, 8.

25. League of Nations Report to the Council by the Advisory Committee on Traffic in Women and Children, First Session, Geneva, 28 June–1 July 1922, pp. 2–12, LNA A.9(1).1922.IV.

26. The governments of Denmark, France, Great Britain, Italy, Japan, Poland, Romania, Spain, and Uruguay were invited to appoint a representative, as well as the following private organizations: the International Bureau for the Suppression of Traffic in Women and Children, the International Catholic Association for the Protection of Girls, the Federation of National Unions for the Protection of Girls, the International Women's Organizations, and the Jewish Association for the Protection of Girls and Women; League of Nations Report to the Third Assembly of the League on the Work of the Council and on the Measures taken to execute the Decisions of the Assembly, Geneva, 1922, pp. 72–73, LNA A.6.1922.

Figure 1. League of Nations Advisory Committee on the Traffic in Women and Children.
*UNOG Library, League of Nations Archives, Geneva. Used with permission.*

labour legislation, and (increasingly by the mid-1930s) psychiatrists. Like
government delegates, non-official assessors were entitled to sponsor
resolutions, propose reforms, add subjects to the annual agenda, and
initiate debates, but they had no voting rights.[27]

During its first years of activity, the Committee focused on the tasks
appointed by the League's Council: compilation of information on traffic;
supervision of the efforts made by the signatories to conform to the international agreements on traffic; control of the situation with regard to the
signatures of the 1921 Convention; and the monitoring of agencies engaged
in finding employment for women abroad. It also urged competent national
authorities and voluntary associations to keep an eye on the movements of
women and girls who secured situations abroad independently of such
agencies. In particular, engagements in theatres, music halls, and other places
of entertainment were perceived as potential threats that could lead women

27. Barbara Metzger, "Towards an International Human Rights Regime during the Inter-War
Years: The League of Nations' Combat of Traffic in Women and Children", in Kevin Grant,
Philippa Levine, and Frank Trentmann (eds), *Beyond Sovereignty: Britain, Empire and
Transnationalism, c.1880–1950* (New York, 2007), pp. 54–79, 59–61; League of Nations, *Report
of the Special Body of Experts*: Part 1, p. 8; Report of the Sub-Committee [...] Second Draft of a
Convention for Suppressing the Exploitation of the Prostitution of Others, August 1937, p. 3.

to prostitution. Besides these core issues, the Committee paid great attention to female migration and the employment of foreign women in licensed brothels, which were considered to have a strong link with trafficking. The members of the Committee were sharply divided on these issues, but the gender dynamics of the debates did not always follow the lines one might expect. Not all female representatives to the Committee advocated the protection of women's rights and not all male delegates supported preventive measures that could have ended up depriving women of their freedom.[28]

The Committee was at odds over a proposal to prohibit the employment of foreign prostitutes in licensed brothels. Feminist abolitionists such as Paulina Luisi (Uruguayan delegate) and Avril de Sainte-Croix (representing the International Women's Organizations)[29] refused to support the proposal because it implied condoning licensed houses of prostitution, which they viewed as a "social evil" degrading to all women irrespective of their nationality.[30] Gaston Bourgois[31] (French representative) also opposed the proposal because he saw in it an infringement of national sovereignty. Yet a large group within the Committee accepted the proposal as an "immediate compromise", which could lead to the abolition of the regulation of prostitution. Because of the established link between traffic and regulated prostitution, the Committee insisted on the necessity of obtaining detailed information about national legal systems with regard to commercial sex and about the prostitution milieu in general.[32]

28. See for example the contrasting views on female migration of Annie Baker (International Anti-Traffic Bureau's representative), who insisted on the need for strict migration legislation for young women, and of Samuel Cohen (Jewish Association for the Protection of Girls and Women) and Paulina Luisi (Uruguayan delegate), who called for the promotion of gender-neutral policies that would not interfere with the personal freedom of adult women; Committee, Minutes of the First Session, 1922, pp. 12, 24; Committee, Minutes of the Third Session, 1924, pp. 27, 39.

29. For Luisi's role within the Uruguayan feminist movement, see Christine Ehrick, "*Madrinas* and Missionaries: Uruguay and the Pan-American Women's Movement", in Mrinalini Sinha, Donna Guy, and Angela Woollacott (eds), *Feminisms and Internationalism* (Oxford, 1999), pp. 62–80. For an overview of Avril de Sainte-Croix's activism, see Karen Offen, "Madame Ghénia Avril de Sainte-Croix, the Josephine Butler of France", *Women's History Review*, 17 (2008), pp. 239–255. My findings on Avril de Sainte-Croix's opinions within the Committee sharply contrast with those of Karen Offen, who describes her views as "staunchly liberal, even radical, and secular in the tradition of the Declaration of Rights of Man as viewed through a feminist lens" (p. 242).

30. The following quotations are taken from: Reports on the Work of the Advisory Committee during its Second Session held at Geneva 22–27 March 1923, Geneva, August 1923, p. 10, LNA A.36.1923.IV; Committee, Minutes of the Second Session, Geneva, 22-27 March 1923, pp. 19, 24–25, LNA C.225.M.129.1923.IV.

31. Not to be confused with Léon Bourgeois (d. 1925), first President of the Council of the League of Nations and Nobel Peace Prize winner (1920).

32. Jessica Pliley, "Claims to Protection: The Rise and Fall of Feminist Abolitionism in the League of Nations' Committee on the Traffic in Women and Children, 1919-1936", *Journal of Women's History*, 22 (2010), pp. 90–113, 91–105.

## THE 1927 *REPORT OF THE BODY OF EXPERTS*

In 1923, Grace Abbott (US delegate)[33] proposed a thorough investigation of
the nature of international traffic. In her view, the League of Nations needed
to respond to the desire of world public opinion "to know the truth" about
the traffic and the legal tools to combat it.[34] The initiative followed the logic
of what Michel Foucault called "the great procedure of investigation", in
which "three conditions [make] it possible to ground judgement in truth:
knowledge of the offence, knowledge of the offender and knowledge of the
law".[35] The proposed investigation aimed at establishing: the crime of
trafficking, its authors, and measures for the legal punishment of recruiters
and the protection of women and children. The League approved the US
proposal and appointed a Special Body of Experts. It consisted of members
of the League's Committee and the Director of the American Social
Hygiene Association, the organization that provided the financial and
human resources for the field enquiries. Undercover agents travelled to 112
cities and districts to compile official and unofficial information from the
prostitution milieu; they interviewed some 6,500 persons, including 5,000
people directly connected with the "underworld".[36] The results of the
investigation were summarized by the Body of Experts in a two-volume
final report. It was the latter, rather than the unpublished field reports
proper,[37] that proved vital for the Committee's affirmation of the existence
of trafficking and for its awakening to the question of recruitment.[38]

Until 1927, references to the issue of recruitment for prostitution were
sporadic and almost exclusively made by the Committee's non-government

33. Germany and the United States were not (yet, in the German case) members of the League
of Nations, but the Committee recommended that the Council invite those two countries to
appoint representatives.
34. Committee, Minutes of the Second Session, 1923, pp. 6, 27, 61.
35. Michel Foucault, *Discipline and Punish: The Birth of the Prison* (Oxford, 1977), p. 19.
36. League of Nations, *Report of the Special Body of Experts*: Part 1, pp. 5–6; Paul Knepper,
"Spotlight and Shadow: The League of Nations and Human Trafficking in the 1920s", paper
presented to the European Social Science History Conference, Glasgow, 11–14 April 2012.
37. The field reports of the First Enquiry on Traffic in Women and Children are classified per
country and city in the LNA, boxes S171 to S181.
38. Katarina Leppänen, "Movement of Women: Trafficking in the Interwar Era", *Women's
Studies International Forum*, 30 (2007), pp. 523–533, 528, argues that the "League of Nations
took a non-moralising stand on the issue of prostitution and trafficking. Throughout the reports
and investigations, it was the procurers and traffickers, if anyone, who were considered criminal
or immoral – not the women". While it is true that the Body of Experts did not condemn
prostitutes, it described trafficking as the "vilest of trades" and prostitution as a "public evil to
be kept within the narrowest possible limits". Following this logic, prostitutes were victimized,
while intermediaries of prostitution were described as "pests of society" and "real parasites";
League of Nations, *Report of the Special Body of Experts*: Part 1, pp. 9, 48. For a dissection of
the work of the Body of Experts, see Jean-Michel Chaumont, *Le mythe de la traite des
blanches. Enquête sur la fabrication d'un fléau* (Paris, 2009).

members. In its early activism, the Committee built from a foundation of its binary belief in weak and passive victims (or deviants in a few cases) on the one hand, and brutal and immoral perpetrators on the other. In the Committee's view, trafficking and prostitution in general constituted a world of unequal power relations. Although the 1921 Convention attempted to discover and prosecute whoever – men or women – engaged in the traffic of women and children of either sex,[39] the Committee focused on female victims and male offenders. Furthermore, procurers, *souteneurs*, and traffickers were often identified as "alien",[40] "men of foreign race",[41] or linked to Jewish identity.[42]

Gendered stereotypes were magnified by the *Report of the Body of Experts*. These experts established a close relationship between international traffic and "the national aspect of commercialised prostitution", and defined it in the widest possible sense:

> [...] international traffic has been taken as meaning primarily the direct or indirect procuration of one or more other persons. This definition covers the cases in which girls have been procured and transported to become mistresses of wealthy men. It also covers certain cases of the procuring of women as entertainers and artists, and exploiting them for the purposes of prostitution in foreign countries under degrading and demoralising conditions.

So as to gain credibility, the Body of Experts attempted to avoid the sensationalism that characterized the earlier anti-trafficking campaign. Nonetheless, the shock value of the report was high. The Body of Experts admitted that trafficking did not involve the literal kidnapping of girls and stressed that it "did not wish to give the impression that all or most of these were unsuspecting and defenceless women who had been decoyed to a foreign country in ignorance of the real purpose of their journey".

---

39. International Convention for the Suppression of the Traffic in Women and Children, Geneva, 30 September 1921, available at http://treaties.un.org/doc/Treaties/1921/09/19210930%2005-59%20AM/Ch_VII_3p.pdf; last accessed 29 November 2011.

40. Committee, Minutes of the First Session, 1922, pp. 37–38.

41. The following quotations are taken from League of Nations, *Report of the Special Body of Experts*: Part 1, pp. 9, 18–19, 22, 43–44.

42. Knepper, *International Crime in the 20th Century*, pp. 107–112. See also *idem*, "'Jewish Trafficking' and London Jews in the Age of Migration", *Journal of Modern Jewish Studies*, 6 (2007), pp. 239–256. It is interesting to note the similarities in the picturing of the "victims" and "perpetrators" in the sex trade during the interwar period and in the past few decades. In the Netherlands, for example, the term "loverboy" was recently introduced to describe the actions of young, dark males (often of Moroccan or Antillean origin) who "entice" young, white, Dutch women to enter into prostitution. Current anxieties about human trafficking, however, focus primarily on women from low-income countries and the former Soviet bloc; Frank Bovenkerk *et al.*, *Loverboys of modern pooierschap* (Amsterdam, 2006); Jo Doezema, "Loose Women or Lost Women? The Re-emergence of the Myth of 'White Slavery' in Contemporary Discourses of 'Trafficking in Women'", *Gender Issues*, 18 (2000), pp. 23–50.

However, the experts emphasized "that the practices of those now engaged in the traffic in women [...] still involve heartless fraud and cruelty". The report's authors estimated that about 10 per cent of the traffic was in minor girls and admitted that "a large number of foreign women met with were prostitutes before they went abroad". But, they added, "there is ample evidence for believing that a considerable proportion of them were originally induced to become prostitutes by some form of deceit or false pretence". A rationale suggesting that deceit and agency are necessarily exclusionary led the experts – along with many contemporary scholars and radical feminists[43] – to conclude that most women found in foreign brothels were not free agents and thus that "a traffic of considerable dimensions" did exist.

Close reading of the final report, and more importantly of the original field reports, leads me to believe that the Body of Experts did not recognize that not all illegal migrants were victims of human trafficking. The undercover investigators did confirm the existence of a large migratory movement of men and women, as well as of informal networks that facilitated the recruitment and entrance of women into prostitution. They provided full details of the vast array of methods men and women had at hand to arrange the movement of females to overseas brothels: smuggling, marriage, employment contracts, facilitation of boat or train tickets, and provision of forged documents (visas, birth certificates, passports, invitation letters from family members living abroad, and so on).[44] Furthermore, the undercover agents often reported on the existence of "sexual excesses" or "perversion" and debt bondage in the sex industry; references to "conditions of slavery" or "slave-girls" for prostitution, however, appear mainly in the experts' final report.[45]

---

43. The list of authors who concur with the definition and general findings of the Body of Experts with regard to sex trafficking is long. Most of these authors draw parallels between today's "sexual exploitation" and that of the second half of the nineteenth century and interwar period. A few examples are: Sheila Jeffreys, *The Idea of Prostitution* (North Melbourne, VIC, 1997); Leppänen, "Movement of Women"; Limoncelli, *Politics of Trafficking*; Metzger, "Towards an International Human Rights Regime"; Mumm, "Josephine Butler and the International Traffic in Women"; Pliley, "Claims to Protection".
44. League of Nations, *Report of the Special Body of Experts*: Part 1, pp. 31–35.
45. *Ibid.*, pp. 10, 14, 23; League of Nations, *Report of the Special Body of Experts*: Part 2, p. 177, LNA C.52(2).M.52.(1).1927.IV; Havana report, December 1924, LNA box S173; Chaumont, *Le mythe de la traite des blanches*, pp. 181–201. Allusions to slavery were infrequent. Contrary to radical feminists, the Committee did not tend to refer to prostitution or trafficking as forms of slavery. The change in terminology in the anti-traffic conventions from "white slave traffic" to "traffic in women and children" reflected the reluctance of the League's experts to treat this form of labour as identical with slavery. Similarly, the League's Advisory Committee of Experts on Slavery focused on issues related to domestic slavery and slave-dealing proper (such as the legal ownership of persons, compulsory labour, and the transfer and inheritance of slaves) and made therefore no references to the forced recruitment of women for prostitution abroad.

Yet, as with the debates on and campaigns against traffic in the late nineteenth and early twenty-first centuries, the interwar experts failed to distinguish between exploitative working conditions and actual trafficking. All cases of abuse in the sex trade were identified as traffic. This perspective denied women's agency, except when they decided to leave prostitution and consented to rehabilitation.[46] Statements such as "even if a woman over age freely consents to being the object of the traffic, in the majority of cases she is not fully aware of the disaster to which she is being led"[47] symbolized the Committee's gendered and moralist view on so-called victims and perpetrators. Hence the Body of Experts and the Committee concluded not only that the crime of trafficking existed but also that its authors needed to be identified and prosecuted. Procurers and *souteneurs* were perceived as the main "agents of the traffic" because "prostitutes would not move from one country to the other on their own initiative".[48] Therefore, it was of paramount importance to punish severely the intermediaries and to protect the victims and potential victims of trafficking.

## SUPPRESSION OF WOMEN'S RECRUITERS

The Body of Experts treated the traffic in women and children as an illegal business activity governed by the laws of supply and demand. However, neither the experts nor the Committee as a whole focused on the demand for foreign prostitutes. Only towards the end of the 1930s did the Committee very timidly tackle the issue of demand, concluding that "it is generally agreed that whatever the force of the natural sex impulse which lies at the root of prostitution, it is artificially stimulated by third parties who make their living by its exploitation".[49] In its view, the

---

For a historical overview of the concept of "slavery" and the inclusion of prostitution, see Kevin Bales and Peter T. Robbins, "'No One Shall Be Held in Slavery or Servitude': A Critical Analysis of International Slavery Agreements and Concepts of Slavery", *Human Rights Review*, 2 (2001), pp. 18–45.

46. The Italian representative, Princess Cristina Giustiniani Bandini, stressed the importance of consent for a successful rehabilitation of prostitutes; Committee, Minutes of the Fourteenth Session, Third Meeting, Geneva, 3 May 1935, p. 3, LNA CTFE/14th Session/PV.3.

47. Committee, Minutes of the Twelfth Session, Third Meeting, Geneva, 7 April 1933, p. 5, LNA CTFE/12th Session/PV.3.

48. Société des Nations. Sous-comité de la répression des agissements des souteneurs, Genève, 20 janvier 1933, p. 2, LNA CTFE/CJ/2ème Session/PV.1; translations from French are mine.

49. Committee on Social Questions, Prevention of Prostitution, Geneva, 17 February 1938, p. 4, LNA CQS/A/16. In a 1947 brochure, a member of the abolitionist movement admitted that it was "high time that the International Abolitionist Federation should recognise the part men play in prostitution", and thanked the League's Committee for paying attention to this issue during one of its last sessions; A. Bouman, "The Part Men Play in Prostitution", International Abolitionist Federation Congress, Brussels, 8 September 1947, p. 1.

demand could be reduced by suppressing all forms of procuring, by providing counter-attractions to men (such as cultural centres, public libraries, cinemas, playing fields, and swimming pools), and by facilitating early marriage.[50]

The undercover investigators provided sufficient proof that transactions in the sex trade most often involved "intermediaries whose business is to recruit prostitutes".[51] Prostitutes, pimps, traffickers, and madams all confirmed that many sex workers had "a boy" or "a sweetie" (often prostitutes' boyfriends or husbands, but invariably identified as regular "pimps" by the undercover agents) or had arranged their trip to another country through a third person, often a male. Many other prostitutes, however, also mentioned prostituted girlfriends, female relatives, or acquaintances who had persuaded them to enter into prostitution or helped them to go abroad.[52] When or where women had not yet acquired sufficient political and socio-economic power to work as independent prostitutes, the tripartite organization of prostitution seemed practically inevitable. Furthermore, migratory impediments and labour restrictions, as well as stigma, marginalization, and violence, encouraged the involvement of third parties in the organization of prostitution. Bascom Johnson, Legal Director of the American Social Hygiene Association and Director of Investigations of the Body of Experts, claimed that only "prostitutes of the better class [...] go it alone and never have pimps".[53]

However, the relationship between prostitutes and *souteneurs* seems not to have been as asymmetric as generally assumed. Pimps moved from city to city to "secure recruits", while prostitutes actively looked for "boys" to help them out with travel tickets, money, forged documents, contacts with brothel keepers, and clients, and so on.[54] The undercover agents also found various cases in which the traditional view of recruiting

50. Committee on Social Questions, Prevention of Prostitution, Geneva, 15 May 1939, p. 23, LNA CQS/A/19(a); Committee on Social Questions, 1938, pp. 2, 11, LNA CQS/A/16, CQS/A/16(1).
51. League of Nations, *Report of the Special Body of Experts*: Part 1, p. 24.
52. See for example these field reports: Buenos Aires, June 1924 and Algiers, February 1925, LNA box S171; Havana, December 1924, LNA box S173; Lyon, December 1924, Marseille, October 1924, and Paris, June–July 1926, LNA box S174. See also Knepper, *International Crime in the 20th Century*, p. 99. In their introduction to Maria Jaschok and Suzanne Miers (eds), *Women & Chinese Patriarchy: Submission, Servitude and Escape* (London [etc.], 1994), pp. 1–24, 14–15, the editors also stress that the role played by women in the exploitation of other women within the Chinese patriarchal system should not be overlooked.
53. Legal Sub-Committee, Activities of Souteneurs, Geneva, 11 January 1933, p. 17, LNA CTFE/CJ/3. Academic studies on pimps are even scarcer than those on prostitutes. As Ronald Weitzer, "New Directions in Research on Prostitution", *Crime, Law and Social Change*, 43 (2005), pp. 211–235, 227, observes, "the little we know about pimps comes mainly from prostitutes, rather than from the pimps themselves".
54. Paris report, September 1924–September 1926, pp. 3, 5, LNA box S174.

for prostitution was turned upside down. For instance, French police and emigration officials stated that recruitment often went in two directions:

> This recruitment of girls for prostitution, whether by souteneurs or others, is well known to the police of all countries and to the public generally. What is not so well known is the influence which professional prostitutes have in the recruitment of souteneurs [...]. Cases are known to exist of good-looking young men who, though of weak and idle natures, were not bad until infatuated by some experienced prostitute whose only means of keeping a companion and protector is to support him in the idleness to which he is naturally inclined.[55]

Johnson added to the confusion about the "strange relationship" between prostitutes and *souteneurs* by stating that "in America, at least, as many pimps are created by prostitutes as there are prostitutes created by pimps, probably more, because, since the strengthening of our laws against third parties, they don't take any more chances than necessary".[56] Johnson also argued that his international experience had taught him that the pimp–prostitute relationship was often as varied (respectful or abusive) as conventional relations between men and women or as common (either affectionate, violent, or degrading) as real marriages. Similarly, in his history of modern prostitution in France, Alain Corbin pointed to the "marital behaviour" of some pimp–prostitute relationships, as well as to the different ways persons involved in the prostitution milieu expressed their feelings.[57]

Indeed, members of the Committee seem to have had great difficulty in understanding the way that prostitutes and intermediaries of prostitution related to each other. Classist and stigmatizing statements often slipped into the discussion on the intimate bond and the refusal of many prostitutes to press charges against pimps. According to the Italian delegate to the Committee, Princess Cristina Giustiniani Bandini, "witnesses usually refused to speak, as they belonged to the same low ranks of society, and prostitutes retracted their own evidence under influence of fear, affection or some other feeling towards the *souteneur*".[58] Therefore, none of the first-hand statements coming from prostitutes and pimps provoked a change in the Committee's gendered view of the division of labour, consisting of exploited women and exploitative men, in the sex industry. Between 1927 and 1939, when the League's activities stopped as a result of the outbreak of World War II, the Committee did its best to stamp out the direct or indirect recruitment of women for prostitution.

55. French report, December 1924–January 1925, pp. 10–11, LNA box S174.
56. Legal Sub-Committee, Activities of Souteneurs, 1933, pp. 16–18.
57. Alain Corbin, *Women for Hire: Prostitution and Sexuality in France after 1850* (Cambridge, MA, 1990), p. 156.
58. Committee, Minutes of the Twelfth Session, Fourth Meeting, Geneva, 7 April 1933, p. 7, LNA CTFE/12th Session/PV.4(1).

Figure 2. Photograph album of traffickers, *souteneurs*, and prostitutes, obtained from the chief of the judicial police, Havana (c.1927), "Souteneurs. Luis Lombardi – white race – son of Pedro and Rosa, born in Italy, 30 years old, single, con inst, unknown address, no more data." *UNOG Library, League of Nations Archives, Geneva. Used with permission.*

The Committee's first target was the *souteneur*. After all, the *Report of the Body of Experts* made it clear that the prevailing international anti-traffic conventions already covered procuration (i.e. obtaining a person as a prostitute for another person) but did not yet cover pimping (i.e. controlling, protecting, and living on the earnings of a prostitute). Moreover, the experts stressed that by 1928 only a few countries (Canada and Great Britain for example) had "effective legislative measures" – such as flogging – to punish the *souteneurs*.[59] In other cases (Belgium being one), the offence of pimping fell under the heading of vagabondage, which allowed for the segregation of anyone with no visible means of existence.[60]

The need for order, normalization, and control moved the members of the Committee to focus on *souteneurs*. More so than procurers, pimps were considered particularly dangerous offenders because they were "obstinately averse to all honest work", "always outside the moral law and on the fringe of organised society".[61] Supported by legal experts, the Committee also believed that most *souteneurs* sooner or later would become traffickers. Pre-emptive legal action was thus mandatory. Foucault would have interpreted the Committee's actions as an attempt to "provide the mechanisms of legal punishment with a justifiable hold not only on offences, but on individuals; not only on what they do, but also on what they are, will be, may be".[62]

All members of the Committee concurred in the need to punish *souteneurs* and to institutionalize the offence as an international crime. However, it seemed remarkably difficult to reach agreement on a precise definition of the offence. The difficulty arose because in many national legislations procurement and pimping were merged in the same clause. Thus, the difference between procurers and pimps was not always clear. Some Committee members used a comprehensive definition and perceived a *souteneur* as being guilty of three "violations": aiding and protecting

59. Great Britain reintroduced flogging for *souteneurs* in 1898 (under the Vagrancy Act) and for procurers in 1912 (under the Criminal Law Amendment Act). The Belgian delegate to the Committee, Count Carton de Wiart, was particularly interested in this British law. He claimed not to be in favour of such measures, but he agreed that it might be necessary in dealing with extreme cases. Miss Wall, a British substitute delegate, seemed embarrassed and stressed that the infliction of corporal punishment was very rare and that her government had approved the law hoping that the possibility of such punishment would serve as a deterrent. For a brief analysis of the flogging campaign in Britain at the end of the nineteenth century and its connection with the "white slave panic" of the early twentieth century, see Angus McLaren, *The Trials of Masculinity: Policing Sexual Boundaries, 1870–1930* (Chicago, IL, 1997), pp. 17–19.
60. Committee, Minutes of the Seventh Session, Geneva, 12–17 March 1928, pp. 34, 36, LNA C.184.M.59.1928.IV; League of Nations, *Report of the Special Body of Experts*: Part 1, p. 39.
61. Report of the Sub-Committee of the Traffic in Women and Children Committee, Geneva, 7 February 1931, pp. 2, 13–14, LNA CTFE/CJ/2.
62. Foucault, *Discipline and Punish*, p. 18.

prostitutes; living on the earnings of a prostitute; and recruiting "inmates" for foreign brothels. Other members were inclined to focus solely on the second accusation, namely making the prostitution of another person a source of livelihood. According to Estrid Hein (Danish delegate), all qualified as pimps. She classified the first category as "active" and the second one as "passive" *souteneurs*. To find a workable solution, the Committee proposed the establishment of a legal subcommittee.[63]

But the legal subcommittee too found it hard to define the factors constituting the offence of pimping. Like the League's Committee, the legal experts held differing opinions on the scope of the offence. However, they agreed on one issue: individuals who drew from the prostitution of others the whole or part of their livelihood ought to be "punished with particular severity".[64] Technically, this elasticity meant that not only the prostitute's partner but also her maid, parents, children, doctor, or landlord who were living with her, or who received financial gain as a result of her activities could be punished on the basis of this definition. Profit, exploitation, and the close liaison between the prostitute and the *souteneur* were therefore emphasized in the additional protocol to the 1921 Convention proposed by the legal subcommittee.[65]

An interesting gender dynamic arose from this debate. While most male members of the committees wished to prosecute any person guilty of pimping, female delegates insisted on applying the word "*souteneur*" exclusively to men. Male delegates protested and the phrase "person of either sex" was included in the protocol. However, during the debates pimps were invariably linked to the male sex. Elizabeth Zillken (German expert) and Estrid Hein explained this by claiming that "the very exact description given of a *souteneur*'s character from the psychological point of view [that is, the intimate pimp–prostitute relationship] made it clear that a woman could not carry on the profession of *souteneur*".[66] A woman could commit the same offence and be punished as a procuress but not as a *souteneur*. Hein's viewpoint was, however, more moderate. She thought that a distinction should be made between various categories of offender: "a brutal individual living on the immoral earnings of a

63. Committee, Minutes of the Eighth Session, Geneva, 19–27 April 1929, pp. 54, 58–59, LNA C.294.M.97.1929.IV; Committee, Minutes of the Twelfth Session, Fourth Meeting, 1933, pp. 7–8; Report of the Sub-Committee of the Traffic in Women and Children Committee, 1931, p. 2. The sub-committee was composed of government representatives serving on the Legal Sub-Committee of the Child Welfare Committee, and academic and international police experts.
64. Report of the Sub-Committee of the Traffic in Women and Children Committee, 1931, p. 3.
65. Legal Sub-Committee, Preliminary Draft International Convention on the Punishment of Persons who Live on the Immoral Earnings of Women, Geneva, 9 December 1930, p. 2, LNA CTFE/CJ/1.
66. This and the following quotes are taken from Committee, Minutes of the Tenth Session, Geneva, 21–27 April 1931, pp. 21–22, 25–26, 28, 87, LNA C.401.M.163.1931.IV.

woman should not be allowed bail, but other cases, for instance that of a wife who in desperation engaged in prostitution to provide for her unemployed husband and children, might call for a degree of clemency".

Furthermore, some Committee members pointed to another important difficulty with the draft protocol. The double aspect of the definition of a *souteneur* (intermediary of prostitution and profiteer) meant that it could include in its application the owners or managers of regulated brothels. As the protocol would indirectly lead to the suppression of licensed houses, it could be interpreted in abolitionist terms and meet with the opposition of regulationist countries. Self-proclaimed abolitionist members within the Committee such as Samuel Cohen (assessor representing the Jewish Association for the Protection of Girls and Women), Avril de Sainte-Croix, Estrid Hein, and Paulina Luisi had no objection to brothel keepers and pimps being treated similarly, "since they were also procurers and were always in agreement with the *souteneurs*".

After years of discussion and disagreement on the meaning of *souteneur*, Cohen provoked the Committee to shift its attention to an issue closely related to the recruitment of women for prostitution: the elimination of the age limit in the 1910 and 1921 anti-traffic conventions. Like the question of penalizing third parties, the idea of punishing procuring regardless of age had first been raised in 1927, when Part 1 of the *Report of the Special Body of Experts* was under discussion. Seeing that forged passports and birth certificates were ubiquitous in the sex trade, that the age of consent was fixed as low as ten in some countries, and that it seemed extremely difficult to produce legal evidence that intermediaries had employed fraudulent means or coercion, the experts suggested the removal of any mention of age from the existing conventions. The distinction drawn between adult women and minors was thus perceived as a legal tool with a perverse effect, as it facilitated the operations of intermediaries of prostitution. Hence it needed to be expunged from the international conventions.[67]

Most members of the Committee supported the elimination of the age limit. However, a few of them pointed to the objections some governments would pose to the proposal. Estrid Hein, for instance, explained that the Danish government would not support such an amendment "for it held the view that the liberty of action of adults should be respected".[68] Isidore Maus too hoped that all governments would respond favourably to the elimination of the age limit, but pointed out that it was very probable that certain difficulties would arise in regulationist countries such as his own, Belgium. He explained that if the age limit was abolished,

67. Committee, Minutes of the Seventh Session, 1928, p. 37; Committee, Minutes of the Twelfth Session, Third Meeting, 1933, p. 4; League of Nations, *Report of the Special Body of Experts*: Part 1, pp. 44–45.
68. Committee, Minutes of the Eighth Session, 1929, p. 60.

keepers of licensed houses or those who recruited women for regulated brothels would become subject to legal penalties. Yet Maus also thought that it was the Committee's duty to recommend the action it thought necessary, irrespective of the reservations of governments.[69]

The most moderate voice within this debate was (once again) that of Estrid Hein. She preferred a limited recommendation that would apply only to international traffic. Hein feared that an unconditional amendment to the conventions might lead to the prosecution of innocent third parties and indirectly to the infringement of the liberty of adult women who consent to prostitution.[70] In her view, "it was not felt desirable to protect adults against the consequences of acts they voluntarily committed".[71] However, Hein's allusion to the necessity of protecting the freedom of individuals was deprecated by the rest of the Committee. F.A.R. Sempkins (International Anti-Traffic Bureau) thought that "the principle at stake took priority over the interests of the individual". Paulina Luisi, an otherwise outspoken defender of women's rights, was also convinced that the "abolition of the age limit would certainly interfere with the freedom of adults [...], but it was the Committee's duty to combat the crime of procuring whatever the age of those concerned". Individual choice of prostitution abroad was inconceivable. As a French delegate argued, "it could not be maintained that these unfortunate women ever really gave their consent".[72]

Nonetheless, Hein's suggestion of restricting the elimination of the age limit to international traffic did not pass unnoticed, particularly by representatives of regulationist countries. The French delegation readily picked up the idea and stressed that international traffic could easily be identified and represented a far greater danger than national traffic. By launching a proposal that restricted the abolition of the age limit to cases of adult and minor women being recruited for prostitution abroad, the French could score twice, both on the domestic and the international level. On the one hand, the sovereignty of regulationist countries would remain intact as recruiters for or owners of licensed brothels would not be convicted on the basis of the new convention; on the other, limiting the issue to all women going abroad would deal a blow to the so-called international traffic, as the recruitment of foreign females of every age

---

69. Committee, Minutes of the Ninth Session, Geneva, 2–9 April 1930, p. 37, LNA C.246.M.121.1930.IV.

70. Committee, Minutes of the Eleventh Session, Fifth Meeting, Geneva, 6 April 1932, p. 3, LNA CTFE/11th Session/PV.5; Committee, Minutes of the Twelfth Session, Third Meeting, 1933, p. 7.

71. The following quotations are taken from Committee, Minutes of the Eleventh Session, 1932, pp. 3, 5–6, 8.

72. Committee, Minutes of the Twelfth Session, Fourth Meeting, Geneva, 7 April 1933, p. 2, LNA CTFE/12th Session/PV.4(1).

would henceforth be criminalized.[73] Abolitionist members within the Committee unanimously supported the French amendment and declared themselves prepared "to compromise and to accept the immediate international remedy now proposed, as a step towards a complete abolition of the *souteneur* from national as well as from international traffic".[74]

In 1933, the League's Assembly approved the International Convention for the Suppression of the Traffic in Women of Full Age. It covered "the offence of procuring, enticing or leading away, even with her consent, a woman or girl of full age for immoral purposes in another country".[75] This approval was perceived as a triumph of the Committee's joint action – between state and non-state actors – to combat the traffic in women and children. As the Spanish delegate to the Committee observed, "the restriction of the export traffic from France would have the beneficial effect in Spain of preventing the entry of French women, for whom there was a special demand", and "action by the Spanish authorities would prevent the export of Spanish women to South America".[76] Whether the 1933 Convention helped to prosecute genuine offenders of human trafficking and whether it was beneficial to the women it sought to protect is doubtful. As Marjan Wijers argues, restrictive measures easily give rise to increased clandestine action, punishment of innocent people, restriction of personal freedom, stigmatization, and the social exclusion of the men and women engaged in the sex trade.[77]

The campaign for the protection of foreign women of all ages did not distract the Committee from its earlier effort to punish intermediaries of prostitution. During the early 1930s, the Committee debated the best way to transcend the main difficulty – whether or not to penalize the manager of licensed brothels – and to draft a convention that would be acceptable to as many countries as possible – abolitionist and regulationist. Seeing that the Committee could not find a suitable solution to this issue, the League's Assembly called on the International Bureau for the Unification of Criminal Law for assistance. The Committee would provide the "moral substance" and the Bureau the legal form.[78]

73. Committee, Minutes of the Eleventh Session, 1932, pp. 7, 9–10; Committee, Minutes of the Twelfth Session, Third Meeting, 1933, pp. 2–4, 7, 9.
74. Committee, Minutes of the Twelfth Session, Third Meeting, 1933, pp. 5–7.
75. *Ibid.*, p. 7; Report of the Sub-Committee […] Second Draft of a Convention for Suppressing the Exploitation of the Prostitution of Others, 1937, p. 3.
76. Committee, Minutes of the Twelfth Session, Third Meeting, 1933, p. 6.
77. Marjan Wijers, "European Union Policies on Trafficking in Women", in Mariagrazia Rossilli (ed.), *Gender Policies in the European Union* (New York, 2000), pp. 209–229, 219, 227. Wijers analyses recent European policies on traffic but draws many parallels with the campaigns and policies of the early twentieth century.
78. Committee, Minutes of the Thirteenth Session, Geneva, 4–12 April 1934, pp. 4–5, 83, 94–95, LNA CTFE/13th Session/PV (revised).

By the mid-1930s, the Committee's enquiry into the system of regulation provided sufficient ammunition for the criminalization of all forms of recruitment for prostitution. Since the system of licensed or tolerated brothels had not attained its main objective (the prevention of venereal diseases), the Committee reached three important conclusions: regulation of prostitution could not be justified; brothels of all kinds ought to be prohibited; and brothel keepers, procurers, and *souteneurs* should be punished.[79] A new draft convention was prepared to make all procurement illegal, but some Committee members did not support it, for two reasons. Sidney West Harris (British representative) thought that there could be "no effective convention for the punishment of souteneurs if the problem of licensed houses was not first solved". For his part, the International Anti-Traffic Bureau's delegate, Sempkins, regretted that the Convention "made little provision for dealing with the souteneurs and was mainly concerned with procuring".[80]

In 1935, a legal subcommittee was appointed to find a solution to the impasse. To obtain the approval of regulationist countries, the new draft convention omitted the term "*souteneur*". At the same time, it wished to give immediate satisfaction to the aspirations of abolitionist countries and supporters by implicitly targeting "all those who recruited women for the purpose of immorality".[81] The draft Convention for Suppressing the Exploitation of the Prostitution of Others (1937) was intended to fill the gap in the existing conventions by protecting adults of either sex against procuration, even when they consented and were not taken abroad.[82] The outbreak of World War II prevented its approval by the Assembly, but many of the ideas included in the draft convention were taken up by the United Nations in 1949.[83]

One of the two pillars that sustained the League's moral recruitment of women – repression of offenders – remained thus intact throughout the 1920s and 1930s. By 1939, however, as the Committee started to treat

---

79. Abolition of Licensed Houses, Geneva, 15 June 1934, pp. 94–95, LNA C.221.M.88.1934.IV; Committee, Minutes of the Fourteenth Session, Fourth Meeting, Geneva, 4 May 1935, pp. 2–3, LNA CTFE/14th Session/PV.4.
80. Committee, Minutes of the Fourteenth Session, Fifth Meeting, Geneva, 1935, pp. 2–3, 6, LNA CTFE/14th Session/PV.5.
81. Sub-Committee on the suppression of the activities of souteneurs, Geneva, 25 January 1936, p. 9, LNA CTFE/CS.4.
82. Report of the Sub-Committee [...] Second Draft of a Convention for Suppressing the Exploitation of the Prostitution of Others, 1937, pp. 2–3.
83. The UN Convention for the Suppression of the Traffic in Persons and of the Exploitation of the Prostitution of Others called on states to suppress trafficking and prostitution, regardless of the consent of the people involved. But as Harris had predicted, not many states ratified the 1949 Convention, partly because of its abolitionist goal; Joyce Outshoorn, "Introduction: Prostitution, Women's Movements and Democratic Politics", in *idem* (ed.), *The Politics of Prostitution: Women's Movements, Democratic States and the Globalisation of Sex Commerce* (Cambridge, 2004), pp. 1–20, 8; the Convention's text is available at http://www2.ohchr.org/english/law/trafficpersons.htm, last accessed 6 December 2011.

prostitution from a psychiatric viewpoint, its perception of intermediaries for prostitution altered slightly. Backed by the expertise of the Director of the University Institute for Human Genetics (Copenhagen), Dr Tage Kemp, the Committee observed a strong parallelism between the "mental state of prostitutes" and that of *souteneurs*. The Committee discovered that, like many prostitutes, a large percentage of *souteneurs* could be classified as "dull, feeble-minded, or clearly even psychopathic".[84] Hence the Committee wished not only to criminalize but also to investigate the social conditions under which the phenomenon of pimping appeared. Regardless of the motives and mental attributes of recruiters, the Committee invariably thought that females needed to be protected.

Concrete action for the protection of women had been the competence of voluntary organizations since the second half of the nineteenth century. From its origins, the Committee paid due attention to the issue. However, it was especially after the publication of the investigations on trafficking and regulated brothels that all of its members (governmental and non-governmental) showed great interest in the protection of women. Particularly during the 1930s, the Committee formulated strong views on rehabilitation and the prevention of prostitution. The following pages illustrate the Committee's ideas in more detail.

## PROTECTION OF WOMEN

International organized women were divided on issues such as the urgency of moral reform and the need to protect women. Feminists such as Paulina Luisi feared that protective measures would result in discriminatory control of women.[85] Although Luisi regularly aired these concerns within the League of Nations, most members of the Committee agreed on the need to establish protection strategies that would prevent women and young girls from entering into prostitution and from becoming victims of traffic. Contrary to what some authors suggest,[86] the majority of women's groups represented at the Committee did support initiatives for the protection of women. Furthermore, "rescue missions" were not only endorsed by religious or secular organizations associated with the (rather conservative) International Anti-Traffic Bureau but also by women's organizations closely linked to the International Abolitionist Federation (commonly viewed as more progressive).

---

84. Committee on Social Questions, Report on the work of the Committee in 1939 (Third Session), Geneva, July 1939, p. 16, LNA C.214.M.142.1939.IV.
85. Rupp, *Worlds of Women*, pp. 151–152; Summers, "Which Women?", p. 223.
86. Carol Miller, "The Social Section and Advisory Committee on Social Questions of the League of Nations", in Paul Weindling (ed.), *International Health Organisations and Movements, 1918–1939* (Cambridge, 1995), pp. 154–174, 158–159; Limoncelli, *The Politics of Trafficking*, pp. 75–76.

Figure 3. Photograph album of traffickers, *souteneurs*, and prostitutes, obtained from the chief of the judicial police, Havana (c.1927), "PROSTITUTE. Lonya Vavionsha. Born in Poland, 25 years of age. Father – Adolph, mother – Anna. Prostitute at 9 Bernat Street, Havana, Cuba. Was imported for purposes of prostitution by trafficker ANNA GRIEF SEIMAN." *UNOG Library, League of Nations Archives, Geneva. Used with permission.*

The yearly reports of the non-governmental associations represented in the Committee are testimony to the continuation and strengthening of protective measures. For instance, Avril de Sainte-Croix proudly informed her peers that the International Council of Women (ICW) had agreed to organize "an international system of female supervision" on board ships.[87] The ICW hoped to reach an agreement with shipping companies, as it felt that women were relatively well protected in stations and ports but not en route.[88] Similarly, Samuel Cohen informed the Committee on the successful activities of the Jewish Association for the Protection of Girls and Women in ports, railway stations, and long-distance coach termini which had led to the prosecution and conviction of men, and to the restoration of girls "to a respectable life".[89] Like de Sainte-Croix, Cohen wished to obtain better arrangements with transport companies to refuse passage to those suspected of trafficking, to patrol stations, ports, and ships, and to be allowed to post warning notices on vessels pointing to "the dangers that might be encountered on the particular route".[90] For his part, the French delegate Bourgois regretted that many of the questions dealt with by voluntary organizations were "more concerned with social hygiene than with traffic".

Indeed, a moral rather than a liberal-feminist or humanitarian perspective dominated the debate on rescue work. Avril de Sainte-Croix, for example, shared Paulina Luisi's concern about restrictive regulations governing the travel of adult women, but insisted at the same time on the need to "afford protection to unprotected women and to girls and children in moral danger". From the evidence found in the Committee's documents, one gets the impression that many female members within the Committee had a generally negative perception of men – or at least of male migrants – that was often based on speculation. For example, Mrs Curchod-Secretan (Fédération des Unions Nationales des Amies de la Jeune Fille) reported to the Committee that:

[...] one of our station representatives sees a charming young girl get out of the train one morning, followed by a suspicious-looking man who appears to be taking great care of her. "Where are you going?", asks our representative. "I am going to B.", replies the girl, "but not at once; this gentleman has offered to show me round the town, and we are going to dine together". Our representative puts the girl back into the train and points out to her the danger of changing one's plans. Meanwhile, the disreputable gentleman disappears.[91]

87. Committee, Minutes of the First Session, 1922, pp. 46–47.
88. Monitoring of places of departure was already included in the 1904 International Agreement for the Suppression of White Slave Traffic (see above).
89. Committee, Minutes of the First Session, 1922, p. 46.
90. The following quotation are taken from Committee, Minutes of the Third Session, 1924, pp. 26–27, 80.
91. Committee, Minutes of the Fifth Session, 1926, p. 92.

Hence Avril de Sainte-Croix applauded the initiative of women's organizations to establish separate clubs, canteens, and *"foyer féminins"* to provide young working women with cheap food and lodging, and stressed that "by offering them a refuge from men's attentions in the restaurants, [these organizations] have saved many [women] from the great dangers to which bad company exposes young girls".[92] Adéle Thurler (International Catholic Association for the Protection of Girls) too described her organization's rescue work as "an outpost, preventing the treacherous enemy from penetrating to the citadel".[93] A strong gendered logic of men being a danger for women and of women being in danger of men guided the thought and actions of many female delegates and assessors. For their part, male representatives were more inclined to stress female vulnerability rather than male menace.

Influenced by these fears, the more permissive climate of the 1920s and 1930s was not interpreted in terms of opportunity for women's empowerment. On the contrary, the sexual revolution of the early twentieth century only aggravated the Committee's preoccupation with moral degradation and female libertarianism. Many female representatives showed great concern about the relaxation of parental authority and excess of liberty granted to young people, which "was creating a problem not of commercialized traffic but of promiscuity".[94] A Canadian assessor regretted that the single moral standard was approached by a route that had not been anticipated and that "increased knowledge of contraceptives and greater freedom tended [...] to diminish the seriousness of immorality and irregular sexual relations in the eyes of women". What was needed, she said, was "intensive education, character training and attention to the attitude, especially that adopted by women, towards morality, chastity and virtue".

Moreover, following in the footsteps of international women's organizations, many within the Committee seemed convinced that moral and sexual education was not only of paramount importance but also a right and responsibility of women.[95] For instance, through the League of Nations, Avril de Sainte-Croix successfully propagated the ICW campaign for the worldwide establishment of a women's police force, which they considered essential for any serious reform of public morals.

92. Committee, Minutes of the Third Session, 1924, p. 81.
93. Committee, Minutes of the First Session, 1922, p. 41.
94. The following quotation are taken from Committee, Minutes of the Fifteenth Session, Fifth Meeting, 22 April 1936, pp. 10–12, LNA CTFE/15th Session/PV.5.
95. Catherine Jacques and Sylvie Lefebvre, "From Philanthropy to Social Commitment", in Éliane Gubin and Leen Van Molle (eds), *Women Changing the World: A History of the International Council of Women, 1888–1988* (Brussels, 2005), pp. 149–169, 149, 161; Rupp, *Worlds of Women*, p. 154.

In their opinion, in questions concerning the defence of women and children "women should be called upon to lend their abilities and devotion".[96] Avril de Sainte-Croix also praised the efforts of the Société française de prophylaxie sanitaire et morale, in particular its campaign against venereal diseases and the importance attached to the mother in sexual education.[97] It was necessary, in her view, "to impress the young with the dangers of the traffic and of immorality" because "the main cause of prostitution was environment and the evil could be combated only by giving young people of either sex moral education and a sense of responsibility and self-respect".[98]

On the causes of prostitution, the divisions within the Committee were profound. This debate arose for the first time in 1927, after the Body of Experts had presented evidence of the influence of low wages on the development of prostitution and trafficking. The economic depression of the early 1930s intensified the debate, but it did not resolve those divisions. Various governmental and non-governmental members – Paulina Luisi and Isidore Maus, and Avril de Sainte-Croix and Baroness de Montenach respectively – thought that there was a strong relationship between low wages and prostitution and, therefore, wanted a prompt investigation of the subject. To prove her argument, De Sainte-Croix used the example of "a young, refined girl" whom she had asked "whether the life she led did not disgust her", and to which the girl had replied: "my body is my own, and while I am about it I would rather sell it for an hour for 10 francs than for ten hours work a day for a miserable wage".[99] For his part, Sidney Harris (Britain) did not believe the connection between wages and prostitution was clear-cut and, above all, he thought the issue involved a major economic question that lay outside the scope of the Committee's competence. Nonetheless, the Committee recognized that the low wages paid to women in certain branches of employment was a factor that could not be disregarded and suggested that the League's Secretariat should examine the question in cooperation with the International Labour Organization (ILO).[100] To my knowledge, no joint study emerged from this suggestion.

96. Committee, Minutes of the Eighth Session, 1929, p. 116; Committee, Minutes of the Fifth Session, 1926, p. 25.
97. Committee, Minutes of the Sixth Session, Geneva, 25–30 April 1927, p. 41, LNA C.338.M.113.1927.IV.
98. Committee, Minutes of the Fifth Session, 1926, p. 89; Committee, Minutes of the Thirteenth Session, 1934, p. 23.
99. Committee on Social Questions, Reports of voluntary organizations, 27 April 1937, p. 3, LNA CQS/A.10.
100. Reports on the Work of the Advisory Committee during its Sixth Session held at Geneva from 25–30 April 1927, Geneva, July 1927, p. 5, LNA A.25.1927.IV.

No agreement could be reached regarding the influence of unemployment on prostitution. Avril de Sainte-Croix claimed that her enquiries and those from colleagues all over the world had led her to conclude that undue importance was attached to unemployment. Lack of work could not be seen as a direct cause of prostitution since domestic servants, shop girls, stenographers, and so on accounted for a large proportion of prostitutes. In her view, idleness, coquetry, greed, bad company, and sybaritism had more "corrupting" effects. The Danish, German, Polish, and Uruguayan delegates (all female) – Hein, Zillken, Grabinska, and Luisi – strongly disagreed. In their view, want, unemployment, and social inequality were indisputably linked to prostitution.[101]

Whatever the causes of prostitution, the Committee unanimously agreed that providing "a suitable and decent livelihood for the women of the less favoured classes" could safeguard them from being recruited for prostitution and trafficking.[102] A peculiar mix of feminism and conservatism was often discernible in the discussions on the prevention of prostitution through work and the place of women in society in general. At the Committee's fifth session, Avril de Sainte-Croix defended with verve her ideas on gender equality: a woman, she said, deserved the same opportunities as a man to expose her ideas, "without prejudice to her essential mission as guardian of the home".[103] Similarly, a delegate of the International Union of Catholic Women's Leagues urged an enquiry into the effects of female unemployment on prostitution, but wanted at the same time to create social institutions "to facilitate the return of the mother to the home".[104] Yet realizing that economic factors compelled many women to work, all Committee members found it necessary to improve the socio-economic position of women to prevent them from entering into prostitution.

From the nineteenth century on, voluntary associations had established non-profit employment bureaus and rescue homes where training and workrooms for women were organized. Voluntary female workers acted as a link between the "inmates" and the world outside. The yearly reports of the non-governmental assessors informed the Committee of their continuous efforts to secure jobs and to "inculcate in young girls a love of work".[105] As stated in the Committee's study on the prevention of

---

101. *Ibid.*, pp. 16–18, 23, 26–27; Committee, Minutes of the Sixth Session, 1927, pp. 16–17, 37; Committee, Minutes of the Eighth Session, 1929, p. 116; Committee, Minutes of the Eleventh Session, Fourth Meeting, Geneva, 5 April 1932, pp. 3, 7, 9, 16, LNA CTFE/11th Session/PV.4; Committee, Minutes of the Fifteenth Session, Fifth Meeting, 1936, p. 9.
102. Committee, Minutes of the Thirteenth Session, 1934, p. 15.
103. Committee, Minutes of the Fifth Session, 1926, p. 87.
104. Committee, Minutes of the Thirteenth Session, 1934, p. 17.
105. Committee, Minutes of the Fourteenth Session, Third Meeting, 1935, p. 7.

prostitution, the idea was to provide "protection by means of work".[106] The Committee had come to the conclusion that although certain forms of employment (such as domestic service or jobs in bars, dance halls, and other public places) "may cause moral danger", a lack of occupation was no less risky. Furthermore, in addition to unemployment, working conditions also demanded attention. Wages and the status of some occupations needed improvement to protect women against the "temptation to find a way out by taking up a shameful but profitable trade".

Work was thus to be made attractive to women, but it needed to be monitored. The Committee applauded the efforts of voluntary organizations, which sought cooperation with ministries of labour and private employment agencies to obtain not only working permits for foreign girls but also "moral guarantees" for jobs abroad.[107] Another crucial partner for the task of promoting and supervising female labour was the ILO. In the Committee's study on prevention of prostitution, the ILO authored the chapter "Moral Protection of Young Women Workers".[108] Its analysis focused on three measures: regulation of placing operations; protection at the workplace; and protection of female workers during their spare time.

A radical measure for the regulation of job placement was adopted in 1933, when the International Labour Conference adopted a convention to abolish all fee-charging employment agencies and to supervise non-profit bureaus working under the mask of philanthropy. Among the important provisions for the protection of women at the workplace were the conventions on the minimum age for industrial and non-industrial employment. Supervision of employment in the entertainment industry, restaurants, public houses, and domestic service in particular called for greater attention. Because a statistically significant number of prostitutes had previously worked as domestic servants in private households, the ILO wished to strengthen its efforts to improve domestic work, but it admitted that progress was slow.[109] According to the ILO, an increased appreciation of domestic work as a profession was as important as improved working conditions. Women who took up domestic service ought to "feel that they had a real vocation and should not be ashamed of their work".[110]

On the protection of young women outside working hours and during holidays, the ILO had to admit that legislation on the subject was

---

106. The following quotations are taken from Committee on Social Questions, Prevention of Prostitution: A Study of Preventive Measures, Especially Those which Affect Minors, Geneva, 15 May 1939, pp. 60–61, LNA CQS/A/19(a) [hereafter, "Study of Preventive Measures"].
107. Committee, Minutes of the Third Session, 1924, p. 83.
108. The following quotations are taken from "Study of Preventive Measures", pp. 45, 57–63.
109. The ILO Convention Concerning Decent Work for Domestic Workers was adopted in June 2011.
110. Committee, Minutes of the Fifteenth Session, Fifth Meeting, 1936, p. 4.

restricted. Since spare time did not belong to the employer–employee relationship, the recreation activities organized by charitable associations were of crucial importance. The ILO found four types of private initiative that at the time of writing (1939) were apparently worth mentioning: youth hostels; Christian workers' organizations; social service or adult education associations; and institutions organized by political parties, such as the socialist women's groups in Belgium and the Hitler Youth in Germany. Among the activities organized by public authorities, the ILO took the German, Italian, and Soviet tourist services as examples. Obviously, the ILO explained, the objective of all these initiatives was not merely recreational. The educational aim was to teach "young persons of both sexes to live in normal, healthy friendship".[111]

Indeed, one major goal underlay the initiative of the League of Nations with regard to women's safety: the protection of morality. Using the social measures taken by the Cuban government as an exemplary case, the Committee stressed the relation between public morals and the improvement of the economic position of women. Intolerable economic conditions were seen as a menace to the normal functioning of the community. Therefore, the Committee emphasized "the importance of preserving a stable family life as a major factor in prevention", and vehemently insisted on the elimination of the double standard of morals.[112] "Respectable" jobs, education, recreation, and control of the sexual behaviour of the young, both men and women, would contribute to the successful protection of women against the intermediaries of prostitution.

## CONCLUSION

Judging the achievements of the League of Nations is inherently difficult. In theory and on the supranational level, the Committee's efforts in what I have called the "moral recruitment of women" were successful. On the one hand, the interplay between governmental and non-governmental representatives within the Committee contributed to the strengthening of a global prohibition regime against the recruitment of women for prostitution with the approval of the Convention for the Suppression of International Traffic of Consenting Adult Women in 1933, and the draft

---

111. "Study of Preventive Measures", pp. 61, 70–73. In Europe, leisure time became increasingly formalized, regularized, and institutionalized from the eighteenth century onward. During the interwar period, the organization of leisure was a powerful control mechanism of authoritarian regimes. For analyses of the organization of leisure time in Italy and Germany see Victoria de Grazia, *The Culture of Consent: Mass Organisation of Leisure in Fascist Italy* (Cambridge, 2002), and Shelley Baranowski, *Strength Through Joy: Consumerism and Mass Tourism in the Third Reich* (Cambridge, 2007).
112. Committee on Social Questions, Report on the Work of the Committee in 1938 (Second Session), Geneva, 6 May 1938, p. 18, LNA C.147.M.88.1938.IV.

convention against the national and international procurement of consenting adults in 1937, which formed the basis of the 1949 UN Convention. On the other, it bolstered public and private initiatives for the protection of women and developed strong views on the prevention of prostitution and rehabilitation of prostitutes. This moral recruitment of women was meant to provide for both the punishment of undesirable activities and the protection of women and societal order.

However, the actual impact of these policies is hard to measure. As with all international conventions, the differentiation between ratification by member states and de facto implementation at the national level must be emphasized.[113] Whether the Committee's ideas were transformed into concrete reform of domestic legislation and judiciary systems to suppress effectively intermediaries of prostitution remains thus far unclear. As Ethan Nadelmann suggests, activities that require limited resources and no particular expertise, that are easily concealed or unlikely to be reported to the authorities, and for which the demand remains substantial are difficult to repress,[114] and to research. I suspect that the ideas of the League of Nations, reflected in the United Nations after 1945, had at least some impact on countries such as Belgium, France, Greece, Italy, or Japan, which were moving towards abolitionism after the war. Yet the degree to which signatories conformed to the anti-trafficking international agreements and the repercussions of criminal laws on offenders (presumed and otherwise) require further study, particularly in national and local archives.

The Committee's influence on initiatives aimed at the protection of women is equally hard to gauge. Since the Committee did not engage in preventive or rehabilitation programmes, its impact could not have been other than indirect. The League's archives give evidence of the strong appreciation among public authorities and voluntary organizations of the Committee's support, which mainly consisted of information gathering. Akin to other international organizations, the League of Nations played an important role as a clearing-house for the compilation and dissemination of information on international traffic and protective and preventive measures. Furthermore, the Committee's collaboration with the International Labour Organization, psychiatric and legal specialists, as well as international police experts, strengthened the League's credibility. As is the case with contemporary international institutions, the Committee's findings gave "force and symbolic representation to the moral values, beliefs, and prejudices"[115] of all those private associations and state actors

---

113. Magaly Rodríguez García, "Conclusion: The ILO's Impact on the World", in Jasmien Van Daele *et al.* (eds), *ILO Histories: Essays on the International Labour Organization and Its Impact on the World During the Twentieth Century* (Berne, 2010), pp. 461–478, 462.
114. Nadelmann, "Global Prohibition Regimes", p. 525.
115. *Ibid.*, p. 481.

that strove to protect women and eradicate all forms of recruitment of women for prostitution.

How these protective measures affected women is open to question. On the basis of the material found in Geneva, one can only conclude that the discourse of the League of Nations on human traffic turned into a social purity crusade to abolish state regulation and, ideally, prostitution in general. Liberal-feminist, humanitarian, and regulationist points of view within the Committee became increasingly overshadowed by abolitionist arguments that sought to protect women's purity, to persuade men to live virtuously, and to punish all those (men in particular) who threatened these moral goals. Whereas abolitionist and feminist members of the Committee opposed state control of women, they strengthened the idea of private policing or female patrolling through rescue organizations and women's police forces to bring both men and women back on the right track.

Although there were some differences of opinion between female and male members of the Committee, particularly with regard to the identification of danger with the male sex, they unanimously agreed on three issues: prostitution was defined as a social evil that needed to be either controlled according to regulationists or eliminated according to abolitionists; intermediaries of prostitution were considered dangerous to women and society in general; and prostitutes were seen as persons who threatened the ideal image of woman/motherhood and who needed all possible help to escape "immorality". Through its Advisory Committee on Traffic in Women and Children, the League of Nations strengthened the gendered roles and assumptions that surrounded the sex industry and contributed to the stigmatization, marginalization, and social exclusion of the men and women involved in the sector. Several decades would pass before sex workers started to express their own views on the nature and organization of their profession. The voices of intermediaries of prostitution remain thus far silent.

*IRSH* 57 (2012), Special Issue, pp. 129–160 doi:10.1017/S0020859012000454
© 2012 Internationaal Instituut voor Sociale Geschiedenis

# South American Tours: Work Relations in the Entertainment Market in South America*

CRISTIANA SCHETTINI

*National University of General San Martín/*
*University of Buenos Aires*

E-mail: cschettini@hotmail.com

SUMMARY: This article explores the relationships between young European women who worked in the growing entertainment market in Argentine and Brazilian cities, and the many people who from time to time came under suspicion of exploiting them for prostitution. The international travels of young women with contracts to sing or dance in music halls, theatres, and cabarets provide a unique opportunity to reflect on some of the practices of labour intermediation. Fragments of their experiences were recorded by a number of Brazilian police investigations carried out in order to expel "undesirable" foreigners under the Foreigners Expulsion Act of 1907. Such sources shed light on the work arrangements that made it possible for young women to travel overseas. The article discusses how degrees of autonomy, violence, and exploitation in the artists' work contracts were negotiated between parties at the time, especially by travelling young women whose social experiences shaped morally ambiguous identities as artists, prostitutes, and hired workers.

This article explores the relationships between young European women who worked in the growing entertainment market in Argentine and Brazilian cities, and the many people who from time to time came under suspicion of exploiting them for prostitution.[1] I have paid particular attention to the labour arrangements that made it possible for such

---

* Part of this research was conducted thanks to a CONICET postdoctoral fellowship (National Scientific and Technical Research Council of Argentina). I am very grateful for the comments and critiques of readers of previous versions of this text, especially Carolina González Velasco, Valeria Pita, Tiago de Melo Gomes, Fabiane Popinigis, Diego Galeano, and Henrique Espada Lima. I am especially grateful for the careful reading of the editors, and their accurate and detailed critiques. I should also like to thank Alejandra Vassallo for her translation and insights.
1. On the concept of an entertainment market, see Carolina González Velasco, *Gente de Teatro: ocio y espactáculos en la Buenos Aires de los años veinte* (Buenos Aires, 2012).

women to travel by the same regional immigration routes used by many other groups of European workers looking for a better life in South American cities in the early twentieth century. The international travels of young women with contracts to sing or dance in music halls, theatres, and cabarets provide a unique opportunity to reflect on some of the practices of labour intermediation. As their escorts came to be suspected of establishing improper relations with them, the moral dimensions of labour arrangements become visible and allow us a more general reflection on issues that might have been at stake for other groups of immigrant workers.

The article begins with a description of the labour market in the variety branch of show business about the time of World War I, especially in light of the widespread fashion for "white slavery" stories. Such descriptions raise some of the most commonly recurrent images and social meanings attached to the work relations involving women artists in the entertainment market. Work arrangements and women's strategies, though, are not as evident in theatrical accounts as they are in police records of the expulsion of foreigners accused of procuring. In such documents we are reminded of two classic topics in theatre stories at the beginning of the century – those of the mothers of young women artists, and the seducers of chorus girls.

The mercenary spirit of the matrons, at once concerned with the quality of their daughters' contracts and with ensuring their moral protection by appointing appropriate chaperones, was ridiculed throughout the period in the theatrical press. A mother's greatest enemy was the seducer, a young penniless man who regarded every woman in the entertainment business as sexually available.[2] In police records of expulsions, male escorts and parents appear as being suspected of profiting from the prostitution of women artists, thus lending new meanings to such stereotypes. Their stories, as described in police records, reveal much about labour intermediation practices and what they meant for contemporaries.

---

2. There are many examples, conspicuously relating this figure to Spanish mothers. They include *Blanco y Negro* (Madrid), 13 November 1892, "La madre de la tiple" [The Mother of the Soprano], who is featured negotiating contracts on behalf of her daughter. One of the many descriptions of the "soprano's mother" in Argentina can be found in the 9 December 1912 issue of *PBT*, which regretted: "Thus go the mothers, from one stage to the next, from town to town, like the cart of the old show business down dusty roads [...]", while the girl "does not get any applause, nor signs a contract well paid: she is not pretty, she does not sing well, she lacks artistic genius". The stereotypes of male figures surrounding women artists, especially in the early twentieth-century literature, are the lover, the man who seduces her, and the lecher, an old (and impotent) man who paid her bills. For a graphic description in the "risqué" tale, see Homem de Ferro, *O Marchante* (Rio de Janeiro, n.d.) (Coleção contos rápidos, n. 18). On these tales, see Cristiana Schettini, "Um gênero alegre: imprensa e pornografia no Rio de Janeiro (1898–1916)" (Master's thesis, State University of Campinas, 1997).

Whether as suspected prostitutes or as artists of a "lesser genre", as variety was considered at about the time of World War I, the lives of young women artists have not often been the subject of labour history, which has focused rather on other groups of workers and political activists (especially anarchists) travelling along similar routes in the same years.[3] Variety itself does not have an important place in national theatrical accounts, except as a distant background for performers who subsequently became famous actresses or singers. Nevertheless, variety performances were highly appealing to contemporary audiences, and the travels of variety artists had an important role in creating cultural circuits which eventually elevated some genres and particular dances to the level of "national styles", as was the case with the tango in Argentina or the samba in Brazil.[4]

Looking at such women through the lens of labour history, and restating their importance for their contemporaries as entertainers, becomes a strategy to enable us to examine their ambiguous identities and the complex relationships they established with those who mediated their work. We can reflect upon how contemporaries perceived the degrees of autonomy and the moral boundaries in the work relations of women artists, or, in other words, fragments of these women's lives, their work arrangements, and their affective relationships with either family or male escorts can be used to shed light on the various connections between work and sexual morality in some South American cities in the early twentieth century.

The specifics of women artists' work experience, especially the nomadic character of the work and the fact that their activities were hardly easy to classify, make it very difficult to find traces of their lives in the written sources of the entertainment business at the time. One important exception is the records of the Brazilian police, which enforced the Foreigners Expulsion Act of 1907. Police investigations carried out between 1907 and 1920 to secure the expulsion of a wide variety of foreigners viewed as "undesirable" – among them those suspected of procuring – recorded the different experiences of men and women who were suspected of being

---

3. Osvaldo de Sosa Cordero refers to the idea of a "lesser genre", meaning lower than the "low genre", to refer to variety in his classic account, *Historia de las varietés en Buenos Aires, 1900–1925* (Buenos Aires, 1999). For a new analysis of transnational histories of revolutionary trade-union activists in Italy and Brazil, see Edilene Toledo, *Travessias revolucionárias: idéias e militantes sindicalistas em São Paulo e na Itália (1890–1945)* (Campinas, 2004).

4. For an insightful analysis of our ignorance of popular genres of the beginning of the century, styles which became erased by accounts that focus on genres that eventually became national symbols, see Tiago de Melo Gomes, *Um Espelho no Palco. Identidades sociais e massificaçao da cultura no teatro de revista dos anos 1920* (Campinas, 2004), pp. 27–31. For a cultural studies analysis along the same lines, see Sirena Pellarolo, *Sainetes, cabaret, minas y tangos* (Buenos Aires, 2010), pp. 18–39.

involved in the sex trade. Among those cases, a few refer directly to women
who worked in the entertainment business.[5]

The four cases of expulsion analysed here are therefore part of a larger
universe. Although few in number, they attest uniquely to the valuable
aspects of women artists' work arrangements and affective experience.
These were women who attracted police attention because it seemed that
either their escorts or their relatives were exploiting them, and that allows
us to discuss the affective dimension as an inseparable aspect of women
artists' general work experience. Beyond the actual accusations, police
records shed light on the expectations and work arrangements that made
it possible for young women to travel overseas. They also record the
unexpected uses of repressive legislation, such as the Foreigners Expulsion
Act, by individuals who were themselves the obvious targets of the law.
Finally, they suggest that variety artists' international travels were a key
element of their work experience.

## TRAFFICKING AND THE SOUTH AMERICAN ENTERTAINMENT BUSINESS

The dismissal of women performers' lives by labour and theatrical histories
can be partially explained by another specific cluster of contemporary
meanings attached to their activities – those which associated them with
narratives of the "white slave traffic" so widely publicized on Atlantic
immigration routes at the time. Young singers and dancers were recurrently
portrayed as victims of mysterious organizations which specialized in
deceiving young European women with promises of marriage, employment,
or, less specifically, an exciting artistic life overseas in order to force them
into prostitution in distant lands. The famous tango composer and theatre
writer, Enrique Cadícamo, resorts to this cliché in his memoirs, originally
published in 1983. As a major participant in the musical and theatrical scene
that flourished in turn-of-the-century Buenos Aires, Cadícamo revealed
some inside information on one of the most famous variety theatres of the
time, the Casino:

> The source of the following information does not come from police records but
> from what I learned from other tango musicians, now dead [...]. By 1918 [...]

5. I analysed in depth eighty-three police cases of expulsion between 1907 and 1929 related to
procuring, in which defendants or witnesses had been in the Río de la Plata before going to Brazil.
See Cristiana Schettini, *"Que Tenhas Teu Corpo": uma história social da prostituição no Rio de
Janeiro das primeiras décadas republicanas* (Rio de Janeiro, 2006), pp. 105–155, and *idem*, "Viajando
solas: prácticas de vigilancia policial y experiencias de prostitución en la América del Sur", in Jorge
Trujillo Bretón (ed.), *En la Encrucijada. Historia, marginalidad y delito en América Latina y los
Estados Unidos de Norteamérica (siglos XIX y XX)* (Guadalajara, 2010), pp. 331–353. Among them,
only six cases referred to women artists employed in the variety business.

there was in Buenos Aires an obscure underworld criminal organization with headquarters in Marseille, that appeared to be a peaceful international theatrical agency for Latin America. But it was in fact none other than an agency to promote the white slave trade. This organization covered Rio de Janeiro, Chile, and Buenos Aires. Its affiliate in Buenos Aires provided seemingly artistic personnel, such as café-concert singers, pseudo-dancers [*sic*], chorus girls, thus concealing their real work as prostitutes, and mixing this human traffic with companies of famous wrestlers […] for the historic Greek-Roman wrestling tournaments featured in the *Casino* theatre on Maipú Street. This was a way to covertly smuggle women into Buenos Aires.[6]

Cadícamo's statement that the famous Casino theatre on Maipú Street was nothing but a pretext for the sexual exploitation of European women was based on what he had heard from old tango musicians whom he had known in his youth. At the time he wrote that, Cadícamo was considered one of the most important composers of the twentieth century, and a living first-hand witnesses to the bohemian life of 1920s Buenos Aires. His music became popular in the 1920s; later he published poems too, as well as fiction and non-fiction accounts that eventually became an invaluable source for the history of tango and the tango scene, about the theatres, music halls, cabarets, and café concerts at the turn of the century.

The French origin of the "white slavery" organization and its network in South American capitals echoed in part the renowned image of Buenos Aires as an important site of the international traffic in women. Received wisdom stated that white slave traffic was handled by mafia-type organizations, mainly Jewish, although they might include other nationalities, whose actions were never made totally clear.[7] In this particular text, in contrast to other passages in his writings and other testimonies, young women's overseas trips as well as their contracts are portrayed as a front, and the busy artistic scene at the Casino in the 1910s becomes a cover for the exploitation of young European prostitutes.[8]

Cadícamo's account touched upon elements that surely resonated among Buenos Aires readers and that was in turn immersed in a long tradition of "white slave traffic" stories. From 1870, stories of "white slaves" increasingly involved South American cities, especially Buenos Aires, as European immigration to that part of the world grew to unprecedented proportions. As many authors have pointed out, such stories usually expressed anxieties related to immigration and female work in terms of sexual morality. That was

6. Enrique Cadícamo, *Mis memorias* (Buenos Aires, 1995), p. 55.
7. Donna Guy, *Sex and Danger in Buenos Aires: Prostitution, Family, and Nation in Argentina* (Lincoln, NE, 1991); Beatriz Kushnir, *Baile de Máscaras. Mulheres judias e prostituição. As Polacas e suas associações de ajuda mútua* (São Paulo, 1996).
8. See, for instance, the interview he gave to Sergio Pujol, in S. Pujol, *Valentino en Buenos Aires. Los años veinte y el espectáculo* (Buenos Aires, 1994), pp. 267–276.

true for Buenos Aires and also for those Brazilian cities that received a large number of immigrants, such as São Paulo and Rio de Janeiro.[9]

Apart from the common plots shared by white slavery stories (in Buenos Aires, São Paulo, and Rio), each city featured local details related to specific social and political contexts. In Buenos Aires, stories expressed mainly the local tensions triggered by the unwelcome side effects of European immigration, which had completely transformed the city and the country in just a few years. They also justified heavy-handed state intervention in the organization of the sex trade, through regulations issued from 1875 to 1936.[10] In Brazil, similar stories had a different effect as they became widespread alongside public debates on the abolition of actual slavery and the future of labour relations. The gender and racial connotations of the vocabulary inspired by the struggle against black slavery, then coming to be used to refer to the international sex trade, was particularly disquieting for the Brazilian authorities. The social and political conflicts triggered by the increasing state intervention through progressive regulation to abolish general slave labour lent a negative image to the state's potential intervention to regulate another trade that was also viewed as immoral. The situation affected the policy for control of the sex trade, which in Rio de Janeiro was left mainly to the police, resulting in a non-regulating trend which persisted in the Republic after 1889.[11]

If the local uses and meanings were different in Argentina and Brazil, the vocabulary borrowed from slavery to talk about the sexual exploitation of European women had similar connotations in many places. In fact, it was associated not only with a state of backwardness, violence, coercion, and immorality, it also legitimized the public intervention on moral grounds of specific social sectors and organizations, on behalf of the victims. From that perspective, during the years following World War I the League of Nations became a key authority on the subject. The investigations carried out by their Body of Experts in search of the "true" dimensions of human trafficking attest to the importance attributed to the international circulation of women and the anxiety that triggered in many Western countries. Among other things, the interventions by the League of Nations helped consolidate

9. Donna Guy, *White Slavery and Mothers Alive and Dead: The Troubled Meeting of Sex, Gender, Public Health, and Progress in Latin America* (Lincoln, NE, 2000), pp. 17–32, 70–85; Schettini, *"Que Tenhas Teu Corpo"*, pp. 105–155. There is, of course, a large bibliography on narratives of white slavery and their meanings in other contexts. See, for instance, Judith Walkowitz, *City of Dreadful Delight: Narratives of Sexual Danger in Late-Victorian London* (Chicago, IL, 1992).
10. Guy, *Sex and Danger in Buenos Aires*.
11. These points are further developed in Cristiana Schettini, "Esclavitud en blanco y negro: elementos para una historia del trabajo sexual femenino en Buenos Aires y en Río de Janeiro a fines del siglo XIX", *Entrepasados*, 29 (2006), pp. 43–62.

and generalize the causal association between regulation of prostitution and traffic in women. The underlying idea was that in countries where prostitution was regulated, it eventually facilitated the action of procurers and traffic in women flourished. Thus, in the 1920s, the widespread international discrediting of regulated prostitution reinforced the idea that Buenos Aires was a paradise for traffickers, which in turn created a problem for the Argentine authorities.

As a result of such investigations, in 1927 the League of Nations published an experts' report on traffic in women and children.[12] The report shows on what terms and to what extent a large proportion of the international travel experienced by women in pursuit of work contracts and promises of marriage became a matter of real concern to national governments. Stories of trafficking developed a plot that expressed the apprehension triggered by the unprotected international circulation of vulnerable individuals, as women and children were seen to be. Obsessed with determining the real contours of the "white slave trade", the League of Nations observers were mesmerized by various modalities of young women's international travels.

Among the diverse offers of employment and promises of marriage, the experts focused particularly on the modus operandi of an increasingly international entertainment market. The experts' findings reveal how a fear for women travelling alone or "in bad company" exposed a wide suspicion of different work experiences and of intermediaries as being part of the sex trade. By following the steps of many young women who crossed national borders, investigators were able to isolate specific and recurrent cases of what they saw as traffic in women in every European country, as well as in Central and South America – girls engaged as members of troupes to perform in "music-halls, cabarets, cafés, and other amusement venues".[13]

Contemporary observers, who regarded themselves as unbiased, believed that not all travelling companies acted as a disguise for prostitution. For those observers, "some of the troupes are under proper management and supervision, but instances were brought to our notice of deliberate exploitation". But how is one to establish the difference between one and the other? For Cadícamo, talking about it in the 1980s in reference to the Casino theatre, sexual exploitation was undoubtedly the real motive, despite all appearances to the contrary. In 1927, the League of Nations experts were more sensitive to the nuances, as they focused on a variety of situations and work arrangements that were being carried on

---

12. League of Nations, *Report of the Special Body of Experts on Traffic in Women and Children* (Geneva, 1927).
13. *Ibid.*, p. 20.

Figure 1. When he edited *Fighting the Traffic in Young Girls*,[14] the Methodist missionary Ernest Albert Bell publicized the basic lines of his anti-vice crusade as the Secretary of the Illinois Vigilance Association. Illustrations were an important part of the propaganda. The illustration above refers to what the book presented as one of the most successful methods used by traffickers to "lure" young innocent women. Disguised as a theatrical agent or manager, the trafficker promised a factory girl a better life "upon the stage". In the background is the list of what would appeal to a "girl's ambition": promises of a "high salary", "a brilliant career", and "travel enjoyment". When, almost two decades later, the Body of Experts of the League of Nations relied on similar accounts, such stories were already widespread throughout the circuits of international labor immigration.
*Unnamed artist in Bell*, Fighting the Traffic in Young Girls, *Mary Evans Picture Library. Used with permission.*

14. Ernest Albert Bell (ed.), *Fighting the Traffic in Young Girls: War on the White Slave Trade* (Chicago, IL, 1910); Project Gutenberg online e-book at http://www.gutenberg.org/files/ 26081/26081-h/26081-h.htm.

right in front of their eyes. They noted the centrality of contracts for the cases under scrutiny:

> The contracts which these girls sign often conceal the actual conditions and there is nothing to arouse the suspicions of the girls who sign them. In other cases the terms of the contract are so unfair as to place the girls entirely at the mercy of her employer. An investigator secured a copy of a contract made between the proprietor of a music hall and a dancer aged 18. Under this contract she was liable to be transferred at will; she could be discharged for a variety of reasons over which she had no control, such as "indisposition, loss of voice, disease or suspension of work for any reason whatsoever". The hours of work were unlimited and the small salary (5 francs a day) was subject to capricious fines for not obeying rules that are unknown until they are posted on a notice board. The inhumanity of such contract is almost bound to produce disaster in the case of the foreign girl alone in a strange town and without a friend to turn to when summarily dismissed.[15]

Observers were struck by the harshness of that labour market. Descriptions of terrible work conditions, low wages, and of young ages, stressed the women's extreme vulnerability, only worsened by the isolation that resulted from all the travelling required in their trade, and by the brevity of their employment. In that context, the observers saw prostitution as a permanent and almost unavoidable risk. For them, work contracts were proof of immoral exploitation because of the unfair conditions, while at the same time the contract itself was a veil to hide the very exploitation it implied, since the contracts were presented as arrangements between two free parties.

Although to some degree both accounts are similar, in Cadícamo's view there was no possibility of doubt: the organization which owned the Casino theatre in Buenos Aires was simply a criminal gang; the theatre was nothing but a front for the traffic in women. However, the League of Nations observers suggested instead that the situation could be much more ambiguous, as they situated the problem in the nuances of work conditions. Despite such significant differences, both accounts formulate the problem in the same terms – as if it were possible to draw a clear line between proper and improper ways of hiring young women in the entertainment business. Moreover, both views preclude the possibility of posing different questions: first, questions about degrees of autonomy, violence, and exploitation in the artists' work contracts. And, second, about how those degrees were negotiated by the parties involved, especially by the travelling young women whose social experiences shaped morally ambiguous identities as artists, prostitutes, and hired workers.

---

15. League of Nations, *Report of the Special Body of Experts*, p. 21.

## WORK CONDITIONS IN SECOND-RATE THEATRES AND *CAFÉ CANTANTES*

In the early twentieth century, theatres in Buenos Aires, Rio de Janeiro, and São Paulo featuring Portuguese, Spanish, Italian, and a few local companies competed with a variety of café concerts, circus rings, and improvised stages to attract audiences eager for entertainment. Cabarets would be added in the 1910s, and although with local features, the café-concert model or variety theatre was replicated in many Argentine and Brazilian cities, thus shaping a route for touring artists. Although the performances associated with such venues were considered a minor genre, boundaries between styles and between artists were not always clearly definable, despite the efforts of classical accounts of theatrical history to depict a linear evolution culminating in a national theatre.[16] From that perspective, recurrent moral suspicion of women artists – especially from the police – speaks of a wider concern about the impossibility of defining fixed and stable identities for such women.[17] There were significant elements in the organization of the entertainment labour market that prompted the League of Nations observers and Cadícamo to view work relations in the entertainment business as a site for potential sexual exploitation.

In the early years of the century, variety was an expanding theatrical activity. Announcements of new and refurbished show-business establishments in Brazilian and Argentine cities attest to that. News items portrayed theatre owners as risk-taking entrepreneurs and published full-page advertisements of their programmes in the most important magazines of Buenos Aires and Rio de Janeiro. The business involved a broad range of people who sometimes performed multiple functions – as managers, directors, art directors, theatrical agents, and intermediary agencies – as well as a number of additional activities, such as selling drinks and showing silent films in the intervals of stage performances. Entrepreneurs catered to diverse audiences, who expected to have fun, with circus-like attractions, such as wild animals, acrobats, Roman wrestlers, female impersonators, illusionists, and singing and dancing girls.[18]

Performers used names designed to associate them with the "typical" styles of specific regions. Argentine stages featured artists such as "La Argentinita" (although she was actually Spanish), "La Malagueñita", and

---

16. These include Mariano Bosch, *Historia de los orígenes del teatro nacional argentino y la época de Pablo Podestá* (Buenos Aires, 1972).

17. Pellarolo, *Sainetes*, pp. 41–45.

18. For a review of contemporary descriptions in Buenos Aires, see *ibid.*, pp. 19–39. For Rio de Janeiro, see the series "Rio a noite" [Rio by Night], published in the satirical humojournal *Rio Nu* [Naked Rio], around 1905.

"La Sevillita".[19] In Brazilian cities, a magazine dedicated to the entertainment business published advertisements for similar artists announcing their availability for employment. If Spanish singers were all over Buenos Aires, there was a "Bella Diana, Portuguese singer and fado performer" in Rio de Janeiro, but also "La Cubanita, Spanish singer". Some names suggest erotic performances, such as "Martha Cotty, French eccentric", or a combination of genres, including "La Cholita, Spanish singer and suggestive poses". Although some artists were clearly associated with specific performances, such as lyrical singers and classical ballet dancers, somewhat incoherent names and descriptions were abundant. It is hard to imagine what kinds of act were performed by the "Hispanic-French singer René D'Arcy", or the "Hispanic-Brazilian singer called Egyptian Estrellita".[20]

The combination of references to places of origin with elegant, exotic, or "typically regional" styles ultimately reveals how far such theatrical images were carefully constructed, as well as underlining the appeal of an "international" identity with exotic but civilized connotations. It was all very similar to a movement taking place simultaneously in the characterization of foreign prostitutes either as "Frenchwomen", which carried promises of civilizing the local men in elegant and sophisticated sexual relations (and manners), or as "Polish women", which associated them with a degraded sort of exoticism. Rather than designating actual nationalities, the characterization seems to have mirrored local imagination and the interest in consuming foreign – specifically French – products and lifestyles.[21] Sometimes then, reference to the "French" origin of a singer or dancer suggests an intentional play upon the sexual connotation of such identities.

Women artists embodied complex intersections between the new consumer trends (including sex), social status, and nationality. They applied

---

19. Cordero, *Historia de las varietés*. After her death, Encarnación Lopez, "La Argentinita", was remembered because she had "created something modern and of her own" by studying "the tradition of Spanish folklore" in an era when "singers imitated French styles, classical dancers, singers, and lesser artists cultivated simply shamelessness"; Federico de Onís, "La Argentinita", *Revista Hispánica Moderna*, 12:1/2 (January–April 1946), pp. 180–184.

20. These descriptions are taken from *Arte e Artistas*, a magazine published by the theatrical agency Kosmopol to announce their availability for contract. There were four issues, the first dated October 1918, and the last December 1921.

21. Of course, this French obsession was used by local elites to express the kind of modernity and civilization they yearned for; Jeffrey Needell, *A Tropical Belle Époque: Elite Culture and Society in Turn-of-the-Century Rio de Janeiro* (New York, 1987), ch. 5; Lená Medeiros de Menezes, *Os estrangeiros e o comércio do prazer nas ruas do Rio (1890–1930)* (Rio de Janeiro, 1992), p. 44. On mutual aid associations created by actual Jewish prostitutes, see Kushnir, *Baile de máscaras*. For an analysis of São Paulo's elite representations of foreign prostitution, see Margareth Rago, *Os prazeres da noite: prostituição e códigos de sexualidade feminina em São Paulo (1890–1930)* (Rio de Janeiro, 1991). For Buenos Aires, see Guy, *Sex and Danger in Buenos Aires*.

their talents in theatres and similar venues that offered a wide variety of entertainment. In Rio de Janeiro, the most important entrepreneur employing women artists at the turn of the century was the Italian Paschoal Segreto.[22] Since the early 1900s he had been investing in a wide array of entertainment houses, next to bars, restaurants, brothels, café concerts, and improvised music halls that featured shows or films and which functioned as beer parlours. One of his establishments was the Maison Moderne, dedicated to variety shows. Despite the connotations of elegance in the French name, the Maison Moderne was described by an observer as a mixture of fair and theme park, offering "target shooting, a Ferris wheel, and a carousel", which most probably attracted families to its daytime shows. However, at the back there was a small stage featuring evening shows for an adult audience.[23] As early as 1901, advertisements revealed that managers were interested in publicizing their investment in modern furnishings and renewed international attractions.[24] Expanding his investments, Segreto also became the owner of São Paulo's Casino theatre in the 1910s.[25]

Meanwhile, in Buenos Aires too, the most important variety theatre was named the Casino. One of the owners of that Casino was Carlos Seguín, who later sold it to a limited liability company with English capital wishing to expand into Uruguay, Chile, and Brazil. Under the suggestive name of "South American Tour", the company employed variety artists for the Casino and the Scala in Buenos Aires.[26] Some years later, a contemporary recalled "the admirable companies that Seguín brought to the Casino", attesting to its popularity in the pre-war years.[27]

By the time specialized intermediary agencies appeared in that setting, by the end of the 1910s, Argentina and Brazil had already shared cultural circuits for a long time.[28] Their visibility was certainly related to the

22. On Paschoal Segreto and the organization of his business in Rio de Janeiro, see Gomes, *Um Espelho no Palco*, pp. 87–107.
23. Vivaldo Coaracy, *Memórias da cidade do Rio de Janeiro* (Belo Horizonte, 1988), p. 93. The Casino theatre in Buenos Aires publicized matinees for families, featuring similar attractions. See, for example, the Argentine magazine *Fray Mocho*, 5 July 1912.
24. See for instance the advertisement in *O Arara*, 3 January 1901, for the "Moulin Rouge", which had been "totally refurbished", offering audiences a "beautiful garden", "electric light", and "an attractive performance with the beautiful actresses Ignez Alvarez and Guerrerito", featuring "new shows every day". See also advertisements for the Casino theatre in Buenos Aires in the back pages of such famous magazines as *Caras y Caretas*, *PBT*, and *Fray Mocho*, with new announcements every week.
25. Neyde Veneziano, *De pernas para o ar: o teatro de revista em São Paulo* (São Paulo, 2006), p. 121.
26. "Una nueva empresa teatral, South American Tour", *Caras y Caretas*, 22 April 1911.
27. Federico Mertens, *Confidencias de un hombre de teatro. Medio siglo de vida escénica* (Buenos Aires, 1948), p. 160.
28. In the nineteenth century tours by circus troupes were a frequent aspect of those complex links. Many variety and theatre artists actually started working in circus troupes. Moreover, in

ways in which World War I affected such routes, when communications between Europe and the Americas were interrupted. During those years, South American tours brought North American attractions to the Casino theatre in Buenos Aires.

At the same time, in Rio de Janeiro, the theatrical agency Kosmopol published the magazine *Arte e Artistas* [Art and Artists]. Defined as an "intermediary press between show business managers and variety artists", it worked as an "Artists Guide", available to managers eager to engage new attractions. The agency requested performers (who were probably already stuck in South America) to send "photos, conditions, and exact information about their availability", and took responsibility for the fulfilment of their contracts. By October 1921 it announced the opening of a music and dance academy for cabaret artists to improve their craft.[29] The publication allegedly circulated in "Brazil, Argentina, and Europe", although its headquarters were in Rio de Janeiro. Although no more than four numbers were issued, its brief existence attests to the increasing circulation of capital invested in the dynamic world of variety theatre. It also maps the regional artistic route that interested artists, business managers, and audiences. As it was, either with or without that kind of structured intermediation, managers of small theatres and *café cantantes* and the artists they needed found ways to meet each other.

A growing number of travelling artists, who could perform "typical" styles and who were willing to tour different cities, became a crucial part of the South American entertainment market at the beginning of the twentieth century. The blurred borders between artistic styles, flexible artistic identities, and constant travelling were reinforced by another feature of that world – the expectation of becoming rich and famous very quickly, a topic that appeared repeatedly in plays featuring ingenuous local artists on both sides of the Atlantic who dreamed of success overseas.[30]

For instance, the success story of Italian actress Amelia Lopiccolo on the Brazilian stage, as told in a traditional history of Brazilian theatre, can

---

classical histories of national theatre in Argentina, the circus experience occupies a central place as a precedent: national theatre originated in one-act plays full of profanity in circus rings, moving then towards the respectability of theatre stages. Between them came the loosely defined variety genre; Beatriz Seibel, *Historia del teatro argentino. Desde los rituales hasta 1930* (Buenos Aires, 2006), pp. 352–354.

29. *Arte e Artistas*, 3, October 1921.

30. The play "El debut de la piba" [The Girl's Debut] that first opened in 1916 in Buenos Aires is a satire on the "[Argentine] mania of going on alleged international tours. Artists created theatre companies and competed to discover Spain, trusting their status as Argentines or *porteños* (citizens of Buenos Aires) would enchant Spanish audiences"; Tulio Carella, *El sainete criollo* (Buenos Aires, 1957), p. 228. For a tango example, see the lyrics of "Anclao en París" (1928) [Stranded in Paris] by Cadícamo, who regrets being "stranded, penniless, and hopeless" in the European winter after a tour. About the context of economic crisis, see the interview with Cadícamo in Pujol, *Valentino en Buenos Aires*, pp. 274–275.

be read as a tale of social mobility.[31] It begins like the story of many other European girls who had travelled to South America by the end of the nineteenth century. First she crossed the Atlantic with a group of variety performers on tour to a famously picaresque *café cantante* in Buenos Aires, El Pasatiempo. Later she performed at Eldorado, a similar café in Rio de Janeiro. However, quite suddenly everything changed when Jacinto Heller, the manager of the Santana theatre, witnessed her gracious singing and her "fascinating, darting eyes". According to that account, Heller "rescued" her from the *café cantante* and gave her the much-coveted position as the star in a renowned theatre company. By impersonating a famous actress of the time, she won her own place on the national stage, moving from Europe to South America, and from the lesser variety genre to mainstream theatre.

Exemplary stories like Amelia Lopiccolo's touch upon the suspicion of prostitution and the difficult working conditions for female artists merely as vivid details, irrelevant compared to the denouement that always confirmed the actress's ultimate success. The author of Lopiccolo's story chose a brief but significant tale to illustrate that artists never had a day off, had to perform many times a day, and were vulnerable to breaches of contract when tours failed to turn a profit. In a passing reference, he mentions that when Heller's female artists complained about their working conditions in the Santana theatre, the entrepreneur immediately threatened to replace them with "Frenchwomen".[32] Reference to nationality suggests not only a competitive labour market on the supply side and little room for negotiation; it also hints at the sexual availability of hired artists, as the association of Frenchwomen with elegant prostitution indicates.

Amelia Lopiccolo's story, which took place around the 1890s, contrasts with the tale of the Italian Paulista comedian, Nino Nello, from some years later. Recalling his early days in the postwar years, Nello stated that by then the variety genre paid better than the starvation wages of mainstream theatre. He remembered obtaining a contract thanks to the "South American Tour" and performing as an international imitator, not only at the Casino theatre in Buenos Aires, but also "all over Argentina and the Pacific Republics".[33] According to Nello, that agency played a key role in "booking artists, with pre-arranged dates, in several entertainment establishments with which they had agreements".[34]

31. Roberto Ruiz, *O Teatro de Revista no Brasil. Das origens à primeira Guerra mundial* (Rio de Janeiro, 1988), p. 175, based on Lafaiete Silva's *História do teatro brasileiro* (Rio de Janeiro, 1938), and on a manuscript by the theatre manager Souza Bastos.

32. Ruiz, *O Teatro de Revista*, p. 175.

33. Veneziano, *De pernas para o ar*, p. 246.

34. The Kosmopol agency, for example, advertised women artists who were hired for amusement houses in Belo Horizonte (Eden Cinema), Bahia (Palace Club), São Paulo (Teatro Apolo), and in various establishments in Rio de Janeiro.

Accounts of Lopiccolo's and Nello's lives stress that both worked hard and travelled a lot, using all the resources available to them to achieve artistic social mobility. There was a certain amount of strategy and initiative in both careers. There was a significant difference between them, however, and it was not just the period, given that Lopiccolo performed in the late nineteenth century and Nello was active in the 1910s. In Nino Nello's account, the precariousness of work conditions allowed him to develop his talent: as an "international imitator" in other countries, he impersonated all the different "typical types", playing Italian, Portuguese, Spanish, and even Turkish characters. However, for Lopiccolo and for many other women artists of the period, the goal was to attain a less ambiguous identity by acting within the available roles, hoping eventually to become accepted as a recognized artist and, perhaps, an independent entrepreneur herself.[35]

Goals of upward mobility coexisted with other ways of understanding work in the world of entertainment, and that became evident during the 1919 and 1921 strikes by theatre workers in Buenos Aires. The year 1919 was famous in Buenos Aires for the intensity of social conflicts, workers' protests, and police repression. In May, even theatre artists organized a strike, which paralysed entertainment halls in the Argentine capital for almost a month.[36] Foreign and Argentine actors, supported by chorus girls and members of other trades, joined forces to demand, among other things, payment for additional shows and a general wage increase. In the context of the strike, they used the trope of the "theatre family" not to reinforce a hierarchical and unequal organization, but rather to allow different performers – those who worked for wages and those who owned their companies – to unite at least temporarily over a common agenda. Differences still remained though. Some variety performers even sought to form their own organization, the "International Society of Variety Artists". One of its main demands was that agents should donate a percentage of their earnings to create a mutual aid society.[37]

The meanings of intermediation thus varied. In the context of theatre strikes in Buenos Aires, the role of agents had a negative connotation, and performers acknowledged their presence only to demand that their

35. On strategies to build respectability see Angela Reis, *Cinira Polonio. A divette carioca. Estudo da imagem pública e do trabalho de uma atriz no teatro brasileiro da virada do século XX* (Rio de Janeiro, 1999), pp. 57–61.
36. Teodoro Klein, *Una Historia de luchas. La Asociación argentina de actores* (Buenos Aires, 1988), p. 22. The strike has been analysed in detail by Carolina González Velasco, "'Pierrot ha dejado su traje y enarbola la bandera roja que tan mal le sienta'. Conflictos gremiales en el mundo del teatro porteño, 1919-1921", in Lilia Ana Bertoni and Luciano de Privitellio (eds), *Conflictos en democracia. La política en Buenos Aires, 1850–1950* (Buenos Aires, 2009), pp. 124–148, 133.
37. "Los artistas de varietés", *Tan-Tan*, 5 May 1919.

functions be regulated.[38] In contrast, Nello's testimony argues that the intermediary agency offered a chance of survival during a time of crisis. From yet another perspective, intermediation played a different role in the matter of contracts with young women. Travelling women artists playing in dubious café concerts and cabarets, who passed as "Frenchwomen" impersonating renowned artists (as did Lopiccolo), or who worked in places where prostitutes, waitresses, and artists all seemed sexually available to customers, shaped narratives that cast doubts on their "real" identities as well as those of their agents. Overall, gender and class tensions came together in more or less explicit ways in all the accounts of work relations in the entertainment business, acquiring different specific meanings.

For many women who were less successful and who travelled in search of profitable contracts, the instability of their identities (as artists or prostitutes) was part and parcel of their business. Stories of "white slavery" expressed their situation particularly well, by erasing their strategies and actions in favour of a victimizing perspective. The particular organization of the work of female entertainers (of men) attracted the attention of police authorities in all the South American countries where women artists performed. Brazilian police would then put pressure on individuals who might be related to them, raising the suspicion that they were profiting from the women's prostitution. Therefore, in many cases, records of the police investigations of procurers, carried out in order to expel them, might be a valuable source for examining the work experience and strategies of women in the variety business.

## EXPULSION OF FOREIGNERS LEGISLATION

From the beginning of the twentieth century, the internationalization of the public examination of the trafficking of women evolved, with debates on how local police forces should meet the many threats which were increasing internationally, such as organized crime, but most especially anarchist activists.[39] The widespread perception of such danger in different countries justified the approval of new legislation intended to develop a common front against international criminals.

---

38. There was a second theatre strike in 1921, when actors demanded the end of agents' mediation in the signing of contracts. At the same time, recognizing that some such figure was inevitable, they added that "in that case, the employer should be responsible for paying the agent his commission"; Klein, *Una Historia de luchas*, p. 27.

39. Schettini, *"Que Tenhas Teu Corpo"*, pp. 105–155. On South American police efforts to put together a strategy against "travelling criminals", see Diego Galeano, "Las conferencias sudamericanas de policía y la problemática de los delincuentes viajeros, 1905–1920", in Ernesto Bohoslavsky *et al.* (eds), *La Policía en perspectiva histórica. Argentina y Brasil (del siglo XIX a la actualidad)* (Buenos Aires, 2009), CD-rom.

The 1902 Residence Act in Argentina and the Brazilian "Gordo" Act of 1907, which regulated the expulsion of foreigners as a prerogative of the executive, probably had a significant effect in the South American context.[40] The legislation tended to strengthen police powers to the detriment of judicial procedures, so that it became widely denounced as authoritarian and unconstitutional, as it was used to expel the leaders of labour movements. Recent scholarship has also highlighted the use of the same repressive legislation against other groups of foreigners, identified as thieves, vagrants, swindlers, and procurers – virtually anyone who fitted the category of "a threat to national security and public order".[41]

While the Argentine law extended police powers of discretion to act against any kind of "undesirables" without judicial investigation, the Brazilian Expulsion Act demanded that accusations of "vagrancy, begging, and procuring" be "thoroughly checked". In the latter case, it meant that to prove procuring charges the police had to gather "undisputed evidence", or at least "the statement of two undisputed witnesses who could confirm the truth of the fact".[42] That meant that, at least in Brazil, police power over the whole procedure was constrained by a body of regulations, similar to police inquiries in the first stages of any judicial investigation. In a context in which both Argentina and Brazil developed specific legal structures to control prostitution and to punish procuring, the unique characteristic of the Brazilian legislation had specific consequences. While in the early twentieth century Argentina followed a French-inspired model of regulation which barely punished the crime of corruption of minors, in its penal code of 1890 Brazil adopted a broad definition of procuring, to include different ways of inducing women to become prostitutes, such as making a profit from offering them varieties of assistance, for example, with housing, or money.[43]

40. Passed in 1902 in Argentina and known as the Residence Act, it was then supplemented by a 1909 law known as the Social Defence Act. In Brazil, the law acquired the name of the representative who proposed it, "Alfredo Gordo", and it was approved at the beginning of 1907. On Brazilian law, see Lená Medeiros de Menezes, *Os Indesejáveis. Desclassificados da modernidade. Protesto, crime e expulsão na Capital Federal (1890–1930)* (Rio de Janeiro, 1996), pp. 183–187, and Rogerio Bonfá, "'Com lei ou sem lei': as expulsões de estrangeiros na primeira república", *Cadernos AEL*, 14:26 (2009), pp. 181–217. On Argentina, see Juan Suriano, *Trabajadores, anarquismo y estado represor: de la ley de Residencia a la ley de Defensa Social (1902–1910)* (Buenos Aires, 1988); Eduardo Zimmermann, *Los liberales reformistas. La cuestión social en la Argentina, 1890–1916* (Buenos Aires, 1995); Susana Villavicencio (ed.), *Los contornos de la ciudadanía. Nacionales y extranjeros en la Argentina del Centenario* (Buenos Aires, 2003).
41. Menezes, *Os Indesejáveis.*
42. *Ibid.*, p. 207.
43. Schettini, *"Que Tenhas Teu Corpo"*, p. 171.

Thus, the Brazilian police had already had experience of trials of that type, which had been carried out as part of police-led campaigns of "moral cleansing", or when women had lodged complaints against their landlords or landladies, and that experience surely proved useful in collecting evidence for the expulsion of those accused of procuring.[44] Expulsion procedures and criminal trials for procurement were similar up to a point, although the former were quicker and summary, offering the police a wide range of action. In fact, judicial interference only occurred when a defendant succeeded in obtaining a writ of habeas corpus. Accusations of persecution and police tampering with evidence were very common, but, all the same, the documents resulting from such procedures reveal certain aspects of the relationships established between young women travelling with work contracts to perform in variety and many of the people they met along the way. That, in turn, sheds light on a rich network of work intermediaries. Thanks, then, to repressive police action against foreigners they suspected of procuring offences, we are able to recover part of the transnational experience of women's lives, inasmuch as Brazilian police investigations recorded, if indirectly, the past experience of those women in Buenos Aires and other South American cities.

Police repression against certain foreign groups, triggered by the Expulsion Act, was compounded by an increasing concern with keeping under surveillance those who disembarked at South American ports. With the intensification of eugenic and xenophobic feelings after World War I, many countries passed restrictive legislation on immigration in the 1920s. In the ports of Argentina and Brazil, the new legislation was intended to prevent the entry of sick and elderly people, the disabled, the mentally disturbed, and prostitutes. In previous years, there had already been an increasing demand for passports, criminal records, and certificates of mental health and good conduct. Newer and more sophisticated methods of identification, such as photographic records, were used together with older procedures, which included certificates issued by the local police.[45]

---

44. For a detailed analysis of criminal trials for procuring, see *ibid.*, pp. 171–230, and also Cristiana Schettini, "Prostitutes and the Law: The Uses of Court Cases over Pandering in Rio de Janeiro at the Beginning of the Twentieth Century", in Sueann Caulfield, Sarah Chambers, and Lara Putnam (eds), *Honor, Status, and Law in Modern Latin America* (Durham, NC, 2005), pp. 273–294.

45. This was the 1921 Decree no. 4247; Menezes, *Os Indesejáveis*, pp. 212–213. On the complex application of restrictions to the entry of immigrants in postwar Argentina, see F. Devoto, "El revés de la trama: políticas migratorias y prácticas administrativas en la Argentina (1919–1949)", *Desarrollo Económico*, 41 (2001), pp. 281–304. On the meaning of passports in the context of the international crossings of "American girls" through the continent after the war, see Thaddeus Blanchette and Ana Paula Silva, "As American girls: migração, sexo e status imperial em 1918", *Horizontes Antropológicos*, 15 (2009), pp. 75–99.

Figure 2. The illustration on the cover of the Argentine magazine *Fray Mocho* depicts two ugly women talking about a telegram from London in which the English authorities complain that: "It is nearly impossible for English artists to find respectable lodging in Buenos Aires, and that many women artists hired to perform in Buenos Aires stages are forced to live in dens of corruption." The joke is the pair's fear of going out in the streets and being mistaken for "English artists", when there is no chance such a thing could happen.
Fray Mocho, *15 July 1914.*

However, the main problem for police authorities remained – how to identify the "undesirable" type in the midst of great groups of immigrants who arrived in Brazilian and Argentine cities. The requirement for more documents still went hand in hand with a discretionary identification procedure based on a first glance, an expectation of visual recognition. Therefore, the experience of a first meeting between police officers and women travelling on their own was crucial in fixing the women's identities. Throughout the years, foreign women travelling alone could always expect problems when boarding or leaving ships. Female performers travelling with work contracts and return tickets soon appeared in briefings to consulates, police reports, and investigations concerned with expelling "undesirable foreigners" on account of trafficking. And those records also travelled to both sides of the Atlantic.[46] Behind the coexistence of different identification procedures was the presumption that young women were vulnerable to deceit, and the natural victims of sexual exploitation. Therefore, their tra-velling companions came under police scrutiny. Because of that, expulsion investigations produced a revealing record of work relations.

## LOVERS AND LECHERS

The journey of an Italian singer known by the stage name of Lili Bijou in the Casino theatres of both Buenos Aires and São Paulo in 1911 and 1912 reveals different aspects of work routes in the variety business.[47] Lili arrived from Italy with a contract to sing in Carlos Seguín's Casino theatre in Buenos Aires. Once the season was over, she left for Montevideo, and then went on to work in São Paulo's Casino, which probably then still belonged to Paschoal Segreto. In São Paulo, she stayed at the "Maison Dorée", "a regular boarding house for female artists who have contracts in the city", as stated by its Italian owner. The day she arrived, she met Dr Jorge, an Italian engineer who, having seen her at the Maison Dorée, wished, as he put it, "to offer his protection and take care of her lodging expenses, providing her with enough money to cover all her needs".

In turn-of-the-century São Paulo, "artists' boarding houses" were considered to be elegant and sophisticated brothels, patronized by men with enough resources to do what Dr Jorge was doing, which amounted to paying an artist's expenses in exchange for her company for a while. Everything seemed to be going well and most probably Lili's story would never have been recorded anywhere had it not been for the unexpected appearance of a young Italian man, Henrique Resta, who had escorted Lili

46. Ofício do Ministro de Relações Exteriores ao Chefe de Polícia, 23 April 1921. Ofícios – Polícia Expedidos, 303, 3, 9. Historical Archive of Itamarati. For other examples see League of Nations, *Report of the Special Body of Experts*, pp. 33–35.
47. "Henrique Resta", IJJ7–154, Série Interior, National Archive, R.J., Brazil.

from Buenos Aires. When Dr Jorge was told that he was "wasting his time and money" because Lili was already with someone else, his first reaction was to pay for Henrique Resta's return ticket to Italy. The young Italian refused the offer and police intervention ensued.

Although the original accusation Henrique Resta faced was of procuring, instead of laying criminal charges the chief of the local police sought a summary solution. He gathered statements from witnesses claiming that Henrique Resta walked by Lili's boarding house every day, and sent her notes. Witnesses said it seemed that Lili and Henrique were not only lovers, but that she was also paying his expenses in São Paulo with the money obtained from the men she entertained at the Maison Dorée. The police chief therefore concluded that Resta was behaving like a gigolo, while he for his part insisted that he was actually a lawyer, and that he had worked for the prestigious newspaper *La Patria degli Italiani* in Buenos Aires. His family, he said, was sending him money from Italy. However, his claims were to no avail and the brief police investigation resulted in the standard ministerial decree of expulsion.

The only person in São Paulo who seemed to know Henrique Resta well was Lili Bijou. She told the police that they had been together in Italy, but that since her family did not approve of their relationship they had decided to go to Buenos Aires, where she had a contract to sing at the Casino. She backed Resta's explanation that he received money from his family, and so he did not need hers. Her attitude contrasts greatly with other expulsion investigations initiated as the result of explicit accusations of procuring by women against partners or former partners. In Lili's case, it was evident that, whatever the terms of her relationship with Resta, she did not want the police to meddle in it. That might of course have been because she was either in love with him, or too scared.[48]

However, if Lili herself was content in her relationship with Resta, other people were upset by his unforeseen presence. Lili Bijou's arrival in São Paulo had raised many expectations in different men. The manager of the Casino surely expected her to sing in his theatre for the period agreed in the contract. He might have expected her to stay at the same boarding house where the other artists lived. The owner of Maison Dorée might have expected her presence to attract visitors like Dr Jorge, willing to spend money there. As for Dr Jorge, he must have expected Lili to give him her undivided attention in return for the money he was spending on her, so that all those various expectations suggest that the services Lili performed triggered a number of male pastimes that probably included sexual activity, but were not only about that.

48. For an analysis of investigations into expulsions initiated following accusations by women, see Schettini, "*Que Tenhas Teu Corpo*", pp. 150–155.

Lili Bijou's multiple activities indicate that she relied on all of them, everything from her paid performance at the Casino, accepting Dr Jorge's money, to perhaps even a certain amount of gambling, according to witnesses. It all went to make her tour through Brazilian cities profitable, and she might have reasoned that she could keep all her other endeavours going and continue a probably romantic involvement with the young Italian at the same time. Nevertheless, the four main witnesses at the police station, all of them Italian men apart from a Uruguayan woman who also knew Dr Jorge, described how Henrique Resta prevented Lili from doing her job at the Casino theatre as defined by her contract, although it is likely that the contract did not specify quite all that was expected of her. It is interesting to note that the contract was referred to but never seen in the course of the police investigation, which makes us wonder whether it was a written contract at all.

Lili's situation contrasts with that of Henrique Resta. Although she was also unknown in São Paulo, her contract with the Casino turned her into primarily a *café concert* singer who lived in a luxury brothel, and to any inhabitant of the city that meant that men paid her way for her in exchange for her company. Her identity as a variety artist included a combination of her performance at the Casino with her duties as prostitute at the artists' boarding house. In contrast, Resta's identity was rapidly defined in terms of his relationship with the young singer, but because he spent no money on her he was cast in the role of gigolo.

The notion of exploitation in such cases becomes even more clearly evident in another case of expulsion which occurred the following year. In 1912, a troupe arrived from Buenos Aires at the port of Santos, in Brazil. Like Lili Bijou, they too had a contract to perform in São Paulo's Casino theatre. Eighteen-year-old Marcelle Parisy, a Frenchwoman, was a member of the troupe, but her escort, the Belgian Arthur Van Der Elst, was not.[49] In view of the widespread publicity attributed to "white slavery" stories, the port authorities were suspicious of the couple and did not allow Van Der Elst to disembark. Marcelle and Arthur both claimed they had met by chance on the ship, having known each other in Paris when they worked together in the Bouffes Parisiennes theatre. Furthermore, the Belgian introduced himself as a theatrical agent, explaining that he was in Brazil for just a few weeks to negotiate a tour to São Paulo for a dramatic theatre company. We can only speculate as to whether they were finally allowed to disembark because the ship and port authorities found their story convincing, or only because Marcelle refused to disembark without Arthur.

Perhaps it was thanks to the intervention of the Casino's theatre director that all ended well for Marcelle and Arthur, for it was the director

49. "Arthur Van Der Elst", IJJ7–128, 1912, Série Interior, National Archive, R.J., Brazil.

who was in charge of collecting the artists at the port, taking them to São Paulo by train, and dropping them at their hotel. He even recommended a boarding house for Van Der Elst once the port situation had been resolved. The director's presence at the port confirms the multiple responsibilities of some of the key people in the variety business. Although the multiple-show system demanded increasing specialization of tasks, by the 1910s it was still common to find writers who were also in charge of rehearsals, art direction, or who doubled as mediators between multiple players, such as costume designers.[50] In such cases, the director would have to manage logistics.

In the case of Marcelle and Arthur, as the first to make a statement in the subsequent police investigation, it might have been that the director was the one who first accused the Belgian of being Marcelle's procurer. The local police chief heard too the testimony of the owner of the boarding house where the suspect stayed, and his statement was exactly what the police needed to proceed with the expulsion: the boarding house owner had seen Marcelle giving the Belgian all the money she earned from other men's visits. He "supposed that Van Der Elst exploited her and demanded she give him her money". Marcelle Parisy explicitly denied that Arthur was her lover, stating instead that he was "just a client". Nevertheless, in less than a month Van Der Elst had been expelled.

The expulsions of Henrique Resta and Arthur Van Der Elst share important characteristics. In both cases, the male escorts of performers were accused of procuring after a brief police investigation, which consisted of a few statements by witnesses. Having no fixed occupation on account of their travelling, and being romantically involved with women who stayed in houses renowned for being brothels, men such as they were therefore vulnerable to accusations of profiting from those women.[51] In both investigations, witnesses considered that sexual availability seemed to be only natural in relation to the women engaged as performers by the Casino theatre in São Paulo. The fact that their work contract required prostitution, or at least rather implied it, was utterly relevant. In both cases mentioned here, the police focused on proving that exploitation took place between the newly arrived couple. For that, it was as important for them to obtain statements from the women who had been giving

50. On the figure of "writer-stage manager" and other multiple tasks in the mid-1910s in Brazil, see Filomena Chiaradia, "Em revista o teatro ligeiro: os 'autores-ensaiadores' e o 'teatro por sessões' na Companhia do teatro São José", *Sala Preta*, 3 (2003), pp. 153–163, 158.
51. The local police chief and the director referred to Marcelle's pension as a "house of tolerance". Although the expression is originally associated with the French system of regulated prostitution, in Brazil it was used by the police to designate any house of prostitution during the period. For a judicial debate on the use of the expression, see Schettini, *"Que Tenhas Teu Corpo"*, p. 212.

money to the defendants as it was to establish that the men had no other contacts, and that they had no profession nor known position.

Police investigations placed under scrutiny what appeared to be complex affective relationships, although expulsion records are not reliable sources for describing the exact nature of the couples arriving in São Paulo from Buenos Aires. That is partly due to the fact that authorities were interested only in gathering evidence to turn an individual suspected of procuring into an expelled foreigner. In that sense, the records in fact reveal how the police went about actually creating "undesirable" types. Looking at how the police understood the broadly defined Brazilian legislation on procuring, we can see that the blurred lines between life and work in female artists' lives could potentially cause any man associated with them to be suspected of sexual exploitation. In addition, and for reasons that are hard to fathom, in both our cases here the women were more concerned in their testimony with protecting their partners than with explaining what they themselves actually thought of their relationships.

However, police records do reveal some dimensions of women's lives in the entertainment industry. Henrique Resta and Arthur Van Der Elst were accused because the relationships they had with the Casino theatre artists vexed other men who had their own agreements with those women. Because of that, more subtle aspects of the artists' lives and work arrangements come to light. Police authorities considered that there was nothing illegitimate about the relationships women artists established with their employers and landlords, who acted within a virtual network of intermediaries connected to the business of entertainment, which seems to have included prostitution. Because of that, expulsion investigations record the usual goings-on of the world that surrounded women's work, whether that meant singing and dancing at the Casino, or having sexual dealings with a variety of men.

Neither boarding-house owners nor Casino employers were accused of exploiting women artists – even though the former facilitated living conditions for prostitution, which was one of the definitions of procuring contained in Brazil's Penal Code, and the second fitted the description of what the League of Nations would later consider "white slavery", since the low salaries they paid were considered to amount to economic pressure on women artists to turn to prostitution. In the context of expulsion investigations, sexual exploitation did not seem to include the broader notion of facilitating or inducing someone to take up prostitution, but was seen in a rather narrower sense of profiting from prostitution.[52]

52. During the same years, criminal trials for procuring were initiated against owners of houses of prostitution accused by prostitutes of exploiting them by charging exorbitant rents; *ibid.*, pp. 69–82. League of Nations experts defined international traffic as "the direct or indirect procuration and transportation for gain to a foreign country of women and girls for the sexual

Police records also shed light, indirectly, on the artists' perceptions of the agreements established with their intermediaries and employers. Lili Bijou and Marcelle Parisy might have felt they had a certain amount of room for manoeuvre, perhaps even to the point of breaking an implicit rule of working arrangements – not to bring their own men with them, for instance. From that perspective, Casino contracts were not in fact simply a front for the "smuggling of women", simply because such contracts – whether written or verbal – did not have a single function. In fact, the stories of Lili Bijou and Marcelle Parisy suggest that men had competing vested interests in women like them.

In the tours through South America, work contracts were rather a defining element of women's identities as artists during their travel and during their stays. Contracts established the legitimate terms of their relations with others, and accusations of sexual exploitation were applied to relationships deemed unacceptable. Therefore, the moral terms used to define boundaries between acceptable and unacceptable behaviour were established in very particular settings, among the competing interests of men in relation to women's activities as artists and prostitutes. However, and despite their vulnerable position, women artists developed strategies to deal with such relationships. Mobility played a crucial role, as it was part of their contractual obligations, but at the same time it could create the possibility for them to be rid of what they considered to be undesirable escorts.

## FAMILY CONTRACTS

Not all foreigners expelled from Brazil under accusations of procuring were the male escorts of women artists. If the most popular figure of white slavery was the young man playing the role of seducer, in theatrical settings it was quite common to feature the mother as her daughter's career manager. When family structure forms part of labour intermediation practices, it reveals different aspects of contemporary views of female and child labour in the entertainment industry, as well as of the survival strategies of women artists. In such family settings, vulnerability became the major characteristic.

In 1913 Costa Junior, a man of the theatre accustomed to performing multiple tasks in the entertainment world – as composer, writer, teacher, and director – noted something strange about one Max Werman's family, and notified the police.[53] Famous in Rio de Janeiro for composing the music for a successful play in 1909, Costa Junior also worked as an

gratification of one or more other persons"; League of Nations, *Report of the Special Body of Experts*, p. 9.
53. See *Dicionário Cravo Albin da Música Popular Brasileira*, available at http://www.dicionariompb.com.br (last accessed 4 February 2011).

agent for artists. Junior testified that he had known the Wermans for a long time, because a few years earlier he had hired the Werman children for a play. After that, the Wermans had retired to Buenos Aires, and according to Costa Junior their sudden reappearance in Rio de Janeiro, where they wished to negotiate a contract for their daughter Rosita at the Pavilhão Internacional, one of Paschoal Segreto's establishments, raised disturbing rumours. He had heard from other artists that Werman had "traded his daughter's honour in Buenos Aires", and that the police of both Buenos Aires and São Paulo had expelled him from their cities.[54]

The return of the Wermans to Rio offers a glimpse into work relations involving family networks, as stated by witnesses called during police procedures to expel Senhor and Senhora Werman. After Costa Junior filed his complaint, the first person who was keen to say something about the case was a nineteen-year-old carpenter who had worked for the Wermans in Buenos Aires and Rio. As a family employee, he had all kinds of scandalous tales to tell, especially of how Rosita's parents offered her to men who would pay for each rendezvous. Meanwhile, a neighbour was willing to testify that he saw the "young lady copulating (with her clients) in the living room".

Teresa Nelson, a Spanish artist employed at the Maison Moderne (another of Segreto's establishments), also testified against Max Werman. She was married to a painter employed at the Pavilhão Internacional, so the whole family was engaged in the entertainment business. Their daughter used to keep company with Rosita Werman. The two girls frequented places considered by all witnesses as inappropriate for them, such as the Palace Theatre and the Palace Club, featuring not only variety shows but gambling and prostitution too. Teresa Nelson's daughter was mentioned in Costa Junior's and the carpenter's statements, so it is probable that Senhora Nelson had some explaining to do at the police station in order to protect her own daughter's honour. In her defence, she claimed that when she realized that the Wermans were not "honest people" she forbade her daughter from seeing Rosita Werman again. She had first known the Wermans as "poor people and they were now covered in jewellery and had a lot of money provided by the exploitation of their daughter Rosita".

The establishments belonging to Paschoal Segreto mentioned in all the above testimonies were among the most popular in Rio de Janeiro at the time. The Wermans and the Nelsons obtained contracts to perform different jobs there, but while the Nelsons could prove that they were still working, Max and Carmen Werman confessed that they lived exclusively on the money earned by their children as artists. Teresa Nelson's accusations against the Wermans therefore highlighted a moral difference between the

54. "Carmen e Max Werman", IJJ7-145, 1913, Série Interior, National Archive, R.J., Brazil.

two families. Senhora Nelson presented herself and her husband as hard-working people who worried about their daughter's virtue, although it was clear from other testimonies that both girls often went together to places considered by all witnesses as unsuitable. Nevertheless, Teresa Nelson sought to establish a distinction between what she considered workplaces (such as the Maison Moderne or the Pavilhão Internacional) and other places inappropriate for their daughters (such as the Palace Club or the Palace Theatre). Therefore, even if she was unable, or unwilling, to control her daughter's wanderings in the city as the police authority would have expected, she maintained that work for female and child performers in the entertainment business was quite compatible with honest and hard-working family life.[55]

For all witnesses, the immorality of the situation was not in the contract, nor in the fact that the Wermans' children worked in Segreto's establishments. Costa Junior himself had no difficulty in admitting that he hired child artists. Furthermore, the Wermans' son's working conditions were never questioned by the police, even though Senhora Nelson accused the Wermans of "living off the prostitution of their daughter Rosita and the work of their son Luiz". Costa Junior also mentioned that Max Werman used to "exploit" the wrestler Muller, but the police were not interested in that either. Once again, their justification for expelling Werman was that he exploited his own daughter – he forced her to prostitute herself and profited from the money she made from it. Despite the incriminating testimonies, the police chief preferred to send the Wermans away rather than prosecute them for procuring.[56] Although Senhor Werman left the country a few days after the investigation had begun, within a month both the Wermans were facing decrees of expulsion.

As extreme as the Werman case might have been, it nevertheless illuminates common strategies of family work in the entertainment business, many of them probably related to older traditions inherited from circus families who had been travelling throughout South American cities for decades.[57] Families travelled and worked together and it was usual for parents to negotiate their children's contracts in the entertainment business. Many parents, whether more or less successfully than Teresa Nelson,

55. For a keen analysis of generational conflicts between mothers and daughters concerning sexual morality issues in the context of the emergence of new spaces of entertainment in the postwar period, see Sueann Caulfield, *In Defense of Honor: Sexual Morality, Modernity, and Nation in Early-Twentieth-Century Brazil* (Durham, NC, 2000), pp. 136ff. For the previous period, see Martha de Abreu Esteves, *Meninas Perdidas. Os populares e o cotidiano do amor no Rio de Janeiro da Belle Époque* (Rio de Janeiro, 1989).
56. In criminal trials of procuring, not one involved father and daughter, and very few involved legally married couples. The vast majority involved owners of houses of prostitutes and separated couples in conflict with each other. See Schettini, *"Que Tenhas Teu Corpo"*, chs 1 and 3.
57. Seibel, *Historia del teatro argentino*, pp. 352–354.

struggled to define the moral boundaries that separated them from certain places, people, and practices they considered reprehensible. Although night tours of the city by their daughters might have blurred those boundaries, many parents held dear the trope of the "theatre family" and the "circus family".[58]

The confluence of labour intermediation and sexual exploitation in Rosita's parents, particularly her father, makes their case completely different from the expulsions discussed above. Although there is no statement from Rosita herself in the police records and no reference is made to her age, her extreme vulnerability vis-à-vis her father was abundantly clear to everyone involved. While for Lili Bijou and Marcelle Parisy prostitution was part of their activities as artists at the Casino theatre, for Rosita prostitution was a parental imposition. Everyone agreed that Werman's mediation in the prostitution of his own daughter and the fact that he himself did not work was unacceptable.

But even in that extreme case, ambiguities remained. Costa Junior and Teresa Nelson seemed to conceive of a broader notion of exploitation than the one applied by the police (suggesting that the wrestler Muller and Werman's son were also his victims). Although witnesses portrayed Rosita as a victim and the Nelson girl as a somewhat more sheltered daughter, both with little or no room for manoeuvre, the girls actually went willingly to nightclubs, thus blurring the spatial moral boundaries adults insisted on trying to reinforce. Police intervention reduced all those dimensions to the single plot of the abusive father and the victimized daughter.

The investigation that led to the expulsion of the mother of yet another young singer, who coincidentally was also called Rosita, further reveals familial strategies in the international routes of variety entertainment. In addition, this is a rare case that also sheds light on the personal strategy of the young woman concerned in her efforts to confront her intermediary – in this case her own mother. Known as "Bella Rosita", she had been hired as a "Spanish singer" to perform in Buenos Aires, Montevideo, and other Argentine cities before she arrived in São Paulo in 1915.[59] In contrast to the stories discussed above, in this case her tour did not include the Casino, nor any other of Paschoal Segreto's establishments, but rather cabarets. That in itself seems to confirm the growing importance of a new setting, where the mixture of prostitution and variety theatre was more straightforward.[60]

58. José J. Podestá, *Medio Siglo de Farándula. Memorias de José J. Podestá* (Buenos Aires, 2003), pp. 301–302; Regina Horta Duarte, *Noites circenses. Espetáculos de circo e teatro em Minas Gerais do século XIX* (Campinas, 1995).
59. "Mercedes Vaya Ayala", IJJ7–144, 1915, Série Interior, National Archive, R.J., Brazil.
60. Based on Cadícamo's memoirs, Pellarolo argues that there was a continuum connecting cabaret and variety performances; Pellarolo, *Sainetes*, p. 31. For São Paulo cabarets see Rago, *Os prazeres da noite*.

Mother and daughter arrived with a contract for "Bella Rosita" to sing at the Montmartre cabaret, which also doubled as a boarding house, for which she would receive 30,000 réis per night, a sum actually collected by her mother. (It is interesting to note that Señor Werman was accused of receiving 100,000 réis for each rendezvous between his daughter and a client.) Thus, Rosita worked and lived in the same place, and when the contract with the Montmartre was over, Bella Rosita started singing at the Apolo theatre and the Café Paris cabaret three times a week, moving to another boarding house along with her mother. Rosita herself provided the information about her whereabouts to the police, when she accused her mother of keeping all the money she, Rosita, had earned. She also gave the police precinct chief a list of possible witnesses who could attest to her situation, including her landlords and several women, most of them Italian performers who were older than she.

If the statements her co-workers gave were truthful, Rosita's situation was indeed tragic. They mentioned suicide attempts, and regretted that no man who might have been willing to protect her could get near her, because all the money she earned ended up in her mother's pocket. All the witnesses stated that Rosita's mother expected to take advantage of her daughter's youth so that both could return to Buenos Aires as rich women. From five statements by women artists, it becomes clear that they did not expect to become rich through their work as singers, but rather through the protection, favours, and money given them by the patrons of the places where they worked and lived. Thus, many seemed to live in hope that they could benefit from moving from one cabaret to another, or from one boarding house or theatre to the next, just as Lili Bijou had done at the beginning of the decade. Their existence as travelling artists could scarcely be called a lifestyle, but rather a temporary strategy to profit from their work.

The comments from Bella Rosita's friends working on the stages of South America hint at the meanings some of the young women attributed to the sex trade. Maria Fantini, an Italian singer who was staying in the same boarding house as Bella Rosita and her mother, testified that Rosita had told her that she "would work as a prostitute once she got rid of her mother, because the latter had extorted all the money she earned, even to the point of not having a stitch to wear". The Spanish Vicenta Gual, who had known mother and daughter since the time they had lived in Entre Ríos (Argentina), when they had all worked together at the Teatro Variedad Tinti, also stated that Rosita's mother "extorted [*sic*] all the money she earned from her honest work". For her co-workers, Rosita's exploitation lay in her mother's daily "extortion". From their perspective, immorality included both the sexual and the stage work forced on Bella Rosita by her mother, and her appropriation of Rosita's earnings.

As in previous cases, police investigations reveal valuable clues about women artists' work routes. In Entre Ríos, Bella Rosita had sung in a duet with her aunt, while the Spanish Vicenta was a singer of Italian tunes. Italians Guia Caiaffa and Margarita Fabris also knew Rosita from the time they all worked at the Teatro Cosmopolita in Buenos Aires, at least three years earlier. Thus, at eighteen, Rosita was very well acquainted with the life of a variety artist, travelling with her family. She had worked mainly in Argentine cities until her mother decided to broaden their horizons, which showed the cleverness of her mother's timing. Bella Rosita's view of her mother's exploitation would later be partly shared by the police: the biggest problem was not prostitution per se, nor the economic constraints that led Rosita to prostitution, but rather the fact that someone else kept all the money obtained by Rosita's activity.

One of the most relevant aspects of the case – quite different from those discussed above – is that we have first-hand information because it was Bella Rosita herself who made the move against her mother. Contrary to what the League of Nations investigators would find ten years later, although Bella Rosita was in a vulnerable situation she was not isolated at all. If she had been, how could she have managed to find five women willing to go to the police and testify against her mother? The owner of the boarding house might have been persuaded to make a statement because the two women had left his establishment without paying their bill, but the other women seemed genuinely outraged at Rosita's mother's actions and stated that they were prompted by what one of them called "stage camaraderie" and "friendship".

The cases of both Rositas leave no doubt about the violence and abuse that could be involved when direct relatives mediated young women's labour. In those particular situations, the expulsion investigation focused on the tutelage of parents over the work of their daughters as entertainers, which was easily characterized as procuring. However, it is also true, at least in the case of the second of the Rositas, that the experience of crossing borders – due to work contracts that facilitated Bella Rosita's reunion with older friends and previous acquaintances from her stage appearances in Argentine cities – allowed her to use the repressive legislation on the expulsion of foreigners in Brazil to her own benefit. Therefore, in the struggle for autonomy as a young woman artist vis-à-vis her own mother, she was able to enlist many allies.

## EXPLOITATION AND THE MEANINGS OF CONTRACTS

For some historians of national theatre in Argentina and Brazil, the pre-World-War-I era signalled the peak of variety entertainment. In their accounts, the interruption of communications between Europe and the Americas during the war was critical because it allowed for the development of national companies, and therefore of a "true" national theatre.[61] However, considered on its own terms, the prewar period tells us more about the vital role of international routes in the entertainment and cultural market of South American cities. More investment together with the growth of European immigration fostered a significant increase in the circulation of artists during the first two decades of the twentieth century.

Different types of intermediary played a key role in the labour market of the entertainment business in South American cities. Considered a minor genre in the performing industry, variety theatre – featuring travelling artists and hinting at different modalities of male entertainment, including the sexual – involved work relations characterized by moral ambiguity. Thus, the actions of those who were related to women artists and interfered with their earnings came under the scrutiny and suspicion of their contemporaries. In that context, variety theatre becomes then a privileged site for analysing the relationship between work and morality.

Moral boundaries within the business and the degree of autonomy permitted to women artists were negotiated by contemporaries in specific social settings, in answer to a larger concern over the circulation of young women across international borders. Two meanings of immorality seemed to coexist and sometimes mingled in such negotiations. First, the immorality of sexual exploitation in the context of affective (sometimes familial) bonds; and second, the immorality of work exploitation in a wider sense, where prostitution derived from the vulnerability of young women artists who found themselves in harsh and precarious work conditions. In both, work contracts were seen as a guarantee of unequal and coercive relations, but in the end neither the League of Nations experts nor participants in the entertainment world, and certainly not the police, could trace precisely the fine moral line that separated "properly managed troupes" from those which were used to disguise organized prostitution. Whereas many of them believed a genuine separation did in fact exist and could be identified, they could not isolate sexual exploitation from regular work exploitation. Rather, they ended up unveiling, directly or indirectly, the larger context of a growing entertainment labour market.

In order to succeed in their goal of expelling "undesirable" foreigners, the interests of the police lay in emphasizing a single meaning of exploitation – as the expropriation of money gained by women from prostitution. A close reading of police investigations reveals, however, that multiple meanings of exploitation were at stake in labour arrangements. Work and affective relations were far from univocal to witnesses, victims, and suspects.

61. For a contemporary view, see Mertens, *Confidencias de un hombre de teatro*, p. 160: "The European war had closed all seas to navigation. For this reason, Buenos Aires found itself deprived of those great variety shows." This version is widely repeated in national histories of the theatre.

According to police investigations of male escorts of female performers, work contracts drew a distinct line between legitimate (employers, land-lords, stage managers) and illegitimate (escorts who allegedly kept the artists' earnings) intermediaries.

Moral boundaries were also the concern of a number of people in the entertainment world, especially in the face of what they perceived as improper behaviour of the young women artists themselves. As for them, some insisted on crossing boundaries by exploring the city's expanding nightlife, while others rebelled against their mothers for depriving them of the money they made, although not for making them work as prostitutes in the first place, as the League of Nations observers might have imagined.

Apart from detailing the routes and work relations of women artists and their escorts, police records of expulsion also offer a chance to reassess the moral ambiguity that characterized women's experience and their vulnerability in that labour market, as strategies of survival, accumulation, and upward mobility developed by artists and their families. In that sense, the spatial mobility that work contracts guaranteed was far from being univocal. Contracts actually bound young women to fulfil both explicit and implicit work requirements, but they also allowed them, as Bella Rosita proved, to participate in the social fabric of a "stage camaraderie", where they could meet other artists and recognize a shared experience, which was surely made up of more than what those brief records allow us to glimpse. What we can see though is that young women's perceptions of what it meant to cross the morality boundary, and what exploitation meant, might be very far from what the police or League of Nations observers could imagine, even if some meanings could be shared by all.

*IRSH* 57 (2012), Special Issue, pp. 161–189 doi:10.1017/S002085901200048X
© 2012 Internationaal Instituut voor Sociale Geschiedenis

# The Making of Public Labour Intermediation: Job Search, Job Placement, and the State in Europe, 1880–1940\*

SIGRID WADAUER

*Department of Economic and Social History, University of Vienna*

E-mail: sigrid.wadauer@univie.ac.at

THOMAS BUCHNER

*Department of Economic and Social History, University of Vienna*

E-mail: thomas.buchner@univie.ac.at

ALEXANDER MEJSTRIK

*Department of Economic and Social History, University of Vienna*

E-mail: alexander.mejstrik@univie.ac.at

SUMMARY: Since the late nineteenth century, job seeking has become increasingly linked to organizations and facilities that offer information on vacancies, offer placement services, or undertake recruiting. The present article focuses on how job placement became a concern for the emerging European welfare states, and how state-run systems of labour intermediation were established between 1880 and 1940. Even more important was the state's regulation of existing job placement practices, which resulted in a slow process of specialization, codification, and homogenization – in short, a slow process of normalization of practices at national levels. State labour exchanges thereby became the dominant reference point for seeking and finding work.

Since the late nineteenth century, job seeking has become increasingly linked to organizations and facilities that offer information on vacancies,

\* The research leading to these results is funded by the Austrian Science Fund (FWF, Project Y367–G14) and the European Research Council under the European Community's Seventh Framework Programme (FP7/2007–2013)/ERC grant agreement no. 200918. The project "The Production of Work" is hosted by the University of Vienna. We would like to thank Irina Vana and Jessica Richter for their comments.

offer placement services, or undertake recruiting. Labour intermediation became a concern of state policy in Europe and beyond. This was understood, first, as a reaction to social problems – such as poverty, mobility, or unemployment – arising from or exacerbated by industrialization. Second, it was seen as an attempt to organize labour markets, which were perceived as becoming more complex and even chaotic. In that respect, many contemporary experts, politicians, and public servants considered state-run labour intermediation an indispensable tool to match the right person to the right job or position.[1]

Later on, historical research often adopted this view. Yet recent French, British, and US sociological and historical literature[2] has pointed out that labour market policy was not a response to pre-existing socio-economic problems but instead contributed to bringing them into existence. It highlights the importance of job placement for the invention of unemployment and the "birth"[3] of the unemployed. The establishment of labour intermediation therefore has to be discussed as an element of the production of the new regime of *work, non-work, employment, unemployment,* and *unemployability*.[4] Before states began to intervene in labour intermediation, national labour markets did not exist. Rather, there was a variety of different labour markets and labour intermediations, each

---

1. For a recent overview see David H. Autor (ed.), *Studies of Labor Market Intermediation* (Chicago, IL, 2009).
2. See Bénédicte Zimmermann, *Arbeitslosigkeit in Deutschland. Zur Entstehung einer sozialen Kategorie* (Frankfurt, 2006); Christian Topalov, *Naissance du chômeur. 1880–1910* (Paris, 1994); *idem*, "The Invention of Unemployment: Language, Classification and Social Reform 1880–1910", in Bruno Palier (ed.), *Comparing Social Welfare Systems in Europe*, I: *Oxford Conference, France–United Kingdom* (n.p., 1994), pp. 493–507; Jean Luciani, "Logiques du placement ouvrier au XIXe siècle et construction du marché du travail", *Sociétés contemporaines*, 3 (1990), pp. 5–18; John Burnett, *Idle Hands: The Experience of Unemployment, 1790–1990* (London, 1994); John Garraty, *Unemployment in History: Economic Thought and Public Policy* (New York, 1979); William Walters, *Unemployment and Government: Genealogies of the Social* (Cambridge, 2000).
3. Topalov, *Naissance du chômeur*.
4. "Unemployability" denotes the social status of those deemed unable and/or unwilling to work. In late nineteenth-century England, the term "unemployable" was used to describe a residuum of people unable to find work (whether regular or otherwise) due to moral and/or personal defects. Although the interpretation of unemployment as a phenomenon caused by economic forces became more important before 1914, the figure of the unemployable did not disappear from discourse. Beveridge acknowledged the existence of moral and personal unemployability but stressed that only a minority of those without work or regular income could be described as unemployable. The labour market reforms that Beveridge strongly advocated were supposed to lead to a clear separation between the employed, the unemployed, and the unemployable, i.e. those who should be eliminated from the labour market and handed over to poor relief. In the 1920s, unemployability again gained importance as an effect of long-term unemployment. See John Welshman, "The Concept of the Unemployable", *Economic History Review*, 59 (2006), pp. 578–606.

with its own problems and contestations. Nonetheless, the policies of various European states differed significantly. This becomes most evident if we include the efforts made to survey, compare, organize, and equalize these policies at a national and international level.

The present article focuses on how job placement became an agenda for emerging welfare states and how state-run systems of labour intermediation were established in Europe from the late nineteenth century to World War II.[5] Recent literature has described the emergence of public labour intermediation primarily as a project of public servants, politicians, and interest groups such as employers' and workers' organizations. But that is too narrow an approach given the wide range of practices that shaped the emergence of public labour intermediation, including private and commercial labour exchanges and the job seekers themselves, who have been particularly omitted in research so far. Job placement cannot be restricted to actual public employment exchanges and state policy cannot be understood by looking exclusively at the state. Yet, state policy did play a special role in the making of public labour intermediation by establishing public employment offices that conducted increasingly specialized placement services and by universalizing placement beyond particular occupations and places, thus mediating a variety of interests.

In nineteenth- and early twentieth-century Europe, a bewildering multiplicity of terms was used to describe organizations and facilities offering placement services. Both national and international statistics, surveys, and research compiled in the first few decades of the twentieth century had great difficulty in determining what services were meant by specific designations – even within the same country. This ambiguity and the confusing terminology are an integral part of the phenomenon in question. For reasons of readability, we will differentiate as follows. The term "job placement" is used to denote all kinds of placement services provided by states, associations, commercial businesses, or other kinds of organizations. Job placement facilities are referred to as "labour" or "employment exchanges", both terms being used interchangeably. In cases where such a facility was run by a municipality, a province, or a central government, "public" (labour or employment) exchange (or office) is used to distinguish it from private exchanges. The services offered by the

---

5. The present article does not aim at a systematic comparison of national developments. Cohen and Hanagan compare unemployment policies in Britain, France, and the United States but do not pay much attention to labour intermediation; Miriam Cohen and Michael Hanagan, "Politics, Industrialization and Citizenship: Unemployment Policy in England, France and the United States, 1890–1950", in Charles Tilly (ed.), *Citizenship, Identity and Social History* (Cambridge, 1995), pp. 91–129. For another comparative study, see Topalov, *Naissance du chômeur*, and Jan Lucassen, "In Search of Work in Europe, 1800–2000" (IISG Research Paper 39) (Amsterdam, 2000) available at http://socialhistory.org/sites/default/files/docs/publications/insearch.pdf

public offices varied from country to country and changed over time. Sometimes, such changes were marked by a change in the term used (for example in Germany from *Arbeitsnachweis* to *Arbeitsamt*), but more often the names were left unchanged. Finally, the term "public labour intermediation" covers not only public labour exchanges but also the entire repertoire of state policies with respect to job searching as well as the placement and recruitment of workers.

This article has greatly benefited from some early twentieth-century comparative surveys on labour intermediation across Europe and beyond. It also draws on the results of a workshop on the history of job seeking and labour intermediation held in Vienna in 2009.[6] The authors are currently preparing an edited volume that includes papers from this workshop.[7]

## THE EMERGENCE OF AN INTERNATIONAL PROBLEM

In the late nineteenth century, intensive debates emerged in numerous contexts about the existing and future possibilities of job placement as a remedy for social problems (unemployment, vagrancy, begging, for example).[8] Both within and between states, these debates involved experts, social reformers, scholars, politicians, and public servants,[9] as well as officials from trade unions, employers' organizations, and philanthropic associations. Conferences facilitated comparisons between different notions and uses of job placement.[10] Committees of social reformers, experts, politicians, and public servants organized inquiries and visited labour exchanges in cities at home and abroad. They described their findings in numerous reports, articles, and

6. See Norma Deseke, Conference Report on the "History of Labor Intermediation. Institutions and Individual Ways of Finding Employment (19th and Early 20th Centuries)", 27–28 November 2009, University of Vienna, Austria, in H-Soz-u-Kult, 8 December 2010, available at http://hsozkult.geschichte.hu-berlin.de/tagungsberichte/id=3424; last accessed 21 April 2012.

7. See Sigrid Wadauer, Thomas Buchner, and Alexander Mejstrik (eds), *History of Labour Intermediation: Institutions and Individual Ways of Finding Employment* (currently under review).

8. See Nils Edling, "Regulating Unemployment the Continental Way: The Transfer of Municipal Labour Exchanges to Scandinavia, 1890–1914", *European Review of History*, 15 (2008), pp. 23–40; Ronald van Bekkum, *Tussen vraag en aanbod. Op zoek naar de identiteit van de arbeidsvoorzieningsorganisatie* (The Hague, 1996), pp. 151, 173ff., 249, 251ff.

9. See Ewald Frie, *Wohlfahrtsstaat und Provinz. Fürsorgepolitik des Provinzialverbandes Westfalen und des Landes Sachsen 1880–1930* (Paderborn, 1993), p. 48; William Booth, *The Darkest England and the Way Out* (London, 1890), p. 110.

10. An early example of an international conference including a focus on job placement was the International Conference on Unemployment (Paris, 1910). See Garraty, *Unemployment in History*, p. 139; Topalov, *Naissance du chômeur*, pp. 59–115; Sabine Rudischhauser and Bénédicte Zimmermann, "'Öffentliche Arbeitsvermittlung' und 'placement public' (1890–1914). Kategorien der Intervention der öffentlichen Hand. Reflexionen zu einem Vergleich", *Comparativ. Zeitschrift für Globalgeschichte und vergleichende Gesellschaftsforschung*, 5 (1995), pp. 93–120.

books, some of which were comparative in character.[11] Many societies and associations were established at local, national, and international level, ranging from philanthropic associations establishing local employment exchanges to the International Association on Unemployment, which included the question of job placement in its debates and publications.[12]

After World War I, the International Labour Organization (ILO) became an important site for international exchange on the issue of job placement, for instance through worldwide studies of the scope for job placement and related problems.[13] Apart from assembling and providing information, the ILO developed standards for creating and regulating employment exchanges. States ratifying the 1919 Washington Convention agreed to establish "a system of free public employment agencies under the control of a central authority".[14] Moreover, these national systems were aimed at the "total suppression of fee-charging employment agencies",[15] because labour "should not be regarded merely as a commodity or article of commerce".[16] In this vein, further conventions commonly recommended abolishing or at least regulating commercially run placement agencies.[17]

---

11. See, for example, David F. Schloss, *Report to the Board of Trade on Agencies and Methods for Dealing with the Unemployed in Certain Foreign Countries* (London, 1904); Otto Becker and Ernst Bernhard, *Die gesetzliche Regelung der Arbeitsvermittlung in den wichtigsten Ländern der Erde* (Berlin, 1913); "Die Arbeitsvermittlung im Deutschen Reich", *Austria. Archiv für Gesetzgebung und Statistik auf den Gebieten der Gewerbe, des Handels und der Schiffahrt*, X (1895), pp. 1008–1012.

12. This association edited the *Quarterly Journal of the International Association on Unemployment*.

13. See, for example, International Labour Office [hereafter, ILO], *Employment Exchanges: An International Study of Placing Activities* (Geneva, 1933); International Labour Conference, *Unemployment Insurance and Various Forms of Relief for the Unemployed. Seventeenth Session* (Geneva, 1933); *idem, Abolition of Fee-Charging Employment Agencies. Sixteenth Session 1932* (Geneva, 1932).

14. "The States ratifying this convention or acceding thereto shall establish, in their respective countries, a system of free public employment agencies under the control of a central authority. Committees, which shall include representatives of employers and representatives of workers, shall be appointed to advise on matters concerning the carrying on of these agencies. In States in which both public and private free employment agencies engage in the work of finding employment for the unemployed, such States shall take steps to coordinate the operations of any or all such agencies on a national scale"; League of Nations, International Labor Conference, *First Annual Meeting. October, 29 1919–November 29, 1919* (Washington DC, 1920), p. 237.

15. "Not only did legislation for regulation continue to spread, but the principle of total suppression of fee-charging employment agencies, formally enunciated by the International Labour Conference at its Washington Session in 1919 and destined to receive growing recognition in the years that followed, began to be experimented upon"; International Labour Conference, *Abolition of Fee-Charging Employment Agencies*, p. 6.

16. *Ibid.*, p. 1.

17. For example, ILO Convention no. 34 (Fee-Charging Employment Agencies Convention) of 1933; Sergio Ricca, "The Changing Role of Public Employment Services", *International Labour Review*, 127 (1988), pp. 19–34, 30.

These international initiatives frequently focused on concrete "solutions" for job placement and job seeking in a few model countries. The British model constituted state-run labour exchanges at a national level, established by the Labour Exchanges Act of 1909. Combined with the national unemployment insurance enacted by law in 1911,[18] it served as a point of reference for many countries across the world.[19] However, experts and policymakers in the late nineteenth and early twentieth centuries also derived information from elsewhere. Australian social reformers looked not only at the British example but also at early attempts to create public employment exchanges in New Zealand.[20] In the early twentieth-century Netherlands, the British system was discussed as an option, but the German model of municipal labour exchanges was eventually deemed more appropriate.[21] Apart from national preferences, specific models evidently attracted certain interest groups. Before World War I, the example of the French *bourses du travail* – facilities run by trade unions that, *inter alia*, also offered the placement of jobs – served as an important point of reference for trade unions all over Europe.[22]

The intensity of debates on job placement can best be highlighted by the example of German municipal employment exchanges. Inspired by the example of Swiss cities, which had installed public exchanges in the 1880s,[23] a network of municipal exchanges was established in the 1890s that would

18. On unemployment and unemployment policies in Great Britain, see Noel Whiteside, *Bad Times: Unemployment in British Social and Political History* (London, 1991); José Harris, *Unemployment and Politics: A Study in English Social Policy 1886–1914* (Oxford, 1972).

19. This was, for example, the case in the US and Canada. See Udo Sautter, *Three Cheers for the Unemployed: Government and Unemployment before the New Deal* (Cambridge, 1991), pp. 32ff.; *idem*, "The Origins of the Employment Service in Canada, 1900–1920", *Labour/Le Travail*, 6 (1980), pp. 89–112, 101.

20. Anthony O'Donnell, "Organising the Labour Market in a Liberal Welfare State: The Origins of the Public Employment Service in Australia", in Wadauer *et al.*, *History of Labour Intermediation*.

21. However, when unemployment insurance was being discussed, the Danish model appeared to be attractive for the Netherlands. See Van Bekkum, *Tussen vraag en aanbod*, p. 257. According to Daniel Levine, Danish social reform was likewise interested in model solutions abroad, but was strongly inclined to opt for solutions perceived to adhere to the country's existing institutions; Daniel Levine, "Conservatism and Tradition in Danish Social Welfare Legislation, 1890–1933: A Comparative View", *Comparative Studies in Society and History*, 20 (1978), pp. 54–69.

22. See Ad Knotter, "Mediation, Allocation, Control: Trade Unions and the Changing Faces of Labour Market Intermediation in Western Europe in the Nineteenth and Early Twentieth Centuries", and Malcolm Mansfield, "Labour Intermediation, Uncertain Employment and the Bourses du Travail in Late Nineteenth Century France", both in Wadauer *et al.*, *History of Labour Intermediation*.

23. See Wilhelm Lins, "Arbeitsmarkt und Arbeitsnachweis", in Ludwig Elster *et al.* (eds), *Handwörterbuch der Staatswissenschaften*, I: *Abbau bis Assignaten*, 4th edn (Jena, 1923), pp. 824–839, 829; Erich Gruner, "Arbeitsvermittlung und Arbeitslosenversorgung. Das Beispiel

soon cover the entire country. Politicians, scientists, public servants, and social reformers from all over the world travelled to Germany in order to visit municipal labour exchanges there.[24] Particularly before World War I, the Munich labour exchange (*Arbeitsamt*) was one of their favourite destinations. In 1908, the facility reported 125 visitors from Germany and abroad, including experts from the US, Belgium, Great Britain, Finland, France, Greece, Japan, Austria-Hungary, Russia, and Switzerland.[25] One year earlier, William Beveridge[26] had also studied the placement practices of the Munich exchange, which informed his notion of the potential functions of public labour exchanges.[27] The annual reports of the *Arbeitsamt* were regularly sent to labour exchanges not only in Germany but also in Hungary, Italy, France, Belgium, the Netherlands, Denmark, Sweden, Norway, and Russia.[28] The functioning of the labour exchange was presented at numerous national exhibitions and conferences, as well as at the International Hygiene Exhibition (Dresden, 1911),[29] the International Industrial Exhibition (Turin, 1911),[30] the International Exposition of Social Hygiene (Rome, 1912),[31] and the International Urban Exhibition (Lyons, 1914).[32]

Yet even though the international dimensions of this exchange are remarkable, particularly before World War I the primary aims of state bureaucracies were to gather information on placement activities and on the supply of and demand for jobs in their own countries.[33] A major concern was how to count the unemployed. It was a problem that went

der Schweiz", in Hans-Peter Benöhr (ed.), *Arbeitsvermittlung und Arbeitslosenversorgung in der neueren deutschen Rechtsgeschichte* (Tübingen, 1991), pp. 237–256.

24. On the attractiveness for British social reform, see E.P. Hennock, *British Social Reform and German Precedents: The Case of Social Insurance 1880–1914* (Oxford, 1987), pp. 152–167. The German municipal labour exchanges were particularly attractive since their administration included equal representatives of employers and workers (*paritätische Verwaltung*).

25. Städtisches Arbeitsamt München, *13. Geschäftsbericht 1908* (Munich, 1909), p. 3.

26. On Beveridge and his travels to Germany see José Harris, *William Beveridge: A Biography* (Oxford, 1977), pp. 134ff.; William Beveridge, *Power and Influence* (London, 1953), p. 56; David Price, *Office of Hope: A History of the Public Employment Service in Great Britain* (London, 2000), p. 20.

27. Beveridge described his impressions in W.H. Beveridge, "Public Labour Exchanges in Germany", *The Economic Journal*, 18 (March 1908), pp. 1–18, 3–6.

28. Staatsarchiv München, Arbeitsämter no. 1013, Inspektor städtisches Arbeitsamt an das Magistrat der Stadt München (27.10.1903).

29. Städtisches Arbeitsamt München, *15. Geschäftsbericht 1910* (Munich, 1911), p. 4.

30. *Ibid.*

31. Städtisches Arbeitsamt München, *16. Geschäftsbericht 1911* (Munich, 1912), p. 6.

32. Städtisches Arbeitsamt München, *18. Geschäftsbericht 1913* (Munich, 1914), p. 5.

33. See, for example, a survey on the possibilities of job placements within the Cisleithanian part of the Habsburg Monarchy: *Die Arbeitsvermittlung in Österreich. Verfasst und herausgegeben vom statistischen Departement im k.k. Handelsministerium* (Vienna, 1898). For the domestic German comparison, see Kaiserliches Statistisches Amt, *Die Versicherung gegen*

unsolved, since what being *unemployed* actually meant was neither clearly defined nor identifiable. In this respect, the development of mathematical statistics proved its practical and administrative value by redefining the problem and developing ways of measuring unemployment as a social fact. It used and combined various materials, such as monthly reports of union-run labour exchanges (in Great Britain, Germany, as well as France), and developed new statistical tools, such as rates and "index numbers".[34] Labour offices were maintained especially in state-run systems of labour intermediation, along with the administration of unemployment insurance, thus producing the information that administrative statisticians used to construct their barometers of national labour markets.[35]

## OPTIONS FOR JOB SEARCH AND PLACEMENT

The late nineteenth- and early twentieth-century European studies revealed multiple ways to earn a living and make use of organizations that offered job placement.[36] Except for some philanthropic or state-run facilities that provided information on vacancies,[37] public labour exchanges did not exist before the last quarter of the nineteenth century.

A common practice of job seeking was – and still is – to use social networks provided by family, kin, friends, or colleagues.[38] This coincided with the recruiting practices of firms that, either directly or through foremen, labour recruiters, or gang leaders, addressed their workers' personal contacts to fill vacancies.[39] One of the most important ways to

die Folgen der Arbeitslosigkeit im Ausland und im Deutschen Reich, 3 parts (Berlin, 1906), here part 2.

34. See Topalov, *Naissance du chômeur*, pp. 375–406; Roger Davidson, "Official Labour Statistics: A Historical Perspective", *Journal of the Royal Statistical Society. Series A (Statistics in Society)*, 158 (1995), pp. 165–173; Dieter G. Maier, *Anfänge und Brüche der Arbeitsverwaltung bis 1952. Zugleich ein kaum bekanntes Kapitel der deutsch-jüdischen Geschichte* (Brühl, 2004), pp. 31ff.

35. W.R. Garside, *The Measurement of Unemployment: Methods and Sources in Great Britain, 1850–1979* (Oxford, 1980).

36. Walter Licht's study on Philadelphia describes a similar spectrum of job placement possibilities; Walter Licht, *Getting Work: Philadelphia, 1840–1950* (Philadelphia, PA, 1992), pp. 34ff.

37. Georg Hannsen, "Über öffentliche Arbeitsnachweisanstalten", *Archiv der politischen Ökonomie und Polizeiwissenschaft*, N.F. 4 (1846), pp. 296–323.

38. However, the importance of "weak ties" for job search, although difficult to trace in a historical setting, should not be underestimated. See Mark Granovetter, *Getting a Job: A Study of Contacts and Careers*, 2nd edn (Chicago, IL, 1995).

39. See Joshua L. Rosenbloom, *Looking for Work, Searching for Workers: American Labor Markets During Industrialization* (Cambridge, 2002); on foremen see Patricia van den Eeckhout (ed.), *Supervision and Authority in Industry: Western European Experiences, 1830–1939* (New York, 2009); Amit Kumar Mishra, "Sardars, Kanganies and Maistries: Intermediaries in Indian Labour Diaspora during Colonial Period", and Piet Lourens and Jan

find work was to ask at factory gates, building sites, port entrances, or mines. This practice was known as *Umschau* ("looking around") in Germany and Austria, *leuren om werk* in the Netherlands, and "calling around" in Great Britain.[40] Guilds, trade unions, relief funds, and associations (such as the Catholic *Kolpingverein* in central Europe) supported skilled workers who went tramping in search of labour. Servants and agricultural labourers in particular could find a job or position through the "open-air markets" found in some European regions before World War II. Responding to newspapers advertisements became a new way of searching for a job in the nineteenth century, but it never replaced personal ties.

In the final quarter of the nineteenth century, various organizations were established which offered job placement, among other services. At the same time, some existing organizations extended their placement activities. Among the most important organized forms of job placement were commercial placement agencies. According to the available data, in some European countries these agencies were responsible for most of the registered job placements, especially in areas such as domestic service or agricultural work.[41] There is scant documentation available on these commercially run facilities. The research literature and contemporary surveys suggest that, apart from such commercial offices, placement was often practised on the side by innkeepers, concierges, waiters, warehousemen, travelling salesmen, and peddlers.[42]

Apart from that, philanthropic and confessional associations offered placement and other kinds of support. In some cases they can be regarded as direct forerunners of state-run – particularly municipal – employment exchanges.[43] Such associations were founded either as general charitable organizations for the poor or to support specific groups such as apprentices, the homeless, prostitutes, or convicts. They created not only offices but also hostels, asylums, wayfarers' relief stations, and railway missions that offered a variety of services, including job placement.

Lucassen, "Labour Mediation among Seasonal Workers, in Particular the Lippe Brick Makers, 1650–1900", in Wadauer *et al.*, *History of Labour Intermediation*; Albert Rees, "Information Networks in Labor Markets", *American Economic Review*, 56 (1966), pp. 559–566.

40. See Knotter, "Mediation, Allocation, Control"; William Beveridge, *Unemployment: A Problem of History* (London, 1909), pp. 262ff.

41. See Franz Ludwig, *Der gewerbsmäßige Arbeitsnachweis* (Berlin, 1906); Woong Lee, "Private Deception and the Rise of Public Employment Offices in the United States, 1890–1930", in Autor, *Studies of Labor Market Intermediation*, pp. 155–181, 166ff.

42. *Arbeitsvermittlung in Österreich*, pp. 85ff.

43. Some examples are recorded for Berlin, Vienna, Prague, and Amsterdam. See Rudolf von Fürer, *Die Gestaltung des Arbeitsmarktes* (Vienna, 1911), p. 127; Otto Uhlig, *Arbeit amtlich angeboten. Der Mensch auf seinem Markt* (Stuttgart, 1970), pp. 81ff.; Van Bekkum, *Tussen vraag en aanbod*, pp. 166, 181.

Trade unions and employers' organizations likewise founded exchanges as a political tool for industrial action and as an attempt to control the allocation of labour.[44] But although union-run labour exchanges were important when linked to union-based benefit systems like the Ghent system, their impact – as measured by the number of placements – depended ultimately on the ability to organize workers in a certain branch and/or location. Further job placement activities of lesser significance were reported for schools and political parties.[45]

In the early period, job placement was only one of many services offered. The French *bourses du travail* might serve as an example: these institutions also offered travel benefits, lodging for wayfarers, and advanced training courses. Furthermore, they served as trade union meeting places, where strike funds and consumer cooperatives were maintained. In addition, they set the unemployable apart from the employable.[46] Generally speaking, none of these organizations specialized in job placement. At least one of the following services could be found in each of them. Union-run exchanges usually offered services similar to the French *bourses*. Philanthropic exchanges frequently offered lodging for wayfarers, cheap meals, bathing facilities, and some kinds of migrant benefit. Organizations with confessional backgrounds usually linked job placement to proselytizing. Foremen and labour recruiters not only signed up, but also supervised new workers; they offered credits and helped migrants to integrate socially. Commercial placement agencies allegedly exploited job seekers by combining costly placement activities with lodging and, in the worst cases, ultimately forced young women into prostitution.

Clearly, these organizations and facilities exercised multiple functions and tasks, but what they had in common was that they offered some kind of support to those lacking various – especially social and professional – resources. Examples might include: a young girl from the countryside arriving in the big city to earn a living as a domestic servant; a single casual worker standing alone against an industrial entrepreneur; or a poor household containing more children than could be fed. These unspecialized services made sense in the context of either traditional welfare for the poor or a market for personal services. Anything else – such as the specialized administration of all citizens of a welfare state – was clearly neither necessary nor imaginable.

---

44. Knotter, "Mediation, Allocation, Control".
45. In the 1930s some organizations within the German Nazi Party (particularly the SA) offered job placement.
46. See Mansfield, "Labour Intermediation"; Peter Schöttler, *Die Entstehung der "Bourses du Travail". Sozialpolitik und französischer Syndikalismus am Ende des 19. Jahrhunderts* (Frankfurt, 1982); Christopher K. Ansell, "Symbolic Networks: The Realignment of the French Working Class, 1887–1894", *The American Journal of Sociology*, 103 (1997), pp. 359–390, 360ff.

Most of these organizations were established in the late nineteenth and early twentieth centuries and successfully extended their activities. Thus, it would be wrong to reconstruct the history of job seeking and placement only from the perspective of a nascent system of public labour intermediation. It was partly in response to the exploitative practices associated with commercial employment agencies and partly to fight unorganized forms of job seeking that public employment exchanges were founded. Public labour intermediation was thus developed both alongside and in opposition to other possibilities for job placement. Furthermore, it did not necessarily eliminate these alternatives. Even in countries where legislation granted a monopoly to public labour market administration (such as Germany in 1935[47]), informal ways of finding a job remained important. The range of organizations offering job placement nonetheless substantially declined in states where systems of public labour intermediation were launched, though they did not disappear completely.

## PLACEMENT AS A REMEDY: THE EXAMPLE OF MOBILITY

The assumption that job placement entailed important benefits developed in many different contexts. Job placement was seen as a remedy for a variety of social problems. It evolved, for instance, within the most common forms of job searching, such as calling around or tramping without funds, both of which seemed to be unmonitored and (in many respects) risky. Neither mobility nor poverty started with industrialization. Over time, however, increasing numbers of people became predominantly dependent on wages – a condition that became permanent throughout their lives. As a result, they were increasingly exposed to economic slumps. Since there was a high labour turnover in this period of industrialization, employment often being casual,[48] seasonal, and/or temporary,[49] most workers constantly had to find and secure work.[50] It was common practice to look for work in more than one community, which proponents of job placement criticized as ineffective, humiliating, demoralizing, and sometimes even endangering the genuine work seeker.[51] It could, after all, easily slide into begging, vagrancy, or prostitution. As some critics of the absence of job placement argued, it would become a mere cover for avoiding decent work in the first place.

47. Hans-Walter Schmuhl, *Arbeitsmarktpolitik und Arbeitsverwaltung in Deutschland 1871–2002. Zwischen Fürsorge, Hoheit und Markt* (Nuremberg, 2003), pp. 245ff.
48. See, for example, construction work and port labourers: Beveridge, *Unemployment*, pp. 68–110; ILO, *Employment Exchanges*, pp. 102–112.
49. See, for example, Beveridge, *Unemployment*, and Rosenbloom, *Looking for Work*.
50. Licht, *Getting Work*, p. 32.
51. Knotter, "Mediation, Allocation, Control".

Up until the twentieth century, the main assumption behind state efforts to police the indigent had been that a distinction could be made between the deserving and the undeserving poor. Drawing this distinction had been the major concern. At the end of the nineteenth century, however, contemporary social reformers and officials began to perceive not only an increase but also a transformation in mobility and poverty. New distinctions and new practical categories emerged. Historians have shown that social reform at the end of the nineteenth century invented rather than discovered the involuntary *unemployed* and the *unemployable.*[52] The problem of a clear distinction necessary for any kind of policing remained, but the particular solutions had changed. The selection of unemployed, unemployable, and workshy turned out to be more a question of collective and rational treatment than of moral, individual diagnosis.[53]

As a concomitant to debates on job placement, comparative studies and reports now dealt with the question of how to distinguish systematically able-bodied genuine work seekers from those vagabonds avoiding work.[54] Legal repression, punishment, and "re-education" through hard labour remained options for dealing with beggars and vagabonds. Correspondingly though, job placement and support of wayfarers willing to work were regarded as appropriate assistance to the involuntarily unemployed. As a result, wayfarer relief was established in parts of Germany, in the Cisleithanian[55] part of the Habsburg monarchy, and in

52. See Topalov, *The Invention of Unemployment*; Paul T. Ringenbach, *Tramps and Reformers 1873–1916: The Discovery of Unemployment in New York* (Westport, CT, 1973); Zimmermann, *Arbeitslosigkeit in Deutschland*; Burnett, *Idle Hands*, p. 3; Garraty, *Unemployment in History*, p. 4; Barry Eichengreen, "Introduction: Unemployment and Underemployment in Historical Perspective", in Erik Aerts and Barry Eichengreen (eds), *Unemployment and Underemployment in Historical Perspective. Session B-9, Proceedings. Tenth International Economic History Congress. Leuven, August 1990* (Leuven, 1990), pp. 3–13; on the unemployable, see also John Welshman, *Underclass: A History of the Excluded, 1880–2000* (London, 2006).
53. Topalov, *Naissance du chômeur*, pp. 36–58.
54. See, for example, Charles James Ribton-Turner, *A History of Vagrants and Vagrancy, and Beggars and Begging* (London, 1887); William Chance, *Vagrancy: Being a Review of the Report of the Departmental Committee on Vagrancy (1906), with Answers to Certain Criticism* (London, 1906); United States, Bureau of Foreign Commerce, *Vagrancy and Public Charities in Foreign Countries: Reports from the Consuls of the United States in Answer to a Circular from the Department of State* (Washington DC, 1893); Otto Becker (ed.), *Die Regelung der Wanderarmenfürsorge in Europa und Nordamerika* (Berlin, 1918); Edmond Kelly, *The Elimination of the Tramp: By the Introduction into America of the Labour Colony System Already Proved Effective in Holland, Belgium, and Switzerland with the Modifications thereof Necessary to Adapt this System to American Conditions* (New York, 1908); Sigrid Wadauer, "Establishing Distinctions: Unemployment Versus Vagrancy in Austria from the Late Nineteenth Century to 1938", *International Review of Social History*, 56 (2011), pp. 31–70.
55. This was the Austrian part of the Habsburg Monarchy, officially denoted as "The Kingdoms and States Represented in the Imperial Council". Cisleithania consisted of what is more

Switzerland.[56] These *Naturalverpflegsstationen* or *Herbergen* could be initiated and run by charitable religious organizations (as in German provinces) or local communities (as in Cisleithania). While *Naturalverpflegsstationen* in Cisleithania were regulated and supervised by provincial governments, some German provincial and Swiss governments preferred to intervene by subsidizing wayfarers' aid. These facilities provided shelter and provision and were supposed to indicate vacancies for (mostly male) visitors.

Nonetheless, these measures normalized the search for work instead of actually mediating labour. Public labour exchanges either built on available facilities for wayfarer relief or integrated them into their own range of activities. In Bohemia, for instance, the 1903 law on labour intermediation turned *Naturalverpflegsstationen* into labour exchanges, additionally regulating placement procedures and setting up public exchanges where *Naturalverpflegsstationen* did not exist.[57] In Germany as well, the connection between *Herbergen* and public labour exchanges was a constant source of disquiet.[58] In 1927 the German Unemployment Insurance Act regulated support for wayfarers. For workers in certain trades, building up occupational experience by working in different locations was seen as a possible and desirable option.[59] Labour exchanges in various countries facilitated labour mobility as part of national policies not to suppress mobility, but to prohibit vagrancy. Apart from being facilitated by public and charitable organizations, mobility was supported by unions or occupational associations.

Besides protecting work seekers from physical and moral dangers, states were also concerned about where they were heading. Moving, for example, from the countryside to the cities – leading to what was apprehensively observed as baleful "rural depopulation": *Landflucht* – was a prominent

or less Austria, Bohemia, Moravia, parts of Silesia, Bukovina, Galicia, Carniola, Littoral, Dalmatia, and parts of northern Italy.

56. In England, casual wards of workhouses were intended to serve similar functions. See Lionel Rose, *Rogues and Vagabonds: Vagrant Underworld in Britain 1815–1985* (London, 1988).

57. See R. Krejčí, "Über die Bedeutung und die Ergebnisse der öffentlichrechtlichen Arbeitsvermittlung im Königreiche Böhmen im ersten Jahrzehnt der Gültigkeit des Gesetzes vom 29. März 1903, L.-G.-Bl. Nr. 57", in *Öffentlich-Rechtliche Arbeitsvermittlung und Tätigkeit der Naturalverpflegsstationen im Königreiche Böhmen in den Jahren 1911, 1912 und 1913* (Prague, 1915) (= *Mitteilungen des statistischen Landesamtes des Königreiches Böhmen. XXIV/2*), pp. 7–28.

58. See Frie, *Wohlfahrtsstaat und Provinz*; Becker and Bernhard, *Gesetzliche Regelung*, pp. 16ff.; *Das Wanderarbeitsstättengesetz vom 29. Juni 1907 erläutert von Dr. Mauve und v. Gröning* (Berlin, 1909), p. 26.

59. Adolf Schell, *Der wandernde Arbeitslose im Aufgabenkreis der Arbeitsvermittlung und Arbeitslosenversicherung* (Frankfurt, 1927), pp. 20ff.

issue, particularly in Germany.[60] High figures for return migration were commonly ignored, even by later researchers.[61] Beyond internal mobility, transnational and transcontinental migration also became a topic of regulation, at least after the end of the nineteenth century[62] and particularly after World War I. International placement – especially for women and juveniles – was a matter of concern and regulation.

In the interwar period, many countries largely restricted the employment of foreigners. Bilateral agreements regulated not only seasonal labour in agriculture[63] but also in industrial work.[64] In reaction to the demands of organized labourers who feared competition from European immigrants, the US government passed the Alien Contract Labor (or Foran) Law in 1885, which forbade migrants to conclude a contract with a US employer prior to their arrival.[65] Consequently, migration policy was seen as an important tool for regulating movement, protecting national labour markets,[66] and prohibiting the exploitation of migrants, while also preventing epidemics, including cholera. Public job placement was regarded as a crucial remedy in such circumstances.[67]

## RESTRICTING COMMERCIAL PLACEMENT AGENCIES

In contemporary public debates on labour mediation, however, the critique of commercial employment agencies appears as the main starting point for

60. Klaus J. Bade, "Arbeitsmarkt, Bevölkerung und Wanderung in der Weimarer Republik", in Michael Stürmer (ed.), *Die Weimarer Republik. Belagerte Civitas* (Königstein/Ts., 1980), pp. 160–187.
61. See Steve Hochstadt, *Mobility and Modernity: Migration in Germany, 1820–1989* (Ann Arbor, MI, 1999); and Annemarie Steidl, "Ein ewiges Hin und Her. Kontinentale, transatlantische und lokale Migrationsrouten in der Spätphase der Habsburgermonarchie", *Österreichische Zeitschrift für Geschichtswissenschaften*, 19 (2008), pp. 15–42.
62. See, for example, Andreas Fahrmeir, Olivier Faron, and Patrick Weil (eds), *Migration Control in the North Atlantic World: The Evolution of State Practices in Europe and the United States from the French Revolution to the Inter-War Period* (New York, 2003).
63. ILO, *Employment Exchanges*, §5.
64. Cohen and Hanagan, "Politics, Industrialization and Citizenship", p. 101.
65. See Catherine Collomp, "Labour Unions and the Nationalization of Immigration Restriction in the United States, 1880–1924", in Fahrmeir *et al.*, *Migration Control*, p. 245; Annemarie Steidl, "Verwandtschaft und Freundschaft als soziale Netzwerke transatlantischer MigrantInnen in der Spätphase der Habsburgermonarchie", in Margareth Lanzinger and Edith Saurer (eds), *Politiken der Verwandtschaft. Beziehungsnetze, Geschlecht und Recht* (Göttingen, 2007), pp. 117–144, 126ff.
66. Jochen Oltmer, "'Schutz des nationalen Arbeitsmarktes': transnationale Arbeitswanderungen und protektionistische Zuwanderungspolitik in der Weimarer Republik", in *idem* (ed.), *Migration steuern und verwalten. Deutschland vom späten 19. Jahrhundert bis zur Gegenwart* (Göttingen, 2003), pp. 85–122.
67. Emerich Ferenczi, *Die Arbeitslosigkeit und die internationalen Arbeiterwanderungen. Bericht an das internationale Komitee der Internationalen Vereinigung zur Bekämpfung der Arbeitslosigkeit* (Jena, 1913), p. 18.

public measures in most European countries.[68] The numbers of placements available indicate that commercially run agencies played a major role in finding employment, work, or posts.[69] They obviously met the needs, for example, of servants who, as a rule, were not organized in unions or associations and who found it hard to call around for posts. Yet this kind of placement service was expensive for the job seeker, and the information provided on vacancies was often false.

When commercial placement was combined with lodging, the businessman had no interest in placing job seekers quickly. Accordingly, commercial placement allegedly induced workshyness, lured women into prostitution, and drove men to drink. Hence commercial agencies were seen as keen to defraud or exploit the jobless, and – since they also encouraged changing positions – to undermine stable labour relations.[70] Owing both to their significance and their suspected malpractice, commercial agencies were the main targets of criticism by governments, unions, and charitable organizations as well as (partially) by employers. Contemporary critics thus argued that the economic interest of commercial agencies caused harm both to job seekers and the entire economy.[71] As a result, in most European countries legal regulation and restrictions on commercial placement agencies were the state's first steps towards intervention in job placement.[72] France passed such a decree in 1852; Austria in 1863. In 1875 Switzerland agreed to the international placement of young persons and adopted further measures in 1892. Regulations were approved in 1883 in Germany; in 1884 in Hungary and Sweden; in 1891 in Denmark; and in 1896 in Norway. New Zealand, Western Australia, and the US state of Iowa also passed regulations at that time.

By the beginning of the twentieth century, such decrees were often replaced by laws. This happened in France (where a 1904 edict was codified in 1910), in Austria (1907), in England and Wales (1907), and in Germany (1910) – to give just a few examples.[73] Numerous options had to be regulated, and requiring licences was a feature common to most of the laws.[74] Often criteria were issued concerning eligibility for such a licence[75] – not to speak of their location, the requirements for charging

---

68. Becker and Bernhard, *Gesetzliche Regelung*, pp. 2ff., 69–140; International Labour Conference, *Abolition of Fee-Charging Employment Agencies*, p. 14.

69. Becker and Bernhard, *Gesetzliche Regelung*, p. 69.

70. *Arbeitsvermittlung in Österreich*, pp. 77ff.

71. See also Brainard H. Warner Jr, *Die Organisation und Bedeutung der freien öffentlichen Arbeitsnachweisämter in den Vereinigten Staaten von Nordamerika* (Leipzig, 1903), pp. 5–14; and *Arbeitsvermittlung in Österreich*, p. 69.

72. Becker and Bernhard, *Gesetzliche Regelung*, pp. 69–77.

73. International Labour Conference, *Abolition of Fee-Charging Employment Agencies*, pp. 4ff.

74. *Ibid.*, p. 16.

75. Becker and Bernhard, *Gesetzliche Regelung*, pp. 83–86; for example, in Sweden, Bulgaria, and London.

fees, their extent, and so on.[76] A combination with other trades such as inns, restaurants, and boarding houses, or itinerant trades was forbidden, for example in Germany.[77] Granting licences could be made conditional on local or regional demand for job placement facilities, acknowledged by the respective authorities. Business practices were monitored, and reports to the authorities were made obligatory.[78] Special emphasis was often placed on protecting young people, on questions of morality, or on the regulation of international placements, including the trafficking of women.[79] In addition, commercial placement agencies were not supposed to encourage workers to change jobs or breach their contract. Particularly before World War I, the strictness of this policy varied from state to state. In France it was even possible to forbid or abolish agencies, in exchange for compensation.[80]

Outside Europe, where World War I more or less halted this process, such regulations rapidly extended between 1910 and 1920.[81] As mentioned earlier, in 1919 the ILO recommended taking measures to prohibit the establishment of employment agencies that charged fees or carried on their business for profit. In the years to follow, this aim came to be shared by many countries.[82] Together with the establishment of public exchanges, it was regarded as necessary in order to prohibit abuses and to organize national labour markets.

Still, the scope of the enacted regulations varied considerably across Europe. Some countries regulated fee-charging placement only with respect to certain occupations, certain types of employment, or on a gender basis. Others legally abolished commercial placement, yet exceptions were possible. In almost every country, the fees for placement were also subject to legal regulations.[83] In some cases they were fixed, in others it was merely stipulated which party had to pay the fee and under what circumstances. In France, for instance, the fee could be charged only to employers.[84] In other countries – such as Danzig, Finland, Germany, Hungary, Italy, the Netherlands, Poland, Romania, the USSR, and Yugoslavia – legal provisions required the total or partial abolition of fee-charging placement agencies, either gradually or immediately. In France, local authorities had the power to shut down commercial agencies.[85]

---

76. *Ibid.*, pp. 70ff.
77. Ludwig, *Der gewerbsmäßige Arbeitsnachweis*, pp. 126ff.
78. Becker and Bernhard, *Gesetzliche Regelung*, pp. 119ff.
79. *Ibid.*, pp. 117ff.
80. *Ibid.*, p. 70.
81. International Labour Conference, *Abolition of Fee-Charging Employment Agencies*, p. 6.
82. *Ibid.*, p. 1; ILO, *Employment Exchanges*, pp. 15ff.
83. International Labour Conference, *Abolition of Fee-Charging Employment Agencies*, pp. 22ff.
84. *Ibid.*, p. 22.
85. *Ibid.*, p. 53.

## REGULATING AND INTEGRATING: FREE PRIVATE PLACEMENT

Other placement services, defined by the ILO as "private",[86] but free of charge, did not seem to be as problematic. Placement services run by benevolent philanthropic associations in Germany (and to a lesser extent in Austria, the Netherlands, and Belgium) can even be regarded as the precursors of public employment exchanges. Typically, these were increasingly subsidized by the municipalities. And they were integrated step by step into communal administrations until, finally, they were run by those municipalities. At the same time, they turned from being associations for fighting poverty to labour exchanges for combating unemployment and organizing the local labour market.

The importance of union-run labour exchanges varied from country to country. They were particularly significant in Great Britain, where unions had long been established and accepted. In France, unions had been allowed to have their own labour exchanges since 1884. In countries such as Germany, Austria, Romania, and Sweden, craft cooperatives ran (or were obliged to run) their own job placement services, albeit with varying efficiency, prior to World War I.[87] Once public employment exchanges were able to integrate union- or craft-run exchanges, they became more essential in attracting qualified workers.

Similarly, other organizations could be authorized or ordered to conduct placement services. In some countries, such free (non-commercial) labour exchanges were subsidized if they fulfilled certain requirements.[88] That way, the state could influence policy or implement certain rules.

## ESTABLISHING PUBLIC LABOUR INTERMEDIATION

As mentioned before, some effort to establish public facilities that provided information on vacancies can be observed as early as the eighteenth and early nineteenth centuries. Yet these attempts were isolated. In the late nineteenth century, placement services were instituted more broadly, becoming more in the way of modern public employment exchanges. In at least one respect, they were (at least) supposed to contribute to organizing labour markets instead of just offering assorted help to those in need of it.

The comparative surveys carried out in the early twentieth century reveal an impressive variety of options for seeking jobs or placing people, as well as remarkable differences in the practices of public job placement

---

86. *Ibid.*, pp. 12ff.
87. Becker and Bernhard, *Gesetzliche Regelung*, pp. 48–51.
88. This had already been the case before World War I in Denmark, France, Switzerland, and Norway. See *ibid.*, pp, 4, 25, 31, 40ff.

per country. The terms used to describe these exchanges already suggest that: "employment exchange", "labour bureau", "labour bourse", "*arbeidsbeurs*", "*bureau de placement*", "*Arbeitsamt*", "*Arbeitsbörse*", and "*Arbeitsnachweis*". Some of these facilities merely provided information on vacancies, while others were more actively engaged in the process of matching men and women to jobs. Even if the same terms were used to describe organizations, practices within a given country were not necessarily similar. To some extent, like other possibilities for job placement, early public employment exchanges were not specialized organizations, for they also provided bathing facilities, lodging for wayfarers, cheap meals, and legal advice. Furthermore, some countries had transferred the task of public job placement to the railways,[89] the police,[90] the courts, or post offices,[91] since these facilities were already present across the country and could provide modern means of communication, such as the telephone.

The multiple ways of practising public job placement are indicated equally in the broadly formulated justifications for making this problem a state responsibility. Public employment exchanges were expected to organize the labour market(s)[92] by reducing casual labour,[93] and identifying the real unemployed so as to separate them from the unemployable[94] or workshy.[95] They were intended as instruments to enhance national competitiveness by enabling a more efficient use of human resources.[96] Furthermore, they were supposed to fight poverty and thereby relieve the cities of the burden of supporting the poor.[97] Other tasks assigned to these public agencies were to control migration, combat vagrancy, and stabilize employment relations. Public employment exchanges promised to help control labour mobility and help employers deal with labour shortages. Moreover, they were expected to assist in integrating former convicts and reservists as well as in reducing the "malpractices" of which other placement services were accused. In the

---

89. For an example in Canada, see Becker and Bernhard, *Gesetzliche Regelung*, p. 5.
90. According to regulations on servants in Austria, 1810; for Romania, see *ibid.*, pp. 42, 5, 49.
91. For examples in Luxembourg, see *ibid.*, p. 5; Robert Schmölders, "Der Arbeitsmarkt", *Preußische Jahrbücher*, 83 (1896), pp. 145–180, 158ff.
92. This issue was likely to have been raised in the debates taking place in each nation.
93. This was of particular importance in the British context.
94. Welshman, "The Concept of the Unemployable"; Topalov, *Naissance du chômeur*.
95. "Labor exchanges became mechanisms through which American and British governments could enforce a division between worthy and unworthy supplicants for assistance"; Desmond King, *Actively Seeking Work? The Politics of Unemployment and Welfare Policy in the United States and Great Britain* (Chicago, IL, 1995), p. 19.
96. Whiteside, *Bad Times*, p. 56; and David Meskill, *Optimizing the German Workforce: Labor Administration from Bismarck to the Economic Miracle* (New York, 2010).
97. Anselm Faust, *Arbeitsmarktpolitik im Deutschen Kaiserreich. Arbeitsvermittlung, Arbeitsbeschaffung und Arbeitslosenunterstützung 1890–1918* (Stuttgart, 1986), pp. 71, 73.

context of World War I, public employment offices were meant to monitor the labour force, reintegrate war invalids and returnees, and by doing so diminish social unrest.

Although labour intermediation was chiefly a concern of larger cities, some state policies reached out beyond urban economies. Whereas in Great Britain public labour exchanges were designed to cope with predominantly urban problems,[98] their prime function in Italy was to locate work for agricultural labourers.[99] These examples indicate that it would be misleading to describe these facilities as simple national variants of a general system of public labour intermediation. Their objectives and scope could be fundamentally different.[100]

The practical organization of labour intermediation by European states thus differed in two respects at least, namely with regard to the actual involvement of different state levels and with regard to how states organized labour intermediation. No clear and unanimous distinction could be made between state-run and other placement activities. Public labour placement could be initiated, established, or run either by municipalities (in Switzerland,[101] the Netherlands,[102] Belgium,[103] in Germany until 1927, and in some cities of Austria-Hungary[104]), by provincial authorities and/or districts (in Bohemia,[105] and Galicia[106]), or by national authorities (in Great Britain since 1909[107]). In many cases, this implied that the central state would be involved only marginally or hesitantly. In a number of countries, however, the laws stipulated that municipalities of a certain size had to set up labour exchanges. This already happened before World War I in Bohemia.[108] In France, pursuant to a 1910 decree, every city with

---

98. Noel Whiteside, "Between State Monopoly and Institutional Diversity: Finding Jobs in Early Twentieth Century Europe: Organising Labour Markets: The British Experience", in Wadauer *et al.*, *History of Labour Intermediation*.

99. Becker and Bernhard, *Gesetzliche Regelung*, p. 37.

100. Even highly developed systems of public labour intermediation, as in interwar Germany or Austria, were not constituted by homogenous placement practices. See Irina Vana, "The Usage of Public Labour Offices by Job Seekers in Interwar Austria", in Wadauer *et al.*, *History of Labour Intermediation*.

101. Gruner, "Arbeitsvermittlung und Arbeitslosenversorgung".

102. Van Bekkum, *Tussen vraag en aanbod*.

103. Els Deslé, *Arbeidsbemiddeling en/of werklozencontrole. Het voorbeeld van de Gentse arbeidsbeurs (1891–1914)* (Ghent, 1991); Becker and Bernhard, *Gesetzliche Regelung*, p. 23.

104. Hans Hülber, *Weg und Ziel der Arbeitsvermittlung. Studie über das Arbeitsmarktgeschehen in Österreich von 1848 bis 1934* (Vienna, 1965), pp. 19, 39.

105. Becker and Bernhard, *Gesetzliche Regelung*, p. 44.

106. *Arbeitsvermittlung in Österreich*; Richard Boleslawski von der Trenck, *Die Arbeitsvermittlung in Oesterreich* (n.p., n.d.); Becker and Bernhard, *Gesetzliche Regelung*, p. 46.

107. *Ibid.*, p. 33; E.P. Hennock, *The Origin of the Welfare State in England and Germany, 1850–1914: Social Policies Compared* (Cambridge, 2007), pp. 298ff.

108. Becker and Bernhard, *Gesetzliche Regelung*, pp. 5, 44.

more than 10,000 inhabitants was supposed to have a public labour exchange.[109] Finland had a similar regulation from 1930 on; Bulgaria from 1925 on; and Denmark from 1927 on.[110] In Germany, under the 1927 German Unemployment Insurance Act every municipality had to be covered by a public labour exchange.[111]

However, a combination of various forms of exchange, funding, and regulation could often be observed. In pre-World-War-I France, for instance, labour exchanges were primarily financed by municipalities, although the state had started to provide some limited funding in 1911. During the war, nonetheless, every town or city was obliged to set up labour exchanges administered by joint committees. Additionally, *offices régionaux de placement* (regional labour exchanges), *offices départementaux de placement* (district employment exchanges), and a central office in the Ministry of Labour were established.[112] In Italy, commercial job placement was outlawed in 1928–1929.[113] State-run labour exchanges were permitted, as were "acknowledged labour exchanges" – communal labour exchanges, employer/union labour exchanges (either jointly run or run by one if acknowledged by the counterpart), and charitable placement. And there were also joint labour offices in regions without public employment exchanges. Most such placement services were supervised by provincial offices and a central employment office. Districts could be merged so as to combine employment services for certain occupations.[114]

Furthermore, in many European countries trade unions and employer organizations were involved in administering public employment exchanges. In several countries, even private job placements were conceived more as complements to public employment exchanges than as adversaries. According to the 1934 ILO survey, most countries had taken one of the following measures.[115] First, private placement services could be allowed to supplement public placement for certain occupations in certain places (as in Finland, Italy, and Poland). Second, private placement services might be supervised and regulated (as in France, Finland, Germany, Yugoslavia, Romania, and Spain). Third, private and public employment exchanges could cooperate by exchanging information, especially about vacancies that one or the other was not able to fill (as in Denmark, Switzerland, and in Hungary). Fourth, private exchanges might be fully integrated and absorbed

109. *Ibid.*, pp. 29–31.
110. *Ibid.*, pp. 27ff.; ILO, *Employment Exchanges*, pp. 16–18.
111. ILO, *Employment Exchanges*, p. 18.
112. Lins, "Arbeitsmarkt und Arbeitsnachweis", p. 838.
113. International Labour Conference, *Abolition of Fee-Charging Employment Agencies*, pp. 76ff.
114. Lins, "Arbeitsmarkt und Arbeitsnachweis", p. 838.
115. ILO, *Employment Exchanges*, pp. 29–34.

by public systems (as in Belgium and Bulgaria). In the Netherlands, labour exchanges could apply for public recognition. In Great Britain, unions were able to negotiate a contract with public offices in order to administer employment benefits.

Within a national system of placement organizations and facilities, a variety of measures could secure an extensive clientele and supply a pre-ferential position to public employment exchanges.[116] Yet compulsory usage both for employers and employees, as was the case in Italy,[117] was not common. In Germany, a de facto public monopoly for part of the labour market existed even before a monopoly was legally enacted in 1935, inasmuch as public enterprises had to recruit through public employment offices.[118] Private enterprises were not required to use them, but collective agreements might include obligatory clauses (in 1925, this applied to 44 per cent of all such agreements).[119] In Germany, it was also formally possible to impose obligatory reporting of vacancies by employers, but this was not put into practice. In Poland, all enterprises covered by unemployment insurance – with the exception of state-run or municipal enterprises – had to report vacancies.[120] This possibility was at least discussed in other countries as well. In addition, public labour exchanges could openly advertise their services in order to gain the trust of employers and employees.[121] Probably the most important measure for establishing and securing a preferential position for public employment exchanges was to require people to register at a public employment exchange in order to be eligible for unemployment benefits.

On the one hand, authorities acted by regulating, restricting, and funding on the basis of certain principles, especially those of free placement and joint committees. They authorized or delegated intermediation to organizations or municipalities, or they integrated various forms of placement by setting up community or state-based placement. From country to country, public and private placement services were distinguished in different ways.[122]

On the other hand, however, public placement did not simply impose its own rules. It also adopted – and adapted – principles of private placement services: German and Austrian public labour placements attempted to implement "individualized" placement practices for domestic servants that

116. *Ibid.*, §4.
117. *Ibid.*, pp. 19, 40ff.; see, for example, the Labour Charter of 1927 and a royal decree of 1928.
118. *Ibid.*, p. 42.
119. *Ibid.*; the situation in Switzerland was similar: Gruner, "Arbeitsvermittlung und Arbeitslosenversorgung", p. 247.
120. ILO, *Employment Exchanges*, p. 42.
121. *Ibid.*, p. 36.
122. Rudischhauser and Zimmermann, "'Öffentliche Arbeitsvermittlung' und 'placement public'".

seemed to be founded on the attractiveness of commercial employment agencies. This adaptation of principles of alternative placement services also became evident when public employment exchanges were linked with the administration of unemployment benefits. As a result, the willingness to work as a criterion for support was not an invention of state unemployment insurance.[123]

Even before state benefits were introduced, the statutes of occupational associations and union relief funds defined their respective requirements for support. For example, circumstances deemed legitimate included losing or giving up employment, taking on employment, or being obliged to relocate. Moreover, a legal distinction was drawn between people "out of work" and those who were "unemployed". Yet placement and benefits were supposed to enable people to stay within their own profession (at least for a certain period of time) and not to have to accept just any wage or any labour condition. Support was also intended to strengthen union impact in industrial action; hence union members were expected to fit in politically.

Clearly, the state adopted and adapted principles selectively, while sometimes altering them. What is more, national measures and services were not always welcomed or accepted. Unions and labour movements at times mistrusted the state[124] when it attempted to organize labour intermediation, inasmuch as job placement and benefits were crucial when there were strikes. Furthermore, there was widespread concern that state intervention might lead to bureaucratization or to standardized placement without concern for an individual's trade.[125]

Public labour exchanges gained considerable significance in the first few decades of the twentieth century, particularly because they could be used to serve different interests. State-run enterprises, for instance, became key factors in the economies of the emerging welfare states. The modern governmental agencies also established rational recruiting, thereby adopting a principle of regularity crucial for the new employment regime.[126] In the course of World War I, public placement measures were taken up in many countries. Controlling the economy on a nationwide level became indispensable, and joblessness was the problem to be solved. War invalids and former soldiers needed to be economically integrated.[127] Such developments

123. Whiteside, "Between State Monopoly and Institutional Diversity".
124. See, for example, Hülber, *Weg und Ziel*, p. 39.
125. Employers particularly but also unions used these arguments. See Malcolm Mansfield, "Flying to the Moon: Reconsidering the British Labour Exchange System in the Early Twentieth Century", *Labour History Review*, 66 (2001), pp. 24–40, 24, 29, 34; Faust, *Arbeitsmarktpolitik im Deutschen Kaiserreich*, pp. 92, 97.
126. Licht, *Getting Work*, pp. 174ff.
127. Verena Pawlowsky and Harald Wendelin, "Transforming Soldiers into Workers: The Austrian Employment Agency for Disabled Veterans during the First World War", in Wadauer *et al.*, *History of Labour Intermediation*.

were not always sustained though. In the US, state-run employment exchanges were scaled down considerably after demobilization, and Great Britain and Canada both considered the same option.[128] By contrast, a comparatively smooth expansion of public employment exchanges took place in Germany and Austria.

In the course of time, the considerable variety in public job placements in a number of countries began to decline, albeit quite slowly. Comparisons became easier after the 1913 survey by Becker and Bernhard and later ILO surveys. Relevant ILO recommendations, however, were not always put into practice.[129] Yet according to an ILO survey of 1934, most countries either had laws concerning labour exchanges, or they regulated placement laws and decrees pertaining to unemployment insurance (Austria and Germany being two examples). The principles of free placement and joint committees of representatives of employers and employees seemed to have been broadly accepted even if they were realized in different ways and to various extents.[130] Most countries additionally had central labour exchanges for supervising and coordinating local and provincial offices and for exchanging information between various exchanges.

## PUBLIC JOB PLACEMENT AND UNEMPLOYMENT BENEFITS

The crucial step in establishing the predominance of state employment exchanges in the process of organizing national labour markets, both in Europe and the United States, was to connect them to unemployment insurance. In a 1936 survey on recent publications, Harry D. Wolf emphasized:

> In the administration of unemployment insurance, a system of employment offices is necessary to receive claims of applicants and to investigate their validity, to apply the work test and to disburse benefits. On the other hand, experience here and abroad indicates that in the absence of unemployment insurance there is a tendency on part of both employers and employees to ignore the services of the employment offices and thus to defeat their primary purpose, namely, a systematic organization of the labor market, and a more effective use of our resources, human and otherwise.[131]

128. Sautter, *Three Cheers for the Unemployed*, pp. 176ff.; *idem*, "The Origins of the Employment Service", pp. 110ff.; Price, *Office of Hope*, pp. 46ff.; Mansfield, "Flying to the Moon".
129. ILO, *Employment Exchanges*, pp. 15ff.
130. International Labour Conference, *Abolition of Fee-Charging Employment Agencies*, pp. 4–8; ILO, *Employment Exchanges*.
131. Harry D. Wolf, "Public Employment Offices and Unemployment Insurance", *Southern Economic Journal*, 2 (1936), pp. 69–75, 69.

As a result, one ought to distinguish between various forms of unemployment relief. First, some countries established nationwide unemployment relief whereas others subsidized unemployment funds of associations, trade unions, or municipalities.[132] Second, compulsory insurance should be distinguished from voluntary insurance. Up to 1933 compulsory unemployment insurance had been established in Germany, in Queensland (Australia), Austria, Bulgaria, Great Britain and Northern Ireland, in Italy, Poland, and in twelve Swiss cantons. Voluntary insurance had been established in Belgium, Denmark, Finland, France, Norway, the Netherlands, eleven cantons of Switzerland, Czechoslovakia, and in Spain.[133] Apart from that, almost every European country had made provisions for unemployed workers in one form or another. Public employment exchanges varied with the actual form of provision. And by administering unemployment insurance, public placement gained a hitherto unmatched effectiveness in defining unemployment, thus identifying and dealing with those who were involuntarily unemployed.

In fact, choosing the unemployed by administering them collectively and bureaucratically was the only possible solution to the old problem of counting the "real" unemployed – something which had haunted debates on unemployment from the beginning.[134] Unemployment insurance could practically select the employable from among the unemployable, the latter of whom could then be turned over to other institutions of the "welfare state", such as public welfare, old age or disability pension providers, the penal system, and psychiatric institutions. Evidently, these categories remained ambiguous and disputed, as in the case of those elderly unemployed assigned to early retirement. Insurance was effectively dividing the old category of the poor into stratifiable and stratified individuals who continued to be regarded as part of the national economy, and all others.[135] Unemployment insurance and benefits formally defined a status, permitting individuals to understand their situation as unemployment, even if they were casually employed.[136] This resulted in the emergence of *the unemployed* as a phenomenon of the modern economic system and its cycles, thereby personifying a status beyond both a person's responsibility and reach.[137]

In this manner, public employment exchanges became increasingly specialized. Other tasks they had fulfilled at first (like other organizations

132. International Labour Conference, *Unemployment Insurance and Various Forms of Relief for the Unemployed. Seventeenth Session* (Geneva, 1933), pp. 1ff.
133. *Ibid.*, p. 5.
134. Topalov, *Naissance du chômeur*, pp. 269–350.
135. Alain Desrosières, *La politique des grands nombres. Histoire de la raison statistique. Postface inédite de l'auteur* (Paris, 2000), pp. 318ff.
136. See Vana, "The Usage of Public Labour Offices".
137. Topalov, *Naissance du chômeur*, p. 407.

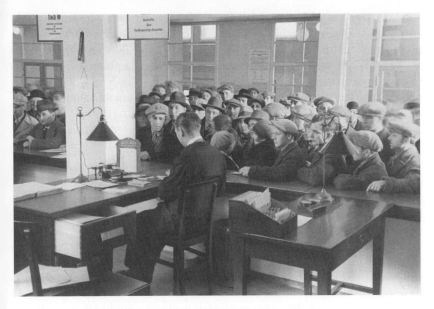

Figure 1. "Arbeitslosenunterstützungsstelle in Steyr" – office administrating unemployment benefits in Steyr (Upper Austria), 1932.
*Photograph: Lothar Rübelt; Österreichische Nationalbibliothek Wien. Used with permission.*

operating as placement services) were now relinquished. Unskilled workers too were overrepresented among those who used public placement.[138] Still, there could be divisions specialized in certain occupations, such as assisting those who were (or were supposed to be) most in need of regular employment. Yet in the course of time, enlarging the clientele was actively promoted. Once it was seen as an urgent problem, more and more kinds of wage earner were addressed. Consequently, public labour exchanges became increasingly generalized. In addition, they developed and formalized methods of placement, such as psychological tests for determining a client's affinity or aptitude for particular occupations (or vocations).

This process of specialization and universalization demonstrates that the old regime of policing "the poor" – a distinct class, almost a world of its own – had lost significance. Instead, a bureaucratic administration of

---

138. In the early communally run employment offices in Switzerland, for example (St Gallen, Berne, Basle), unskilled male day labourers and servants dominated in the 1880s and 1890s; Ernst Laur, "Der kommunale Arbeitsnachweis in der Schweiz", *Zeitschrift für die gesamte Staatswissenschaft*, 52 (1896), pp. 419–455, 420ff. For similar circumstances in the US, see Rosenbloom, *Looking for Work*, pp. 75ff. See also Faust, *Arbeitsmarktpolitik im Deutschen Kaiserreich*, p. 63. After World War I, British trade unions claimed that public employment exchanges were no longer of use for qualified workers; Mansfield, "Flying to the Moon", p. 29.

increasingly unified national labour markets was favoured, which might encompass all employable citizens. In combination with state unemployment benefits, public labour intermediation – like other institutions of the emerging welfare states – could be experienced pragmatically as the relationship between citizens and the state. Accordingly, even more people without work considered their situation as unemployment.[139]

## NORMALIZING LABOUR MARKETS

The predominance of labour intermediation by facilities and organizations in general in the modern labour market and the supremacy of public labour placement in particular (as claimed by many European states in the interwar period) appear to be primarily an effect of the emerging bureaucratic mode of labour market organization. The invention, definition, and administration of labour by institutions of the new welfare states was a consequence of greater (quantitative) importance than might be suggested by contemporary – i.e. state-run – data derived from public labour market policy. Research has often reproduced this official perspective by focusing on those facilities operating as placement services as well as on public labour statistics. Thus, it was assumed that the official perspective amounted to an exhaustive description of the entire phenomenon of labour intermediation. Yet this picture must be expanded to include the entire range of documented and undocumented ways of finding work.

Licht points out that according to a 1936 survey only 10 per cent of respondents in a sample of 2,500 Philadelphia workers of all age groups took advantage of diverse institutional offers, i.e. newspaper and radio advertisements, placement agencies, and school referral services;[140] 90 per cent found work with the help of family intervention, personal initiative, or contacts. According to Licht, the practical importance of "formal agencies and institutions" also varied highly throughout the life course and according to a person's gender and type of occupational training. Although Licht's results are based upon unique sources, his observations on Philadelphia can be complemented by further studies.

In a recent contribution, Woong Lee argues that public labour exchanges in the US were used by 2 million job seekers annually (c.5 per cent of the total labour force) in the 1920s. Yet in the 1930s, due to the 1933 Wagner-Peyser Act and the 1935 Social Security Act, this figure rose to nearly 12 million job seekers per annum.[141] In Great Britain prior to

---

139. See Matthew Cole, "From Employment Exchange to Jobcentre Plus: The Changing Institutional Context of Unemployment", *History of the Human Sciences*, 20 (2007), pp. 129–146.
140. Licht, *Getting Work*, pp. 30–34.
141. Lee, "Private Deception", p. 164.

1914 less than one-third of all placements in insured trades were made by the recently established public labour exchanges.[142] The Ministry of Labour estimated that in the 1920s and 1930s less than one-third of the total labour turnover was organized by public labour exchanges – a share that David Price believes is still too optimistic.[143] For Germany, Anselm Faust estimates that both public and private non-fee charging labour exchanges were responsible for perhaps 30 per cent of the total labour turnover in 1912.[144] By and large, then, people made selective use of public placement.

Unemployment benefits nonetheless treated people selectively, sometimes excluding agricultural labourers, domestic servants, the young and/or elderly, as well as others. In the interwar period, many people were still not insured. Not all kinds of work were equally considered part of the labour market, and not all people without employment understood themselves to be unemployed. Many ways of earning a living did not fit neatly into the idea of gainful employment. Jessica Richter's work on women working in service in interwar Austria, for example, confirms that they frequently changed posts – even alternating with helping out in one's family – which usually meant losing their accommodation as well.[145] Her work and Irina Vana's systematic comparison of autobiographical accounts[146] highlight something similar: the way being out of work was handled and understood depended greatly on how a person made a living – not to speak of their occupational training, the kinds of employment sought, integration in a household, and especially entitlement to unemployment benefits. Yet the emerging official categories of "decent" employment or unemployment became an unavoidable reference. Even those who tried to avoid it had to reckon with it.

To a great extent, employers shaped public employment exchanges. Consistent with Licht's study, enterprises preferred using existing informal contacts and networks.[147] Similar observations can be made for other historical milieus in Europe.[148] Public employment services, as argued

---

142. Price, *Office of Hope*, p. 26.
143. *Ibid.*, p. 81.
144. Faust, *Arbeitsmarktpolitik im Deutschen Kaiserreich*, p. 70.
145. Jessica Richter, "A Vocation in the Family Household? Household Integration, Professionalization and Changes of Employment in Domestic Service (Austria, 1918–1938)", in Wadauer *et al.*, *History of Labour Intermediation*.
146. Vana, "The Usage of Public Labour Offices".
147. Rosenbloom likewise stresses this point; Rosenbloom, *Looking for Work*.
148. See, for example, Reichsverband der allgemeinen Arbeitsvermittlungs-Anstalten Österreichs (ed.), *III. Konferenz der österreichischen Arbeitsvermittlungs-Anstalten (Wien 1.–2. Oktober 1909)* (Toppau, 1910), p. 15; Toni Pierenkemper, "Beschäftigung und Arbeitsmarkt", in Gerold Ambrosius, Dietmar Petzina, and Werner Plumpe (eds), *Moderne Wirtschaftsgeschichte. Eine Einführung für Historiker und Ökonomen* (Munich, 2006), pp. 235–256, 249; Toni

above, often organized help for the supposedly needy along old philanthropic lines. These either operated in niches where informal exchanges of
information did not work,[149] or they addressed persons who had lost
touch with such networks. Specialized job placement emerged only
after state-run job placement had become established. Efforts made to
decasualize the English labour market (Beveridge's central desideratum)
were unsuccessful;[150] if anything, entrepreneurs in the relevant trades
(shipbuilding for example) scarcely used public employment offices.
Similarly, Malcolm Mansfield points to the 1920 Report of the Barnes
Committee, which was charged with evaluating the employment offices.
That report noted that public employment offices were used by 141
shipbuilding companies to recruit 2,500 workers, whereas 21,000 posts
were assigned by "direct contacts".[151]

Hence, even after the formal authority of public placement services had
been established and nationwide labour markets organized (i.e. invented
and defined), state-run job placement remained only one of several possibilities for finding work or recruiting workers. Even in countries such as
Italy or Greece, where a monopoly of public labour exchanges took hold
in the course of the twentieth century, the share of placements made
centrally did not exceed those in countries without a state monopoly.[152]
People in search of employment and those seeking employees not only
utilized institutions for different purposes. They also combined different
methods to achieve these goals. It is difficult to clearly distinguish the
array of practices or relate them to a singular institution, as suggested in
official reports and insinuated by the statistics collected by the welfare
states. Therefore, to include the range of different ways in which labour
exchanges were used or how a person's search for work was perceived in
the historical description of public job placement is neither merely
illustrative nor morally obligatory. It is crucial for comprehending the
social effects of state administrations.

## CONCLUSIONS

This article has highlighted the ways in which labour intermediation
became a concern of the state and how state-run systems of labour
intermediation were established and operated from the late nineteenth

Pierenkemper, *Arbeitsmarkt und Angestellte im Deutschen Kaiserreich 1880–1913. Interessen
und Strategien als Elemente der Integration eines segmentierten Arbeitsmarktes* (Wiesbaden,
1987), p. 289.
149. Rosenbloom, *Looking for Work*, pp. 26ff, 46ff.
150. Noel Whiteside and James A. Gillespie, "Deconstructing Unemployment: Developments
in Britain in the Interwar Years", *Economic History Review*, 44 (1991), pp. 665–682.
151. Mansfield, "Flying to the Moon", pp. 31ff.
152. Ricca, "The Changing Role", pp. 22ff.

century to World War II. Although public labour exchanges were important tools for instituting public labour intermediation, state policies of job placement cannot be reduced to the activities of these facilities. Rather, the state adopted job placement as an agenda by regulating, constraining, prohibiting, or simply influencing the possibilities for job placement. It subsumed and altered the existing options and initiated a slow process of specialization, universalization, codification, and homogenization at national levels.

Amid the appearance of normalized national (and international) labour markets, state labour exchanges became the dominant reference point for all activities – even to those who were excluded from or opposed to them. Fewer and fewer people could avoid dealing with these institutions in one way or another. Accordingly, job placement should be examined as a field of relations between state policies (enacted by local, provincial, and federal levels of state authority), trade unions, employers, philanthropists, scholars, commercially run agencies, and – if nothing else – job seekers. The making of public labour intermediation, a new and crucial type of labour market policy, was a collective process involving activities that were all in one consensual as well as antagonistic. It cannot be reduced to a mere effect of the state changing its mode of governance. The problem of organizing the labour market and the solutions to this problem were produced alongside each other by the same activities.

The establishment of public labour intermediation differed from country to country. This article has attempted to demonstrate this variety by highlighting examples from all over Europe. However, the fact that they emerged concurrently across nations was not their least significant similarity. It is, in fact, a remarkable phenomenon, inasmuch as the problems that systems of public labour intermediation were intended to address were not the same throughout Europe. Moreover, they were addressed in different social-scientific and political contexts, allowing us to conclude that the policies leading to the establishment of public labour intermediation demonstrate also an intrinsic logic (administrative, political, social scientific, for instance) that has to be taken into account.

*IRSH* 57 (2012), Special Issue, pp. 191–224 doi:10.1017/S0020859012000466
© 2012 Internationaal Instituut voor Sociale Geschiedenis

# Temporary Labour Migration and State-Run Recruitment of Foreign Workers in Europe, 1919–1975: A New Migration Regime?

CHRISTOPH RASS

*Institute for Migration Research and Intercultural Studies (IMIS), Osnabrück University*

E-mail: chrass@uos.de

SUMMARY: Temporary labour migration was one of the characteristic phenomena of human mobility in Europe during the twentieth century. The predominant answer in several European countries to the growing economic demand for an external labour supply on the one hand, and political demands to limit the numbers of foreign workers and to protect the native workforce from the competition of "cheap" migrant labour on the other, was a growing direct and active involvement of the nation state in regulatory efforts and recruitment operations abroad. Besides bureaucratic organizations on a national level, bilateral recruitment agreements – starting in their modern form in 1919 – became the most important tool to regulate labour migration between two countries. This article takes a look at the evolving system of bilaterally fixed migration relations in Europe and its implications for sending and receiving countries as well as for the labour migrants involved. It argues that the network of bilateral recruitment agreements provided controlled and selective migration channels in Europe between the 1950s and 1970s. These agreements installed and protected certain minimum standards to migrants and led to a general improvement of the rights and conditions offered to temporary labour migrants in Europe.

## INTRODUCTION

International labour migration and mobility became one of the striking characteristics of the "Trente Glorieuses", the period of unprecedented economic growth and prosperity experienced by most of western Europe during the early decades after World War II. Between 1960 and 1973 alone, labour migration involved more than 30 million people, as foreign workers moved from southern and south-eastern Europe, as well as north African countries, into the core economies of north-western Europe.[1]

---

1. Anthony Fielding, "Mass Migration and Economic Restructuring", in Russell King (ed.), *Mass Migration in Europe: The Legacy and the Future* (Chichester, 1993), pp. 7–18, 10.

Such an enormous movement of population resulted not only in the temporary presence of an extra labour force but also in large-scale immigration into those countries; it also constitutes one of the largest voluntary, peaceful, economically driven migration movements in modern history.[2]

Quite apart from the scale, scope, and consequences of the European migration system of that time and its migration movements, two of its features call for further research. First, after World War I, European states began to assume an unusual role as they not only controlled migration movements across borders but also acted as mediators in the international labour market, which was made up of a growing number of countries bound together by flows of labour migration. In some cases, states restricted themselves to setting up the political and bureaucratic frameworks, while others began to structure those flows more actively. At times, that involved not only the creation of government-run emigration services but also recruitment commissions being sent abroad by government agencies of receiving countries.

The growing involvement of the state in the regulation of migration is in fact a much debated question in migration research,[3] especially considering the advent of the Westphalian system in the mid-seventeenth century, the conception of the nation state in the nineteenth century, and the dawn of the welfare state during the twentieth century. However, the growing importance of the state as a mediator on *international* labour markets has not yet received adequate attention.

Second, the role of the state in shaping labour migration also changed at another level. Between World War I and the oil-price shock of the mid-1970s, bilateral agreements between countries became the institutional backbone of labour migration in Europe as people moved from its peripheries to its economic centres. That turned labour migration policies

The term "core economies of north-western Europe" refers to Belgium, West Germany, France, Luxembourg, the Netherlands, Austria, Sweden, and Switzerland during this period. Denmark and Norway, which also fall into this category, will not be discussed, given their marginal role in the international labour market. Britain too has been excluded from this analysis as labour migration to the UK was structured rather differently. As this text discusses western Europe, the GDR will also not be taken into account. See further John and Rueben Ford, "The United Kingdom", in William J. Serow *et al.* (eds), *Handbook on International Migration* (Westport, CT, 1990), pp. 325–340; Kim Christian Priemel (ed.), *Transit – Transfer: Politik und Praxis der Einwanderung in der DDR 1945–1990* (Berlin, 2011).

2. Philip L. Martin, *Guestworker Programs: Lessons from Europe* (Washington DC, 1980), p. 91; Mark James Miller and Philip L. Martin, *Administering Foreign-Worker Programs: Lessons from Europe* (Lexington, MA, 1982), p. 2.

3. Dietrich Thränhardt, "Der Nationalstaat als migrationspolitischer Akteur", in *idem* and Uwe Hunger (eds), *Migration im Spannungsfeld von Globalisierung und Nationalstaat* (Wiesbaden, 2003), pp. 8–32; Michael Bommes, "Der Mythos des transnationalen Raumes: Oder: Worin besteht die Herausforderung des Transnationalismus für die Migrationsforschung?", in *ibid*, pp. 90–116; Martin Geiger, *Europäische Migrationspolitik und Raumproduktion* (Baden-Baden, 2011).

into matters of international politics and international law. Although treaties to regulate migration had spread throughout the world during the nineteenth century, they were concerned mostly with processes of immigration and settlement.[4] It was only after World War I that governments started to draw up agreements jointly to organize and regulate the temporary transfer of labour between their territories.

Moreover, attempts dating back to the late nineteenth century by a wide circle of actors, including trade unions, internationalists and their societies, socialist movements, and even some governments, to establish internationally recognized social rights and labour standards for workers, including migrants, bore fruit when the International Labour Organization (ILO) was founded in 1919. The new agency immediately began to formulate standards for temporary labour migration. The dissemination of a set of norms to be observed in the regulation of migration combined with an instrument binding governments to those standards through international law – bilateral migration agreements – fundamentally changed the relation of the state towards temporary labour migration. That, therefore, raises questions about the internationalization of migration politics and challenges the so far little-disputed predominance of the nation state and national politics in migration matters throughout the twentieth century.[5]

Bilateral labour agreements, also known as recruitment as well as migration agreements or treaties, have themselves long played only a marginal role in historical migration research.[6] Lately, however, interest in them has been growing and they have been discussed from a variety of different angles.[7] Some authors argue, somewhat strangely, that their

4. Madeleine Herren, *Internationale Sozialpolitik vor dem Ersten Weltkrieg: Die Anfänge europäischer Kooperation aus der Sicht Frankreichs* (Berlin, 1993).

5. Paul-André Rosental, "Gibt es nationale Migrationspolitik? Über einige Lehren aus den zwanziger Jahren", in Steffen Kaudelka, Thomas Serrier, and Rudolf von Thadden (eds), *Europa der Zugehörigkeiten: Integrationswege zwischen Ein- und Auswanderung* (Göttingen, 2007), pp. 69–78, 74; Christoph Rass, "Private und staatliche Anwerbung: Frankreich und Deutschland zwischen den Weltkriegen", in Dittmar Dahlmann (ed.), *Perspektiven in der Fremde? Arbeitsmarkt und Migration von der Frühen Neuzeit bis in die Gegenwart* (Essen, 2011), pp. 259–287.

6. See for instance Maurice Flory, "Accords de main-d'oeuvre et modèle de développement", in Centre de recherches et d'études sur les soc. Méditerranéennes (ed.), *Rapports de dépendance au Maghreb* (Paris, 1976), pp. 263–277; Michel Vincineau, *Les traités bilatéraux relatifs à l'emploi et au séjour en Belgique des travailleurs immigrés* (Brussels, 1984); Erich Noher, *Die internationalen Verträge über die Aus- und Einwanderung* (Affoltern am Albis, 1937); OECD (ed.), *Migration for Employment: Bilateral Agreements at a Crossroads* (Paris, 2004).

7. Janine Ponty, *Polonais méconnus: Histoire des travailleurs immigrés en France dans l'entre-deux-guerre* (Paris, 1988); Karin Hunn, *"Nächstes Jahr kehren wir zurück ...": Die Geschichte der türkischen "Gastarbeiter" in der Bundesrepublik* (Göttingen, 2005); Barbara Sonnenberger, *Nationale Migrationspolitik und regionale Erfahrung: Die Anfänge der Arbeitsmigration in Südhessen (1955–1967)* (Darmstadt, 2003); Carlos Sanz Díaz, *"Illegale", "Halblegale", "Gastarbeiter"*.

application was motivated exclusively by foreign policy and diplomatic strategies.[8] Other researchers, while acknowledging their importance in defending claims of state sovereignty over migration processes,[9] make a case for their limited economic and political effect in comparison with the significance of migration itself as a potent social and political factor.[10] In contrast, the function of such agreements as stepping stones on the road to internationalization and multinational institutions has been under-scored,[11] as has the significant contribution, if not pivotal role, of bilateral agreements in the establishment of transnational social rights and the protection of labour migrants.[12] Finally, the importance has been pointed out of analysing such institutions from above the national or bilateral level in order to appreciate network effects within multipolar structures made up of bilateral links, to unearth their full impact.[13] That approach draws on the belief that networks play a significant role at a meso level between traditional approaches in international relations research, which conceptualize links between sovereign nation states in hierarchical or anarchical models, and suggests reassessing the state as an actor within that frame of reference.[14]

This article therefore examines modern labour migration to continental western Europe from the time of World War I until the 1970s, and will consider the position of the state as an actor in an international labour

*Die irreguläre Migration aus Spanien in die Bundesrepublik Deutschland im Kontext der deutsch-spanischen Beziehungen 1960–1973* (Berlin, 2010); Stefanie Mayer and Mikael Spång (eds), *Debating Migration: Political Discourses on Labor Immigration in Historical Perspective* (Vienna, 2009); Paul-André Rosental, "Migrations, souveraineté, droits sociaux. Protéger et expulser les étrangers en Europe du XIXe siècle á nos jours", *Annales*, 66 (2011), pp. 375–412; Christoph Rass, *Institutionalisierungsprozesse auf einem internationalen Arbeitsmarkt: Bilaterale Wanderungsverträge in Europa 1919–1974* (Paderborn, 2010).

8. Heike Knortz, *Diplomatische Tauschgeschäfte. "Gastarbeiter" in der westdeutschen Diplomatie und Beschäftigungspolitik 1953–1973* (Cologne, 2008).

9. Hélène Thiollet, "Migrations et relations internationales: Les apories de la gestion multilatérale des migrations internationales?", *Transcontinentales*, 8/9 (2010), available at http://transcontinentales.revues.org/787; last accessed 20 March 2012.

10. *Idem*, "Migration as Diplomacy: Labor Migrants, Refugees and Arab Regional Politics in the Oil-Rich Countries", *International Labor and Working-Class History*, 79 (2011), pp. 103–121.

11. Herren, *Internationale Sozialpolitik vor dem Ersten Weltkrieg*.

12. Rosental, "Migrations, souveraineté, droits sociaux".

13. Christoph Rass, "Bilaterale Wanderungsabkommen und die Entwicklung eines internationalen Arbeitsmarktes in Europa 1919-1974", *Geschichte und Gesellschaft*, 35 (2009), pp. 98–134.

14. Barry Buzan and Richard Little, *International Systems in World History: Remaking the Study of International Relations* (Oxford, 2000); Thomas Cayet, Paul-André Rosental, and Marie Thébaud-Sorger, "How International Organisations Compete: Occupational Safety and Health at the ILO, a Diplomacy of Expertise", *Journal of Modern European History*, 7 (2009), pp. 174–194, 192.

market. We shall examine the attempt by European states to extricate themselves from a complex dilemma: faced with their demographic situations, changes in economic as well as social structure, and the advent of what has been called the Fordist system of production and organized labour, none of the leading economies of western Europe was able to sustain economic growth without the inward migration of labour during most of the twentieth century.[15]

While labour mobility *between* European economies tended to shrink, continental western Europe had had to accept labour immigration from its southern and eastern periphery from the late nineteenth century onward, while trying to exclude labour immigration from territories outside Europe and from colonial possessions before they had been decolonized. When France departed from that model during and after World War I, it set up strict mechanisms to regulate migration flows from its possessions in north Africa to control the presence of north African labour migrants in the metropolis.[16] That introduced practices for regulating labour movements which had developed in a colonial context to continental Europe, and crudely shaped a model which, although modified, would be widely adopted to regulate international labour migration during the interwar period.

The increase in state involvement in the management of migration was driven as well by protectionist policies towards wages, working conditions, and the social rights of the domestic workforce, and by the conflict between national social security policies and highly mobile foreign workers. The European answer – brewed from those ingredients – took up the idea of state-regulated temporary labour migration based on bilateral agreements inspired not least by various colonial examples and French practice during World War I.[17] Selective recruitment, the temporary character of labour migration, and the principle of equal treatment of foreign and domestic workers emerged as key elements in correspondence with the ideas of the International Labour Organization, which stated an improvement in the situation of international labour migrants as one of its central aims. The result was an internationally rooted and commonly practised European model of regulated temporary labour migration which promised to solve the key problem of combining protectionism with labour migration while avoiding permanent settlement and immigration. The migration regime to govern the system gained

15. Russell King, "From Guestworkers to Immigrants: Labour Migration From the Mediterranean Periphery", in David Pinder (ed.), *The New Europe: Economy, Society & Environment* (Chichester, 1998), pp. 263–280.
16. Gary S. Cross, *Immigrant Workers in Industrial France: The Making of a New Laboring Class* (Philadelphia, PA, 1983), pp. 35ff.
17. Rass, "Bilaterale Wanderungsabkommen", pp. 82ff. and 348–352.

firmer shape during the interwar years and achieved its greatest momentum between the late 1940s and early 1970s.

While its links to colonial experience are obvious, the European model, which introduced state regulation and control while embracing the ILO's attempts to establish improved conditions for migrant workers through equal treatment and assisted migration, was not intended to be generalized beyond the European context. Though a good deal of regulated and temporary extra-European labour migration before World War II took place within the colonial context,[18] none of the European colonial powers was in the least interested in disseminating the practices developed in Europe to their colonial labour markets. The ILO consequently achieved little in that respect during the interwar years, and it took that organization until well into the 1960s to trigger changes in standards for labour migration beyond Europe.[19]

To analyse how and why the states of Europe became involved in labour migration at an international level during the twentieth century, this article employs a dual model: it will discuss the development of bilateral recruitment agreements as an institution, and their spread as an instrument. Governments acting at a multilateral level in international migration politics will be observed as they created a framework for the governance of labour migration. A look at specific exemplary migration relations based on bilateral recruitment treaties will show what practices ensued between states and how they shaped migration processes. Also, variations in the direct involvement of the state in the international labour market need to be discussed. Finally, interdependencies in the evolution of internationally recognized standards, a system of bilateral treaties, and the state will all be traced in search of their influence on the shape of international labour migration between the 1920s and the 1970s.

## THE SYSTEM OF LABOUR MIGRATION IN TWENTIETH-CENTURY EUROPE

To limit the scope of the migration currents and interconnections to be taken into account, currents of labour migration will be considered which meet four criteria. Firstly, migration movements have to be sparked by

18. Dirk Hoerder, *Cultures in Contact: World Migrations in the Second Millennium* (Durham, NC, 2002), chs 15–17.
19. See Roger Böhning, "A Brief Account of the ILO and Policies on International Migration", in *ILO Century Project* (Geneva, 2008), p. 3, available at: http://www.ilo.org/public/english/century/information_resources/download/bohning.pdf (last accessed 8 December 2011); Oksana Wolfson, Lisa Tortell, and Catarina Pimenta, "Colonialism, Forced Labour and the International Labour Organization: Portugal and the First ILO Commission of Inquiry", in *ibid.*, pp. 6ff., available at: http://www.ilo.org/public/english/century/information_resources/download/wolfson.pdf (last accessed 20 March 2012).

industrialization or demand originating directly or indirectly in the secondary or tertiary sectors of an economy. In turn, the supply of migrant labour has to stem from backwardness in such a process. Secondly, population movements between peripheral and central zones must predominantly be intended as temporary migration. Thirdly, migration patterns have to be increasingly regulated by an institutional framework, and the fourth criterion will be that the overall migration process has a profound effect on the economies and societies of both the sending and the receiving countries. Given all that, an appropriate point of departure will be a chronological look at the migration system constituted by qualified currents of labour migration starting in the late nineteenth century.[20]

Following that compass, five major movements of transnational labour migration can be identified within western Europe prior to World War I. Emigrants from Italy started to gravitate towards some of the major economies of continental Europe, namely France, Belgium, Switzerland, Luxembourg, and Germany.[21] In addition, Germany saw a steady influx of labour migrants also from those parts of Poland which had been annexed by Russia and Austria.[22] The north African territories of France – Algeria, Morocco, and Tunisia – were attached to the system during World War I,[23] and Spain and Portugal developed ties to the labour markets of central Europe at the same time.[24] The interwar years saw the restoration of the Polish state and its incorporation into the international labour market, while newly founded countries and those which gained independence at the time, such as Hungary, Yugoslavia, Romania, and Czechoslovakia, became significant sources of labour for various European economies, before the Cold War excised them from the system after 1945. Among the countries of eastern Europe, Yugoslavia alone managed to revive its labour-market relations with the West in the postwar era.[25]

---

20. Rass, "Bilaterale Wanderungsabkommen", p. 13. For the purpose of this study, Belgium, Germany, France, Luxembourg, The Netherlands, Austria, Sweden, and Switzerland will be discussed as countries of immigration; Algeria, Greece, Italy, Yugoslavia, Morocco, Poland, Portugal, Spain, Turkey, and Tunisia will be discussed as countries of emigration.

21. Antonio Golini and Anna Maria Birindelli, "Italy", in Serow *et al.*, *Handbook on International Migration*, pp. 143–165.

22. Klaus J. Bade, *Migration in European History* (Oxford, 2003), *passim*.

23. Labri Talha (ed.), *Maghrébins en France: Emigrés ou immigrés* (Paris, 1983).

24. Joao Antonio Alpalhao and Victor Pereira Da Rosa, "L'émigration portugaise: Réflexion sur les causes et les conséquences", *International Migration*, 17 (1979), pp. 290–296.

25. Georges Als, "Le Luxembourg et ses étrangers", in Pierre Werner (ed.), *Innovation – Intégration* (Luxembourg, 1993), pp. 485–492; Hans-Joachim Hoffmann-Nowotny, "Switzerland", in Tomas Hammar (ed.), *European Immigration Policy: A Comparative Study* (Cambridge, 1985), pp. 206–238; Gérard Noiriel, *The French Melting Pot: Immigration, Citizenship, and National Identity* (Minneapolis, MN, 1996); Jochen Oltmer, *Migration und Politik in der Weimarer Republik* (Göttingen, 2005); Jean Stengers, *Emigration et immigration en Belgique au XIXe et au XXe siècle* (Brussels, 1978); Ivan Cizmic, "Emigration from Yugoslavia Prior to World War II", in Ira A.

The international labour market was disrupted by Germany through
the occupation of many European countries and their incorporation into
the German system of slave, forced, or otherwise recruited labour as part
of the German war economy between 1939 and 1945, but the market's
reconstruction started as soon as World War II ended.[26] Traditional
migration patterns, such as those between France and Italy, or Belgium
and Italy, were the first to thrive again, but in subsequent decades Sweden,
Austria, and the Netherlands joined the system on the demand side,
although their intra-European labour market relations have earlier roots,
namely in the interwar period.[27] On the other hand, Greece and Turkey
were newly integrated as fresh suppliers of labour migrants only during
the 1950s and 1960s.[28] The western European system of labour migration
reached its highest density and largest size during the late 1960s, with
migration currents peaking between 1967 and 1972.[29]

## THE STATE AND BILATERAL LABOUR AGREEMENTS

### Bilateral agreements regulating temporary labour migration

While the number of countries interconnected by currents of labour
migration expanded steadily, a specific form of bilateral agreement gained
growing importance as a means to regulate the flow of labour between
countries within the system.[30] The idea of bilaterally fixing terms to frame

Glazier and Luigi De Rosa (eds), *Migration Across Time and Nations: Population Mobility in
Historical Contexts* (New York, 1986), pp. 255–270; Idesbald Goddeeris, *De Poolse migratie in
België, 1945–1950: Politieke mobilisatie en sociale differentiatie* (Amsterdam, 2005); Carl-Ulrik
Schierup, *Migration, Socialism, and the International Division of Labour: The Yugoslavian
Experience* (Aldershot, 1990).
26. Mark Spoerer, *Zwangsarbeit unter dem Hakenkreuz: Ausländische Zivilarbeiter, Kriegs-
gefangene und Häftlinge im Deutschen Reich und im besetzten Europa 1939–1945* (Stuttgart,
2001); Ulrich Herbert, *Fremdarbeiter: Politik und Praxis des "Ausländer-Einsatzes" in der
Kriegswirtschaft des Dritten Reiches* (Bonn, 1999).
27. H. ter Heide, "Labour Migration from the Mediterranean Area to the Benelux Countries",
in Hein G. Moors (ed.), *Population and Family in the Low Countries* (Leiden, 1976), pp.
132–148; B. Cornelis, "Migratie naar Nederland", in Han B. Entzinger and P.J.J. Stijnen (eds),
*Etnische minderheden in Nederland* (Heerlen, 1990), pp. 9–30; Heinz Fassmann and Rainer
Münz, *Einwanderungsland Österreich? Historische Migrationsmuster, aktuelle Trends und
politische Maßnahmen* (Vienna, 1995); Tomas Hammar, "Sweden", in *idem, European Immigration Policy*, pp. 17–49.
28. Demetrios Papademetriou, "Greece", in Ronald E. Krane (ed.), *International Labor
Migration in Europe* (New York, 1979), pp. 187–200; Ayfur Barışı Ayda Eraydin, and Ayse
Gedik, "Turkey", in Serow *et al.*, *Handbook on International Migration*, pp. 301–323.
29. Fielding, "Mass Migration and Economic Restructuring", pp. 7–18, 10; Klaus J. Bade *et al.*
(eds), *Enzyklopädie Migration in Europa* (Paderborn, 2007), *passim*.
30. Frank Caestecker, "The Changing Modalities of Regulation in International Migration within
Continental Europe", in Anita Böcker *et al.* (eds), *Regulation of Migration: International*

settlement migration between states by using conventions or treaties had proliferated throughout the nineteenth century. In 1904, France and Italy concluded the first of a series of agreements aimed at establishing certain standards, procedures, and protocols in the context of modern labour migration and its consequences for the transfer of funds or claims against national social security systems.[31] This treaty heralded a new era of bilateral migration agreements, although its form and coverage were not as far-reaching as the agreements that would follow during the interwar years. Nonetheless, it clearly reflected the ideas of social reformers who were trying to protect both migrant workers from exploitation, and domestic workers from the erosion of their social rights which would tend to be the result of the availability of a cheaper and less well protected labour force of foreign, immigrant, workers.[32] The treaty and its successors must be seen also as early attempts by the emerging welfare state to factor international migration into national social security schemes. To arrive at what would finally become the modern bilateral agreement on labour migration after World War I, two more ingredients were required: the regulation of labour transfer between colonial empires through bilateral agreements,[33] and the experience of organizing an external labour supply under conditions of total war, which arose between 1914 and 1918.[34]

A new model for bilateral labour migration agreements finally began to appear across Europe in the 1920s. Now, European states began to intervene thoroughly in regulated labour migration in peacetime, and

*Experiences* (Amsterdam, 1998), pp. 73–98, 79; Thomas Schindlmayr, "Sovereignty, Legal Regimes, and International Migration", *International Migration*, 41 (2003), pp. 109–123.

31. "Accord relatif aux transferts de fonds entre la Caisse d'épargne française et la Caisse d'épargne postale italienne, 15 April 1904", in Clive Parry (ed.), *The Consolidated Treaty Series*, 231 vols (Dobbs Ferry, NY, 1980), 195, pp. 229ff.

32. Dick Geary, "Labour in Western Europe from *c*.1800", in Jan Lucassen (ed.), *Global Labour History: A State of the Art* (Berne, 2006), pp. 227–287; Leo Lucassen, "The Great War and the Origins of Migration Control in Western Europe and the United States", in Böcker *et al.*, *Regulation of Migration*, pp. 45–72, 47ff.; Gertrud Gandenberger, *Die Internationale Arbeitsorganisation: Wirkungen der Normensetzung und Normenkontrolle am Fallbeispiel der Bundesrepublik Deutschland* (Heidelberg, 1996), p. 6; Ulrich Herbert, *Geschichte der Ausländerpolitik in Deutschland: Saisonarbeiter, Zwangsarbeiter, Gastarbeiter, Flüchtlinge* (Munich, 2001), pp. 65ff.; Eva Senghaas-Knobloch *et al.*, *Internationale Arbeitsregulierung in Zeiten der Globalisierung: Politisch-organisatorisches Lernen in der Internationalen Arbeitsorganisation (IAO)* (Münster, 2003), p. 7.

33. International Labour Office, *Migration Laws and Treaties*, 3 vols (Geneva, 1928–1929), I, pp. 263, 265.

34. Lucassen, "Great War and Origins of Migration Control", p. 56; Leslie Page Moch, *Moving Europeans: Migration in Western Europe since 1650* (Bloomington, IN, 1992), pp. 165ff.; Cross, *Immigrant Workers in Industrial France*, p. 34; Bertrand Nogaro and Lucien Weil, *La main-d'oeuvre étrangère et coloniale pendant la guerre* (Paris, 1926), pp. 7ff.

France again took the lead in developing and propagating the new institution.[35] The labour agreement concluded between France and Poland in
1919 can be rated as the first of this new generation of treaties. It became
an internationally accepted standard and provided the nucleus for the
subsequent spread of the institution, its main innovation being its regulative
range and clear structure. In addition to conditions for the admission as well
as the residence of foreign workers and some basic labour standards, the
treaty created protocols for the administration of the recruitment and
transfer of migrants between labour markets. The agreement in fact set up a
new migration channel[36] alongside spontaneous individual migration: the
recruitment of foreign labour, organized or at least regulated by the state,
combined with a dual selection of candidates by the representatives or
authorized agents of both governments involved.[37] In fact, access to the new
migration channel was withdrawn from individual choice and put instead
under state control, direct or indirect.

Furthermore, the process of balancing the demand and supply of labour
power was transferred to the labour markets of the countries which were
providing migrant workers, because selection according to demand was now
executed before the actual migration process began. Along with such far-
reaching means of controlling economically motivated migration, the principle of equal treatment of foreign and domestic workers was anchored and
codified, so that, at least notionally, Polish migrants could expect the same
labour standards as their French co-workers.[38] The increase in control seemed
to work both ways, as stricter rules for immigration meant more reliable –
and at times indeed improved – conditions of work and residence abroad.[39]

### From early treaties to international standards for regulated labour migration

The formation of this new institution can be traced on two levels. In the
multilateral sphere, the International Labour Organization became an important platform on which standards were negotiated, formulated, and promoted
between representatives of member states, trade unions, and employer
associations,[40] even if the actual adoption of those standards remained at

35. "Convention entre la France et la Pologne relative à l'émigration et l'immigration, 7 September
1919", *Legislative Series*, 1 (1920).
36. Allan M. Findlay, "A Migration Channels Approach to the Study of High Level Manpower
Movements: A Theoretical Perspective", *International Migration*, 28 (1990), pp. 15–23, 15ff.
37. Rass, *Institutionalisierungsprozesse auf einem internationalen Arbeitsmarkt*, pp. 298–300.
38. Rosental, "Migrations, souveraineté, droits sociaux".
39. Ponty, *Polonais méconnus*.
40. Martin Senti, *Internationale Regime und nationale Politik: Die Effektivität der Internationalen Arbeitsorganisation (ILO) im Industrieländervergleich* (Berne, 2002), p. 11; George
Foggon, "The Origin and Development of the ILO and International Labour Organisations",

the discretion of each national government. On the second level, the diffusion of labour standards for migrant workers through bilateral agreements can be observed as it actually happened. The core countries of the European migration system concluded thirteen bilateral labour agreements between 1919 and 1934, and a further eleven treaties expanded the system temporarily towards eastern Europe prior to World War II.[41] Even Nazi Germany stuck with the common form of labour agreement in an attempt to create some sort of normality within its sphere of influence while installing a system of forced and slave labour: between 1937 and 1943 it signed a total of sixteen labour treaties with allied states or territories.[42] After 1945 about forty primary and subsequent labour treaties which closely followed the model created by the ILO during the interwar years can be counted within the system, which therefore established firm pathways for labour migration.

When the ILO started to become an effective actor on the international stage in 1919, just weeks after Poland and France had signed their groundbreaking agreement, an organization had been created which for the first time united the three major actors in modern labour markets: state, trade unions, and employer associations.[43] Activities of the ILO concerning international labour migration can be traced right back to the beginning of its operations.[44] To that end a special commission was set up to investigate the conditions of international migration with respect to standards for migration processes.

The report it presented in 1921 lists the main areas of maltreatment or discrimination of migrants in general and labour migrants in particular. It reads like a plea for a general reform and regulation of migration policies and procedures.[45] Indeed, many of the early ILO recommendations – for

in Paul Taylor and A.J.R. Groom (eds), *International Institutions at Work* (New York, 1988), pp. 98–113, 100ff.; Rosental, "Gibt es nationale Migrationspolitik?", p. 77.

41. A register of bilateral labour agreements concluded in Europe between 1919 and 1973 can be found in Rass, *Institutionalisierungsprozesse auf einem internationalen Arbeitsmarkt*, p. 492.

42. *Idem*, "Staatsverträge und 'Gastarbeiter' im Migrationsregime des 'Dritten Reiches'. Motive, Intentionen und Kontinuitäten", in Jochen Oltmer (ed.), *Nationalsozialistisches Migrationsregime und "Volksgemeinschaft"* (Paderborn, 2012), pp. 154–189.

43. Jean-Michel Bonvin, *L'Organisation Internationale du Travail. Etude sur une agence productrice de norms* (Paris, 1998); Michael Wollenschläger, "Die Internationale Arbeitsorganisation (IAO): Entstehen, Entwicklung und Bedeutung für den Schutz der Wanderarbeitnehmer", in Hugo J. Hahn and Albrecht Weber (eds), *Währung und Wirtschaft: Das Geld im Recht* (Baden-Baden, 1997), pp. 573–590; Elspeth Guild, "Who is Entitled to Work and Who is in Charge: Understanding the Legal Framework of European Labour Migration", in Didier Bigo and Elspeth Guild (eds), *Controlling Frontiers: Free Movement into and within Europe* (Aldershot, 2005), pp. 100–139.

44. Böhning, "Brief Account of the ILO and Policies", pp. 6ff.

45. International Labour Office, *The International Labour Code: Appendices* (Geneva, 1952), p. 284; Paul Fauchille, "The International Emigration Commission", *International Labour Review*, 1 (1921), pp. 527–562.

instance cooperation among the national bureaucracies involved, enhanced control over private agencies, the establishment of fixed protocols for the exchange and distribution of information, the use of standardized employment contracts or government-controlled collective recruitment, and transfer of workers – were eventually to become commonly accepted features of regulated labour migration. The ILO translated its standards into several conventions and recommendations which concerned themselves with labour migration, hoping that a growing number of states would accept them and adjust their national legislation, policies, and administrative practice accordingly.[46] It took the ILO until 1949 to construct a grid of such standards and sum up its efforts in Convention 97 and Recommendation 86. In becoming the blueprint for regulating temporary labour migration, that Convention and Recommendation together constituted a model bilateral migration treaty which was to be used by European countries from the end of World War II until the tailing off of recruitment in the early 1970s.[47]

### Structuring an international labour market

Equally important insights can be gained by reflecting on the international labour market itself as an entity in which one group of economies offered workers, and another group of countries needed additional labour. The result was a network of supply and demand relations that effectively created the migration system. In fact, a growing number of countries entered a transnational labour market either to supply labour or because they were in need of it. Through migration streams and bilateral treaties they became entangled in complex market relations: every country of emigration was connected to several countries of immigration and vice versa, which made countries in the same class competitors either for workers or for jobs.

As international standards negotiated by the ILO proliferated after 1945, it can be assumed that a certain collective pressure built up to include the treatment of labour migrants in the formation of general labour standards. First, common international standards, especially on equal treatment, helped to protect advanced national labour standards, such as sophisticated social security systems or collectively negotiated wages. Failure to comply in effect led either to a loss of competitiveness or an erosion of national standards. Second, the amelioration of labour standards for migrants was important in defining one's position on the international labour market as a bidder for labour power. Hence a clear trend can be observed from before World War II and again after it,

46. Wollenschläger, "Die Internationale Arbeitsorganisation (IAO)", pp. 58off.
47. Rass, *Institutionalisierungsprozesse auf einem internationalen Arbeitsmarkt*, pp. 309–332.

indicating that countries entering the system of bilateral labour treaties tended to adopt the ILO's ideas at least partially, or orientated themselves towards the French model. Even Germany, which initially used different forms of bilateral agreement in the 1920s, showed signs of converging with what was to become the mainstream.[48] None of that implies a total concordance of agreements, rather a convergence of structure and content but with some room for manoeuvre, which gradually led to a wider adoption of certain standards, with every new treaty of the kind making further dissemination more likely.[49]

France, for instance, used the model treaty worked out with Poland to regulate many of its other international labour market relations in the 1920s and 1930s. Countries that concluded such agreements with France, in turn, used the set of conditions put in place by France as the basis for labour market relations with other countries. That pattern became even more noticeable after 1945. In composition and range, most European labour recruitment agreements followed the ILO model more or less strictly. Treaties became more similar in their overall makeup, but discrepancies in detail remained. Beside the macro trend of slow convergence, a third force must be taken into account, which could generate rapid progress in standards in certain sectors of the migration system. That force gathered strength whenever rivalry between the most powerful players became acute: sometimes economies competed for foreign labour on the international labour market, or more precisely for labour from a particular labour market within the system of bilateral migratory links.

Such competitive pressure on a contested labour market where many recruiting countries looked for labour migrants could induce structural changes to the migration system, as indicated by its expansion through the inclusion of Turkey in 1961,[50] or the German turn towards recruitment in Greece in 1960 and its acquisition of a dominant position there.[51] Yet most importantly, a third kind of reaction can be identified in the improved competitiveness brought about by improvements in conditions for labour migration and in labour standards through new or modified migration agreements. Each of those decisions had to be made in the political realm, negotiated at the international level as well as codified by bilateral agreements and – at least in part – implemented by one key actor: the state.

---

48. Jochen Oltmer, *Migration und Politik*.
49. Rass, *Institutionalisierungsprozesse auf einem internationalen Arbeitsmarkt*.
50. Ahmet Akgündüz, *Labour Migration from Turkey to Western Europe, 1960–1974: A Multidisciplinary Analysis* (Aldershot, 2008).
51. Johannes-Dieter Steinert, *Migration und Politik: Westdeutschland – Europa – Übersee 1945–1961* (Osnabrück, 1995).

## THE STATE ON THE INTERNATIONAL LABOUR MARKET

*On the ground: actors, procedures, and migrant experiences*

While we have so far concentrated on the international level and international law, it is also important to discuss the practices of regulated migration which resulted from the changing role beginning to be assumed by governments and their agencies. Though this section will focus on labour-receiving countries, the state agencies of labour-exporting countries will be considered as partners, in order to demonstrate how states with a common macro interest in the transfer of labour but differing micro interests interacted.

A model of state involvement derived from the study of practices at the national and international level both before and after the disruption of 1939–1945 reveals government intervention in all phases of regulated labour migration. In labour-receiving countries the state often collected employers' requests for foreign workers centrally in order to try to match demand first through interregional, but internal, migration. They could then determine whether the immigration of foreign workers was economically feasible and subsequently approve the recruitment of required contingents of migrant workers.[52]

Bilateral treaties then obliged governments to carry out recruitment procedures themselves or authorize private or semi-private agencies to do so, and to monitor their operations closely. Such procedures, which were carried out in liaison with partner organizations from the labour-sending side, included dispatching recruitment commissions, medically examining potential migrant workers en masse, as well as testing their professional qualifications to determine their aptitude. Selected candidates were usually transported together by train from central recruitment centres to distribution points in the receiving country and from there taken to their future employers. Once in their place of destination, the conventional mechanisms to control the presence and mobility of foreigners usually took over.

That level of involvement fundamentally changed the position of the state or, in other words, altered its migration regime. To the state, controlling migration was no longer limited to keeping foreigners out nor to controlling their movements or even presence, but also about getting the right ones in, in certain numbers at a certain time and for certain periods. Moreover, recruiting those migrant workers could become a competitive business which involved much more than opening or closing the gates.[53]

52. Rass, *Institutionalisierungsprozesse auf einem internationalen Arbeitsmarkt*, pp. 85ff.
53. *Ibid.*, pp. 295ff.

Fig. 1. The Spanish Ambassador Marqués de Bolarque and State Secretary Van Scherpenberg of the German Foreign Office sign the recruitment agreement between Spain and Germany, Bonn, 29 March 1960.
*Photograph: Rolf Unterberg. Bundesarchiv Bildarchiv, Berlin. Used with permission.*

Within Europe, the presence of government-run as well as private or semi-private but government-licensed recruitment agencies on the labour markets of emigration countries can be traced back to the early twentieth century. Prussia, for instance, had set up the Deutsche Feldarbeiterzentrale, which worked under the auspices of the Chambers of Agriculture and the Prussian Ministry for Agriculture from 1905 to hire agricultural workers from eastern Europe.[54] A semi-official organization, it managed labour recruitment throughout World War I and during the interwar years before the state-run labour administration, which had come into being in

54. Bade *et al.*, *Enzyklopädie Migration in Europa*, p. 475.

1927, took over recruitment operations directly in 1935.[55] Labour recruitment by the state labour administration became an integral part of the Nazi system of forced labour during World War II.[56] In the 1950s the agency (by then the Bundesanstalt für Arbeitsvermittlung und Arbeitslosenversicherung) managed to reclaim its monopoly of labour recruitment abroad when Germany returned to the international labour market and organized recruitment campaigns in almost every country with which Germany concluded bilateral labour agreements.[57]

Other countries went down a similar path. During World War I, France, for instance, had set up government-run recruitment services as well as licensing private organizations to attract workers from Spain as well as other allied countries, and from its overseas territories.[58] Nonetheless, when France started to build up a vast network of bilateral migration agreements in the 1920s to provide an adequate labour supply for postwar reconstruction, recruitment operations abroad were passed into the hands of a private company, the Société générale d'immigration, established by employer associations in 1924. Only those parts of the migration process which had to be managed within French territory were kept under direct state control.[59]

Although the idea of creating a national Office public d'immigration gained popularity during the 1930s, it took until after World War II before a government agency gained control over the management of all stages of the migration process, when the Office national d'immigration (ONI) came into being in 1946.[60] The French government insisted on setting up offices in most of the European countries with which it had concluded bilateral treaties, but the ONI proved so bureaucratic and inefficient that private recruitment and

55. Christian Westerhoff, *Zwangsarbeit im Ersten Weltkrieg. Deutsche Arbeitskräftepolitik im besetzten Polen und Litauen 1914–1918* (Paderborn, 2012), pp. 87–120; Oltmer, *Migration und Politik*, pp. 448ff.

56. Volker Herrmann, *Vom Arbeitsmarkt zum Arbeitseinsatz: Zur Geschichte der Reichsanstalt für Arbeitsvermittlung und Arbeitslosenversicherung 1929 bis 1939* (Frankfurt, 1993), pp. 129ff.

57. Rass, *Institutionalisierungsprozesse auf einem internationalen Arbeitsmarkt*, pp. 74ff.

58. Pierre Sicsic, "Foreign Immigration and the French Labour Force, 1896–1926", in Timothy J. Hatton and Jeffrey G. Williamson (eds), *Migration and the International Labor Market, 1850–1939* (London, 1994), pp. 119–138, 136; Cross, *Immigrant Workers in Industrial France*, pp. 27ff.; Marie Christine Volovitch-Tavarès, "Les phases de l'immigration portugaise, des années vingt aux années soixante-dix", *Actes de l'histoire de l'immigration*, 1 (2001), p. 2, available at http://barthes.ens.fr/clio/revues/AHI/articles/volumes/volovitch.html (last accessed 20 March 2012); Vincent Viet, *La France immigrée: Construction d'une politique, 1914–1997* (Paris, 1998), p. 34.

59. Marianne Amar and Pierre Milza, *L'immigration en France au XXe siècle* (Paris, 1990), pp. 289ff.; Jeffrey M. Togman, *The Ramparts of Nations: Institutions and Immigration Policies in France and the United States* (New York, 2002), p. 83.

60. Don Dignan, "Europe's Melting Pot: A Century of Large-Scale Immigration into France", *Ethnic and Racial Studies*, 4 (1981), pp. 137–152, 145.

individual immigration soon became commonly accepted. In fact, it was even promoted by the French government through its liberal practice of regularizing irregular migrants after they had found jobs.[61]

In contrast to France and Germany, smaller countries too among the labour-receiving economies of Europe experienced growing involvement of the state after World War II, but they relied on private or semi-private organizations to recruit workers abroad. Belgium, which initially needed foreign workers predominantly for its mining industries, relied on the Fédération des Associations Charbonnières, an association of mining companies, during almost the entire period. The federation had started to recruit workers privately in Italy in 1922–1923 and soon became the agency authorized by the Belgian government to conduct recruitment operations abroad, which it carried on doing until the early 1970s.[62] Luxembourg for its part tried to switch recruitment operations from the private sector to a government agency after World War II, and sent a recruitment commission from its national labour administration to Italy, though it soon returned to allowing private-sector recruitment within the framework of bilateral agreements, because the intended process of state-run recruitment proved too slow to fulfil employers' requests for foreign workers.[63] Similarly, the Netherlands used a mixed system of labour recruitment through official posts and private-sector agencies in various countries when it built up its network of bilateral agreements during the 1960s.[64] Other attempts to increase direct government involvement in the recruitment process eventually leading to heavy reliance on monitored private-sector recruitment can be discovered in Austria,[65] Sweden,[66] and Switzerland.[67]

61. Togman, *The Ramparts of Nations*, p. 93.
62. Anne Morelli, "L'immigration italienne en Belgique aux XIXe et XXe siècles", in *idem* (ed.), *Histoire des étrangers et de l'immigration en Belgique de la préhistoire à nos jours* (Brussels, 1992), pp. 195–206, 197; Frank Caestecker, *Alien Policy in Belgium, 1840–1940: The Creation of Guest Workers, Refugees and Illegal Aliens* (New York, 2000), pp. 60ff.
63. Marcel Barnich, "Les débuts du Service de l'immigration", in Michel Pauly (ed.), *Letzebuerg de Letzebuerger? Le Luxembourg face à l'immigration* (Luxembourg-Bonnevoie, 1985), p. 80; Nadia Piazza, *Accueil et intégration des immigrés italiens au Luxembourg de 1945 à la création du Service de l'Immigration en 1964* (Luxembourg, 2002), p. 33.
64. Frank Bovenkerk, "The Netherlands", in Krane, *International Labor Migration in Europe*, pp. 118–132, 126.
65. Christof Parnreiter, *Migration und Arbeitsteilung: AusländerInnenbeschäftigung in der Weltwirtschaftskrise* (Vienna, 1994), pp. 117ff.
66. Tommy Bengtsson, C. Lundh, and K. Scott, "From Boom to Bust: The Economic Integration of Immigrants in Post War Sweden", in Klaus F. Zimmermann (ed.), *European Migration: What Do We Know?* (Oxford, 2005), pp. 15–58.
67. Marc Perrenoud, "La politique de la Suisse face à l'immigration italienne (1943–1953)", in Michel Dumoulin (ed.), *Mouvements et politiques migratoires en Europe depuis 1945: Le cas italien* (Brussels, 1989), pp. 113–141, 121ff.

Such observations can be put into perspective with regard to the strategic purpose of government-run recruitment and regulation of migration between two countries. Generally speaking, four types of migration channels[68] can be distinguished, between two labour markets, which relate to large-scale migration of low-skilled workers in the European context. The first is direct recruitment of workers specified only by certain characteristics such as age, sex, health, and qualifications. The second is the individual recruitment of persons known by name to recruitment agencies or employers. A third channel encompasses the unassisted individual migration of workers who have already found a job abroad or are allowed to search for one during a fixed period. Fourthly, irregular migration with subsequent illegal presence and employment, or its regularization, constitutes a specific migration channel as well.[69]

Most countries tried not only to coordinate migration and/or recruitment from different sources but also to operate migration channels in parallel to cater to their needs for labour market related immigration. Governments intending to encourage labour immigration while maintaining a certain degree of control over it often relied on government-run or government-assisted recruitment to begin with, in order to initiate the process. In case of a lasting demand for migrant workers, more liberal countries often chose to withdraw temporarily from an active role by granting greater leeway to private recruitment as well as to individual migration – regular or irregular – once a migration movement had gained momentum. Countries preferring more restrictive migration policies had the option of maintaining a higher degree of official involvement but had to build up an effective recruitment apparatus in order to meet demand for an external labour supply efficiently. In any case, maintaining an official recruitment operation preserved the opportunity to close or restrict alternative channels quickly, and limit labour migration to direct recruitment as soon as demand began to dwindle. That way, migration currents could be cut off quickly, as happened in 1967 and 1973 in Germany as well as in most other countries of continental western Europe.[70]

All labour-sending countries at the European periphery basically shared similar expectations, namely to export unemployment temporarily, gain foreign currency by remittances as well as qualified re-migrants, and factored those into their economic plans.[71] Some of them had already

68. Findlay, "Migration Channels Approach", pp. 683ff.
69. Monika Mattes, *"Gastarbeiterinnen" in der Bundesrepublik: Anwerbepolitik, Migration und Geschlecht in den 50er bis 70er Jahren* (Frankfurt, 2005), pp. 137ff.
70. Klaus J. Bade and Jochen Oltmer, "Deutschland", in Bade *et al.*, *Enzyklopädie Migration in Europa*, pp. 141–170, 160.
71. Robert Miles, *Capitalism and Unfree Labour: Anomaly or Necessity?* (New York, 1987), p. 150.

been countries of emigration long before temporary labour migration to western Europe became a major current within their emigration movements. Hence, the governments of Italy, Portugal, or Spain could draw on their experience in the management of migration processes and used their emigration services – in some cases long established – to put their migration regimes into action.[72] Other countries, such as Turkey, Greece, and Yugoslavia, which lacked such a background, entrusted their labour administration with the task of guiding the process according to their political, economic, and social objectives.[73]

Given the structure of regulated labour migration set up by bilateral agreements, agencies of emigration countries largely worked on their own territory as they participated in mobilizing and selecting potential migrants. Two main branches of their activities were tied to the international arena, since many of the bilateral agreements allowed officials from labour-sending countries to monitor the treatment of their compatriots working abroad, to set up agencies intended to provide certain social services, and to monitor the migration process. They were intended not only to protect a nation's own citizens but, in many cases, it was hoped that cultural and social links could be kept alive in order to foster labour migration that would turn out to be temporary rather than permanent.[74]

Other than that, the influence of the state became most apparent in the selective mobilization of migrant workers. In Spain, for instance, the Instituto Español de Emigración, founded in 1956, tried to force labour-recruiting countries to concentrate their efforts on Spain's under-developed regions. It went so far as to assign certain territories to the recruitment campaigns of France and Germany, and aimed to restrict all other forms of labour emigration other than official recruitment controlled by both countries involved.[75] The Portuguese Junta da Emigração strove to implement a similar policy of strict control in an attempt to allocate migration opportunities in pursuance of Portugal's own economic and social policies.[76] That certainly implied quite restrictive migration

72. The Spanish case is discussed by Luis M. Calvo Salgado *et al.*, *Historia del Instituto Español de Emigración: La política migratoria exterior de España y el IEE del Franquismo a la Transición* (Madrid, 2009).

73. Akgündüz, *Labour Migration from Turkey to Western Europe*; Ulf Brunnbauer (ed.), *Transnational Societies, Transterritorial Politics: Migrations in the (Post-)Yugoslav Region 19th–21st Century* (Munich, 2009); Theodore P. Lianos, "Greece: Waning of Labor Migration", in Daniel Kubat, *The Politics of Migration Policies. Settlement and Integration – The First World into the 1990s* (New York, 1993), pp. 249–261.

74. Various countries are discussed by Bade *et al.*, *Enzyklopädie Migration in Europa*.

75. Calvo Salgado, *Historia del Instituto Español de Emigración*.

76. Victor Pereira, "La politique d'émigration de l'Estado Novo entre 1958 et 1974", *Cahiers de l'Urmis*, 9 (2004), available at http://urmis.revues.org/document.html?id=31 (last accessed 20 March 2012); Carminda Cavaco, "A Place in the Sun: Return Migration and Rural Change in

Fig. 2. German officials looking down at potential labour migrants gathered in the courtyard of
the German recruitment post in Istanbul, 1972.
*Photograph: Jean Mohr. DomiD Archive, Cologne. Used with permission.*

regimes and forced willing migrants to accept a rather limited set of
choices once they had decided to participate in the official recruitment
schemes.[77] Such attempts to tailor temporary labour migration to fit social
policies and economic planning actually left an imprint on migration
currents which often bore distinct geographical, demographic, and gender
characteristics as far as the origin of migrants was concerned.[78]

Yugoslavia did not establish a designated migration service when it
integrated itself into the western European migration system, but it did
arrange its labour administration to link up with foreign recruiting services.
Probably mindful of German labour recruitment during World War II, it
successfully managed to hold its foreign partners at bay.[79] When a bilateral

Portugal", in King, *Mass Migration in Europe*, pp. 174–194, 176; Michel Poinard, "L'émigration
portugaise de 1960 à 1969", *Revue géographique des Pyrénées et du Sud-Ouest*, 42 (1971),
pp. 293–304, 294ff.; Pierre Guibentif, "Le Portugal face à l'immigration", *Revue européenne de
migrations internationales*, 12 (1996), pp. 121–139, 129.
77. Maria José Fernández Vicente and Victor Pereira, "Les États portugais et espagnols et
l'émigration (1950–1970)", *Actes de l'histoire de l'immigration*, 8 (2008), pp. 21–44.
78. R. Mansell Prothero, "Labor Recruiting Organizations in the Developing World: Introduction", *International Migration Review*, 24 (1990), pp. 221–228.
79. Anna Maria Grünfelder, *Arbeitseinsatz für die Neuordnung Europas: Zivil- und Zwangs-
arbeiterInnen aus Jugoslawien in der "Ostmark" 1938/41–1945* (Vienna, 2010), pp. 234ff.;

labour agreement came into being in 1968, the German recruitment commission was not allowed to work as an independent body but had to be integrated into the Yugoslavian labour administration and was required to transfer control over the recruitment process almost entirely to Yugoslavian hands.[80] Of course, in all three examples many migrants were simply driven into irregular emigration or tried to gain access to alternative migration channels. Such stratagems were even implicitly acknowledged by many labour-sending countries, which recognized that official emigration agencies often worked with a great lack of efficiency and seldom met the intended emigration rates, while anyway the by-passing by emigrants of official recruitment could not be prevented.[81]

Labour-sending countries were therefore effectively obliged to manoeuvre between two extremes. Granting potential migrants liberal access to all principal migration channels maximized the magnitude of migration and thus its relieving effect on their own social problems as well as on the reflux of remittances. The downside of the strategy lay in the uncontrolled drain of qualified workers who, of course, were the most sought after by recruiting agencies from the "other side". In contrast, maintaining a high degree of control by granting access to the recruitment channel only to preselected candidates seemed to prevent undesired emigration but usually drove people into illegal emigration, and could cause countries wishing to import labour to turn towards more liberal partners on the international labour market.[82]

Such observations indicate the significance of relations between state agencies and other actors in labour-sending and labour-receiving countries alike. Designated as partners in the regulation of labour migration by bilateral treaties and charged with monitoring and organizing the process, they shared an overall interest in the temporary transfer of migrant workers, although actually they largely disagreed on whom to admit. As national business cycles in Europe tended to synchronize themselves after World War II, labour-receiving countries looked for foreign workers during economic upswings when the internal demand for workers in the labour-sending countries also began to surge. During downswings, however, when sending countries strove to rely on emigration to relieve their domestic labour markets, receiving countries tried to limit the influx of migrants. By the same token, sending countries were interested in

Holm Sundhaussen, *Wirtschaftsgeschichte Kroatiens im nationalsozialistischen Großraum 1941–1945: Das Scheitern einer Ausbeutungsstrategie* (Stuttgart, 1983), pp. 179ff.

80. Senad Hadžić, "Die Geschichte der jugoslawischen Arbeitsmigration", in Kölnischer Kunstverein (ed.), *Projekt Migration* (Cologne, 2005), pp. 812–815, 813ff.

81. Salustiano del Campo, "Spain", in Krane, *International Labor Migration in Europe*, pp. 156–163, 159; Sanz Díaz, "*Illegale*", "*Halblegale*", "*Gastarbeiter*", pp. 54ff.

82. Rass, *Institutionalisierungsprozesse auf einem internationalen Arbeitsmarkt*, pp. 474ff.

sending abroad those sections of their workforce with low qualifications as well as unemployed workers and wanted to keep qualified workers to themselves. Of course qualified migrants enjoyed by far the best chance of being admitted to the labour market of a recruiting country and then being allowed to stay there for a prolonged period. In fact, during recruitment operations, the emigration services of labour-sending countries tended to offer employment candidates who would fit their own agenda, while in turn the recruitment agencies of the receiving countries were in the market for migrants with their preferred profile.

Results were mixed. Germany and Portugal, for instance, shared a common interest in tightly controlled labour migration and limited family reunion. Both countries agreed to limit the process largely to state-controlled recruitment. At the same time, it emerged that a large proportion of labour migrants from Portugal to France simply went to avoid official recruitment, because geographical proximity facilitated individual migration, which was often irregular. Likewise, Spain tried to implement a controlled recruitment and migration process, while France made no effort to enforce the ONI's recruitment scheme in order to maximize its gain of Spanish workers.[83]

In other cases, however, organizations entrusted with the management of labour migration in labour-sending countries never gained proper control of the process in the first place. In Turkey, the national labour administration was simply overrun by workers wanting to register for emigration, and only very few of its programmes designed to create a strategic structure for migration flows actually succeeded.[84] Greece fared even worse, as domestic political actors neither agreed on an emigration policy nor succeeded in setting up an organization to manage the process. Consequently Germany, which turned out to be the most important destination for Greek labour migration during the 1960s, enjoyed a great deal of leeway in which it tailored the extraction of migrant workers to its own needs.[85]

With respect to Greece, Turkey, Spain, and Portugal, as well as Yugoslavia, labour recruitment also gained a political dimension, because the first four countries were, at least for a number of years, authoritarian regimes or actual dictatorships, and the fifth was regarded as a socialist country and almost part of the Eastern bloc. Framed by the conflict between the West and the East, political questions seldom appeared to be at issue when bilateral treaties were negotiated, nor while recruitment operations ran in close cooperation

83. *Ibid.*, pp. 239ff.

84. Akgündüz, *Labour Migration from Turkey to Western Europe*, pp. 62–64.

85. Christoph Rass, "Die Anwerbeabkommen der Bundesrepublik Deutschland mit Griechenland und Spanien im Kontext eines europäischen Migrationssystems", in Jochen Oltmer *et al.* (eds), *Das "Gastarbeiter"-System nach dem Zweiten Weltkrieg: Westdeutschland und Europa* (Munich, 2012).

with the institutions of Western dictatorships. In contrast, labour migrants from Yugoslavia who travelled to Germany were at times seen through the ideological prism of the Cold War as a fifth column, poised to strike.[86] In fact Yugoslavia – like some other rather authoritarian regimes – tried to implement a degree of control over its expatriates to ensure their political loyalty during a migration process which was largely perceived as a temporary phenomenon.[87]

How then did the expansion of state interference with labour migration affect the migrants themselves and shape their experience? Regulated labour migration as set up by bilateral agreements subjected migrants to a highly organized and controlled migration regime which possessed a Janus-faced character. Direct contact with recruitment services or migration officials often left migrants with degrading experiences. They were subjected to processes of selection by agencies of their own country as well as those of potential destination countries. Medical examinations were organized rather like musterings for military service and were carried out with little thought for privacy or discretion.

Many receiving and sending countries implemented procedures to check the political backgrounds of potential migrants. Sending countries typically tried to prevent evasion of compulsory military service, and the authoritarian regimes attempted to control or restrict the movements of political opponents. They faced a more or less permanent dilemma over whether to allow opponents to leave, thereby making their job of ruling easier at home, or to keep them at home in a bid to control their activities. Following that logic, access to regulated labour migration was to be granted first and foremost to loyal subjects.[88]

Receiving countries for their part tried to prevent criminals or "radicals" from entering disguised as labour migrants. Such fears mainly had to do with the "threat" of communist intruders, but in practice many attempts to monitor migration streams closely were doomed, given their sheer magnitude and the inability of security organizations to keep pace with them. Nonetheless, the entanglements of politically and economically driven migration during the recruitment phase as well as the role of oppression, political conflict, and the Cold War in general remain fields deserving renewed research efforts.[89]

86. See for instance Barch [Bundesarchiv] B 199 3026, vol. 2, Exchange of letters between the German Labour Administration and a board member of Daimler Benz AG in 1962.
87. Pascal Goeke, "Jugoslawische Arbeitswanderer seit dem Zweiten Weltkrieg", in Bade *et al.*, *Enzyklopädie Migration in Europa*, pp. 731–735.
88. Sanz Díaz, *"Illegale", "Halblegale", "Gastarbeiter"*, pp. 63ff.
89. Georges Prevelakis, "Greek Diaspora", in Matthew J. Gibney and Randal Hansen (eds), *Immigration and Asylum from 1900 to the Present*, 3 vols (Santa Barbara, CA, 2005), I, pp. 272–275.

Finally, organized collective transport – mostly by rail – to host countries, to say nothing of the bureaucratic procedures required to register for and then obtain a work permit, often left bitter memories. Moreover, the experience of being rejected from recruitment, or of undertaking to migrate through other channels, was shattering for individuals. Even well-intended efforts to support migrants – for instance through brochures providing information about the host country – sometimes contributed to the asymmetries between expectations and the realities of migration. Informing potential migrants about what they could expect and helping them to cope with their journey and residence were in fact integral parts of regulated and assisted migration, and were anchored in almost every bilateral agreement which followed the ILO model. At the same time, advertising potential host countries as attractive destinations for well-qualified migrants was the cornerstone of what recruitment services did, and they often created expectations which would subsequently be sharply contrasted by the harsh realities of living in western Europe as a temporarily admitted labour migrant.[90]

The ambiguous character of regulated labour migration also shaped the experience of female migrants. According to the ILO standards, assisted migration, the promise of equal treatment, and special initiatives to protect female migrants should have reduced discrimination.[91] However, the realities of managed migration often proved not to fulfil those promises. The migration regime installed by bilateral treaties and government-run recruitment actually implemented a gender bias: while female migrants became a significant group involved in the recruitment scheme, the system failed to provide for conditions equal to those offered to male migrants in many places. Loopholes in the system allowing discrimination against women rather created incentives which reinforced structural discrimination.

While the emigration of single women often became a contested issue in the countries of emigration in southern Europe, female migrant workers quickly became much sought after by recruitment agencies.[92] Since it was easy for employers in the countries receiving immigrants to avoid paying equal wages to women, the recruitment process was characterized by an extremely high demand for female migrants, especially after World War II when collective bargaining and rising wages for domestic male workers drove up labour costs.[93] As a consequence, during the 1960s German

90. Aytac Eryilmaz and Karin Hunn, "Einwanderer wider Willen. Die Arbeitsmigration aus der Türkei", in Kölnischer Kunstverein, *Projekt Migration*, pp. 809–811, 809ff.
91. Christiane Harzig, "Immigration Policies: A Gendered Historical Comparison", in Mirjana Morokvasic-Müller, Umut Erel, and Shinozaki Kyoko (eds), *Crossing Borders and Shifting Boundaries*, I: *Gender on the Move* (Opladen, 2003), pp. 35–58, 50.
92. Sanz Díaz, "*Illegale*", "*Halblegale*", "*Gastarbeiter*", pp. 47ff.
93. Mattes, "*Gastarbeiterinnen*", pp. 97ff.

employers who asked recruitment agencies to provide female workers sometimes had to wait several months before the first applicants arrived for work. In an almost frantic hunt for female workers, German recruitment officials, for example, hectically forwarded such requests from country to country trying to find suitable candidates quickly.[94]

Among the many degrading experiences of women caught up in the recruitment process, the handling of pregnancy soon became a major concern for employers and recruitment officials alike. For instance, German employers reserved the right to refuse work to female migrants who arrived pregnant, and sometimes denied pregnant migrant workers appropriate health and safety measures while at work. As late as 1971, a company from Aachen forced female migrant workers to give up newborn babies for adoption under the threat of evicting mother and child from company housing.[95] Despite such questionable and frankly inhumane practices, female migrant workers made up an increasingly large proportion of the people moving through the European migration system after 1945.

When recruitment came to an end in the early 1970s, women made up about 25 per cent of all migrants who had passed through that migration channel. Many had managed to turn into agents of change and used their increased mobility to move towards self-determination.[96] At another level, women entered the migration process through family reunion, which also turned out to be contested ground. Throughout the interwar years, and especially after World War II, countries recruiting labour could choose either to reject family reunion to minimize the settlement resulting from temporary labour immigration, or to welcome families in order to draw more migrant workers into their labour markets. Countries of emigration had the opposite choice, between facilitating family emigration

94. Rass, "Die Anwerbeabkommen der Bundesrepublik Deutschland".

95. Marc Engels and Christoph Rass, "Eine Stadt in Bewegung. Mit einer Ausstellung Stadt-geschichte als Migrationsgeschichte erzählen", in Helmut König, Manfred Sicking, and Elke Ariens (eds), *Multikulturalität* (Aachen, forthcoming).

96. María do Mar Castro Varela, "Zur Skandalisierung und Re-Politisierung eines bekannten Themas. 'Migrantinnen auf dem Arbeitsmarkt', in *idem* and Dimitra Clayton (eds), *Migration, Gender, Arbeitsmarkt. Neue Beiträge zu Frauen und Globalisierung* (Königstein/Taunus, 2003), pp. 8–29, 16ff.; Marina Liakova, "'Ausländerinnen', 'Migrantinnen' und 'Frauen mit Migra-tionshintergrund' in Deutschland. Wissenschaftliche Rezeption und mediale Darstellung", in Edeltraud Aubele and Gabriele Pieri (eds), *Femina Migrans. Frauen in Migrationsprozessen (18.–20. Jahrhundert)* (Sulzbach/Taunus 2011), pp. 129–152; Umut Erel and Eleonore Kofman, "Female Professional Immigration in Post-War Europe: Counteracting an Historical Amnesia", in Rainer Ohliger, Karen Schönwälder, and Triadafilos Triadafilopoulos (eds), *European Encounters: Migrants, Migration and European Societies since 1945* (Aldershot 2003), pp. 71–95; Esra Erdem and Monika Mattes, "Gendered Policies – Gendered Patterns: Female Labour Migration from Turkey to Germany from the 1960s to the 1990s", in Ohliger *et al.*, *European Encounters*, pp. 167–185.

and hampering it. One important reason for the latter was to secure the reflux of remittances by keeping the families of migrant workers at home, which was what Portugal tried to do. On the other side, restrictive migration policies of immigration countries regarding female migrant workers and female migration within the context of family reunion often put them in a most difficult position – as has been shown in the case of the Netherlands since 1945, for instance.[97]

Some important features of regulated migration tend to be concealed behind such experiences and memories, which naturally dominate the image and interpretation of labour recruitment. In fact, millions of male as well as female labour migrants went through a thoroughly organized process which attenuated many of the most notorious dangers of international labour migration, reduced insecurity, and lowered migration barriers. Regulated migration based on bilateral treaties provided standard work contracts in the migrants' own languages and – at least nominally – secured equal treatment in working conditions and social security. Migrants had jobs waiting for them before even setting off and were guided from their points of departure to their new workplaces, where housing had to be provided and the cost of travel was, at least in part, lifted from their shoulders.

Medical and professional examinations could even be interpreted as measures designed to make sure that anybody who began a journey had a good chance of fulfilling their contract, which was in the interests of migrants themselves as much as it was of the other parties involved. Of course, rejection was disappointing; but whoever made it through the gates to the channels of regulated migration was better protected and cared for than generations of labour migrants who had gone before.[98] It certainly did not prevent exploitation, nor did it shield migrants from discrimination and racism, but it marked an advance when compared with circumstances in the periods prior to the implementation of bilateral migration agreements.

In addition, the aspiration of governments to extend their control over international labour migration by no means left the migrants themselves without agency. Alongside their ingenuity in gaining access to alternative migration channels, migrants were well aware of the various alternative destinations that were open to them.[99] As the system of bilateral agreements expanded and more and more recruitment services became established in the

---

97. Marlou Schrouver, "Why Make a Difference? Migration Policy and Making Differences between Migrant Men and Women (The Netherlands 1945–2005)", in *idem* and Eileen Janes Yeo (eds), *Gender, Migration and the Public Sphere, 1850–2005* (New York, 2011), pp. 76–96, 84ff.
98. Rass, *Institutionalisierungsprozesse auf einem internationalen Arbeitsmarkt*, pp. 479ff.
99. Sanz Díaz, "*Illegale*", "*Halblegale*", "*Gastarbeiter*", pp. 53ff.

Fig. 3. Italian labour migrants begin their return journey at Cologne main station, 21 December 1973.
*Photograph: Ludwig Wegmann. Bundesarchiv Bildarchiv, Berlin. Used with permission.*

urban centres of labour-sending countries, competition among them became a factor of which migrants could take advantage.[100]

In Milan, for example, recruiters from France, Belgium, Switzerland, and Luxembourg were already present when Germany opened its recruitment post in 1955–1956, and their Austrian and Dutch colleagues entered the arena during the 1960s. One consequence of the situation was fierce competition among the representatives of those countries for Italian migrants. Recruitment services tried to grasp as much as they could of the market for workers by aggressive advertising campaigns and by making improvements in the conditions they offered. On the opposite side, Italians exploited their options cleverly by registering with several recruitment campaigns simultaneously, so that if they passed more than one examination they could choose the most attractive offer.[101]

There is similar evidence from north Africa that Moroccan migrants balanced registering for a job in the Netherlands, where, in the event of their being laid off, unemployment benefits became available to them more quickly, against going to Germany, which offered higher wages but where it was harder to qualify for unemployment benefits.[102] Finally, government officials as well as agents of private companies conducting recruitment operations were immune neither to bribes nor cheating, and buying one's way through the examinations of the domestic emigration services or on to lists of accepted candidates became not only a sport but practically a branch of organized crime in some countries of emigration.[103]

## THE IMPACT OF COMPETITION FOR MIGRANT LABOUR

The effects of competition and choice as they become apparent at the micro level shed light on a neglected aspect of labour migration. It is usually assumed – and in many cases it was true – that because migrants were in competition for jobs they were easy to exploit since they enjoyed little protection. However, the institutionalization of regulated labour migration and the almost continuously growing demand for migrant workers in western Europe throughout most of the twentieth century sometimes turned the wheel of fortune in their favour. Besides its effect of expanding the options open to migrants and their use of them, the impact of competition can be traced through the history of bilateral treaties. Three examples will be used in this section to illustrate that process, one selected from the interwar years, two from after 1945.

100. Cindy Hahamovitch, "Creating Perfect Immigrants: Guestworkers of the World in Historical Perspective", *Labor History*, 44 (2003), pp. 69–94, 85.
101. Rass, *Institutionalisierungsprozesse auf einem internationalen Arbeitsmarkt*, pp. 184ff.
102. *Ibid.*, pp. 199ff.
103. Sanz Díaz, *"Illegale"*, *"Halblegale"*, *"Gastarbeiter"*, pp. 71ff.

When France and Poland began to organize large-scale labour migration in 1919, which resulted in the immigration of more than half a million Poles to France during the 1920s, Germany's position in the Polish labour market was severely weakened. A quasi-monopoly was lost, and although that did not prove too harmful during the crisis-shaken early 1920s, it was to become a problem when the demand for Polish labour migrants in Germany rose again during the second half of the decade. Simultaneously, the advantageousness of the Polish position, with what had been a virtually unlimited demand for migrant workers in France, was diminished in the late 1920s by a tightening of French migration policies. Consequently, when Poland and Germany concluded their first labour recruitment agreement in 1927 the treaty bore signs of both those developments.

Germany was neither ready to depart fully from its own tradition of labour agreements nor openly to adopt the French model of bilateral treaties, but it had to make certain concessions. Poland became entitled to send workers to Germany within a quota framework and mandatory model contracts negotiated yearly, which enhanced the equality of treatment. In turn, the agreement entitled Germany – for the first time – to send official agents of its own labour administration into Poland to conduct recruitment operations. The recruitment itself had to be carried out under the strict control of Polish governmental agencies, which were allowed to determine recruitment areas and influence the selection of candidates. Also, protocols for a periodic evaluation of regulations and practices were introduced, which mimicked the Franco-Polish agreements. Interestingly, Poland used its amended labour relations with Germany to start fresh negotiations with France on a further enhancement of migration standards, until finally even the French association of agriculturalists pleaded for a new agreement with Poland, to be modelled on the German treaty. Its operatives mistakenly believed that Germany had granted Poland even better conditions than France had.[104]

A second example concerns the actions of Belgium and France in the Italian labour market after 1945. Both countries were short of miners in the early postwar years and turned to Italy as the classic source for migrant workers. France put forward its first migration agreement in February 1946, but established a bureaucratic and frustrating recruitment procedure without explicitly granting equality of treatment. On top of that, a complicated system for transferring funds back to Italy – essentially allowing for the shipment only of goods purchased in France – lessened the attractiveness of France as a migration destination. Only four months

---

104. A contemporary account is provided by G.S. Rabinovitch, "The Seasonal Emigration of Polish Agricultural Workers to Germany: I", *International Labour Review*, 25 (1932), pp. 213–235, and *idem*, "The Seasonal Emigration of Polish Agricultural Workers to Germany: II", *ibid.*, pp. 332–367.

later, Belgium entered the arena with its own migration accord. It defined detailed migration and labour standards – though not total equality of treatment – and allowed for the swift transfer of savings from Belgium to Italy.

France countered in November 1946 with a novel labour agreement with Italy which made recruitment easier and promised a lump sum for Italian workers as soon as they crossed the French border. Belgium in turn improved its position on the Italian labour market in February 1948. The Fédération des Associations Charbonnières, which conducted recruitment in Italy, presented a model contract for Italian miners that decisively strengthened the equality of treatment and smoothed their path to permanent settlement in Belgium. France relied on its two most powerful levers to regain the lead. In March of the same year, it signed an agreement with Italy on social security, which established equality of treatment. In 1951, a new migration accord between Italy and France followed, marking the transition from the ad hoc agreements concluded in the late 1940s to a full-scale international treaty modelled on the example given by the ILO conventions. The bonus for Italian miners was raised significantly, as it was for other workers.

But while France continued to upgrade migration conditions for Italians in the 1950s, the competition in Italy had already begun to widen further with the arrival of yet more recruitment commissions sent from western Europe. The accumulating pressure of a rising demand on the Italian labour market finally proved to be a strong incentive for labour-importing countries not only to improve the conditions they offered but also to expand the range of their recruitment activities to new foreign labour markets.[105]

That leads to the third example demonstrating the effects of growing competition. When Germany turned to Turkey as a source of labour power in 1961 it became the first European nation to employ labourers from the Turkish labour market. From that position, Germany could push through a recruitment agreement, which installed a migration protocol of inferior quality when compared to the standards established for labour migration to Germany from other countries.

Not only did the Germans initially use an exchange of notes instead of a bilateral agreement, and thus a less binding diplomatic channel, to seal the agreement, they also severely limited the period of residence for Turkish workers in Germany. Exceptional amounts of leeway were given to German recruiters in the selection of candidates, and for the first time criteria were established which led to the automatic exclusion of a sub-group of potential migrants. On top of that, the agreement omitted family

105. Christoph Rass, "Westeuropäische Industriestaaten und transnationaler Arbeitsmarkt im 20. Jahrhundert: Nationale Strategien in einem internationalen Handlungsfeld", in Rolf Walter (ed.), *Geschichte der Arbeitsmärkte* (Stuttgart, 2009), pp. 287–312.

reunion entirely, which was unprecedented in German agreements after 1945. Three years later, the situation in Turkey changed fundamentally when Austria, the Netherlands, and Belgium entered the market and established their own migration agreements in 1964. The three treaties closely followed examples set by other labour agreements involving the three labour-importing countries and, in contrast to the German case, showed no significant departures from agreements the Netherlands and Belgium had concluded a little earlier with Spain.

However, by no means did that rule out differences between the different agreements. Belgium, for instance, tended to grant more liberal standards of migration control than did the Netherlands. Indeed, the Dutch often suffered severe disadvantages when competing in foreign labour markets as a consequence of the strict regulation of migration and the inferior options for migrants arriving on the Dutch labour market which resulted from it.[106] Germany reacted at the end of 1964. A new draft of the migration agreement was prepared which ruled out the most painful grievances. Turkey was allowed to send its own personnel for social care and counselling to Germany, and a special commission was set up to conduct an annual evaluation of the migration process. Both features had become internationally accepted standards by that time, and the German-Turkish agreement of 1961 is one of the few examples to ignore them. More importantly, the Germans dropped from their work permits for Turkish workers in Germany the limitation which had restricted Turks to a maximum of two one-year work periods.

Maintaining such discrimination against Turkish migrants to the German labour market would have been possible only at the price of diminishing the influx of labour migrants from Turkey, given the options that had opened up for them in the mid-1960s. As competition in Turkey tended to increase when France and Sweden started recruiting workers there in 1965 and 1967 respectively, the trend to more liberal migration agreements continued. The French and Swedish agreements proved to grant better conditions to Turkish migrants, putting pressure on Germany, Austria, and the Netherlands to rethink their regulations and to improve labour immigration from Turkey, either formally or informally.[107]

## CONCLUSION

This article has traced the changing role of nation states in an international labour market on two levels, by looking first at bilateral and multilateral international politics and then at the practice of regulating the migration process itself. The first section has shown that from the interwar period onward, rather restrictive paradigms in migration politics could be followed

---

106. Hunn, *"Nächstes Jahr kehren wir zurück ..."*, pp. 66ff.
107. Rass, *Institutionalisierungsprozesse auf einem internationalen Arbeitsmarkt*, pp. 415ff.

through only by extending the direct and indirect involvement of states in the proactive management of migration and the recruitment of migrants. In that respect, taking over the mobilization of migrants can certainly be interpreted as an extension of control too. Together with the second major current in the arena – the implementation of international labour and migration standards – the outcome, however, is somewhat surprising.

Extending the range of nation states as mediators on the international labour market of Europe required treaties which had to obey international law. The resulting bilateral migration agreements allowed states wishing to establish migration relations to fix terms on the one hand, but then converged towards an internationalized model which bound them to a set of international standards on the other. Those standards were promoted by the ILO, an organization in which nation states cooperated multilaterally as well as with potent third parties, namely trade unions and employer associations. In the end, attempts to extend control led nation states to an internationalization of migration policies, which created networks of structurally standardized bilateral relations between a set of partners. That in turn to a certain degree limited their sovereignty over migration processes and even national migration policies.

On the practical side of migration management, the process required nation states to take over a whole array of new responsibilities. Bureaucracies to control foreigners within national borders were complemented by organizations which enlisted those foreigners abroad through selective recruitment – which often included advertising one's own country as a favourable destination to attract desired workers. Such organizations might be state-run or state-licensed and usually cooperated with their counterparts from the labour-sending countries. Both sides shared a common agenda but competed fiercely to steer the whole process to maximize their specific interests. Such findings can be given context from two perspectives. At the institutional or organizational level, almost every country which became part of the European system of labour migration went down a path of growing direct state involvement, stretching from setting up and operating recruitment posts to orchestrating migration currents through various migration channels as well as from a growing range of partners. Empirical examination of the resulting cooperation of complementary organizations has revealed a great variety of models and degrees of success. The resulting framework can be seen as a transition from predominantly national migration regimes to hybrid ones in which no single nation state could entirely govern migration processes either originating from or targeting its territory.

In that respect, the ILO's struggle to embed standards for the regulation of labour migration must be rated highly not only as a major effort to improve labour and migration standards but also as bringing about seminal changes concerning the management of international migration within the European context. The implementation of such standards within the European system, however, has been shown to rest upon the interaction of several forces beyond the sole command of the ILO or individual countries.

Undoubtedly, the steady spread of a set of rules pursued by the ILO actually contributed to the international convergence of labour migration standards. Although the process slowly gained pace and even significantly changed national politics at times, national paradigms of migration politics were never entirely overruled but always imprinted their character on the way individual states acted within the system. That became visible also in the refusal, well into the 1960s, to extend the principles increasingly applied to regulate temporary labour migration within Europe to include colonial labour markets, and to convert the migration standards defined by the ILO into globally enforced and applied norms. The interplay of the experience of European states as mediators on colonial labour markets, the development of regulated labour migration in Europe, and the development of standards for labour migration in the extra-European world, which is to say the study of migration regimes alongside migration systems, deserve renewed attention.

The significance of the European framing conditions between the 1920s and the 1970s in shaping the combination of state-run recruitment, managed migration, and equality of treatment became obvious when a long-term recession struck the economies of Western Europe and the importance of labour migration dwindled in the face of rising domestic unemployment. This fundamentally changed the situation as soon as the "economic miracle" ended in the early 1970s and the pressure of supply and demand on the international labour market shifted, so that the bargaining position of migrants and sending states became weaker. After recruitment finished, most channels for labour migration were closed or severely narrowed; bilateral agreements for the recruitment of unqualified or lowly qualified migrants played thenceforward only a marginal role. Europe instead embarked on internal labour mobility and began to seal off its borders to immigration in general.[108] The diminished importance of bilateral migration treaties after the recruitment of "guest workers"[109] in the European context clearly reflects this seminal turn.

While bilateral labour agreements still play a considerable role as an instrument to regulate temporary labour migration in the non-European world, within Europe they have begun to serve other purposes, for the most part. Although in recent times fears about future demographic development and its consequences for the labour market in some European countries – among them Germany – have stirred up renewed interest in

---

108. Bernd Parusel, *Abschottungs- und Anwerbungsstrategien. EU-Institutionen und Arbeits-migration* (Wiesbaden, 2010); Sabine Hess and Bernd Kasparek (eds), *Grenzregime: Diskurse, Praktiken, Institutionen in Europa* (Berlin, 2010).
109. For a brief history of this term and its use during the Nazi period, see Rass, *Institutio-nalisierungsprozesse auf einem internationalen Arbeitsmarkt*, pp. 70ff.

temporary labour migration programmes, bilateral migration treaties have been used since the 1980s predominantly as a tool to manage migration within the context of EU expansion. At the same time, they have become an instrument to fend off refugee migration from Africa and Asia towards Europe and its southern member states.[110] It could indeed be argued that despite the renewed and even growing importance of temporary work programmes the degraded bargaining position of low-skilled migrant workers on international labour markets has not only ended the international upward convergence of migration standards for temporary workers but also dramatically eroded conditions offered to them by many of their destination countries.[111]

Nonetheless, the remarkable trend during the heyday of the state-run recruitment of temporary labour in western Europe, especially between 1945 and 1973–1974, is worth noting. In an arena framed by national politics and international standards, competition, which is usually expected to work in favour of those countries offering work to migrants, could actually induce a significant shift in the division of bargaining power from which migrants and labour-sending countries benefited. That observation on the institutional level neither rules out nor denies the de facto existence of double standards and discrimination against migrant workers.

Yet their experiences while passing through a regulated migration process which brought them in contact both with their own governments and the governments of their destination country with unprecedented intensity has to be interpreted carefully. The many bitter memories migrants of the "guest worker" period bear with them have to be weighed against the improvement in security and rights brought about by assisted migration during the interwar years and the "Trente Glorieuses" as compared to all previous models. The exchange of individual freedom against such improvements, which resulted in an extension of state control, certainly was a critical price which had to be paid. In the end the strategy employed by many nation states to extend control over migration by turning themselves into key mediators on the international labour market turned out to be at least partially a self-delusion, not only because migrants proved to be tremendously ingenious in reclaiming agency, but also because the idea proved illusory of preventing permanent immigration and settlement by keeping labour migration entirely temporary and controlled. That illusion lured many countries into a self-image as nations of non-immigration, and so postponed policies of integration for far too long.

110. Aderanti Adepoju, Femke Van Noorloos, and Annelies Zoomers, "Europe's Migration Agreements with Migrant-Sending Countries in the Global South: A Critical Review", *International Migration*, 48 (2010), pp. 42–75.
111. Christoph Rass, "Globale Mobilität und unfreie Arbeit", in Joachim Rückert (ed.), *Arbeit und Recht im 19. und 20. Jahrhundert* (forthcoming).

*IRSH* 57 (2012), Special Issue, pp. 225–252 doi:10.1017/S0020859012000478

# Labour Brokers in Migration: Understanding Historical and Contemporary Transnational Migration Regimes in Malaya/Malaysia

A MARJIT  K AUR

*University of New England, Armidale, NSW*

Email: akaur@une.edu.au

SUMMARY: Labour brokerage and its salient role in the mobility of workers across borders in Asia has been the subject of recent debate on the continuing usefulness of intermediaries in labour mobility and migration processes. Some researchers believe that labour brokerage will decline with the expansion of migrant networks, resulting in reduced transaction costs and a better deal for migrant workers. From an economic standpoint, however, reliance on brokers does not appear to have a "use-by date" in south-east Asia. Labour brokers have played an important role in organizing and facilitating officially authorized migration, particularly during the contemporary period. They undertake marketing and recruitment tasks, finance migrant workers' travel, and enable transnational labour migration to take place. Consequently, both sending and destination states have been able to concentrate on their role as regulatory "agencies", managing migration and ensuring compliance with state regulatory standards and providing labour protection. Private recruitment firms have simultaneously focused on handling the actual recruitment and placement of migrant workers. Notwithstanding this, the division of responsibilities in the migration regimes has also led to uncontrolled migration and necessitated intervention by the state during both periods. These interventions mirror the ethos of the times and are essential for understanding past and present political environments and transnational labour migration in south-east Asia.

## INTRODUCTION: GLOBAL-REGIONAL CONNECTIONS AND ASIAN LABOUR MIGRATIONS

In the late nineteenth and early twentieth centuries the British Colonial Office (London) and the India Office's imperial web of connections resulted in the creation of migration corridors between Malaya, India, and China, transforming mobility in the region. Britain dominated this first wave of globalization and played a major role in Malaya and south-east Asia's greater incorporation into the new globalized system of production, trade, and investment. In most south-east Asian countries populations were sparse, and, initially, East India Company traders and administrators in

Malaya turned to India and China for their labour needs. After Britain intervened in the Malay States in the 1870s, the British created a demand for migrant workers and also developed "manpower supply chains" connecting India, China, and Malaya. Colonial Malaya's economy subsequently became part of the Old International Division of Labour, producing commodities for industrializing Britain and other northern hemisphere countries. This migration phase marked a new chapter in international labour migration in south-east Asia.

The Malayan government also became the official state agency for organizing Indian labour recruitment after the 1870s and developed a migration infrastructure to expand labour mobility and ensure compliance with Indian legislation. This task involved managing emigration procedures at ports, legislating on shipboard conditions, ensuring that migrants emigrated "willingly", and also that they met minimum health standards. Furthermore, the government generated migration by improving transport infrastructures, subsidizing travel, initiating liberal migration regulations, and establishing indentured labour regimes. Concurrently, Chinese merchants who had a long history of trade connections in south-east Asia also facilitated and encouraged Chinese immigration to Malaya. Most of them had obtained mineral or agricultural concessions from local rulers in frontier zones prior to British hegemony in Malaya. Their contacts and familiarity with conditions in Malaya enabled them to conduct their business without relying on the British. Thus, unlike Indian labour recruitment and employment, the Malayan establishment did not play a key role in either the recruitment or employment of Chinese labour migrants.

By the late 1930s and 1940s, wars and globally depressed trade conditions resulted in reduced transnational movements to Malaya, following the Malayan government's implementation of border control systems and legislation to restrict immigration. Then, after World War II and subsequent decolonization measures, universal travel documents became standardized and the independent Malayan nation state introduced stringent regulations to control cross-border movements. During this phase, the United States emerged as the dominant economic power in a second wave of globalization characterized by the further integration of economic activities and labour markets. Additionally, since the 1970s and 1980s, and following Singapore's separation from Malaysia in 1965, a cheap labour supply in the context of the New International Division of Labour became an integral factor in attracting foreign investment and enabling economic growth. Immigration was again seen by both Malaysia and Singapore as a viable solution to increase their labour supply against the backdrop of demographic decline and an ageing workforce.

Labour mobility in south-east Asia/Malaysia is presently recognizable by its predominantly intra- and sub-regional features, but also by wider

Asian movements, thus indicating a new chapter in transnational labour movements. Regional cooperation in the economic arena has further promoted both regionalized as well as global labour mobility, encompassing a greater number of source countries. Migration has thus expanded exponentially and includes both highly skilled and low-skilled labour movements. The state unilaterally regulates migration through specific governance measures which include state legislation and policies on foreign labour employment; a constructed legality of movement through documents such as passports and work visas; and labour agreements. Most importantly, labour brokerage has expanded considerably in both destination and sending states and comprises both large and small private labour agencies that operate at the hub of new transnational labour migration regimes.

This article examines comparatively the role of the state and labour brokers in migration regimes in Malaya/Malaysia in historical and contemporary perspectives. It also assesses the connections between the state and labour brokers in the migration infrastructure. Finally, it considers why a detailed knowledge of the specific recruitment practices of labour brokers is necessary to understand the rise in contemporary labour mobility in the region.

### The British Empire and labour migration in south-east Asia, 1870s–1930s

From about the late nineteenth century the growth of the international economy and associated demand for Asian commodities for the world market corresponded with the region's greater integration into the new globalized system of production, trade, and investment. The political map of south-east Asia was redrawn by the European colonizers and the ensuing new geographical and administrative frameworks comprised six major countries – British Burma, British Malaya, French Indo-China, Dutch Indonesia, the Spanish (later American) Philippines, and independent Thailand. British imperialism and the spread of capitalism in Asia also linked China and India more directly with south-east Asia. The new economic corridors, extending from southern China and southern India to south-east Asia, facilitated labour market integration, resulting in mass proletarian migration to south-east Asia. These economic corridors also helped create a demand for migrant workers in the colonies. The British thus transformed mobility in the region through their open border policy and officially authorized opportunities for Chinese and Indian labour migration.

Prior to these developments, the British East India Company had established settlements in Malaya and Sumatra for plantation agriculture and imported Indian slave and convict labour to cultivate the crops. After British slave emancipation in 1834, and especially the provisions of the Indian Penal Code of 1860, the slave trade and slavery in India and

Malaya ended.[1] It was thus essential to secure new labour sources for the economic development of British Malaya, which comprised three political units: the East India Company's existing Straits Settlements ports – Singapore, Penang, and Malacca (now colonies); the Federated Malay States (FMS); and the Unfederated Malay States (UMS).

The Malay states were effectively governed as colonies, though they were regarded as protectorates, and remained nominally under their own rulers. Singapore was transformed into the leading port city in the region and became the main commercial and financial centre, and administrative capital, of British Malaya. Globalization and the complex exchanges and interconnections with industrial processes in Europe and elsewhere and commodities of empire were accordingly decisive issues in promoting labour mobility and the building up of a viable "freer" labour supply in the region. Simultaneously, the increased taxes on peasants and new land regulations in India had impoverished the peasantry and were a driver of labour migration.

These factors foreshadowed the coordination and regulation of migration in the form of voluntary indentured labour contracts and the organization of travel arrangements. The growth of this new form of labour engagement is usually considered as marking the start of the modern system of wage contract labour in south-east Asia.[2] The new sources of labour supply corresponded with earlier migrant flows. As noted previously, Chinese enterprises had drawn on workers from China, and this pattern continued. Similarly, European employers had a preference for Indian labour based on their experiences with them in the Straits Settlements and elsewhere. Indian and Chinese mass migration was thus interwoven with imperialism, social transformation, and the new economic organizations of plantations, mines, and markets.

From the outset, labour intermediaries played an integral role in Asian migration. Labour brokers (or employers as intermediaries) paid the migrants' passage and travel costs and the migrants had to work for a set period until they had cleared their debts. Indian migrants moved largely between two colonial establishments – India and Malaya – under the overall jurisdiction of the Colonial Office in London. Hence the "British establishment" played an important role in policing migration processes and regulated employment and labour conditions in consultation with employers. Chinese migrants, who have variously been described as "self-driven", "self-organized", and "speculative", went to a wide range of countries. Their migration overseas could best be described as being

1. I.M. Cumpston, *Indians Overseas in British Territories, 1834–1854* (London, 1953), p. 85.
2. Amarjit Kaur, *Wage Labour in Southeast Asia since 1840: Globalisation, the International Division of Labour, and Labour Transformations* (Basingstoke, 2004), chs 3–4.

organized by intermediaries under both a personal recruitment system and a mixture of recruitment arrangements, and largely directed by Chinese business interests. There was no recognized "establishment body", and the influence of secret societies was ubiquitous.

According to Huff and Caggiano, the immigration rate (immigrants per 1,000 population) for Malaya (Peninsula Malaysia and Singapore) was the highest in the world throughout the period 1881–1939.[3] They have also estimated that between 1911 and 1929 Chinese and Indian gross migration to Burma, Malaya, and Thailand was twice as high as gross migration to the United States.[4] While European migrations were voluntary and largely free, Chinese and Indian labour migration took place under free and semi-free arrangements, some of which, though technically legal, had elements of illegality. Additionally, labour brokers played a pivotal role in migration.

The following account of Indian and Chinese recruitment and employment in the rubber and tin industries respectively broadens the scope of the role of the state and labour brokers in Malaya and underlines the contrasts between the migration experiences of the two groups.

## IMPERIAL HEGEMONIES AND LABOUR INTERMEDIARIES

After the collapse of the East India Company in 1858, the Straits Settlements were placed under the direct control of the British government and constitutionally separated from India in 1867. This action was followed by a ban on Indian labour migration to the Straits Settlements. The ban was then lifted in 1872 at the request of European planters, on condition that the Straits Settlements colonial government take over the regulation of Indian labour emigration to Malaya. Henceforth, emigration to the Straits Settlements was permitted under a modified version of the Indian Act XIII of 1864. The Magistrate at Nagapattinam (the main embarkation port in southern India) was appointed Protector of Indian Labour to ensure that professional recruiters did not engage in speculative recruitment and misrepresent employment and working conditions overseas. The professional recruiters included private labour brokers in the Straits Settlements and India and ship owners and merchants who had previously recruited Indians for the East India Company and European sugar planters.

Other conditions included the screening of prospective emigrants by medical emigration agents and an evaluation of migrants' motivations and

---

3. Gregg Huff and Giovanni Caggiano, "Globalization and Labor Market Integration in Late Nineteenth and Early Twentieth-Century Asia", *Research in Economic History*, 25 (2008), pp. 255–317.
4. *Idem*, "Globalization, Immigration, and Lewisian Elastic Labor in Pre-World War II Southeast Asia", *Journal of Economic History*, 67 (2007), pp. 33–68, Table 1.

their ability to work in Malaya. Indian migrants were allowed to travel only as free individuals, and Indian nationalists and social reformers entered the debate about this, thus adding a "new set of imperatives and agendas" to the conversation.[5] Subsequently, the Straits Settlements government compiled its own labour code in 1876, to regulate indentured labour migration to Malaya.[6] The code laid down the labour contract's salient terms and the labour conditions for Indian emigrants. Henceforth, Indian labour recruits arriving at Penang (the port of disembarkation in Malaya) arrived with a debt obligation of Straits $17 to cover their passage costs and an advance on their pay, which was recoverable from their wages.[7] The Malayan coffee planters meanwhile developed an alternative recruitment method, the *kangani* method, to recruit Indian labour (see below).

This code was also considered restrictive, and the Straits Settlements administration subsequently requested that it be revoked. The Indian government then rescinded the legislation in 1881, effectively removing restrictions on Indian emigration to Malaya. In 1884 new legislation, the Indian Immigration Ordinance, was approved in the Straits Settlements to replace the previous legislation. Thus, the Indian indentured labourer was no longer obliged to sign a contract until his arrival in the Straits Settlements. Moreover, in 1887 the Straits Settlements and several Malay States governments agreed to provide a steamship subsidy to transport Indian labour emigrants to Malaya. The Indian government was also progressively persuaded to instigate new measures to encourage emigration to Malaya, to revise recruitment regulations to end the monopoly of the Indian recruiting agents, and to facilitate emigration by establishing labour depots for receiving and processing Indian emigrants in southern India.[8]

In 1897 all restrictions on Indian emigration to Malaya were abolished and the India Office's jurisdiction over Indian emigration to Malaya ended. Britain's larger political agenda for both India and Malaya was thus secured. More importantly, Malaya's future economic growth, with a continuous supply of Indian labour for plantations, railway, road construction, and other public projects, was guaranteed. Politically too, the British extended their hold over Malaya and contributed to the spread of Western enterprise there. Between 1874 and 1914, Britain brought the

5. R.N. Jackson, *Immigrant Labour and the Development of Malaya, 1786–1920* (Kuala Lumpur, 1961), p. 163; Sunil Amrith, "Indians Overseas? Governing Tamil Migration to Malaya, 1870–1941", *Past and Present*, 208 (2010), pp. 239–241.
6. Straits Settlements Ordinance No. 1, also known as the Indian Immigrants Protection Ordinance of 1876, or the Indian Act No. 5 of 1877.
7. Hugh Tinker, *A New System of Slavery: The Export of Indian Labour Overseas, 1830–1920* (London, 1974), p. 12.
8. Jackson, *Immigrant Labour and the Development of Malaya*, pp. 62–69; Virginia Thompson, *Labor Problems in Southeast Asia* (New Haven, CT, 1947), pp. 62–65.

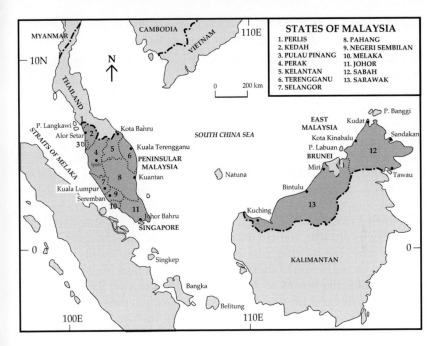

Figure 1. Map of Malaysia.

Malay States (the FMS and the UMS) under formal protectorate status (see Figure 1).

The moving frontier in Malaya both supported and advanced the development of a "permanent" wage labour force in the country in connection with the expansion of the tin and rubber industries. The state also helped transform the cost structure and capacity of the rubber industry by privileging plantation production and Western (mainly British) investors. Afterwards, Western capital dominated too in the tin sector. The state also established modern bureaucratic structures, introduced new administrative and legal frameworks, and built a unified transport system in the country.[9] By 1910, rubber covered approximately 225,000 hectares, rising to 891,000 hectares in 1921. This accounted for 53 per cent of the total land under rubber in south and south-east Asia; and Malayan rubber exports also rose from 6,500 to 204,000 tonnes between 1910 and 1919.[10] The remarkable expansion of the rubber and tin industries was due largely to an unlimited supply of mainly Indian and Chinese migrant labour.

9. Amarjit Kaur, *Bridge and Barrier: Transport and Communications in Colonial Malaya, 1870–1957* (Singapore, 1985).
10. John Drabble, *An Economic History of Malaysia, c.1800–1990* (London, 2000), pp. 53–54.

*The colonial state as regulatory agency, labour broker, and employer:*
*The case of Indian migrant workers*

The principal Indian labour migrations were to Malaya, Burma, and Thailand, while the port cities of Singapore and Penang functioned as important transit hubs. The state and planters (as employers) essentially regarded Indian labourers headed for Malaya as another tradable commodity in the production cycle. All the necessary arrangements for their sojourn abroad – recruitment, transportation, and employment – were made by four parties: the sub-imperial Indian government (or India Office); the Colonial Office in London; the Malayan (Straits Settlements and FMS) government; and Western entrepreneurs. Indian labour migrants comprised low-caste men, mainly from the Tanjore, Trichinopoly, and North Arcot districts in southern India. These districts were particularly vulnerable to drought, and famine and landlessness was widespread.[11]

Since most Indian emigrants lacked the funds for spontaneous mass migration, the sub-imperial India Office regulated Indian labour recruitment for Malaya for the benefit of the Malayan administration. In Malaya, governance structures for the plantation labour regime and public projects rested on two pillars – the mobilization of a largely migrant labour force that facilitated the use of economic and extra-economic measures to maintain low wage bills; and an ethnic (and gender) differentiation of the labour force that enabled the manipulation of both workers and wages.

Private labour brokers/intermediaries were "entrusted" with the important task of facilitating and driving labour migration under the auspices of two recruitment methods – the indenture system and its variant, the *kangani* system. The indenture recruitment method authorized employers to utilize enforceable, written labour contracts. Prior to the abolition of indenture, Malayan planters either engaged the services of one of the labour recruitment firms in Nagapattinam or Madras, or sent their own agents to southern India to recruit labourers directly. The agents advanced money to individuals wanting to migrate to Malaya, the advance being conditional on the intending migrants signing a contract on arrival in the country. The migrants were then considered to be under indenture to their employers for a fixed period, varying from three to five years. (The indenture period was reduced to three years after the 1904 Labour Ordinance took effect.)[12] Once the workers' indenture period had been completed, they were given the option of re-indenture for a further period or released from indenture, providing they had settled their recruitment and other passage costs.

11. Kernail Singh Sandhu, *Indians in Malaya: Some Aspects of their Immigration and Settlement, 1786–1957* (Cambridge, 1969), p. 164.
12. Tinker, *A New System of Slavery*, p. 179.

Employers were responsible for all recruitment charges and expenses involved in transporting workers to Malaya. Wages were fixed at the time of recruitment and were not negotiable. Indian workers' wages were calculated after deducting this outlay from their wages.[13] Most planters regarded this migration method as an essential tool for labour retention and circulation to maintain a stable workforce on rubber plantations. The low wages meant that workers were forced to extend their contracts and re-indenture themselves. Crucially, workers were "bound" to employers during their period of indenture and were treated as unfree men. Employers further used sanctions to enforce labour contracts, and breaches of these contracts were regarded as criminal, not civil offences.

Subsequently, rubber planters started utilizing their own "trusted" workers as labour brokers to recruit Indian labour, thus introducing a chain-migration outcome based on specific recruitment areas in southern India. This system, known as the *kangani* recruitment system, was primarily a personal or informal recruitment system and it became the preferred recruitment method after 1910. The word *kangani* means "overseer" or "foreman" in Tamil, and the *kangani*, typically a labourer already employed on the plantation, was delegated by his employer to recruit workers from his village. This system was preferred by most planters due to the lower costs incurred in using the *kangani*'s services compared with the higher costs incurred under the indenture method, which involved payment of fees to recruitment agencies. Indian labour intermediaries were also often blamed for restrictions in labour supply. Crucially, the *kangani* provided the vital connection between poverty stricken rural southern India and the frontier regions of Malaya, and enabled Indian migration to take place. Planters preferred this method given that the prospect of workers absconding became less likely, especially since the *kangani* had a vested interest in ensuring that the labourers did not abscond.

The *kangani* method utilized social capital or migration networks to assist workers' transition to plantation life in Malaya. These networks were essentially sending networks that articulated with the particular receiving plantation networks in Malaya. The *kangani* was not only a powerful intermediary, he also received "head money" for each day worked by the workers, and stood to forfeit that if workers absconded.[14] The *kangani* also related to the labourers in his roles as plantation storeowner and moneylender, and workers frequently became indebted to him. Arudsothy argues that the *kangani* system was a "variant of the indenture system, as in effect, the debt-bondage relationship between

13. C. Kondapi, *Indians Overseas, 1838–1949* (New Delhi, 1951), pp. 8–29.
14. Sandhu, *Indians in Malaya*, p. 101.

servant and master still remained, although indirectly".[15] Nevertheless, although planters delegated the actual recruitment task to the *kangani*, it is important to bear in mind that employers were the "true" labour intermediaries in Indian labour recruitment to Malaya, and were unhampered by any Indian legislation. The Malayan government, however, considered the *kangani* method a major improvement on the indenture system because, theoretically, labourers were no longer required to have written contracts, were "free" workers, and had greater personal (as opposed to "occupational") mobility.

On the plantation the new migrants lived in compound accommodation and their social life revolved around plantation activities and society. Nevertheless, the isolation of plantations, timidity of the workers, and the plantation boundary reduced this mobility. Furthermore, the labour force comprised mainly male workers. Married men were discouraged from emigrating because, since wages were low, they could not afford to bring their families; the payment norm was a single-person wage; working conditions were harsh; and accommodation was available for single men only. In its 1864 legislation (Act XIII), the Indian government had stipulated that female recruits had to be included in all labour shipments overseas in the following proportion: 25 women to 100 men.[16] However, Malaya was repeatedly exempted from this gender-ratio stipulation due to a dualism in recruitment/regulation procedures governing Indian labour in Malaya. As noted earlier, the India Office had lost its jurisdiction over Indian emigration to Malaya in 1897, consistent with Britain's emphasis on the wider British Empire interests.

The Malayan government's expanding labour requirements for public works development, the growing competition for labour, and an upsurge in labour "poaching" activity signalled a change in the state's role as both a regulatory agency and a labour broker. In 1907 the Malayan government established a centralized quasi-official body, the Indian Immigration Committee (IIC), to facilitate and regulate southern Indian labour recruitment for Malaya. This move foreshadowed two key changes in the Indian migration regime. First, the Malayan state officially became the "sole" labour broker and had jurisdiction over all Indian labour recruitment for Malaya. It may even be considered to have been a "labour-brokerage" state for Indian labour recruitment. Second, the state then gave itself greater regulatory powers in the Indian migration regime.

In 1908 too a Tamil Immigration Fund (later Indian Immigration Fund) was established to recruit Indian labour *directly* for the government and

---

15. P. Arudsothy, "The Labour Force in a Dual Economy" (Ph.D., Glasgow University, 1986), p. 75.
16. Major G. St John Orde-Browne, *Labour Conditions in Ceylon, Mauritius and Malaya* (Cmd. 6423) (London, 1943).

to meet the plantation sector's needs, and to provide free passage for labourers destined for Malaya. All employers of Indian labour were required to pay a quarterly levy or tax to the fund to cover the travel and related costs of Indian migrants to Malaya. This meant that Indian labour, once recruited under the auspices of the fund, was subsequently either confined to plantations or state development projects in emerging townships. In return, Indian workers headed for Malaya were no longer required to pay their travel costs and were free of debt obligations. The actual recruitment was entrusted to *kanganis*. The Malayan administration introduced new legislation as the system developed, including the licensing of *kanganis* to minimize potential abuse of migrants and the stipulation that migrants be employed on a monthly basis only.

These developments also encouraged voluntary migration, and prospective migrants went to the Indian depots for assisted migration to Malaya. Additionally, the indenture recruitment method was phased out in 1910, with the last contracts ending in 1913. For planters this centralized recruitment system cost less than the "old" *kangani* method since other intermediaries were circumvented, and the *kangani*'s power over workers gradually declined. Nevertheless, although workers arrived in Malaya without any debt obligations, they continued to be considered under contract to plantation owners and under the supervision of the *kangani*. Until 1923, the state also upheld penal sanctions for breaches of labour contracts under the new regulations. *Kangani*-assisted recruitment gradually declined in the late 1920s, was suspended during the Great Depression, and was formally abolished in 1938. In the 1930s government assistance in labour recruitment was regarded as inappropriate and the Tamil Immigration Fund was utilized to repatriate unemployed workers. After the Great Depression there was less pressure from planters for a centrally managed labour recruitment system since government-assisted migration was well publicized and most repatriated workers could finance their own return trips.

Thousands of Indian migrants arrived annually in Malaya under the two recruitment systems. Between 1844 and 1910, about 250,000 indentured labourers came to Malaya.[17] The peak of *kangani*-assisted recruitment occurred in the 1910s, when about 50,000 to 80,000 Indian workers per annum arrived. During the period 1844–1938, *kangani*-assisted migration accounted for 62.2 per cent of total Indian labour migration, compared with 13 per cent of indentured labour migration. Moreover, whereas in 1920 only 12 per cent of Indian workers had not been recruited, this proportion had increased to over 91 per cent by the 1930s.[18] In the first

17. Sandhu, *Indians in Malaya*, p. 81; Sinnappah Arasaratnam, *Indians in Malaysia and Singapore* (Kuala Lumpur, 1979, rev. edn).
18. Virginia Thompson, *Postmortem on Malaya* (New York, 1943), p. 123.

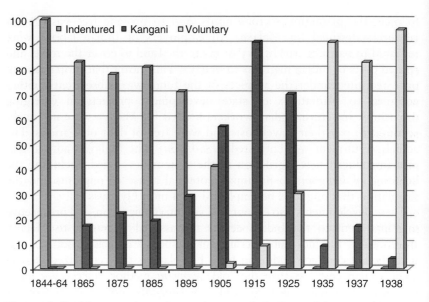

Figure 2. Indian labour recruitment by recruitment method, 1844–1938 (percentage). *Adapted from Sandhu,* Indians in Malaya, *Appendix 2, pp. 306–309.*

four decades of the twentieth century, Indians accounted for between 70 to 80 per cent of the FMS plantation labour force.[19]

The shift in recruitment patterns and breakdown of Indian migrant workers by recruitment system is shown in Figure 2. Most Indian migrants were single men and were taken to frontier plantations won from the jungle. The Indian sex ratio improved under the *kangani* method of recruitment. As plantation work became differentiated and specialized as well, with differing pay scales for tapping, weeding, and factory tasks, women's migration was encouraged and assisted through the *kangani* system. The *kangani* also earned a higher commission for women workers as well as for married couples. Female immigration was also intended to facilitate the reproduction of workers and facilitate the settlement of Indians on plantations.

Two events subsequently impacted on the state's premier regulatory and intermediary roles. First, by the early 1920s Indian nationalists and social reformers had become more vocal in their demands for better protection for Indian workers overseas and the issue of continuing emigration of Indians. Indians comprised about 75 per cent of the estate

19. J. Norman Parmer, *Colonial Labor Policy and Administration: A History of Labor in the Rubber Plantation Industry in Malaya, c.1910–1941* (Locust Valley, NY, 1960), p. 273.

(plantation) labour force, a figure that had remained fairly constant since 1907. Hence in 1922, when the Indian Emigration Act was scheduled to be implemented in India, the question arose as to whether Indian emigration to Malaya should continue after March 1923 (when Malaya truly came under the act's provisions). Since the demand for Indian labour was still huge, the Malayan government implemented five major reforms that had broad implications for Indian welfare and the Indian sex ratio in Malaya.

First, the state adopted the principle of a standard wage, as opposed to a minimum wage. Second, an "improved" sex ratio on the plantations, in line with earlier emigration acts, was also endorsed. Rule 23 of the Indian Emigration Act (Act VII of 1922) specified that there should be at least one female emigrant for every 1.5 males assisted to immigrate as labourers to Malaya. Third, all penal provisions relating to Indian workers were abolished in the Malayan Labour Codes of 1921 and 1923.[20] Fourth, the state commissioned a report on Indian workers' health on plantations to investigate the high mortality rates there and recommended the provision of improved healthcare facilities.[21] This led to "better" facilities on plantations. Fifth, an agent of the Indian government was appointed by India to report on health and general labour conditions on the estates. Although he and successive agents had little authority in Malaya, the appointment represented a small step in the Indian government's attempts to ensure compliance with Indian regulations on workers' welfare.

Generally, by the 1930s the labour-brokerage-cum-regulatory role of the state for Indian labour had undergone some transformations. The impetus for these reforms came from external forces – from India and Indian nationalists. This development mirrors the important role of NGOs in present-day Malaysia in undertaking associational activity for and on behalf of foreign labour in the country.

### Chinese mining labour and labour brokers

Chinese merchants had a long history of trade connections in south-east Asia and obtained mineral or agricultural concessions from local rulers in frontier zones prior to the establishment of British rule in Malaya. Their contacts and familiarity with conditions in Malaya enabled them to conduct their business largely without the intervention and assistance of the British. Thus, unlike the case of Indian labour recruitment and

---

20. Orde-Browne, *Labour Conditions in Ceylon, Mauritius and Malaya.*
21. *Report of the Commission Appointed to Enquire into Certain Matters Affecting the Health of Estates in the Federated Malay States 1924*, 2 vols (Singapore, 1924), cited in Amarjit Kaur, "Indian Labour, Labour Standards, and Workers' Health in Burma and Malaya, 1900–1940", *Modern Asian Studies*, 40 (2006), pp. 425–475.

Figure 3. Indian rubber tappers in a rubber plantation in Pahang (Malaysia), 1978.
*Photograph: Ian Metcalfe.*

employment, the Malayan establishment did not play a key role in either the recruitment or employment of Chinese labour migrants. However, private labour brokers played a major role in Chinese labour migration.

The development of large-scale tin mining in Malaya in the second half of the nineteenth century was due mainly to the existence of merchant capital in the Straits Settlements and the enterprise of certain Malay chiefs who invited the Chinese merchants to develop tin mining in their territories. These Straits Chinese merchants initially obtained Chinese labour from the Straits Settlements. When demand outstripped supply, the merchants turned to southern China to recruit new migrants to work in the mines. The Chinese originated mostly from the coastal districts of Fujian Province, the Chaozhou-speaking districts in north-eastern Guangdong Province, and the Pearl River Delta counties in southern Guangdong. Their journeys took place through Chinese ports that had been annexed as colonies, for example Hong Kong and Macau, and the Chinese treaty ports opened to British and other Western traders following China's defeat in the Anglo-Chinese trade conflicts known as the First and Second Opium Wars. The Chinese government did not support Chinese emigration until the late nineteenth century, making it difficult to utilize open, regulated recruitment arrangements.

The Chinese migration method included a "kinship-based" migration network in China and the credit-ticket network in the destination country, both of which involved labour brokers. The kinship-based migration network involved recruiter-couriers, who recruited migrants from their own villages and regions, and relatives or friends from the migrants' home town normally guaranteed the passage costs and travel expenses. The credit-ticket system, which the bulk of migrants relied upon, necessitated the passage costs and travel expenses being paid by labour brokers, captains of junks, or labour agencies. The crux of their labour contract revolved around the question of how, when, and to whom the passage costs would be repaid. The system exemplified the coolie trade that supplied the bulk of Chinese labour migrants. This trade was controlled by both Chinese and foreign agencies, including British, American, and Dutch firms in the Chinese treaty ports. Prior to 1876, there were at least six coolie agencies operating in the treaty ports that supplied coolies bound for Singapore. Three of these were Chinese-owned, two of which were based at Swatow in Guangdong Province, while the third was based in Amoy in Fujian Province. Two of these also had branch offices in Singapore for receiving coolies.[22]

22. Yen Ching-Hwang, *A Social History of the Chinese in Singapore and Malaya, 1800–1911* (Singapore, 1986), p. 7; Carl Trocki, *Opium and Empire: Chinese Society in Colonial Singapore 1800–1910* (Ithaca, NY, 1990), p. 11.

The labourers were held at receiving depots in Singapore upon arrival at their destination, until their potential employers had paid the passage costs owed by them to either the labour brokers, junk captains, or labour agencies. The immigrants then normally entered into verbal or written contracts for the repayment of their debts in the form of labour service. If no employer came forward to hire the labourer, they were often "sold off" to other employers in adjoining territories. Moreover, there were no conventions for regulating the migrants' subsequent destiny or determining their working conditions. The influence of Chinese secret societies was pervasive and migrants continued to be controlled by secret society members, who prevented them from escaping. When the labourers had repaid their debt (with interest), they were released from their obligations and free to choose their next employer and place of employment.[23]

Tin mining was organized under the auspices of the Chinese *kongsi*, which was a Chinese business cooperative that integrated the maintenance of social control and solidarity.[24] The *kongsi* also functioned as a resilient organization in a frontier society, based on bonds of brotherhood and partnership in economic activity. The isolation of the tin mines from colonial towns, Malay settlement areas, or ports meant that the *kongsi* had to provide a multiplicity of ancillary services required by workers and an institutional framework into which new arrivals, the workers, were inducted. The *kongsi* thus offered a sense of security and identity – it relied on a variety of mechanisms, including a personal recruitment system, kinship links, and clan ties and provincial connections. Membership of secret societies was often obligatory – the society offered protection and established its own law and code of conduct.[25] The labour-intensive nature of the tin industry ensured the continuing dominance of labour brokers in the industry in the second decade of the twentieth century.[26]

The British viewed the credit-ticket system with suspicion owing to reports of abuse of labourers, and gradually took measures to free up the Chinese labour market. This variant of indentured servitude gradually came under government scrutiny, and in 1877 the Straits Settlements administration established Chinese protectorates to regulate Chinese labour recruitment, license the recruiting agents, and register labour contracts. However, the recruitment system did not show much improvement, despite a treaty between China and Britain in 1904. This treaty also permitted the British to recruit any number of Chinese workers at a set fee. But there were no clauses protecting these workers.[27] Nevertheless, by the 1890s secret societies had also been banned and the degree of control exerted over

23. Yen, *Social History of the Chinese in Singapore and Malaya*; Trocki, *Opium and Empire*.
24. *Ibid.*, p. 1.
25. Yen, *Social History of the Chinese in Singapore and Malaya*, pp. 117–118.
26. Kaur, *Wage Labour in Southeast Asia since 1840*, ch. 3.
27. Li Dun Jen, *British Malaya: An Economic Analysis* (Kuala Lumpur, 1982), pp. 137–140.

Figure 4. Chinese miners working on a *palong* at a Chinese gravel pump tin mine in the Kinta Valley (Malaysia), 1978.
*Photograph: Ian Metcalfe.*

workers by mine owners reduced. The power of the *Kapitan China* (the Chinese community head) also weakened, and the position was abolished in 1902. Furthermore, following the abolition of the indenture contract system for Indian labour in 1910 the system was also officially abolished for Chinese labour recruitment in 1914.

Chinese migrants were more advantaged compared to Indian migrants because of their long-standing links and social capital in the Straits

Settlements; their migration method was more speculative; and they were bound only by their financial obligations – once these had been settled they were free to move elsewhere. Given that the larger mining areas in the Malay Peninsula evolved into colonial townships with associated facilities, these emerging towns opened new opportunities for them. By 1931 most Chinese immigrants were employed as traders and shopkeepers rather than in mining and agriculture.[28] The characteristics of the tin supply were a contributory factor. Since tin is a non-renewable asset, workers moved on to other ventures once a mine had been worked. Moreover, as the mining industry was progressively mechanized in the 1920s, control of the industry also shifted to Western entrepreneurs, thus contributing to the growth of a freer Chinese labour force in this industry.

The *Kapitan China* also manoeuvred between the British administrators, Malay rulers, and Chinese communities. Some Chinese went into urban occupations or became smallholders; others worked as contract plantation workers under "contractor intermediaries" who hired out their services to planters.[29] As a temporary contract workforce they were not subject to the paternalistic structures of plantations or of their Western/Asian owners, but remained under the authority of their own contractors and also earned higher wages. These contractors were responsible for the workers' accommodation and other facilities and often moved them around in search of better-paying opportunities. Personal profit, not ethnicity or solidarity, typified their employment status in Malaya and assisted them in advancing their personal economic interests. Consequently, the Chinese miners' migration method gave them additional occupational and personal mobility entwined with a greater sense of freedom, and the nature of their employment and urban settlement enabled them to make the transition to a freer workforce sooner than Indian migrant workers.

The Indian migration method came under the purview of British India and ultimately Britain, and the Malayan establishment was both the regulatory agency and labour broker. All three parties enforced labour control and subjugation in the context of a settled labour force. They thus immobilized the mobile Indian migrant in Malaya whether in "private" plantation work or "official" public works projects and housing. Indians also took a much longer period to repay their travel and passage obligations. The paternalistic policies further ensured that Indians remained powerless, and since the plantation was the boundary of their existence they were denied access to English education in the townships as well as better medical services and contact with other communities.

28. T.E. Smith, "Immigration and Permanent Settlement of Chinese and Indians in Malaya, and the Future Growth of the Malay and Chinese Communities", in C.D. Cowan (ed.), *The Economic Development of South-East Asia* (London, 1964), p. 176.
29. Kaur, *Wage Labour in Southeast Asia since 1840*, ch. 3.

Table 1. *Malayan population by racial group, 1911–1947 (in 000s, percentages as a proportion of total population).*

| Year | Malaysians* | | Chinese | | Indians | |
|------|------|-----|------|-----|------|-----|
|  | No | % | No | % | No | % |
| 1911 | 1,438 | 54 | 917 | 34 | 267 | 10 |
| 1921 | 1,651 | 49 | 1,175 | 35 | 472 | 14 |
| 1931 | 1,962 | 45 | 1,709 | 39 | 624 | 14 |
| 1947 | 2,544 | 43 | 2,615 | 45 | 600 | 10 |

*"Malaysians" include Malays and Indonesians. The table excludes "other" races.
Source: *Malaya: Census Reports 1911–1947.*

### Border controls and immigrant labour

As outlined above, the Malayan Administration had adopted an open immigration policy that led to permanent settlement by foreign workers. The state had also encouraged Javanese immigration, and most Javanese had become settlers and were recorded as Malaysians in census reports. Despite an earlier commitment to unrestricted immigration in the first three decades of the twentieth century, the British introduced legislation in the 1930s that placed restrictions first on the entry of adult male Chinese and, in 1938, on all Chinese. This legislation was consistent with depressed economic conditions and the introduction of international commodity restriction schemes. The British were also able to turn off the immigration tap for Indians by repatriating a sizeable number to India using IIC funds. Thus the state, as both the regulatory agency and the labour broker (for Indians), was able to manipulate Indian migration flows to its advantage, facilitating migrant inflows during good times and repatriating/limiting their entry during bad times.

This period was also marked by a growing national consciousness based on race and ethnicity. From the standpoint of the Malays, and in the context of understanding contemporary immigration policy in Malaysia, Malay indigenism, which reared its head in the 1930s, became even more strident in the 1950s and 1960s. By 1947 Chinese and Indians out-numbered the Malays (and Indonesians). Malaya's changing demographic structure is shown in Table 1.

Malaysia's present immigration policies may be traced to the Malayan state's chauvinistic and selective immigration policies instituted after it became independent in 1957. The Immigration Act of 1959 resulted in a tightening of admission rules under the reunification of families clause, and prohibited entry of spouses and children of Malaysian Chinese and Indian residents who had been living apart from their husbands for a continuous period of five years after December 1954. Subsequently, the state passed the 1968 Employment Restriction Act, which made admission to the labour market for non-citizens conditional on their possessing work permits or labour contracts. The work permit system was also intended to ensure that only skilled non-citizens would be allowed admission into the country. Foreigners or "aliens" who had not taken out citizenship had to leave or were repatriated. A new era thus unfolded in Malaysia for international labour migration.

## THE ROLE OF THE STATE AND LABOUR BROKERS IN MALAYSIA SINCE THE 1970S: CONTINUITY AND CHANGE

The colonial history of Peninsular Malaysia sets the stage for some nuanced discussion of present migration policies, of what has changed, and what has remained the same, to better understand migration regimes and the role of labour brokers in the country.

As noted earlier, after independence in 1957 the Malayan/Malaysian state introduced immigration controls to stop Chinese and Indian immigrants entering the country. The 1968 Employment Restriction Act was intended to restrict the quantity and manipulate the "quality" of migrants and ensure that only skilled non-citizens were permitted entry into the country. Thus, the new Malaysian nation state became a closed labour market, and citizenship conferred both the right to reside and work in the country. Concurrently, a large number of Chinese and some Indians migrated to Singapore after it was expelled from the Malaysian federation in 1965. Although low-skilled immigration was restricted, low-skilled Indonesian workers spontaneously migrated to Malaya since they were not classified as aliens. The Indonesians utilized informal entry channels, building on their pre-World-War-II networks, and Malaysian firms recruited a large number locally, particularly for the plantation, construction, and domestic work sectors. Occupational mobility was high among these migrants, especially in the construction and agricultural sectors, and labour brokers continued to play an important role in the transportation and job placement of new migrants.

After 1987 Malaysia was transformed from a net labour exporter to a labour importer. This transition was also very rapid and occurred long before Malaysia achieved full employment and when its GNP per capita was only about US\$ 1,800.[30] Malaya's dependence on labour migration also occurred against the backdrop of a pro-natalist population policy and domestic labour force growth of 2 to 3 per cent.

Next, following race riots on 13 May 1969 Malaysia adopted an interventionist regulatory policy known as the New Economic Policy, which inaugurated an affirmative action strategy for the Malays (and other

30. Lim Lin Lean, "The Migration Transition in Malaysia", *Asian and Pacific Migration Journal*, 5 (1996), pp. 319, 327.

indigenous communities). The state also became the pre-eminent player in economic development, implementing poverty reduction and income redistribution schemes for the Malays. Apart from the industrialization programme, large-scale development projects including infrastructure and land development schemes were commenced under the management of government agencies. The construction and plantation sectors also expanded, and this growth took place against the backdrop of a tight labour market, consistent with sustained fertility decline and restrictive immigration policies. According to a World Bank Report,[31] 14 million new jobs were created during the period 1987–1993, while the labour market growth rate was 3.9 per cent per annum. The domestic labour force growth rate during this period was 3.1 per cent per annum. Thus the only realistic alternative for the Malaysian government was to implement a temporary worker policy for labour force growth.

The analogies between the colonial and independent Malaysian migration policies are remarkable. The main features of the new policy are: a guest-worker rotation system; employment through intermediaries and offshore recruitment procedures; the provision of assisted passage for workers; repayment of advances through salary deductions; employment with a spe-cified employer; fixed-term employment; and the obligatory return to the country of origin upon completion of the contract. The guest-worker pro-grammes guarantee labour market flexibility and include restrictive admis-sion policies to limit the size of migrant labour flows. The state, labour brokers, and migration agents consequently play a far more important role in the present period compared with the earlier period, due to increased risks in migration processes. The major risks faced by prospective migrants, particularly low-skilled migrants, include a lack of detailed information on where jobs are available, Malaysia's legal system, employment laws, working conditions, and where they can seek redress from unscrupulous employers who falsify information or refuse to pay them.

Unlike the colonial period, gender is an integral part of contemporary labour mobility, and most low-skilled migrant women work in gender-specific jobs, principally as domestic workers and caregivers. They are employed in the private home and are beyond the radar of official state oversight and associated legal protection. Essentially, the entry of more women into the waged economy in higher-income south-east Asian countries, coupled with the commodification of domestic service work (housework, childcare and elderly care), has resulted in the transfer of these tasks to less-well-off women from poorer countries in the region. This arrangement absolves the state from providing state-funded childcare and elderly care services. The rise in

31. World Bank, *Malaysia – Meeting Labor Needs, More Workers and Better Skills* (Washington DC, 1995), p. 58.

dual-career families and the construction of middle-class identity and status has also led to a pattern of assigning responsibility for hiring/supervising domestic service workers from the state to prospective employers.

### The Malaysian state, labour migration policy, and state regulation

Against the backdrop of continuing spontaneous migration by Indonesians, the state instigated institutional and policy changes which led to new programmes for managing labour migration, engaging constructively with migrant-sending countries, and achieving good outcomes for Malaysia. Importantly, the state's immigration reforms and the need for controls prompted the realignment of the Malaysian immigration system, from an earlier "liberal" recruitment policy for Indonesian labour to evolving border controls to prevent unauthorized migration and the official regulation of migration. The revised policy included a law enforcement strategy and securing borders alongside regulating and managing an expanded foreign labour programme and addressing workforce needs. Crucially, it involved participation by the private sector.

Malaysia's immigration policies and programmes, foreign labour recruitment methods, and labour migration are best observed through four fairly distinct phases since the 1970s. During the first phase, 1970–1979, the Malaysian government did not have a comprehensive policy to address labour shortages, nor did it utilize one for foreign labour recruitment. Malaysia espoused a "liberal" approach, which saw minimal intervention in the recruitment of low-skilled foreign labour by employers. Much of this foreign labour comprised undocumented Indonesian workers who lived in the Indonesian squatter settlements in Kuala Lumpur.[32]

Three broad trends relating to changes in labour supply and mobility soon became evident in the country. First, there was increased internal migration from rural to urban districts by both men and women. Malaysian women's economic participation in the manufacturing sector, particularly in manufacturing industries in export-processing zones, also expanded rapidly. Second, the rural–urban migration resulted in labour shortages in the agricultural and construction sectors, at a time when the state had launched massive land development schemes in both Peninsular Malaysia and East Malaysia. Third, as demand for low-skilled labour expanded, the existing social networks and pre-existing channels for long-standing informal Indonesian immigration flows were reinvigorated and led to new influxes of irregular migrants.

During the second phase, 1980–1990, the state addressed the issue of labour force growth and its need for a guest worker policy in two main ways. First, in 1981 Malaysia introduced a Private Employment Agencies

32. Azizah Kassim, "Illegal Alien Labour in Malaysia: Its Influx, Utilization and Ramifications", *Indonesia and the Malay World*, 71 (1997), pp. 50–82.

Act allowing private labour brokers and agencies to recruit foreign labour for Malaysian employers. The agencies had to be licensed and their recruitment fees had to comply with government schedules. The foreign workers had to be provided with work permits and their employment had to be regulated under the 1968 Employment Restriction Act and the 1957 Immigration Act. This recruitment policy tied workers to particular employers and localities. The government also formed a Committee for the Recruitment of Foreign Workers in 1982 that was tasked with the allocation of work permits to guest workers.

Next, the government signed labour accords with labour-sending countries to streamline recruitment procedures and establish legal recruitment channels. In 1984, for example, Malaysia signed the Medan Agreement with Indonesia to recruit Indonesian workers for the agri-plantation and domestic work sectors. In 1985 Malaysia signed a labour accord with the Philippines for the recruitment of domestic workers. Subsequently, employers were permitted to recruit workers from Bangladesh and Thailand for the plantation and construction sectors, and the employment of Indonesians in the plantation sector was also formalized. The labour accords also established formal recruitment channels between source countries and Malaysia. Crucially, the state authorized employers and private recruitment agencies to handle recruitment, and an offshore recruitment policy was developed with the state's role confined largely to immigration formalities and regulations. Despite these measures, unauthorized immigration continued to increase, especially from Indonesia, despite worsening economic conditions in Malaysia. The need to impose some control over labour moves also led to a regularization programme for undocumented Indonesians in the plantation sector in 1989, followed by the suspension of Indonesian labour recruitment in January 1990.

During the third phase, 1991–1996, Malaysia's growing labour needs were further evaluated in the context of strengthened border controls. Thus border controls were largely understood in the framework of the movement of migrant workers. New policy measures were also formulated for the importation of foreign labour. The state's immigration policy centred on the recruitment of highly educated and skilled migrants, together with the recruitment of low-skilled workers for the labour-intensive sectors. In 1991 a Cabinet Committee on Foreign Workers was formed to coordinate and regulate foreign labour recruitment procedures and monitor foreign worker arrivals. The heightened security focus was tied to better data collection and the state also introduced an annual levy (or tax) on migrant workers. This tax on migrant workers varied by sector and skill category (general, semi-skilled, and unskilled) and was payable by either the employer or the foreign employee.

Figure 5 provides information on the criteria used by the state in the selection of migrant workers in certain sectors.

| MANUFACTURING SECTOR |
| --- |
| **1. Export-oriented companies**<br>Eligibility criteria:<br>– Minimum export value: RM 50 million.<br>*Eligibility ratio of local workers to foreign workers 1:3. |
| **2. Non-export-oriented companies**<br>Eligibility criteria:<br>– Minimum paid-up capital: RM 100,000.<br>– Sales RM 2 million<br>*Eligibility ratio of local workers to foreign workers 1:1. |
| **3. Companies in the electrical or electronics sectors**<br>Eligibility criteria: None<br>– Ratio of local workers to foreign workers is 1:2, irrespective of whether the company is designated "export-oriented" or "non-export-oriented". |
| **PLANTATION SECTOR**<br>Eligibility: Owner or lessee of plantation<br>Type of cultivation or nursery: oil palm, rubber, cocoa, teak, and other species of forest<br>Approval criteria – dependent on two factors: land area and number of existing workers (local and foreign). For example, for every 8 hectares of oil palm, 1 foreign worker; for every 4 hectares of rubber, 1 foreign worker. |
| **CONSTRUCTION SECTOR**<br>For construction workers <50<br>– Employer needs to get approval from the Construction Labour Exchange Centre.<br>For construction workers >50<br>– Employer needs to get approval from the Ministry of Home Affairs. |

*Note*: A foreign worker is initially allowed to work for three years only and the worker's application may be extended on an annual basis until the fifth year. Further extensions are allowed only upon application to the relevant certifying authorities after the fifth year, and on the worker's status being upgraded to that of a skilled worker. This classification also promotes circular migration.

Figure 5. Malaysia: criteria for employment of foreign workers in selected sectors. *Adapted from Haji Shamsuddin Bardan, "Terms and Conditions of Employment (Foreign Workers)/Unionism" (typescript, 2006).*

From November 1991 to June 1992 the government also commenced a regularization programme (referred as Ops *Nyah* [Expunge] 1 and Ops *Nyah* [Expunge] 2) to stop "illegal infiltration", weed out "illegal immigrants", and regularize undocumented foreign workers in Peninsular Malaysia. The regularization programme inadvertently led to labour shortages in the manufacturing sector, which were considered too risky for the country's industrialization strategy. Thus, in 1995 the government established a Special Task Force on Foreign Labour as the sole agency responsible for recruiting foreign labour (excepting domestic workers and shop assistants). This task force was set up as a "one-stop agency" to deal with the recruitment and processing of migrant labour. This measure explicitly established the role of the state as the sole institution authorized to organize the importation of foreign labour. It was also intended to reduce exploitation of migrant workers by private recruitment agents. Kanapathy considers this move as both an "explicit" policy on labour importation and "an interim solution to meet excess demand for low-skilled labour".[33]

The state also expanded the Immigration Department's role to include implementation of Malaysia's foreign labour policy; to identify "suitable" labour-source countries; and to determine the eligibility of sectors applying for foreign workers. The department was also assigned to advise on the duration of labour contracts and on levies imposed on foreign workers. Briefly, a foreign labour recruitment policy, based solely on an offshore recruitment system, was implemented by the state to replace the "on-site" recruitment of undocumented and irregular labour. Licensed employment agencies were no longer permitted to recruit foreign workers, with the exception of domestic workers. Domestic workers were seen as a special case, since they were not covered by Malaysia's employment regulations.

The Asian financial and economic crisis of 1997–1998 marked the start of the fourth major phase in Malaysia's evolving immigration policy. The crisis triggered a steep recession in the country in 1998, resulting in a greatly revitalized focus on security issues and overdue reforms for labour recruitment. Data collection on migrant workers to determine their legal status was also increased. In view of the large numbers of irregular migrants, the government established detention centres to detain them "judicially", followed by administrative detention of undocumented workers in detention depots. The state also relied on amnesties and regularization programmes to encourage undocumented workers to register with the authorities and to have their status in Malaysia legalized.

In March 1997 the Task Force on Foreign Labour was disbanded and foreign labour recruitment was placed under the Foreign Workers Division of the Immigration Department. The Malaysian government also amended the Immigration Act in 1997 and again in 2002 to remove ambiguities and tighten regulations; it also further increased the penalties on both employers and workers in breach of immigration regulations. It thus became a criminal offence for foreign workers to work without a work permit or visa, and the state introduced punitive measures, including judicial caning of workers.[34]

33. Vijayakumari Kanapathy, "Migrant Workers in Malaysia: An Overview", country paper prepared for the Workshop on an East Asian Cooperation Framework for Migrant Labour, Kuala Lumpur, 6–7 December 2006, available at http://www.isis.org.my/attachments/381_VK_MIGRATION-NEAT_6Dec06.pdf; last accessed 12 May 2012.
34. Amarjit Kaur, "Order (and Disorder) at the Borders: International Labour Migration and Border Controls in Southeast Asia", in *idem* and I. Metcalfe (eds), *Mobility, Labour Migration and Border Controls in Asia* (Basingstoke, 2006), pp. 23–51.

The government also continued with its periodic expulsion of irregular migrants within specified timeframes.

The state recruited the services of a non-state actor, the Ikatan Relawan Rakyat Malaysia (RELA), or Peoples' Voluntary Corps, in its campaign or "war" against irregular migrants (including refugees and asylum seekers). RELA had been formed in 1972 to assist, maintain, and safeguard peace and security in the country and to undertake community projects. Volunteers were given training and were "expected to act against virtually all types of anti-government activity", and promote government objectives.[35] The state subsequently allowed RELA personnel to be armed, and their new duties included instructions to "stop, search and demand documents, arrest without a warrant, and enter houses or premises believed to house irregular migrants".[36] Consequently, the state has transformed RELA into a valuable ally in Malaysia's war against irregular migrants. RELA personnel also humiliate and carry out judicial caning of undocumented migrants, and "destroy the ID [identification cards] of legal migrants to justify the raids". They are also "immune from prosecution in relation to their conduct".[37]

The state has further created a climate of fear, and forces unauthorized migrants to depart "voluntarily" during trade downturns. Thus, instead of utilizing the services of public law enforcement officials the government continues to criminalize migrant workers, deny them natural justice, and compel them to rely on intermediaries and precarious boats to escape. The saga continues. It is clear that the Malaysian state relies heavily on migrant workers, but vacillates between indecision and repression since it is sensitive to electoral cycles.

Crucially, since Malaysia's share of foreign investment has been dropping, the state has promoted the formation of labour-hire or outsourcing companies to encourage investment in small and medium enterprises (SMEs) that require fewer than fifty workers. The rise of these SMEs correlates with the push by multinationals such as Nike to outsource production to supply chains or "boutique" contract factories in Malaysia for the manufacture of clothes and sports shoes that carry their brand names. According to media and other reports,[38] a Malaysian firm (Hytex)

35. John Funston, *Malay Politics in Malaysia: A Study of the United Malay National Organization and Party Islam* (Kuala Lumpur, 1980).
36. Suaram (Suara Rakyat Malaysia), *Malaysia Human Rights Report 2005: Civil and Political Rights* (Petaling Jaya, 2006), pp. 120–121.
37. FIDH-Suaram, "Undocumented Migrants and Refugees in Malaysia: Raids, Detention and Discrimination" (2007), p. 12, available at http://www.fidh.org/IMG/pdf/MalaisieCONJ489 eng.pdf; last accessed 12 May 2012.
38. BSR International, "International Labor Migration: A Responsible Role for Business" (October 2008), p. 6, available at www.bsr.org/reports/BSR_LaborMigrationRoleforBusiness.pdf (last accessed 12 May 2012); Oxfam Australia, "Forced Labour by Nike Supplier", https://www.oxfam.org.au/2008/07/forced-labour-by-nike-supplier (last accessed 12 May 2012).

used labour brokers in Burma, Bangladesh, and Vietnam to recruit migrant workers for a Nike supply factory in Malaysia. These workers subsequently paid about a year's wages to the labour hire company for the privilege of employment and were rewarded with extremely poor housing, confiscation of passports, and forced labour conditions, since they could not leave without documentation. Simultaneously, "niche" agricultural farms employing fewer than fifty workers also mushroomed. The incentive to hire workers under this recruitment method had arisen because employers in the manufacturing (and agricultural sectors) found it difficult to obtain local workers in the country's segmented labour market. These enterprises allegedly have less attractive labour conditions and fewer enterprise accountability concerns.[39]

Effectively, the outsourcing system has transformed the migrant workers into bonded labour,[40] and horror stories of their exploitation have been reported in the media. A large number of workers, who sold off their family plot or borrowed heavily to "pay" for the privilege of employment in Malaysia, were left stranded at the airport in 2008, or were paid a fraction of what they had been promised.[41] The Malaysian Trades Union Congress has reported that the activities of these labour-hire firms "has worsened the problem of human trafficking" in Malaysia since they "bring in as many as 500 workers each", who are then "sold or out-sourced".[42] According to Human Rights Defenders, the outsourcing agencies also weaken protections since they have become the "employers" and most hold workers' passports, pay on an irregular basis, and charge workers for sub-standard housing and food.

In the past four decades, there has been a marked shift in Malaysia's foreign labour recruitment policy. From a "weak", or rather ad hoc, start in the 1970s, when Indonesian workers were freely allowed to move to Malaysia, the state subsequently permitted private labour brokers to carry out recruitment and placement tasks. Subsequently, hundreds of small recruitment agencies flourished, functioning as labour brokers in a highly competitive environment. This policy measure resulted in a rise in irregular migration, and the more visible presence of migrant workers in the cities as well. Consequently, these workers have been blamed for rising levels of crime in the country.

---

39. Tenaganita, "Fact Finding Report: Outsourcing in Labor or Trafficking in Migrant Labor?" (typescript, 2007).
40. Irene Fernandez, "Recruitment and Placement of Migrant Workers in Malaysia", paper presented at the Malaysian Bar Council Conference on Developing a Comprehensive Policy Framework for Migrant Labour, 18–19 February 2008, Kuala Lumpur.
41. "Worker Rights Violations at Nike Factory in Malaysia", *Associated News*, 1 August 2008.
42. Humantrafficking.org, "Malaysia Reconceptualizes its Assumptions about Human Trafficking", 17 May 2007, available at http://www.humantrafficking.org/updates/622; last accessed 12 May 2012.

In 1995 the Malaysian state legislated to manage directly the movement of foreign workers by taking over all regulatory functions, and it became the sole regulatory agency in the state for almost all categories of less-skilled migrant worker. Apart from the outsourcing firms, private labour brokers are also allowed to recruit domestic workers, and have formed an umbrella organization known as PAPA. Since women have less educational and social capital, they are recruited through "sister" agencies in source countries. They do not have to pay any money to travel abroad, but they are required to attend training in the use of appliances and some language instruction. All their travel costs are paid. However, Malaysian employers are charged for this and the domestic workers are not paid for three months, so that the agency and employers can recover their recruitment costs. This highlights the gendered dimensions of women's migration in south-east Asia.

Crucially, Malaysia's foreign labour policy, labour brokerage practices, and the high levies imposed on guest workers have also contributed to the expansion of irregular migration. The government has introduced some reforms to regulate foreign labour inflows and crafted policy tools based on labour accords to attract low-skilled migrant workers. Like other countries, Malaysia also utilizes the regularization of irregular migrants as a policy instrument to extend legal status to undocumented migrants. These policy changes underpin the state's increased drive for labour flexibility and reduced employment entitlements to migrant labour.